Tender Offers FOR CORPORATE CONTROL

Tender Offers FOR CORPORATE CONTROL

A TREATISE ON THE LEGAL AND PRACTICAL PROBLEMS OF THE OFFEROR, THE OFFEREE, AND THE MANAGEMENT OF THE TARGET COMPANY IN CASH TENDERS AND EXCHANGE OFFERS

By EDWARD ROSS ARANOW

& HERBERT A. EINHORN

EDITORIAL ASSISTANTS:
GEORGE BERLSTEIN
& ALAN STEINBERG

Columbia University Press NEW YORK

Library of Congress Cataloging in Publication Data

Aranow, Edward Ross.
Tender offers for corporate control.

Includes legislation.
Includes bibliographical references.
1. Tender offers (Securities) 2. Consolidation and merger of corporations—United States. I. Einhorn, Herbert A., joint author. II. Title.
KF1477.A96 346'.73'0662 72-10557
ISBN 0-231-03671-X

Printed in the United States of America

10 9 8 7 6 5

PREFACE

The publication of our two editions of *Proxy Contests for Corporate Control* [1] and our active participation in many proxy contests have led us, quite inevitably, into the area of tender offers. Tender offers, often called takeover bids, have long been known as an available technique for acquiring control of publicly held corporations. This technique was most commonly used in England and it was not until the 1960s that it came into frequent use in the United States.

While proxy contests and tender offers generally have the same ultimate objective, viz., control of a publicly held corporation, the applicable methods and strategies, as well as law and regulations, have been quite different. Moreover, the proliferation of tender offers in the United States in the 1960s produced public and congressional reactions which resulted in the new amendments to the Securities Exchange Act of 1934 contained in the Williams bills of 1968 and 1970 [2] as well as other legislation.[3] These new laws and the regulations thereunder changed the rules of the game in important respects. Nevertheless, the statistics seem to show that tender offers continue to be an important weapon of acquiring control.

We have been informed that while the SEC, in the fiscal year ending June 30, 1970, was involved in 24 proxy contests subject to its proxy rules, it had occasion to look into 34 tender offers filed under the Williams Act; and that in the 1971 fiscal year, the comparative figures were: tender offers—43; proxy contests—31.

[1] Copyright © 1957, 1968 Columbia University Press.
[2] Pub. L. No. 90–439 (July 29, 1968); Pub. L. No. 91–567 (December 22, 1970).
[3] E.g., the so-called Mills Tax Bill of 1969; Pub. L. No. 91–172.

Georgeson & Co., the nation's leading proxy solicitation firm, reports that in 1969 it participated in 25 tender or exchange offers and 8 proxy contests for control; and that in 1970 it participated in 18 tender or exchange offers and 8 such proxy contests.[4] These figures, of course, do not reflect the many situations in which tender offers or proxy contests were seriously considered and, for various reasons, postponed or abandoned.

It is clear that the tender offer is here to stay. The more than four years that have passed since the passage of the Williams Act have given us some opportunity to see the new ground rules at work. We therefore felt that this was an appropriate time to attempt a practical guide in this ever-growing area and to take stock of where we are, how far we have come, and where we seem to be going. As in our treatise on proxy contests, we have tried to combine a discussion of the practical problems that must be faced with sufficient legal analysis to make it useful to members of the bar and bench as well as to businessmen involved with tender offers.

The writing of this book would not have been possible without the scholarly assistance of Alan Steinberg, a member of the District of Columbia bar, whose analytical research and imaginative original drafting of a substantial part of this book have been invaluable. In addition, we again wish to acknowledge the able assistance, analytical and editorial, of our partner, George Berlstein, who has shared with us a wealth of experience in this complicated field.

Many others deserve our sincere thanks. The Honorable William J. Casey, Chairman of the Securities and Exchange Commission, has taken the time from his busy schedule and responsibilities to prepare the thoughtful Introduction. Members of the staff of the SEC, because of their scholarly interest and on a strictly personal basis, have made many helpful suggestions. Officers of Georgeson & Co., of New York, have shared with us their invaluable fund of practical knowledge and experience.

Finally, we again express our appreciation and acknowledge our indebtedness to our families, law partners, office associates

[4] Annual Reports, "Report to Our Clients," Georgeson and Co., 1969 and 1970.

and staff who patiently suffered with us during the evolution and completion of this work.

EDWARD ROSS ARANOW
HERBERT A. EINHORN *

New York
October, 1972

* The authors have selected August 31, 1972, as a cut-off date for the material to be included in this treatise.

CONTENTS

INTRODUCTION

BY WILLIAM J. CASEY, CHAIRMAN
SECURITIES AND EXCHANGE COMMISSION *

The older brother of this book, *Proxy Contests for Corporate Control,* has served as a basic tool for all of us involved in proxy contests—latent, threatened and actual. Beyond that, the work has been a guide for all of those concerned with the broad processes of corporate democracy.

Much has happened since the last revision of *Proxy Contests* in 1968. The period of conglomeration reached its peak and began to fade. Tender offers and takeover bids, for a time, became as pervasive in the United States as they were in England shortly after the end of World War II. Legislation governing tender offers has been enacted and the courts have begun to interpret it. The proxy rules have been more aggressively used not only to seek corporate control but also to influence the policy of corporate management, these two objectives being not always separate and distinct. The application and interpretation of the proxy rules and the rules themselves have evolved in a variety of ways. New accounting rules, new disclosure rules, and new court decisions have had a powerful impact on strategy and tactics in the search for corporate acquisitions and in the struggle for corporate control.

Earlier examples of secret aggregation of blocks of stock, of "parking" control blocks with friendly institutions pending a

* The U.S. Securities and Exchange Commission, as a matter of policy, disclaims responsibility for any private publication by any of its members. The views expressed in this Introduction are those of the author and do not necessarily reflect the views of the Commission, nor do they imply agreement with, or acceptance of, the views expressed in the remainder of this volume.

tender offer, of "sweetheart" deals with the management of target companies, of exorbitant borrowings conditioned on repayment out of the assets of the target company and other abuses, which often resulted in special interests obtaining a better deal than the public, have been subjected to disclosure. The Williams Act of 1968 and the amendment to it passed in 1970 have now forced persons tendering cash for the stock of a company to disclose their plans for the target company if the tender is successful, any arrangements made with substantial holders or management, the nature of their own business and management, and the mode of obtaining financing for the tender. This disclosure has to be made through Schedule 13D promulgated by the Commission in response to the Williams Act. Tender offers using securities such as the so-called "Chinese preferred" have, of course, always been subject to 1933 Act disclosure requirements.

In addition, Rule 10b–13 of the Commission prohibits special arrangements with substantial holders of the stock of a target company to give them a better deal than the public. This is accomplished by forbidding purchases of any stock outside of the tender offer during the period it is outstanding. These statutes and the regulations existing under them do not guarantee that a management will be protected from every form of corporate raider but they have provided that the arena of the battle for corporate control is at least more open to public scrutiny.

Accordingly, this companion volume to *Proxy Contests*, covering as it does the how-to as well as the how-not-to of the tender offer, should be most useful to practitioners and companies that find themselves in a tender offer situation. The concern of the Commission as a neutral umpire in these contests cannot be overemphasized. Awhile back an article appeared in *New York* magazine describing how a fanciful young man with only a company name (in this case, "Synergistics, Inc.") could use the tender offer and exchange offer machinery provided by the pre-Williams Act statutory scheme, together with the greed of certain arbitrageurs, to bootstrap that name into control of General Motors by using GM's own funds to finance the purchase. As farfetched as that article seemed, at the time many corporate giants were swallowed whole, or at least given a terrific scare, by small tendering companies using this technique. Stockholders in the target companies were usually given little idea of the maneuvering. Hopefully, under the new scheme these results will not recur.

The Securities and Exchange Commission has placed great emphasis on upgrading the quality of information available in the secondary trading markets. Both the Commission and the courts have substantially expanded and strengthened the obligation which insiders have to public stockholders. New technologies are making possible the broader dissemination of information and news of new developments to stockholders in all parts of the nation.

There have been changes in the tax law that limit the amount of debt that may be incurred to finance a takeover and still qualify for deduction of interest payments. Also, accounting rule changes have limited the use of the "pooling of interests" method of dealing with acquired earnings with the result that premiums paid in excess of book value will more frequently have to be charged against income. This makes straight stock acquisitions less attractive. Finally, the federal government is moving more aggressively to block mergers. Corporate aggression, finding these directions increasingly blocked off, seems likely to seek other outlets, and proxy fights for control will be prominent among them.

Moreover, much of the conglomeration achieved over the last half dozen years has produced disappointment and dissatisfaction. Men who gave up their companies for stock and who are disappointed either with the value of the stock they received, the effectiveness of the management to which they subordinated themselves, or with their own role in the new scheme of things, have responded by challenging for control of the acquiring company through the proxy rules. This development will continue and probably expand.

All of this has created a new atmosphere in which businessmen, securities firms, financial institutions and their professional advisers will be called upon to make more sophisticated analysis and judgment on matters of corporate control and steps taken or contemplated to protect or acquire corporate control. This new work of Messrs. Aranow and Einhorn comes at a propitious time and should be of immense value to those involved in this important and complicated sphere of affairs.

Washington, D. C.
November 1, 1972.

Tender Offers FOR CORPORATE CONTROL

CHAPTER 1. CHARACTERISTICS OF A POTENTIAL TARGET COMPANY

This treatise on corporate tender offers is intended to assist the business community as well as the legal profession. The applicable laws—statutes, regulations, judicial and administrative decisions—are often of decisive importance in furthering or opposing a tender offer. However, the initial decision whether to make a tender offer for the stock of a particular target company is usually based on economic and business, rather than legal, considerations. The same to a large extent is true of the decision of the target's management on whether to oppose the tender offer—colored sometimes by personal considerations. For these reasons, the authors have undertaken to discuss many of the economic and "practical" factors that come into play and must be weighed by the principal participants.

The first item for consideration is the target company itself. Companies having certain characteristics are the more likely targets. Prospective offerors look for such companies; and the management of such companies should be aware of their vulnerability. Thus, before embarking on the legal intricacies involved in tender offers, it would appear appropriate to review the basic characteristics of potential target companies.

While the degree of vulnerability of a corporation to a takeover attempt by means of a tender offer cannot be measured with any scientific or statistical precision, there are a number of characteristics which tend to make a company a more attractive candidate as a potential target. Many of these characteristics either create an economic incentive for the offeror to attempt the takeover or contribute to the offeror's prospects for success by motivating investors to tender their shares. Accordingly, these characteristics will play an important role in the strategy of the tender solicitation as well as the structuring of the offer itself. The potential target, although it may ultimately be able to take defensive action and defeat the offer, is often unable to eliminate the factors which initially give rise to its vulnerability.[1]

Section 1. *THE PRICE/EARNINGS RATIO* [2]

Perhaps the most important factor in assessing the vulnerability of a particular company is the price/earnings ("p/e") ratio of its common stock. While surprisingly little attention has been given to this factor in the statistical studies made on tender offers,[3] there can be no doubt that companies selling at comparatively low "p/e multiples" are generally the choicest targets.

In essence, the decision on whether to make a tender offer is one of fundamental economics. Where the costs of acquisition do not preclude either a present or potential return on invested capital which is substantially in line with or above prevailing rates, the number of potential offerors can be expected to increase. Thus, the lower a company's p/e ratio the more attractive it becomes as a potential target. Conversely, as the p/e ratio increases, the costs of acquisition may begin to exceed the anticipated economic benefits to be derived.

The increasing use of the exchange offer has further emphasized the vulnerability of a company selling at a low p/e ratio. Where the offeror's shares are selling at a higher p/e ratio

[1] For some interesting empirical analyses of some of the characteristics of potential target companies, *see* Austin and Fishman, Corporations in Conflict—The Tender Offer (Masterco 1970); Hayes and Taussig, *Tactics of Cash Takeover Bids,* 45 Harv. Bus. Rev. 135 (March–April 1967); Morse, *Economic Realities of Cash Tender Offers,* 20 Me. L. Rev. 237 (1968).

[2] The price/earnings ratio is the market price divided by the earnings per share.

[3] *But see* Morse, *supra* note 1, an excellent study of all cash tender offers made during the first six months of 1967 involving NYSE-listed companies. Although the statistical sample of the study is rather limited, the results regarding the p/e ratios of target companies are nevertheless revealing. Of the contested offers, the p/e ratios of the targets were lower than the p/e ratios of comparable "control group" companies in 8 out of 10 cases. The market prices of the target companies ranged from 7X–16X earnings with 5 of the 10 companies having p/e ratios of 10 or less. The average p/e ratio of the 500 stocks comprising the Standard & Poor's NYSE Composite Index for the corresponding period was 17.435.

than the shares of the target, an exchange offer may enable the offeror to increase its earnings per share without any real corresponding earnings growth. The following examples indicate how an acquisition of a low multiple target by a higher multiple offeror by means of an exchange offer can increase the offeror's earnings per share.

TABLE 1

THE SIGNIFICANCE OF THE PRICE/EARNINGS RATIO ("P/E") AS A FACTOR IN DETERMINING THE VULNERABILITY OF A POTENTIAL TARGET COMPANY

A. BEFORE THE OFFER

	Offeror			*Target*
	Example 1	*Example 2*	*Example 3*	
Shares outstanding	1,000,000	1,000,000	1,000,000	1,000,000
Earnings	$1,000,000	$1,000,000	$1,000,000	$1,000,000
Earnings per share	$1.00	$1.00	$1.00	$1.00
p/e ratio	20X	30X	40X	10X
Price per share	$20	$30	$40	$10

B. EXCHANGE OFFERS:

Example 1 .7 shares of offeror for each share of target;
Example 2 .466 shares of offeror for each share of target;
Example 3 .35 shares of offeror for each share of target.
(Exchange offer will increase market value of target's shares to approximately $14 per share.)

C. AFTER THE OFFER

	Example 1	*Example 2*	*Example 3*
Shares outstanding	1,700,000	1,466,666	1,350,000
Earnings	$2,000,000	$2,000,000	$2,000,000
Earnings per share	$1.18	$1.36	$1.48
*p/e ratio**	20X	30X	40X
*Price per share**	$33.60	$40.80	$59.20

* Assuming the market continues to place the same p/e ratios after the offer.

It must be noted, however, that a relatively high p/e ratio will not necessarily provide immunity from a tender offer. Where the net asset or liquidating value of the potential target exceeds its market price (after factoring in an offering premium), the p/e ratio may become relatively unimportant because the acquisition of control may enable the offeror to liquidate the target at a profit.[4] Similarly, the offeror may be willing to "pay up" for the stock where the target has excess liquid assets which will be the ultimate source of funds for the purchase of the shares.

SECTION 2. *SIGNIFICANTLY LOWER OR DECLINING EARNINGS WHEN COMPARED WITH COMPETITION*

The inability of a company to generate earning power comparable to its competition may tend to inspire potential offerors where the prospective target's lack of success appears to be caused simply by inept management and where the price of its shares reflects an opportunity to make a bargain purchase in light of the company's potential.[5] While none of the statistical studies found by the authors attempted to compare either the (a) p/e ratios of target companies generating poor earnings with poorly performing comparable companies which were not targets or (b) p/e ratios of target companies generating poor earnings with better performing comparable companies, there is some statistical evidence supporting the conclusion that companies with lower or declining earnings are generally more vulnerable to attack.

The Austin-Fishman study of all cash and exchange tender offers for which data were available between 1956 and 1965 revealed that approximately 60 percent of the target companies showed either decreasing or static earnings trends.[6] Analysis of

[4] A sampling of some eighty-one target companies during the period 1956–1965 revealed that over 54 percent of the targets had book values exceeding their respective market prices per share. *See* AUSTIN AND FISHMAN, *supra* note 1, at 52–53.

[5] The decision to attempt a takeover of a company with apparent weak management because of assumed potential must be recognized as essentially a visceral or subjective rather than an objective decision.

Even where the company's earnings reflect a favorable growth pattern, management should not be surprised by a takeover attempt where the p/e ratio of its shares does not approximate that of comparable companies.

[6] AUSTIN AND FISHMAN, *supra* note 1, at 48–49. While 60 percent of the targets showed disappointing earnings, 58 percent of these same companies evidenced some increase in sales volume. *Id.* at 46–49. On the other hand there was a

the return on stockholders' equity reveals somewhat similar results.[7] The Hayes-Taussig study of contested cash tender offers involving some fifty target companies from 1956 through 1966 indicated that the return on stockholders' equity of approximately two-thirds of the target companies was significantly lower than the comparable "control" group of companies for which no offer was made.[8] The Austin-Fishman study concluded that targets generally perform below their competition in terms of both profits on sales and returns on shareholders' equity.[9]

SECTION 3. *SURPLUS LIQUID ASSETS*

Corporations which maintain substantial liquid assets in excess of that needed for operations or required by law are often prime candidates for a takeover attempt. Where the offeror has limited flexibility because of its own financial position, a successful exchange offer for a company with surplus liquidity may enable the offeror to take advantage of opportunities which it could not previously consider. Similarly, cash tenders which can be financed by the target's own funds following a merger of the offeror and the target will be a powerful attraction to many potential offerors.[10]

The correlation between liquidity and vulnerability is highlighted in the Austin-Fishman study.[11] For the years 1956–1967, 71.5 percent of the targets had "current ratios"[12] higher than

---

strong correlation between earnings and market performance with over 65 percent of the targets failing to show any price appreciation during the three years prior to the offer. *Id.* at 54–55.

[7] The return on stockholders' equity is computed by dividing net income by net worth. The words "stockholders" and "shareholders" are used interchangeably within this treatise.

[8] Hayes and Taussig, *supra* note 1, at 142.

[9] AUSTIN AND FISHMAN, *supra* note 1, at 46. *Compare* the ten contested takeover attempts in the Morse study, *supra* note 1, which revealed that the return on stockholders' equity of the target was lower than the "control" company in only 50 percent of the cases. In only 3 of the 10 cases was the percentage return on the "control" company significantly higher than on the target.

[10] Even where the offeror and the target do not merge, the offeror may still be able to finance at least part of its offer by using the dividends paid on the target's stock.

[11] AUSTIN AND FISHMAN, *supra* note 1.

[12] The current ratio is the current assets divided by the current liabilities.

2.25, which was considered the break-point between normal and high liquidity.[13] Over 45 percent of the targets had current ratios greater than 3.00, and in none of these cases was the industry's ratio as high as that of the target.[14] The results of the Morse study,[15] however, which relied upon a more limited statistical sample, were inconclusive. Five of the ten targets in contested tender offer contests had current ratios below that of their comparable control company.[16]

The "quick ratio," [17] which is a more meaningful test of liquidity, was analyzed in both the Hayes-Taussig and the Morse studies.[18] The Hayes-Taussig study concluded that the average quick ratio of the targets (1.74) was significantly higher than that of the comparable control group companies (1.20).[19] The Morse study revealed that six of the ten targets in the contested tender offer contests had higher quick ratios than that of their comparable control company.[20] The extent of the differences between the sample and the control companies, however, was not significant.

Section 4. *CONCENTRATED SHARE OWNERSHIP*

Where the majority of a corporation's shares are concentrated in the hands of a relatively limited number of independent investors, the risks of a takeover are increased simply because the offeror has fewer people to persuade to make its offer successful. To minimize the risks of undue concentration, efforts should always be made to seek representative distributions of shares in public offerings. In addition, consideration should be given to a rights offering, splitting the stock or issuing stock dividends where there is some obvious pattern of concentrated ownership.[21] While a pro rata increase in the number of shares outstanding will not by itself diffuse share ownership, the increase may well generate wider distribution by creating greater share liquidity. It is interesting to note also that companies with relatively limited amounts of shares outstanding appear to be more

[13] Austin and Fishman, *supra* note 1, at 14–16.

[14] *Id.* [15] Morse, *supra* note 1. [16] *Id.* at 256.

[17] The quick ratio is the cash and cash equivalent items plus receivables divided by the current liabilities.

[18] *Supra* note 1. [19] *Supra* note 1, at 142. [20] *Supra* note 1, at 256.

[21] See Chapter 9, "Defensive Tactics to Thwart a Tender Offer."

likely targets of tender offers. While the number of shares outstanding may simply be a function of the size of the issuer,[22] the statistics are nevertheless revealing. The following tabulation sets forth the approximate shares outstanding of target companies for cash tender offers filed under the Williams Act through February 1970.[23]

	Approx. Shares Outstanding (in thousands)				
	0–499	*500–999*	*1,000–4,999*	*5,000 and over*	*Total*
Number of Target Companies	26	23	29	10	88

SECTION 5. *ASSET SIZE*

Although it is difficult to measure the vulnerability of a corporation to a tender offer strictly in terms of its total assets, it has generally been assumed that the larger American corporations are less vulnerable to attack than their more moderate-sized

[22] Correlation of approximate total assets and shares outstanding of target companies for cash tender offers filed under the Williams Act through February, 1970. Compiled from the SEC list of tender offers reproduced in *Hearing on H. R. 4285, S. 3431 and S. 336 Before the Subcomm. on Commerce and Finance of the House Comm. on Interstate and Foreign Commerce*, 91st Cong., 2d Sess. 15–17 (1970). The table does not include an additional ten tender offers filed through February, 1970 which were apparently inadvertently omitted from the SEC list. See also Chapter 4, note 17.

	Approximate Total Assets (in millions)					
Approximate Shares Outstanding (in thousands)	*0–9*	*10–24*	*25–49*	*50–99*	*100 & Over*	*Total No. of Target Companies*
0–499	14	7	2	1	–	24
500–999	4	7	5	3	2	21
1,000–4,999	5	7	4	3	5	24
5,000 and over	–	–	–	2	7	9
Total No. of Target Companies	23	21	11	9	14	78

[23] Compilation of approximate shares outstanding of target companies for cash tender offers filed under the Williams Act through February 1970, compiled from the SEC list of tender offers reproduced in *Hearings on S. 336 and S. 3431 Before the Subcomm. on Sec. of the Senate Comm. on Banking and Currency*, 91st Cong., 2d Sess. 91–93 (1970).

counterparts. This assumption has been based primarily on the theory that as the total assets of a corporation increase there are simply fewer firms with the necessary financial resources to attempt a tender offer.[24] Furthermore, the probable effect on competition of a major corporation acquiring another company of comparable size is almost certain to raise imposing anti-trust implications. The use of the exchange offer, however, has reduced the significance of size as an impediment to a tender offer and has enabled relatively small companies to acquire much larger concerns. In addition, attempted takeovers of such giants as Commercial Credit Corp. with over $3 billion in assets and Sinclair Oil Corp. with assets in excess of $1.8 billion have underscored the fact that sheer size will not by itself grant immunity from attack.[25]

The Austin-Fishman study of cash and exchange offers for the period 1956–1967 found that approximately 60 percent of some 235 target companies had assets of less than $50 million while only about 5 percent of the targets had assets exceeding $100 million.[26] A breakdown of the total assets of target companies for cash offers only filed under the Williams Act through February 1970 reveals, however, that a significantly higher percentage of companies with assets in excess of $100 million were tender offer targets when compared with the Austin-Fishman results.[27]

[24] It must be noted, however, that equity ownership of 5–10 percent in large corporations may be sufficient to acquire control. *See* introductory remarks of Sen. H. Williams on S. 3431, 115 CONG. REC. S 1529 (daily ed. Feb. 10, 1970).

[25] For the period 1946–1966, only 5 successful tender offers for companies with assets exceeding $250 million were reported. In 1967 there were 6 such successful offers while in 1968 there were 12. 115 CONG. REC. S 1529 (daily ed. Feb. 10, 1970). From the effective date of the original Williams Act (July 29, 1968) through December 31, 1969, exchange offers approximated $18 billion in registered amount far exceeding cash tender offers in number and dollar amount. MEMORANDUM OF THE SECURITIES EXCHANGE COMMISSION, *Hearing on H. R. 4285, S. 3431 and S. 336 Before the Subcomm. on Commerce and Finance of the House Comm. on Interstate and Foreign Commerce*, 91st Cong., 2d Sess. 5–6 (1970).

[26] AUSTIN AND FISHMAN, *supra* note 1, at 13.

[27] *Total assets of Target Companies for Cash Tender Offers Filed under Williams Bill, Through February 1970*

	Total Assets (in millions)					
	0–9	*10–24*	*25–49*	*50–99*	*100 and Over*	*Total*
Number of Target Companies	27	17	11	9	14	78

While the Austin-Fishman study concluded that most tender offer targets are relatively small corporations,[28] it is important to note that the great majority of public companies are small corporations. Absent any statistical evidence that the smaller corporations are tender offer targets in any greater proportion than the larger firms, it is questionable whether size alone has any significance in determining the vulnerability of a particular corporation.

SECTION 6. *OTHER CHARACTERISTICS*

In addition to the factors noted above, there are a number of other characteristics which may contribute to the vulnerability of a corporation to a tender offer. The following list identifies some of the more commonly acknowledged characteristics: [29]

(1) Nominal stock ownership by management in comparison with the total outstanding shares and trading volume;
(2) Substantial cash flow from depreciation;
(3) Undervalued fixed assets;
(4) Nominal debt and contingent liability;
(5) Poor shareholder and professional investment community relations;
(6) Cumulative voting where all directors come up for re-election at the same time;
(7) Unwillingness to consider merger proposals;
(8) Declining dividends;
(9) Poor market performance of the target's stock;
(10) Absence of strong leadership in management; and
(11) Absence of extensive federal or state regulation of the target's business.

Compiled from the SEC list of tender offers reproduced in *House Hearings, supra* note 22, at 15–17. The table does not include an additional ten tender offers filed through February 1970 which were apparently inadvertently omitted from the SEC list. See also Chapter 4, note 17.

[28] AUSTIN AND FISHMAN, *supra* note 1, at 13.

[29] *See also* Abele, *Tender Offer: For Some It Is a Boom and for Others a Threat,* N. Y. Times, April 2, 1967, Financial Section at 1, 16.

CHAPTER 2. PRACTICAL AND LEGAL CONSIDERATIONS OF THE OFFEROR IN PREPARING ITS TAKEOVER ATTEMPT

SECTION 1. *ORGANIZING THE TEAM OF SPECIALISTS*

A successful takeover attempt by means of a tender offer will normally require the combined efforts and talents of a lawyer, an investment banker, a professional "proxy" solicitor, and a network of soliciting banks, trust companies, and securities dealers. In addition, the offeror may be expected to retain the services of one or more banks to act as depositaries and/or forwarding agents to facilitate the actual transfer of shares from the tendering shareholders to the offeror. In many instances, the assistance of a certified public accountant and a public relations expert may also be required. While the offeror may have the in-house capability to supply some of the skills and experience necessary to analyze and plan the general parameters of the offer, it nevertheless is advisable that the assistance and advice of the basic experts be obtained at the very outset so that they can provide the know-how and imagination required to effectively devise and carry out the takeover attempt.

The lawyer should be thoroughly familiar with the applicable federal and state statutes and regulations as well as the judicial and administrative decisions pertaining to tender offers. He should be fully prepared to plan both the strategy of the offer as well as the counteroffensive, should the target undertake defensive tactics to thwart the offer. The lawyer must also be well acquainted with SEC administrative practice and procedure and the various ways of avoiding the complications which result in costly delay when time is of the essence. The lawyer's ability to evaluate and coordinate the takeover attempt will be immeasurably enhanced if he has a thorough working knowledge of the practical mechanics and machinations of the securities markets.

The retention of an investment banking firm is particularly important where the prospective offeror proposes an exchange tender offer. The investment banker will be primarily responsible for structuring an attractive exchange offer package. Where the package consists of a new class or classes of securities, the investment banker's evaluation of the anticipated market value of the package may well be the most important factor in the ultimate success or failure of the offer.

The professional solicitor's function will be that of contacting the stockholders and persuading them to tender their shares. The professional solicitor is often of great help in locating the beneficial owners of shares held in nominee or street name. There are several well-known companies which specialize in such work.

The aggressive solicitation of tenders by banks, trust companies, and securities dealers is an integral part of a successful tender offer. The cooperation of these institutions is obtained through the payment of "soliciting dealer's fees" for shares tendered through such firms and accepted by the offeror. In many instances, the offeror will employ the services of a brokerage firm to act as dealer-manager to coordinate the solicitation effort.

The accountant, together with the lawyer, must be prepared to advise the offeror with regard to the tax consequences of the offer on both the offeror and the tendering shareholders. In addition, the accountant's evaluation of the significance of data which are buried in the footnotes to the target's financial statements is often of great importance.

The public relations expert is generally responsible for insuring the most effective use of the communications media in publicizing the offer. The importance of the public relations expert may manifest itself most dramatically in connection with the generation of creative publicity to counter the target's defensive action.

SECTION 2. *DETERMINING THE OWNERSHIP DISTRIBUTION OF THE TARGET'S EQUITY SECURITIES*

A. INSPECTION OF THE TARGET'S STOCK LEDGER OR STOCKHOLDERS' LIST

(1) *General Principles and Background.* Any realistic appraisal of an offeror's prospects for success necessarily requires a careful analysis of the ownership distribution of the target's equity securities prior to undertaking the tender offer. Obviously, the best starting point for obtaining such information would be through access to either the target's stock ledger or stockholders' list.[1] In addition to enabling the offeror intelligently to evaluate its chances for success, access to the stock ledger will provide the offeror with the address and number of shares held by each stockholder, thereby facilitating both a direct mail and personal solicitation of tenders.

A request for inspection of a corporation's stock ledger will normally require the assertion by a stockholder of a common law or state statutory right to examine the corporation's books and records.[2] This right must be distinguished from the unconditional statutory right of stockholders in certain states to inspect an alphabetical list of stockholders, showing the address and number of shares held by each stockholder, within a specified number of days (normally ten days) prior to a meeting of shareholders.[3]

In most instances the right of inspection or examination of a corporation's books and records pursuant to common law or state statute will be recognized only if the request is for a proper pur-

[1] With regard to the inspection of stock ledgers and shareholders' lists generally, see ARANOW AND EINHORN, PROXY CONTESTS FOR CORPORATE CONTROL 40–58 (2d Ed. 1968).

[2] *See, e.g.,* DEL. CORP. L. ANN. § 220; 15 PA. STAT. ANN. § 1308 (Purdon); OHIO REV. CODE ANN. § 1701.37 (Page); N.Y. BUS. CORP. L. § 624; CAL. CORP. CODE ANN. §§ 3003; 3005 (Deering). With respect to a stockholder's common law right of inspection, *see* Durnin v. Allentown Federal Savings & Loan Assn., 218 F. Supp. 716 (E.D. Pa. 1963); Tucson Gas & Electric Co. v. Schantz, 428 P.2d 686 (Ariz. Ct. App. 1967); Rosenbaum v. Holthausen, 9 N.J. Super. 484, 75 A.2d 760 (Ch. Div. 1950). *See also* cases cited in ARANOW AND EINHORN, *supra* note 1, at 40, n. 13.

[3] *See, e.g.,* DEL. CORP. L. ANN. § 219; ILL. BUS. CORP. ACT, § 32.

pose reasonably related to a person's interest as a stockholder.[4] Some states impose additional statutory qualifications on stockholders seeking to establish a right of inspection. The New York Business Corporation Law, for example, grants a right of inspection only to a person who has been a stockholder of record for at least six months preceding his demand, or who is the holder of at least 5 percent of the outstanding stock, or who has written authorizations from the holders of that amount of stock.[5] An Illinois statutory provision imposes similar qualifications, but provides that the courts may compel inspection upon proof by a stockholder of proper purpose, regardless of the holding period or amount of his stock ownership.[6]

The right to inspect the stock ledger or a stockholders' list at a proper time and for a proper purpose also carries with it the right to make copies thereof.[7]

A court cannot be expected to order an inspection of stock records until there has been a refusal by the corporation to comply with or respond to a proper demand for production of such records.[8] Where the demand for inspection is properly made, the corporation generally has the burden of proof to establish that the inspection is for an improper purpose.[9] In some states, an unjustifiable refusal to permit inspection will subject the corporation to monetary penalties as well as injunctive action.[10] The

[4] See text accompanying notes 17–27, *infra*. *See also* ANNOT. 15 A.L.R.2d 11 (1951) for an excellent discussion of proper and improper purposes with citations to the leading cases in most states.

[5] N.Y. BUS. CORP. L. § 624(b). [6] ILL. BUS. CORP. ACT § 45.

[7] *See, e.g.,* DEL. CORP. L. ANN. § 220(c); N.Y. BUS. CORP. L. § 624(b). Even in the absence of a specific statutory provision, the right to inspect includes the right to make copies and have the assistance of counsel and secretarial help. *See* Shea v. Parker, 234 Mass. 592, 126 N.E. 47 (1920); McGahan v. United Engineering Corp., 118 N.J. Eq. 410, 180 A. 195 (Ch. 1935); State *ex rel.* Healy v. Superior Oil Corp., 13A.2d 453 (Del. Super. Ct. 1940).

Query, whether the right to make copies limits the stockholder to a handwritten transcription or entitles him to use a camera?

[8] *See* Roth v. Bank of Suffolk County, 123 N.Y.L.J. 987 (N.Y. Sup. Ct. March 20, 1950).

Where the substantive law of a state provides for a right of inspection, a federal district court, with jurisdiction by virtue of diversity of citizenship, has the power to issue an order compelling the corporation to permit such an inspection. *See* Stern v. South Chester Tube Co., 390 U.S. 606 (1968).

[9] *See, e.g.,* DEL. CORP. L. ANN. § 220(c).

[10] *See* Nationwide Corp. v. Northwestern Nat. Life Ins. Co., 251 Minn. 255, 87 N.W.2d 671 (1958).

Illinois Business Corporation Act, for example, makes the corporation or an officer or agent thereof liable to the stockholder who has been unjustifiably refused an inspection to the extent of 10 percent of the value of the stockholder's shares in addition to any other damages or remedies afforded by law.[11]

Where a takeover is attempted by means of a proxy contest, the insurgents may be able to obtain the requisite information regarding the target's stockholders pursuant to federal law. Thus, as required by Rule 14a–7 under the 1934 Act,[12] management of the target must distribute the insurgents' solicitation materials or alternatively provide the insurgents with the names and addresses of all stockholders of record together with a statement of the approximate number of beneficial owners to be solicited through each bank, broker, or other person.

In contrast, the Williams Act and the rules promulgated thereunder contain no such provision for the benefit of insurgents in a contested tender offer. Since the underlying purpose of federal tender offer regulation is to insure that shareholders have full disclosure of all pertinent information regarding tender offers, it is surprising that neither Congress nor the Commission has provided for the mailing of the tender offer to stockholders if the offeror does not have a stockholders' list.[13]

On the other hand, it has been argued that since management of the target is not required by the Williams Act or the rules thereunder to make any recommendations regarding a tender offer or to take any other action in favor of or in opposition to a tender offer, there should be no requirement compelling the incumbents to aid the offeror by supplying it with a shareholders' list. However, if the federal tender rules were consistent with the rationale of Rule 14a–7, there would at least be a requirement that the target company furnish the offeror with a shareholders' list or alternatively, to distribute the tender solicitation materi-

[11] ILL. BUS. CORP. ACT § 45.

[12] 17 C.F.R. § 240.14a–7. With regard to a demand for a stockholders list based on Rule 14a–7, *see* ARANOW AND EINHORN, *supra* note 1, at 31–39. Rule 14a–7 does not preempt the field of access to stockholders' lists. *See* Wood, Walker & Co. v. Evans, 300 F. Supp. 171 (D. Col. 1969).

[13] *See* note 14, *infra*.
The authors urged the inclusion of such a rule on the staff personnel of the Commission responsible for drafting the initial regulations in July 1968.

als where it intended to resist the bid.[14] It thus would seem appropriate for the Commission to adopt a rule pursuant to Section 14(d)(4) of the 1934 Act [15] providing that if management of the target intends to make any recommendation or take any other action in opposition to a tender offer, it should either furnish the offeror with a shareholders' list or alternatively, distribute the offeror's solicitation materials to the stockholders. Such a rule would serve the best interests of the investing public by insuring that stockholders will receive the necessary information to make an informed investment decision.[16]

(2) *Inspection to facilitate a tender offer as a "proper purpose."* Proxy contests have given rise to a long line of cases in many jurisdictions supporting the view that a request for a stockholders' list for the purpose of soliciting proxies in opposition to management is a proper purpose.[17] In the tender offer area, while there have been fewer cases, the courts have generally held that a request for a stockholders' list for the purpose of facilitating the purchase of shares held by other stockholders is a proper pur-

[14] *See* Matter of Houston Oil Field Material Co., Inc. v. Holly Sugar Corp., N.Y.L.J., March 14, 1967, p. 16, col. 1, 31 CLARK'S DIG. ANN 210 [350.624.6(2)], *aff'd* 27 App. Div.2d 906, 280 N.Y.S.2d 536 (1967), where a tender offeror's request for inspection of a shareholders' list was held to be for a proper purpose under N.Y. law, based primarily upon the court's finding that "the affirmative steps taken by management in communicating to all shareholders its reasons for their rejecting petitioner's offer required that, in the interest of the stockholders, petitioner have the same opportunity to tell its side of the story."

[15] 15 U.S.C. § 78n(d)(4).

[16] *See* Cohen, *A Note on Takeover Bids and Corporate Purchases of Stock*, 22 BUS. LAW 149, 151–54 (Nov. 1966).

[17] *See* General Time Corp. v. Talley Industries, Inc., 240 A.2d 755 (Del. Sup. Ct. 1968); E. L. Bruce Co. v. State *ex rel.* Gilbert, 144 A.2d 533 (Del. Sup. Ct. 1958); Kerkorian v. Western Air Lines, Inc., 253 A.2d 221 (Del. Ch.), *aff'd*, 254 A.2d 240 (Del. Sup. Ct. 1969); State *ex rel.* Theile v. Cities Service Co., 31 Del. 346, 114 A. 463 (Del. Super. Ct. 1921), *aff'd* 31 Del. 514, 115 A. 773 (1922); Feist v. Joseph Dixon Crucible Co., 30 N.J. Super. 153, 103 A.2d 893 (App. Div. 1954); *In re* Joslyn, 191 Misc. 512, 78 N.Y.S.2d 183 (Sup. Ct.), *aff'd, sub nom.*, Joslyn. v. Universal Laboratories, 273 App. Div. 945, 78 N.Y.S.2d 923 (1st Dept. 1948); Murchison v. Alleghany Corp., 27 Misc. 2d 290, 210 N.Y.S.2d 153 (Sup. Ct. 1960) (dictum), *aff'd without opinion*, 12 App. Div.2d 753, 210 N.Y.S.2d 975 (1st Dept. 1961); Steinberg v. American Bantam Car Co., 76 F. Supp. 426 (W.D. Pa. 1948) (Pa. law applied), *appeal dismissed as moot*, 173 F.2d 179 (3d Cir. 1949); Powelson v. Tennessee Eastern Electric Co., 220 Mass. 380, 107 N.E. 997 (1915); Hanrahan v. Puget Sound Power & Light Co., 332 Mass. 586, 126 N.E.2d 499 (1955); Nationwide Corp. v. Northwestern Nat. Life Ins. Co., 251 Minn. 255, 87 N.W.2d 671 (1958); George v. International Breweries, Inc., 1 Mich. App. 129, 134 N.W.2d 381 (1965); Wood, Walker & Co. v. Evans, *supra* note 12.

pose.[18] This view, however, has not received the same uniform approval as is found in the proxy cases. The cases granting inspection in the tender offer context are based primarily on the theory that the tender offer, like the proxy contest, involves a contest for control which may result in benefit to the corporation and its stockholders through better management and more profitable operations.

In contrast, courts which have denied inspection where the purpose of the request is to facilitate the purchase of shares held by others have based their decisions primarily on the theory that such purchases are for the personal benefit of the purchaser rather than the corporation or its stockholders.[19] Thus, it has been held that a request for inspection by a prospective offeror was for the purpose of furthering the offeror's own business interests and that such interest is an interest adverse to other stockholders since the offeror will seek to obtain control of the target on the most favorable terms and conditions to itself rather than upon those most favorable to the target's other shareholders.[20] Accordingly, the court denied the request for inspection upon finding that the request was not reasonably related to the petitioner's interests as a stockholder.

In *Laidlaw & Co. v. Pacific Ins. Co. of N.Y.*,[21] the court, in denying inspection of a stockholders' list where the *sole* purpose of the inspection was the solicitation of sales of stock to the petitioner, indicated that there was a basic distinction between proxy contests and tender offers for corporate control:

[18] *See* NVF Co. v. Sharon Steel Corp., 294 F. Supp. 1091 (W.D. Pa. 1969); Mite Corp. v. Heli-Coil Corp., 256 A.2d 855 (Del. Ch. 1969); E. L. Bruce Co. v. State *ex rel.* Gilbert, *supra* note 17; Murchison v. Alleghany Corp., *supra* note 17; Feist v. Joseph Dixon Crucible Co., *supra* note 17; Florida Telephone Co. v. State *ex rel.* Peninsular Telephone Co. of Florida, 111 So.2d 677 (Fla. App., 1st Dist., 1959); Crouse v. Rogers Park Apts., Inc., 343 Ill. App. 319, 99 N.E.2d 404 (1951); Matter of Houston Oil Field Material Co., Inc. v. Holly Sugar Corp., *supra* note 14; State v. Crookston Trust Co., 222 Minn. 17, 22 N.W.2d 911 (1946); Lawshe v. Royal Baking Powder Co., 54 Misc. 220, 104 N.Y.S. 361 (1907). *See also* Weber v. Continental Motors Corp., 305 F. Supp. 404 (S.D.N.Y. 1969) (Va. law applied).

[19] Pacific Southwest Airlines, Inc. v. Western Airlines, Inc., No. 946724, Dept. 65 (Superior Ct., L.A., 1969) (reporter's partial transcript of proceedings); Laidlaw & Co. v. Pacific Ins. Co. of N.Y., 52 Misc. 2d 122, 275 N.Y.S. 2d 125 (Sup. Ct. N.Y. 1966); Newman v. Smith, 263 App. Div. 85, 31 N.Y. Supp. 2d 576 (1st Dept. 1941), *aff'd without opinion*, 289 N.Y. 545, 43 N.E. 2d 527 (1942).

[20] Pacific Southwest Airlines, Inc. v. Western Airlines, Inc., *supra* note 19.

[21] *Supra* note 19.

Proxy fights for corporate control may result in benefit to the corporation; purchases of the corporate stock, for the purpose of gaining control, are at least one additional step removed from that end, and may be as consistent with the end of seeking personal gain for the purchaser as with the end of benefiting the corporation.[22]

The *Laidlaw* case, however, has posed little, if any, practical difficulty for tender offerors seeking to obtain a stockholders' list. To avoid confronting the courts with the narrow question of whether a request for inspection of a shareholders' list for the sole purpose of facilitating a tender offer is a proper purpose, offerors have simply framed their requests more broadly.[23]

Thus, a request for inspection under New York law was granted to a tender offeror during the course of its offer, where the avowed purpose of the request was to enable the offeror to "determine whether it should communicate with other stockholders with respect to the election of new directors and with respect to the management, to permit it to estimate the expense of proxy solicitation, as well as to enable it to communicate with the stockholders with respect to its tender offer."[24] Similarly, a request for inspection under New York law by a prospective offeror

[22] 15 Misc. 2d 122, 123, 275 N.Y.S.2d 125, 126. For a critical analysis of the *Laidlaw* case, *see* Weeks, *Business Associations,* 19 Syr. L. Rev. 353, 354–55 (1967).

[23] The *Laidlaw* case appears expressly to approve of this approach as reflected in the following statement in the court's opinion:

"It is true, as urged by petitioner, that some recent cases have held that the allowance of the inspection, where the purposes advanced therefor are proper, will not be denied because 'another purpose may be behind the request—that purpose being [petitioner's] . . . solicitation of the sale to him of shares now held by other shareholders . . .' (Siegel v. Paramount Pictures Corp., N.Y.L.J., May 13, 1965, p. 15, col. 5 [avowed purpose of inspection being solicitation of votes for director]; accord, Matter of Murchison v. Alleghany Corp., 27 Misc. 2d 290, 210 N.Y.S. 2d 153 [avowed purpose being similar to that in Siegel].) These holdings are not, however, authority for directing an inspection where the sole purpose is the solicitation of sales . . ." *Id.* at 126.

In broadly framing a request for a stockholders' list, counsel must nevertheless be sufficiently specific with regard to the purpose of the request. Thus a request for inspection "to communicate with the other stockholders of company with reference to a special meeting of the stockholders" was denied because the request failed to disclose any reasonable relationship between the purpose and the stockholder's interest. *See* Northwest Industries Inc. v. B. F. Goodrich Co., 260 A.2d 428 (Del. 1969); Bank of Giles County v. Mason, 199 Va. 176, 98 S.E.2d 905 (Va. 1957). *Cf.* Henshaw v. American Cement Corp., 252 A.2d 125 (Del. Ch. 1969). *See also* Folk, *Corporation Law Developments*—1969, 56 Va. L. Rev. 755, 757–59 (1970).

[24] *Matter of* Houston Oil Field Material Co., Inc. v. Holly Sugar Corp., *supra* note 14.

seeking to enlist opposition to a contemplated defensive merger by the target was held to be for a proper purpose.[25] Along these same lines, inspection of a shareholders' list was granted under Delaware law where the request was for the purpose of soliciting support for the petitioners' slate of directors at the forthcoming stockholders' meeting of the target company *or* to attempt to buy additional stock from other stockholders, or both.[26] The Delaware cases, however, indicate that inspection will be granted even where the sole purpose of the request is to facilitate a tender offer.[27]

B. Other Methods of Determining the Ownership Distribution of the Target's Securities

Where a prospective offeror does not wish to disclose his intentions with regard to the offer or is unable to obtain a stockholders' list from the target company, he will rely upon a variety of other sources to obtain information concerning the target's shareholders. In many instances, tender offerors depend upon their contacts within the professional investment community to locate the holders of the target's shares. This source of information is important even where a stockholders' list has been obtained because substantial number of the target's shares may be held in "street" or nominee names. Accordingly, contacts within the professional investment community may be the only source of determining the beneficial ownership of such shares.

A thorough review of public sources of information may also enable the prospective offeror to piece together a meaningful approximation of the ownership distribution of the target's shares. Thus, an examination of "insiders' reports" filed pursuant to Section 16(a) of the 1934 Act will enable the prospective offeror to

[25] *In the Matter of* Crane Co. v. Westinghouse Air Brake Co., 56 Misc. 2d 538, 288 N.Y.S.2d 984 (Sup. Ct. 1968).

[26] E. L. Bruce Co. v. State *ex rel.* Gilbert, *supra* note 17.

[27] Mite Corp. v. Heli-Coil Corp., *supra* note 18, discussed in 1970 Duke L. J. 393; 17 BNA Sec. Reg & L. Rep. A-6 (Sept. 24, 1969) (request by offeror for stockholders' list for purpose of making an exchange offer held to be a proper purpose; similarly, counterclaim by target company requesting stockholders' list of offeror for the purpose of communicating with stockholders regarding the exchange offer to be submitted for stockholder approval held to be a proper purpose); E. L. Bruce Co. v. State *ex rel.* Gilbert, *supra* note 17.

determine the holdings of officers, directors, and beneficial owners of more than 10 percent of the target's outstanding equity securities. Similarly, reports filed on Schedule 13D [28] pursuant to Section 13(d)(1) of the 1934 Act [29] will reveal pertinent information regarding those persons or "*groups*" which hold more than 5 percent of the target's outstanding equity securities.

Research and advisory services are also relied upon by prospective offerors in identifying the holders of the target's shares. "Vickers Guide to Investment Company Portfolios," [30] for example, is one well-recognized compendium which will enable the prospective offeror to determine quickly the most recent reported holdings of the target's shares by most registered investment companies.

Section 3. *ESTABLISHING A POSITION IN THE TARGET'S SECURITIES PRIOR TO THE OFFER*

a. Purchases by the Offeror

In preparing for the takeover attempt, it is fundamental that the offeror evaluate the efficacy of taking a position in the target's securities in advance of the actual bid. In this regard, the offeror must carefully consider both the extent and effect of its pre-offer participation in an effort to insure that such purchases will actually further its objective of purchasing the aggregate number of shares sought at the lowest possible cost.

In many instances, offerors have attempted to acquire a relatively large initial block of the target's securities in advance of its bid in order to provide a solid base from which to attempt the takeover. However, if the offeror intends to take the target company by surprise, thereby lessening the latter's ability successfully to employ defensive tactics, it is essential that the offeror limit its holdings in the target company to 5 percent or less of the latter's outstanding equity securities. Purchases and resultant

[28] 17 C.F.R. § 240.13d–101. [29] 15 U.S.C. § 78m(d)(1).

[30] Vickers Associates, Inc., Huntington, L.I., N.Y., publishers. Another valuable reference source is the "International Securities Locator" (Scheinman Ciaramella International Ltd., N.Y., N.Y., publishers) which identifies the positions in some 8,000 U.S. and Canadian securities held by more than 1900 investment companies and trusts in the U.S. and abroad.

ownership of more than 5 percent of such securities will oblige the offeror to file a Schedule 13D statement in which the offeror will be required to disclose its identity and the purpose of the purchases.[31] The 1970 Williams Act amendment reducing the requisite ownership needed to trigger the Schedule 13D filing requirement from 10 percent to 5 percent was prompted by the practice of some offerors taking positions of just under 10 percent in order to avoid disclosure. Accordingly, Congress concluded that the reduction of the triggering figure from 10 percent to 5 percent would provide public disclosure of potential takeover attempts "at a more meaningful level." [32]

Purchases of the target's shares by the offeror in advance of the tender offer can be effected by the acquisition of a block or blocks of such shares from one or more institutional investors, by a series of open-market purchases or by a combination of both. During the 1960s, portfolio managers who were sufficiently astute to recognize the interest of prospective offerors in their blocks as the first step in a takeover attempt were often able to extract "most favored shareholder" treatment as a condition of the sale of such blocks.[33] Pursuant to such an arrangement, the portfolio manager was given certain options which created a virtually riskless opportunity to profit from a subsequent increase in the value of the security he was selling.

If, subsequent to the sale of the block, the offeror made a cash tender offer, the offeror would pay the institutional investor the difference between the block sale price and any higher price offered pursuant to the cash offer. If the offeror made an exchange tender offer, the institutional investor would have the right to repay the cash price it received for the sale of its block and accept instead any higher valued package of securities offered pur-

[31] *See* Item 4, Schedule 13D.

[32] H.R. Rep. No. 91-1655, 91st Cong., 2d Sess. 3 (1970). *See also Hearing on H.R. 4285, S. 3431, and S. 336 Before the Subcomm. on Commerce & Finance of the House Comm. on Interstate & Foreign Commerce*, 91st Cong., 2d Sess. 20 (1970).

[33] *See* Institutional Investor Study Report of the Securities and Exchange Commission (hereinafter cited as "Institutional Investor Study"), H.R. Doc. No. 92-64, Part 5, 92d Cong., 1st Sess. (1971) at 2780. For a fascinating description of the behind-the-scenes machinations in some of the more highly publicized tender offers involving institutional investor participation, *see* Institutional Investor Study at 2771–2849.

suant to the exchange offer. In some instances, the institution was able to obtain the right to require the offeror to repurchase its own securities issued pursuant to the exchange offer.

In other cases, institutional investors were able to obtain additional benefits even if a tender offer was not subsequently made. In such cases, institutional investors were given rights to share in profits realized from the resale of the blocks to third parties or to receive a portion of any prevailing higher market value at some later date.[34]

Where the offeror proposes to purchase the target's shares directly from a regulated investment company, careful consideration must be given to whether such purchases may be lawfully effected without prior SEC approval. Section 17(a) of the Investment Company Act of 1940 [35] provides in relevant part that it is unlawful for an "affiliated person" of a registered investment company or an "affiliate of an affiliate," acting as principal, to purchase any securities from a registered investment company. Section 2(a)(3) of the 1940 Act defines an "affiliated person" of another person to include:

(a) any person directly or indirectly owning, controlling, or holding with power to vote, 5 per centum or more of the outstanding voting securities of such other person; and
(b) any person 5 per centum or more of whose outstanding voting securities are directly or indirectly owned, controlled, or held with power to vote by such other person.

Notwithstanding Section 17(a), Section 17(b) of the 1940 Act provides that:

(a) any person may file with the Commission an application for an order exempting a proposed transaction of the applicant from one

[34] See INSTITUTIONAL INVESTOR STUDY, *supra* note 33, at 2780.

Rule 10b–13 (17 C.F.R. § 240. 10b–13, eff. Nov. 10, 1969) provides that no tender offeror shall, directly or indirectly, purchase, or make any arrangement to purchase, any equity security which is the subject of the offer other than pursuant to the offer itself, from the time such offer is publicly announced or otherwise made known to security holders until the expiration of the offering period. It is clear that Rule 10b–13 prohibits arrangements or understandings made during the course of the offer for the offeror to purchase the securities after termination of the offer. Query, however, whether a "most favored shareholder" arrangement made prior to announcement of the tender offer and providing for the purchase of such shares by the offeror immediately upon the expiration of the offer constitutes a violation of Rule 10b–13.

[35] 15 U.S.C. § 80a–17(a).

or more provisions of that subsection. The Commission shall grant such application and issue such order of exemption if evidence establishes that—

(1) the terms of the proposed transaction, including the consideration to be paid or received, are reasonable and fair and do not involve overreaching on the part of any person concerned.

(2) the proposed transaction is consistent with the policy of each registered investment company concerned, as recited in its registration statement and reports filed under this title; and

(3) the proposed transaction is consistent with the general purposes of this title.

A practical example of the application and mechanics of these provisions is found in the case of *In the Matter of Fifth Ave. Coach Lines, Inc.*[36] In that case, Fifth Ave., a prospective offeror, sought to purchase securities of a target company directly from a registered investment company and, together with the investment company, sought an exemptive order under Section 17(b). At the time of the proposed transaction, both Fifth Ave. and the investment company owned more than 5 percent of the target's voting securities. The proposed purchase by Fifth Ave. therefore came within the prohibition of Section 17(a) since Fifth Ave. was deemed to be an affiliate of an affiliate (the target company) of the investment company. In this particular case, the Commission denied the application upon findings that while the proposed transaction may have been fair to the shareholders *of the investment company,* the applicants did not sustain the burden of proof that the transaction did not involve any overreaching with regard *to the shareholders of Fifth Ave.*[37]

If the offeror intends to establish its position through open-market purchases, the probable impact on the market price of the target's securities must be carefully considered prior to such purchases. If, for example, the trading market for the target's securities is such that substantial or concentrated purchases will have a volatile effect on the market price, the offeror may unwit-

[36] Investment Company Act Release No. 5214 (Dec. 27, 1967), CCH FED. SEC. L. REP. ¶ 77,522.

[37] *Cf.* Bangor Punta Corp. v. Chris-Craft Industries, Inc., 337 F. Supp. 1147, 1152–1153 (S.D.N.Y. 1970).

tingly drive up the price of the target's shares, thereby increasing the price it must ultimately pay for shares purchased pursuant to the tender offer.

The practice of prospective offerors making open-market purchases of the target's shares in advance of the tender offer has raised the question of whether the failure of the offeror publicly to disclose its intention to make a tender offer prior to such open-market purchases will subject the offeror to liability under Section 10(b) of the 1934 Act and Rule 10b–5 thereunder.[38] The issue is perhaps more appropriately framed in terms of whether an open market purchaser is legally required, prior to its initial purchase of an issuer's shares, to disclose its intention to thereafter purchase a substantial amount of additional shares. Simply stated, if the initial purchases are effected solely for the purpose of establishing an investment position prior to making a tender offer, the offeror would appear to have no legal obligation to disclose its intention subsequently to purchase additional shares.[39] The uncertainty which has arisen with regard to the conclusion that an open market purchaser has no duty to disclose its intention to subsequently purchase additional shares derives in large measure from the inappropriate application of the generally recognized prohibition against purchasing securities based upon material nondisclosed information regarding the affairs of an

[38] Section 14(e) of the 1934 Act, which is limited by its terms to fraudulent or manipulative conduct "in connection with any tender offer," may not apply to open-market pruchases made prior to the actual offer. See text accompanying notes 148–157, Chapter 4.

[39] *See* Mills v. Sarjem Corp., 133 F. Supp. 753 (D.N.J. 1955); General Time Corp. v. Talley Industries, Inc., 403 F.2d 159, 164 (2d Cir. 1968), *cert. denied,* 393 U.S. 1026 (1969); BROMBERG, SECURITIES LAW, FRAUD, SEC RULE 10b–5, at 120.6 (§ 6.3(622)) (1969); Wander, "Takeovers: Preparing the Attack," Second Annual Securities Regulation Institute Handbook, PLI (1970) at 9–14. *See also* Schoenbaum v. Firstbrook, 405 F.2d 215 (2d Cir. 1968) (*en banc*), *cert. denied,* 395 U.S. 906 (1969); Penn Mart Realty Co. v. Becker, 300 F. Supp. 731 (S.D.N.Y. 1969).

Disclosure of such purchases may, of course, be required under Section 13(d) of the 1934 Act. In addition, if open market purchases are effected for a purpose other than first to establish an investment position prior to making a tender offer (e.g., to drive up the price of the target's shares in an effort to defeat a competing offer), the failure to make appropriate disclosures may constitute violations of Section 10(b) and Rule 10b–5 as well as other federal anti-fraud provisions. *See, e.g.,* Crane Co. v. Westinghouse Air Brake Co., 419 F.2d 787 (2d Cir. 1969), *cert. denied,* 400 U.S. 822 (1970).

issuer.[40] As a result it is important to note that while the prospective offeror's intention to make a tender offer may be both material and nonpublic, it is information which relates to the plans of the offeror rather than the affairs of the target company. Accordingly, the prospective offeror should have no fiduciary duty under Section 10(b) and Rule 10b–5 to reveal its plans to purchase additional shares despite the fact that disclosure of such information would obviously affect the decision of sellers to dispose of their shares at the then current market price.[41] The law could hardly be otherwise unless one were willing to accept the ludicrous result of requiring every investor that intended to make substantial purchases of a security to disclose such intention prior to its initial purchase. It would therefore appear that any duty of a prospective offeror to make disclosures prior to its open market purchases would derive only from its access to insider information regarding the target and not from its intention subsequently to make a tender offer.[42]

Similarly, open market purchases by selected institutional "tippees" that have been advised of the prospective offeror's intention to make a tender offer would apparently not violate Section 10(b) and Rule 10b–5 thereunder since there can be little, if any, basis for prohibiting a "tippee" from doing what a "tippor" may lawfully do.[43] To date, however, the courts have not had occasion to consider this specific issue and given the expansive reading applied to Section 10(b) in recent years, the Commission or a private litigant may well be able successfully to attack this practice.[44] Such a result, however, would not appear appropriate.

[40] *See, e.g.*, Speed v. Transamerica Corp., 71 F. Supp. 457 (D. Del. 1947); *In re* Cady, Roberts & Co., 40 S.E.C. 907 (1961); SEC v. Texas Gulf Sulphur Co., 401 F.2d 833 (2d Cir. 1968) (*en banc*), *cert. denied, sub nom.*, Kline v. SEC, 394 U.S. 976 (1969); *In re* Investors Management Co., Inc., SEC Admin. Proc. File No. 3–1680 (June 26, 1970), CCH FED. SEC. L. REP. ¶ 77,832; *In re* Merrill Lynch, Pierce, Fenner & Smith, Inc., SEC Securities Exchange Act Release No. 8459 (Nov. 25, 1968), CCH FED. SEC. L. REP. ¶ 77,629. *See also In re* Investors Management Co., Inc., SEC Securities Exchange Act Release No. 8947 (June 30, 1970), CCH FED. SEC. L. REP. ¶ 77,844; Complaint in SEC v. Lums, Inc., 70 Civ. 5280 (S.D.N.Y. 1970); SEC v. Glen Alden Corp., *infra* note 44; Astor v. Texas Gulf Sulphur Co., 306 F. Supp. 1333 (S.D.N.Y. 1969); De Lancey, *Rule 10b–5—A Recent Profile*, 25 BUS. LAW 1355 (July 1970).

[41] *See* note 40, *supra*.

[42] *See* Speed v. Transamerica Corp., *supra* note 40.

[43] *Cf.* Thomas, *Warehousing*, REV. OF SEC. REG. 975, 977 (Feb. 5, 1970); Wander, *supra* note 39, at 13–14.

[44] The Commission, in at least one instance, has alleged that the disclosure of

B. PURCHASES BY FRIENDLY THIRD PARTIES

A number of offerors, either lacking the resources to make purchases of the target's securities or desiring to avoid the disclosure requirements of the Williams Act, have sought the aid of friendly third parties in accumulating positions in the target's securities in advance of the actual bid. In some such instances, institutional investors have received advance information that a tender offer would be made, thereby providing an incentive for the institution to purchase the target's shares before the announcement of the tender offer affected the open market price of the shares.[45] Institutions providing assistance to the offeror, either by way of purchases and subsequent tenders of the target's shares or by loans enabling the offeror to purchase the target's shares, have also received additional inducements in the form of assurances (assuming the offer is successful) regarding the future management of the target's investment portfolio or commercial banking arrangements with the offeror or the target company. In other instances, third parties have purchased shares of the target pursuant to arrangements whereby the offeror agreed subsequently to repurchase the shares at a price in excess of such third party's cost.[46] The practice of parking the target's shares with third parties, commonly referred to as "warehousing," has created huge profit potentials for the institutions involved and has benefited the offeror by assuring the placement of large blocks of the target's shares in the hands of parties who most likely would tender their shares.[47]

---

nonpublic information to an investment company regarding, among other things, projected acquisitions by a prospective offeror constituted a violation of Section 10(b) and Rule 10b-5. *See* SEC v. Glen Alden Corp., 68 Civ. 3203 (S.D.N.Y. 1968), CCH FED. SEC. L. REP. ¶ 92,280 (consent injunction).

[45] *See* INSTITUTIONAL INVESTOR STUDY, *supra* note 33, at 2773, 2848.

[46] *Id.* at 2848.

[47] In view of recent judicial pronouncements regarding "group" activity as that term has been interpreted under Section 13(d) and Section 14(d) of the 1934 Act [*see* particularly GAF Corp. v. Milstein, 453 F.2d 709 (2d Cir. 1971), *cert. denied*, 406 U.S. 910 (1972), discussed in text accompanying notes 45–76, Chapter 4], query, whether the activities and arrangements described above subject both the offeror and the institutional investor to potential liability under the Investment Company Act of 1940 as well as the 1934 Act? *See* INSTITUTIONAL INVESTOR STUDY, *supra* note 33, at 2835.

The purchase of the target's shares by friendly third parties, however, is not without its pitfalls and problems. The case of *SEC v. Madison Square Garden Corp.*[48] illustrates the range of problems which may develop in a contested tender offer. In that case, G & W Land and Development Corp. made a cash tender offer for shares of Roosevelt Raceway, Inc. Immediately thereafter, Madison Square Garden Corp., which apparently intended to make its own tender offer for Roosevelt shares, issued a press release advising that it had reached agreement with a broker-dealer pursuant to which the broker and certain of its institutional clients would purchase a large block of Roosevelt shares with the right after one year to require the Garden to purchase such shares at a price equal to 120 percent of their cost. The SEC alleged that the series of purchases of Roosevelt stock effected by the broker-dealer, the Garden's press release, and the financing arrangement were undertaken to defeat the G & W offer and that such conduct constituted violations of Sections 10(b) and 14(e) of the 1934 Act. Such conduct was also alleged to constitute a solicitation of the Roosevelt shareholders to reject the tender offer, made without the filing of the disclosures required by Schedule 14D of the 1934 Act. The Commission also claimed that the defendants had acted as a "group" without the filing of the necessary disclosures required by Schedule 13D and that the Agreement with the broker constituted an unlawful extension of credit in violation of Regulation T promulgated by the Board of Governors of the Federal Reserve System.[49] Pursuant to a consent injunction, the defendants were enjoined from further violations of the specified statutory provisions, rules, and regulations and ordered to file appropriate Schedule 13D and Schedule 14D statements. In addition, the court declared the financing agree-

[48] 69 Civ. 4364 (S.D.N.Y. 1970), CCH FED. SEC. L. REP. § 92, 649. For a summary of the complaint, *see* 19 BNA SEC. REG. & L. REP. A–2, A–3 (Oct. 8, 1969).

[49] Prior to announcement of an exchange offer by National General Corp. for shares of Great American Holding Corp., the investment broker for National General proposed a block purchase of the target's shares by the offeror. In view of National General's temporary lack of cash, the broker purchased a substantial block of the target's shares on a "21-day delivery buyer's option." Thereafter, a portion of the shares were resold to National General and other clients of the broker. The New York Stock Exchange fined and censured the broker who had effected the transition upon findings that the option constituted a violation of Regulation T. *See* INSTITUTIONAL INVESTOR STUDY *supra* note 33, at 2783.

ment to be null and void and ordered the broker-dealer and its clients who participated in the agreement to dispose of their shares in Roosevelt, with any profits realized by the broker-dealer on the sale of its shares to be donated to a charitable institution approved by the court.[50]

Where the friendly third party happens to be a regulated investment company, additional problems may develop. Section 17(d) of the Investment Company Act of 1940 and Rule 17d-1 thereunder make it unlawful, without prior Commission approval, to effect any transaction in which a registered investment company is a joint or a joint and several participant with an "affiliate" or "an affiliate of an affiliate" of such investment company.[51] Thus, it may be unlawful for an investment company, without prior Commission approval, to purchase more than 5 percent of the target's shares at the request or suggestion of a prospective offeror which already owns more than 5 percent of the target's shares since the prospective offeror may be deemed to be an "affiliate of an affiliate" (the target company) of the investment company. Similarly, acquisitions of the target shares made at the request or suggestion of the prospective offeror by an investment company which already owns 5 percent or more of *the prospective offeror's shares* may be prohibited unless the Commission has first approved the proposed transactions, since the prospective offeror may be deemed an affiliate of the investment company.[52] While there are many difficulties in proving a joint

[50] The method of disposition ordered by the court in connection with the shares held by the broker-dealer deserves special note. During the course of the proceedings in this case, Transnation Development Corp. (formerly G & W Land and Development Corp.) announced its intention to make another tender offer for shares of Roosevelt. The court order provided that should Transnation make a tender offer within sixty days after entry of judgment in this case at a price equal to or in excess of the broker's cost, the broker would be required to tender such shares pursuant to the offer.

The comprehensive nature of the sanctions in this case prompted two commentators to remark that "In an exercise of discretion, the defendants were not required to adorn themselves with scarlet letters." *See* Robinson and Mahoney, *Schedule 13D: Wild Card in the Takeover Deck,* 27 BUS. LAW 107 (July 1972).

[51] With regard to the definition of an "affiliate," see text accompanying notes 35–36, *supra*.

[52] Acquisitions by an investment company of more than 5 percent of the target shares for the purpose of aiding the target in defeating a takeover attempt may be similarly prohibited by Section 17(d) and Rule 17d–1.

participation between an investment company and the offeror, such an arrangement may be inferred from recommendations made by the offeror to the investment company, the use of the same broker, and the exchange of information regarding the investment company's holdings in the target.[53] The existence of a written agreement requiring the offeror to repurchase the shares from the investment company would clearly establish such joint participation and may also constitute an unlawful extension of credit in violation of the margin rules. Even where there are no Section 17(d) or margin regulation problems, an investment company must carefully consider its role in a takeover attempt as any active participation may constitute a violation of its fundamental investment policy prohibiting investments for the purpose of exercising control.[54] In addition, active participation in a takeover

[53] *See* SEC v. Talley Industries, Inc., 399 F.2d 396 (2d Cir. 1968), *cert. denied,* 393 U.S. 1015 (1969). For subsequent proceedings, *see* SEC v. General Time Corp., 407 F.2d 65 (2d Cir. 1968), *cert. denied,* 393 U.S. 1026 (1969). *See also* General Time Corp. v. Talley Industries, Inc., 403 F.2d 159 (2d Cir. 1968), *cert. denied,* 393 U.S. 1026 (1969).

[54] *See also, In the Matter of* Provident Management Corp., SEC Securities Act Release No. 5115 (Dec. 1, 1970) CCH FED. SEC. L. REP. ¶ 77,937, where the Commission found that the receipt of soliciting dealers fees by an affiliated broker-dealer of a registered investment company for shares tendered by the investment company constituted violations of: (a) Section 17 (e)(1) of the Investment Company Act of 1940 by such broker-dealer (wholly owned by the president of the investment company); and (b) Section 17(a) of the 1933 Act, Section 10(b) and Rule 10b–5 of the 1934 Act, and Section 206 of the Investment Adviser's Act of 1940 by (i) the investment adviser and principal underwriter of the investment company and (ii) the president of the investment company.

Section 17(e)(1) of the 1940 Act makes it unlawful for an affiliated person of a registered investment company, acting as agent, to accept from any source any compensation for the purchase or sale of any securities by such investment company, except in the course of such person's business as an underwriter or broker.

The Commission found that the retention of the soliciting dealers fees by the broker-dealer in connection with securities tendered by the investment company "constituted an impermissible form of personal enrichment derived from Fund's portfolio transactions," since the broker-dealer in effect performed no compensable services for the Fund. The Commission noted further that "to countenance such conduct would permit the determination whether an investment company's portfolio securities should be tendered to be influenced by considerations relating to the affiliate's compensation, and thereby create a conflict of interest between those acting in a fiduciary capacity for the investment company and the fund." *Cf.* Moses v. Burgin, 445 F.2d 369 (1st Cir. 1971), *rev'g* 316 F. Supp. 31 (D. Mass. 1970), *cert. denied, sub nom.* Johnson v. Moses, 92 S. Ct. 532 (1972). *See also* Butowsky, *Fiduciary Standards of Conduct Revisited—Moses v. Burgin and Rosenfeld v. Black,* 17 N.Y.L.F. 735 (1971).

contest may well result in the investment company being considered a member of a takeover "group." [55]

SECTION 4. *CONSIDERATIONS IN DETERMINING THE TYPE OF OFFER TO BE MADE*

A. GENERAL CONSIDERATIONS

There are three basic types of tender offers that a prospective offeror will consider before reaching a decision as to the best method of proceeding with its takeover attempt:

(a) A cash tender offer;

(b) An exchange tender offer whereby the offeror issues either its common or preferred stock, convertible or nonconvertible subordinated debentures, bonds, warrants or some combination thereof:

(c) A combination cash and exchange tender offer.

Where adequate financing is available, many tender offerors favor the cash offer as the best method of achieving their objectives. The cash tender offer has the advantage of being "readily comprehensible to the average investor" and is also "considerably easier to make from the standpoint of the federal securities laws." [56]

Perhaps the main advantage of the cash tender is the element of surprise. The cash offeror, for example, can commence his offer contemporaneously with the filing of his disclosure statement under the Williams Act. In a contested struggle for control, the offeror thereby obtains a distinct advantage during the crucial first days of the offer while the target company is still mobilizing its forces. In contrast, the exchange offeror, by virtue of the registration and filing requirements of the Securities Act of 1933, must disclose his hand well in advance of the effective date of the offer.

The cash tender offeror also has a distinct psychological ad-

[55] *See* Thomas, *Warehousing, supra* note 43 at 975. See text accompanying notes 45–76, Chapter 4.

With regard to the practice of "warehousing" as a violation of Section 10(b) and Rule 10b–5 thereunder, see text accompanying notes 38–44, *supra*.

[56] *See* INSTITUTIONAL INVESTOR STUDY, *supra* note 33, at 2833.

vantage in that he is not required to convince the stockholder that he can do a more efficient job in managing the target company because the tendering shareholder disposes of his investment interest for cash and need not evaluate the relative efficiency of the incumbent management and the insurgent offeror. In contrast, the interests of prudent investment judgment would necessarily require the tendering shareholder to make such an evaluation in an exchange offer because he will, in effect, be exchanging an interest in the target for one in the offeror. Thus, the almost primitive appeal to stockholders in straight dollars and cents language can prove to be a decided advantage in attempting to acquire control.

There are several basic considerations in determining the type of securities to be issued pursuant to an exchange offer. A convertible debenture offering, or an exchange offer package consisting of both debt and equity securities, for example, may have greater appeal to stockholders than a straight equity package, as it will enable them to combine the greater certainty of a specified return on their investment with the opportunity to participate in the future growth of the offeror. On the other hand, the use of a straight debt offering may enable the offeror to show a substantial increase in reported earnings per share. (As discussed below, this may be particularly important to the offeror who intends to make future acquisitions by means of exchange offers.)

The combination cash and exchange offer, while rather uncommon, has been used with varying degrees of success over the years. This type of offer has been used primarily where the offeror does not have sufficient financing to make a full cash tender offer. Moreover, the combination offer has the added appeal of providing a little something for everyone (sometimes referred to as the smorgasbord approach), thereby increasing the spectrum of potential tendering stockholders who may be attracted to the offer.[57]

[57] *Cf.* "Notice of Special Meeting of Shareholders," Standard Prudential Corp. (March 27, 1969) at 4, describing a proposal to make an exchange offer which provided, *inter alia,* that shareholders who previously tendered shares pursuant to a Standard cash tender offer could elect to receive the exchange package in lieu of cash.

B. Tax and Accounting Considerations [58]

In an effort to structure a tender offer which will best promote the offeror's interests and objectives, it will be necessary to consider the tax impact of the offer on both the offeror and the tendering shareholder.[59] The acceptance of a cash offer creates a taxable event resulting in a recognizable gain or loss to the tendering shareholder.[60] The same will be true of an exchange offer where the offeror does not own after the offer at least 80 percent of the total combined voting power of all classes of the target's stock entitled to vote and at least 80 percent of the total number of shares of all other classes of stock of the target.[61] An exchange offer involving the issuance of any amount of non-voting securities of the offeror, or indeed any securities or other property other than voting stock of the offeror will also result in a recognizable gain or loss to the tendering shareholder.[62] Where the tendering shareholder recognizes a taxable gain or loss on the tender, the offeror's basis for the shares accepted will be the price paid for such shares in a cash offer or, in the case of an exchange offer, the value of the securities issued. Where the offer does not result in a taxable gain or loss to the tendering shareholder, the offeror's basis for tax purposes will generally be the tendering shareholder's cost or other basis for such shares. Thus, if the offeror subsequently decides to dispose of shares acquired pursuant to a tax free exchange offer, he may well be subject to a greater tax burden than that imposed if the exchange offer had itself resulted in a recognizable gain or loss.[63]

[58] Extensive discussion on the full range of tax and accounting problems involved in tender offers is beyond the scope of this treatise. The following discussion is limited to highlighting some of the more basic problems confronting the tender offeror.

[59] For articles on the tax and accounting problems of tender offers, *see* Fox, *Tender Offers: An Analysis of the Related Tax Considerations Involved*, 30 J. TAX 340 (June 1969); Lipman, *Cooling Mergers*, 4 REV. OF SEC. REG. 921 (May 21, 1971); Shop Talk, *Possible Traps for Shareholders in Tender Offers*, 28 J. TAX 256 (April 1968).

For a fascinating discussion of the use of a private tax ruling as a defensive tactic, *see* Shop Talk, *Interesting Use of Private Ruling in Tender Offer*, 28 J. TAX 319 (May 1968).

[60] *See* Int. Rev. Code § 368(a)(1)(B); Treas. Reg. § 1.368–2(c).

[61] *Id.* [62] *Id.*

[63] With regard to the practical difficulties in determining the basis for securities acquired pursuant to an exchange offer, *see* BNA Tax Management Portfolios, No. 78–2nd, at A–43, A–44 (1969).

Expenses incurred in connection with the acquisition of shares must be capitalized.[64] Such expenses would include brokerage commissions and soliciting dealers fees, as well as legal, accounting and other fees which can be considered as expenses incurred in connection with or incidental to the acquisition process itself.[65] On the other hand, most expenses incurred in connection with an unsuccessful offer can be deducted as an ordinary expense.[66]

In recent years there have been several significant changes in both the tax laws and generally accepted accounting principles which have had an effect on tender offers. A brief review of these developments follows.

(1) Tax Reform Act of 1969 [67]

One of the more striking characteristics of takeover activity during the 1960's was the extensive issuance of bonds and debentures for the purpose of effecting mergers and acquisitions. The use of debt securities rather than stock was attributed, in part, to certain inducements generated by the tax laws, which in turn acted as a stimulant to merger and acquisition activity in general.[68] The unhealthy economic implications of highly leveraged capital structures, coupled with the significant increase in the number of mergers and acquisitions as well as the size of the corporations involved in such transactions, resulted in a predictable clamor for remedial legislation. Accordingly, Congress turned its attention to those provisions of the tax laws which it felt created undesirable inducements to the issuance of debt securities in corporate acquisitions. The following paragraphs summarize the two major changes under the Tax Reform Act of 1969 affecting the issuance of debt securities in tender offers.[69]

[64] *See* Woodward v. Commissioner, 397 U.S. 572 (1970); U.S. v. Hilton Hotels Corp., 397 U.S. 580 (1970).

[65] *See supra* note 64; Rev. Rul. 69–561, 1969–2 Cum. Bull. 25; Rev. Rul. 69–330, 1969–1 Cum. Bull. 51; Treas. Reg. § 1.263(a)–2(e).

[66] *See* Rev. Rul. 67–125, 1967–1 Cum. Bull. 31, 32; Bittker and Eustice, Federal Income Taxation of Corporations and Shareholders at ¶ 5.04, 5–11, ¶ 5.07, 5–29 (3d ed. 1971).

[67] Pub. L. No. 91–172.

[68] H.R. Rep. No. 91–413 (Pt. 1), 91st Cong., 1st Sess. 101, 102 (1969).

[69] In addition to the provisions discussed below, the Tax Reform Act of 1969 provided for revisions in the rules governing original issue discounts. Since these revisions may affect the issuance of debt securities in tender offers, they should be carefully reviewed prior to undertaking such an offer.

(a) Interest Deduction Limitations on Debt Incurred in Connection with Acquisitions

It is well recognized that the tax laws permit the deduction of interest paid on debt securities in contrast to the nondeductibility of dividends paid on stock. Where the characteristics of a security classified as a "debt obligation" more closely resemble a stockholder's interest rather than a creditor's interest, the distinction between debt and equity becomes somewhat obscure. Convertible subordinated debentures, for example, which are frequently issued in connection with mergers and acquisitions, contain elements of both debt and equity securities.[70] To discourage the issuance of substantial amounts of such securities, Congress chose to restrict the availability of interest deductions thereon. Accordingly, Section 411 of the Tax Reform Act of 1969 [71] provides, in essence, that annual interest charges in excess of $5 million [72] on debt incurred after October 9, 1969, by a corporation for the purpose of making an acquisition will be disallowed as an expense if the debt is:

(a) issued for stock (or two-thirds of the assets of the "acquired" corporation);
(b) subordinated to the claims of general creditors or to any substantial amount of unsecured debt;
(c) convertible into stock of the offeror or part of an investment unit which includes a warrant or other option to acquire stock of the offeror; and
(d) the debt-equity ratio of the offeror as of a date specified in the statute exceeds two-to-one, or the average annual earn-

[70] Exchange offer packages consisting of combinations of convertible subordinated debentures and warrants and/or other hybrid securities have sometimes been referred to as "funny money." The term has also been used to describe exchange offer packages where there is a substantial question regarding the offeror's ability to meet its obligations under the terms of the instruments.

[71] Int. Rev. Code § 279.

[72] The $5 million allowable is reduced by the amount of annual interest charges incurred by the offeror on obligations issued after December 31, 1967, for the purpose of acquiring stock or two-thirds of the assets of the acquired corporation but which is not "corporate acquisition indebtedness" as that term is defined in § 279(b) of the Int. Rev. Code. *See* Int. Rev. Code § 279(a).

ings for a specified three-year period do not exceed three times the annual interest to be paid or accrued.[73]

(b) Limitations on Reporting Gains on the Installment Method

Security holders who receive debentures in exchange for their stock in a target corporation are generally treated as having a taxable gain in the amount by which the value of the debentures received exceeds the holder's tax basis of the stock exchanged. Prior to the Tax Reform Act, however, stockholders electing to report the gain on the installment method could effectively defer any tax until the debentures were redeemed. The installment method of reporting was available if the sales price was in excess of $1,000 and the payments received by the seller in the year of sale (excluding the debt obligation itself) did not exceed 30 percent of the sales price. Thus, the target's stockholders could, in most instances, receive the benefits of long-term deferral while the offeror would get the benefit of a stepped-up cost basis which generally is not available in a transaction in which there is no recognizable gain.

Presumably the installment method of reporting gains was initially permitted because the seller received a debt obligation which, in theory, did not provide him with the cash to pay the tax.[74] Debentures issued in exchange offers, however, are in most cases readily marketable and can be properly considered as a "cash equivalent." Accordingly, Section 412 of the Tax Reform Act [75] provides, in effect, that for purposes of determining whether 30 percent or less of the selling price is received in the year of sale, bonds or debentures in a form designed to make it possible to readily trade such securities "on an established securities market," shall be considered as payments received in the year of sale. This limitation effectively eliminates the availability

[73] Section 411 contains special rules for banks and finance companies as well as certain exemptions from the application of the prohibitions set forth therein. Accordingly, specific reference to the statute is essential before any determination is made with regard to any particular problem arising thereunder.

[74] H.R. Rep. No. 91–413 (Pt. 1), 91st Cong., 1st Sess. 107 (1969).

[75] Int. Rev. Code § 453(b).

of the installment method of reporting gains in most all exchange tender offers involving the issuance of debentures.

(2) Recent Changes in Generally Accepted Accounting Principles

In 1970, the Accounting Principles Board ("APB") of the American Institute of Certified Public Accountants adopted certain new rules which were ostensibly designed to eliminate certain abuses resulting from accounting practices employed in connection with business combinations.[76] The area of particular concern was the abuses which were said to result from the use of "pooling of interest" accounting, as compared with the "purchase" method of accounting.

APB Opinion No. 16 describes the pooling-of-interests method of accounting as follows:

> The pooling of interests method accounts for a business combination as the uniting of the ownership interests of two or more companies by exchange of equity securities. No acquisition is recognized because the combination is accomplished without disbursing resources of the constituents. Ownership interests continue and the former bases of accounting are retained. The recorded assets and liabilities of the constituents are carried forward to the combined corporation at their recorded amounts. Income of the combined corporation includes income of the constituents for the entire fiscal period in which the combination occurs. The reported income of the constituents for prior periods is combined and restated as income of the combined corporation.

The purchase method of accounting is described in APB Opinion No. 16 as follows:

> The purchase method accounts for a business combination as the acquisition of one company by another. The acquiring corporation records at its cost the acquired assets less liabilities assumed. A difference between the cost of an acquired company and the sum of the fair values of tangible and identifiable intangible assets less liabilities is recorded as goodwill. The reported income of an acquiring corporation includes the operations of the acquired company after acquisition, based on the cost to the acquiring corporation.

[76] *See* APB Opinions Nos. 16 and 17, issued August 1970. *See also* APB Opinion No 15, issued May 1969, regarding the reporting of per share earnings.

The distinct advantage of the pooling method of accounting is that it can result in higher reportable earnings per share as compared with the purchase method.[77] Since increases in earnings per share from operations generally are believed to reflect "growth," such increases can be expected to contribute to a higher market value as well as a higher price/earnings ratio for a company's stock. Accordingly, acquisition-minded companies are often partial to the pooling method of reporting, particularly where future acquisitions by means of exchange offers are contemplated.[78]

The two principal abuses which were said to exist under pooling accounting and the APB's responses thereto are as follows:

(1) The practice of an acquiring company selling assets of an acquired company at a price substantially in excess of book value shortly after consummating an acquisition. Since the pooling method permitted the recording of the acquired company's assets at book rather than market value, the effect of the sale was to generate "instant earnings" for financial reporting purposes. APB Opinion No. 16 now provides, with certain exceptions, that an acquiring corporation cannot use pooling accounting if it plans to dispose of a significant portion of the assets of the combined company within two years after the combination.

(2) The practice of making acquisitions after the end of the acquiring company's fiscal year but prior to the issuance of the acquiring company's annual report. This practice enabled the earnings of the acquired company to be pooled

[77] The reasons for this are as follows: (a) Under the purchase method of accounting, only earnings of the acquired corporation from the date of acquisition can be consolidated with those of the acquiring company. Pursuant to pooling of interests accounting, however, the acquiring company can consolidate at least a portion of the target's earnings which were generated prior to the acquisition date; and (b) under the purchase method of accounting, depreciable assets are written up to market values and the value of goodwill must be established and amortized over a period not to exceed forty years. Under pooling accounting, depreciable assets are carried forward to the acquiring corporation at the values recorded on the books of the acquired corporation. In addition, no goodwill is created under pooling accounting. *See* APB Opinions Nos. 16 and 17.

[78] Stated in other words, the cost of acquisitions by means of an exchange offer will be reduced as the market value of the offeror's shares increases, since the number of shares which the offeror will be required to issue pursuant to the exchange offer will be correspondingly less.

for the prior fiscal year in the annual report. APB Opinion No. 16 permits pooling of earnings only for the fiscal year in which the combination is effected.

Significantly, APB Opinion No. 16 sets forth additional limitations regarding the use of pooling of interests accounting.[79] The practical effect of these limitations has been to eliminate the use of pooling accounting in many exchange tender offers. APB Opinion No. 16 provides, for example, that pooling accounting may be used only where a corporation offers and issues only voting common stock[80] in exchange for substantially all of the voting common stock of the company to be acquired.[81] For purposes of this condition, "substantially all of the voting common stock" means 90 percent or more of the voting common of the company to be acquired.[82]

In addition, pooling accounting may only be used where, at the dates the plan of combination is initiated and consummated, the combining companies hold as intercorporate dividends no more than 10 percent in total of the outstanding voting common stock of any combining company.[83] Thus, the purchase of more than 10 percent of the offeror's stock by the target company may constitute an effective method of thwarting the offer where the efficacy of consummating the takeover attempt is largely dependent on the availability of pooling accounting.

In summary, APB Opinion No. 16 will now compel many offerors to use the purchase method of accounting in effecting business combinations which previously could be reported on a pooling basis. As previously noted, the effect of purchase accounting when compared to pooling accounting may be to reduce the reported earnings per share of the offeror, thereby possibly adversely affecting the offeror's ability to consummate additional acquisitions.[84] In this regard, APB Opinion No. 16 can be expected to dampen some of the enthusiasm of prospective exchange offerors.

[79] *See* ¶¶ 45–48, APB Opinion No. 16.

[80] Previously pooling was normally permitted where an exchange offer package contained up to 10 percent cash.

[81] *See* ¶ 47, APB Opinion No. 16. [82] *Id.* [83] *See* ¶ 46, APB Opinion No. 16.

[84] See text and accompanying notes 77–78, *supra*.

SECTION 5. *PRICING THE OFFERING*

A. GENERAL PRINCIPLES AND PRACTICES

The determination of the premium over market price which will be offered for tendered shares represents one of the most important decisions which the prospective tender offeror will be required to make in planning its offer. While the ultimate success or failure of an offer often depends upon a variety of economic and psychological factors, the extent of the premium can prove to be the most important. A handsome premium above market, for example, can compensate for an ineffective solicitation effort [85] or overcome active opposition by the management of the target company, and in some instances may even influence the position taken by the target's management with regard to the offer.

The prospective offeror will initially consider the premium issue in terms of both the maximum it would be willing to pay and the minimum it believes necessary to attract tenders for the aggregate number of shares which it seeks to obtain. Once these parameters are established, the prospective offeror can begin to consider the economic feasibility of undertaking the offer. One leading study of cash tender offers has stated that some experts start with a 20 percent premium as a rule of thumb and then refine this figure to reflect the special circumstances of the particular offer.[86] A number of these special factors are outlined in subsection B below.

Tender offers involving an exchange of securities or a combination of cash and securities present additional problems in properly pricing the offering. A number of exchange offers, for exam-

[85] The extent of the solicitation effort can be expected to bear some relationship to the fees which are paid to broker-dealers for soliciting tenders. If the fees are comparatively high, broker-dealers will obviously be inspired to extend their solicitation efforts. The importance of the solicitation effort has apparently prompted some offerors to pay relatively high solicitation fees as an alternative to higher premiums. *See* Hayes and Taussig, *Tactics of Cash Takeover Bids*, 45 HARV. BUS. REV. 135, 141 (March/April 1967).

[86] *See* Hayes and Taussig, *supra* note 85, at 139–40.

Where the market price has substantially increased by virtue of an existing competing offer, it generally will not be economically feasible to offer a large premium over the current market price of the target's shares.

ple, have consisted of varying combinations of common stock, warrants, and newly issued classes of income-producing convertible or nonconvertible debt or equity securities which are extremely difficult to appraise in terms of realistic market values.[87] The added risks to shareholders in accepting securities of uncertain values in a newly structured corporation will generally compel an exchange offeror, in order to attract tenders, to offer a greater premium than would be required in a comparable cash offer.

B. Factors to Be Considered in Determining the Premium

(1) Current Market Price of the Target's Shares

Lower-priced stocks often command proportionately higher premiums than shares selling at higher levels. There is no economic justification for such a result. It apparently derives from the fact that a $12 bid for a security currently selling at $10 will have less visceral appeal than a $60 bid for a $50 security—despite identical 20 percent premiums for both offers.

(2) Market Conditions

Depressed market conditions stimulate the appetite of acquisition-minded companies seeking to take over successful companies whose stocks have fallen upon hard times. While such conditions can create excellent opportunities to make some bargain cash purchases, a prospective offeror cannot be certain that a significant number of shares will be tendered at depressed prices, because many investors will be reluctant to take large capital losses on their investments. Under such circumstances, a prospective offeror should seriously consider offering a premium in excess of that which would be necessary during better times, thereby enabling shareholders to recoup a greater portion of their unrealized losses.

[87] Prospective offerors considering offers of this type will normally find it essential to retain the services of a leading investment banking house to furnish a confidential valuation of the exchange offer package in advance of the actual offer.

(3) Number of Shares to Be Acquired; Turnover of Shares; Floating Supply

In determining the extent of the premium, consideration should also be given to the number of shares sought to be acquired in relation to both the outstanding "float" and the average turnover of the target's shares. Thus, for example, where the number of shares sought to be acquired is comparatively small in relation to the float and the turnover, the prospective offeror may be able to achieve its objectives by offering only a modest premium above market. Conversely, the greater the number of shares sought in relation to these factors, the greater the economic incentive which will normally be required to attract the desired tenders.

(4) The Position of the Target's Management with Regard to the Offer

Careful consideration must also be given to the probable position of the target's management with regard to the offer. Where there is evidence to indicate that the target will actively oppose the bid, the offeror should consider offering a greater premium in an effort to counteract the target's opposition. The offeror may also choose to offer a comparatively high premium where the decision of the target's management to recommend acceptance or to oppose the bid may conceivably be determined by the size of the premium.

(5) Corporate Image

The corporate image of both the offeror and the target company may also have an impact on the price which must be paid to induce shareholders to tender. Thus, where an offeror of limited accomplishment and reputation attempts to take over a respected and well-run financial or industrial corporation, shareholders may be reluctant, for reasons dictated by other than financial considerations, to tender their shares. In such circumstances, the offeror may decide to offer an unusually large premium on the theory that generous economic incentives will aid in severing the emotional attachments which some investors have to corporate entities.

(6) Contingent Nature of the Offering

Where the terms of an offer contain a number of qualifications which condition or make uncertain the offeror's obligation to purchase shares, shareholders may be reluctant to tie up their shares when there is a substantial possibility that they will not be accepted. Thus, where the offeror is not obliged to purchase any shares unless a relatively large number of the outstanding shares are tendered, it may be advisable to offer a premium which exceeds that which might be offered if the offeror unconditionally committed itself to purchase all shares tendered. Similarly, a pro rata offer may have to carry a greater economic inducement than an offer in which the offeror agrees to purchase all shares tendered.

Section 6. *REGULATORY CONSIDERATIONS IN CONNECTION WITH FINANCING THE CASH TENDER OFFER*

Perhaps the most fundamental decision confronting the cash tender offeror, once an approximation of the cost of the takeover has been determined, will be the method of financing the bid. Where the offeror has surplus cash which is not otherwise needed for current or anticipated future operations, the bid may be financed internally. However, where internal sources of financing are not available, the offeror will consider various methods of third party financing.

One form of third party financing has been through private placements. It has not been uncommon, for example, for prospective offerors to finance their bids through the private sale of their own stock, warrants, and/or other securities to institutional investors, thereby generating the cash needed to purchase the target's shares.[88] To a more limited extent, tender offerors have relied on broker-dealers and insurance companies for the financing of tender offers.

Where third party financing is necessary, tender offerors have generally relied upon loans from commercial banks. Financing by commercial banks usually consists of "stand-by" financing, in

[88] *See* Institutional Investor Study, *supra* note 33, at 2836.

that the funds are only borrowed if the tender offer is consummated. If the tender offer is unsuccessful, the offeror's only obligation is to pay a "stand-by" or "commitment" fee, which will generally range from 1/4 of 1 percent to 1/2 of 1 percent of the aggregate lending commitment.

Extensions of credit by banks, broker-dealers, and other lenders such as insurance companies may be subject to the Federal Reserve Board margin rules as set forth in Regulations G, T, or U.[89] Regulation U, for example, places certain restrictions upon banks which extend "purpose credit,"[90] including loans made for the "business purpose of purchasing a controlling interest in a corporation."[91] Some banks, however, have apparently made large "non-purpose" or "unsecured" loans to tender offerors in an effort to avoid the margin restrictions.[92] Such financing of takeover bids has been characterized by the chairman of one of the larger U. S. conglomerates as "imaginative lending."[93]

[89] *See* Regulation U, 12 C.F.R. ¶ 221 (1971)(banks); Regulation T, 12 C.F.R. § 220 (1971)(broker-dealers); and Regulation G, 12 C.F.R. § 207 (1971)(persons other than banks and broker-dealers).

[90] "Purpose credit" is defined as: "Credit which is for the purpose, whether immediate, incidental, or ultimate, of purchasing or carrying a margin stock . . . despite any temporary application of funds otherwise." 12 C.F.R. § 221.3 (b)(1).

"The term 'margin stock' means any stock which is (1) a stock registered on a national securities exchange, (2) an OTC margin stock, (3) a debt security (i) convertible with or without consideration, presently or in the future, into a margin stock, or (ii) carrying any warrant or right to subscribe to or purchase, presently or in the future, a margin stock, (4) any such warrant or right, (5) any security issued by an investment company other than a small business investment company. . . ." 12 C.F.R. § 221.3 (v).

[91] 12 C.F.R. § 221.110(b)(2).

[92] It should be noted that Regulation U prohibits extensions of purpose credit which are directly or indirectly secured by any stock in an amount exceeding the maximum loan value of the collateral, as prescribed from time to time for stocks in 12 C.F.R. § 221.4. *See* 12 C.F.R. § 221.1(a). At present, the maximum loan value for a margin stock is 35 percent of its current market value. 12 C.F.R. § 221.4. For extensions of purpose credit secured by collateral other than stock, Regulation U merely limits banks to a good-faith determination. 12 C.F.R. § 221.3(s). Regulation U places no restrictions on unsecured loans. *Cf.* Regulation G, 12 C.F.R. § 207. *See* Comment, *Application of Margin Requirements to the Cash Tender Offer*, 116 U. PA. L. REV. 103 (1968).

As a practical matter, banks rarely make unsecured loans for the purpose of purchasing securities. Thus, even in cases where loans are denominated as unsecured, banks have retained custody of the securities purchased, and have relied upon such shares for repayment of the loan. *See* INSTITUTIONAL INVESTOR STUDY, *supra* note 33, at 2836. *See also S.E.C. Staff Asks Action On Banks Over Margins*, N. Y. Times, May 2, 1972, at 57.

[93] *See Hearings of the Antitrust Subcomm. (No. 5) of the House Committee on the Judiciary*, 91st Cong., 2d Sess., No. 23, Part 1 at 468 (1969), discussed in IN-

In order to avoid the margin restrictions, as well as to obtain the lowest possible interest rates, some tender offerors have sought to finance their bids through foreign sources. Extensions of credit by foreign lenders, exceeding permissible credit arrangements available to tender offerors through United States lenders under the margin rules, were upheld in *Metro-Goldwyn-Mayer, Inc. v. Transamerica Corp.*[94] In that case the United States District Court for the Southern District of New York held, *inter alia,* that neither the Securities Exchange Act of 1934 nor the margin regulations promulgated thereunder extended the jurisdiction of the federal courts to foreign lenders. The court's opinion was based primarily on the ground that the registration provisions of Regulation G, requiring registration with the Federal Reserve Bank of the district in which the lender's principal place of business is located, applied only to those lenders who could so register. For those who could not so register, the court reasoned that the regulation was inapplicable, and since no such Federal Reserve districts exist for foreign lenders the court held that Regulation G did not apply.[95]

Unfavorable reaction to the holding in the *MGM* case led to the enactment in 1970 of Section 7(f) of the Securities Exchange Act.[96] This new statutory provision differed markedly from the existing law in that it extended the coverage of the margin rules to borrowers as well as to lenders.[97] Thus, a United States borrower seeking funds or credit abroad in order to purchase securities must comply with the applicable margin requirements as if his lender were a domestic lender covered by already existing margin requirements.

VESTIGATION OF CONGLOMERATE CORPORATIONS—A REPORT BY THE STAFF OF THE ANTITRUST SUBCOMM. (No. 5) OF THE HOUSE COMM. ON THE JUDICIARY, 92d Cong., 1st Sess. at 168–69 (1971).

[94] 303 F. Supp. 1354 (S.D.N.Y. 1969).

[95] *Id.* at 1357–58. For a critical analysis of the *MGM* decision, *see* Comment, *Eurodollar Financing of Cash Tender Offers: A New Challenge to the Margin Requirements,* 118 U.PA.L. REV. 768 (1970); Recent decisions, *Extraterritorial Application of the Securities Exchange Act of 1934,* 1–2 LAW AND POLICY IN INTERNATIONAL BUSINESS 168 (1969–70).

[96] Foreign Bank Secrecy Act, Pub. L. 91–508, Title III, § 301(a); 15 U.S.C. § 78g(f) (Supp. IV 1970).

[97] Prior to enactment of Section 7(f) borrowers could have been found guilty of the margin rules on a conspiracy, or "aiding and abetting" theory.

Pursuant to Section 7(f), the Federal Reserve Board promulgated Regulation X [98] which implements the statute by specifically incorporating the margin requirements of Regulations G, T, and U. Subsection (a) of Regulation X [99] makes it mandatory for a borrower obtaining credit within the United States, from a Regulation G, T, or U lender, to conform its credit arrangements to the applicable margin rules.[100]

Subsection (b) of Regulation X implements Section 7(f) as it pertains to credit obtained from foreign sources.[101] This subsection provides that if purpose credit is obtained from a foreign branch of a U. S. bank, or a foreign branch or subsidiary of a U. S. broker-dealer, or a foreign branch of a U. S. "G-lender," such credit must comply with the applicable margin regulations as set forth in Regulations U, T, and G.[102] In addition, if credit is

[98] 12 C.F.R. § 224 (1971). [99] 12 C.F.R. § 224.2(a).

[100] One commentator has stated that although Regulation X does not explicitly prohibit borrowing from other, nonregulated lenders, the language of subsection (a) is "sufficiently ambiguous" to imply such a prohibition. *See* Karmel, *Margin Regulations Updated*, 4 Rev. of Sec. Reg. 832 (Dec. 8, 1971).

Subsection (a) of Regulation X provides in pertinent part as follows:

> A borrower shall not obtain any purpose credit from within the United States unless he does so in compliance with the following conditions:
>
> (1) Credit obtained from a G-lender shall conform to the provisions of Part 207 (Regulation G), which is hereby incorporated in this part (Regulation X). . . .
>
> (2) Credit obtained from a broker-dealer shall conform to the provisions of Part 220 (Regulation T), which is hereby incorporated in this part (Regulation X). . . .
>
> (3) Credit obtained from a bank shall be subject to the provisions of Part 221 (Regulation U), except for section 221.2(i). Except for such section, Part 221 (Regulation U) is hereby incorporated in this part (Regulation X).

There is nothing in the language of Section 7(f), nor in subsection (a) of Regulation X promulgated thereunder, which indicates any intention on the part of Congress or the Federal Reserve Board to regulate a borrower obtaining credit from a person other than a G, T, or U type lender. Stated in other words, there appears to be no intention to make G, T, or U type lenders the exclusive source of credit for purchasers of securities. Thus, borrowing from nonregulated lenders does not appear to create any lack of compliance with the conditions set forth in subsection (a) of Regulation X. In the normal situation involving tender offers, however, the occasion for borrowing from a nonregulated lender would be rare indeed. *See* 12 C.F.R. § 207.1 defining a G-lender.

[101] 12 C.F.R. § 224.2(b).

[102] 12 C.F.R. §§ 224.2(b)(1)(i)-(iii). Thus, for example, if a borrower obtains a loan or extension of credit from a foreign branch of a domestic bank, the borrower must comply with the provisions of Regulation U. 12 C.F.R. § 224.2(b) (1)(iii).

obtained from a foreign lender,[103] credit arrangements must conform to the provisions of Regulation G as if the person extending or arranging such credit were a domestic lender meeting the prerequisites of Regulation G.[104]

The effect of Section 7(f) and Regulation X on tender offerors is clear. Recourse to foreign banks to obtain financing, although perhaps advantageous for other reasons, is no longer a means by which the margin requirements may be circumvented.

[103] "The term 'foreign lender' means a person, other than a United States person, who in the ordinary course of his business extends, maintains, or arranges purpose credit outside the United States and who is not a foreign branch or subsidiary of a broker-dealer, a foreign branch of a bank, or a foreign branch of a G-lender." 12 C.F.R. § 224.2(b)(1)(iv).

[104] *Id.*

CHAPTER 3. ESSENTIAL INGREDIENTS OF THE CASH TENDER INVITATION

The tender invitation or announcement advising shareholders of the cash tender offer serves as the offeror's "prospectus" and is the basic tool employed in the solicitation of tenders.[1] As such, it is essential that the invitation contain all the information necessary to enable any shareholder to evaluate the offer and properly tender his shares. Where access to the shareholders' list has been obtained, the offeror can be expected to transmit copies of the invitation to each registered owner of the target's shares. Arrangements will also be made with broker-dealers to provide beneficial owners of securities held in street name with the tender invitation. To assure maximum exposure for the offer, the bidder will usually publish the invitation in general and financial newspapers of national daily circulation. Regional or local publications may also be used where there is some evidence of concentrated share ownership in a particular geographic area.

Invitations for cash tenders generally consist of three principal parts:

1. The basic terms and conditions of the offer;
2. The mechanics of tendering shares; and

[1] In an exchange offer (as distinguished from a cash offer), where the very length of the prospectus may numb potential tenderors into inaction, the tender invitation may serve as a valuable summary of the more important aspects of the bid. However, a tender invitation or advertisement used in connection with an exchange offer must comply with the publicity and promotion limitations applied to registered offerings. (*See* Rule 134 (17 C.F.R. § 230.134) and Rule 135 (17 C.F.R. § 230.135) promulgated pursuant to the Securities Act of 1933.) Accordingly, the announcement in the case of the exchange offer will be less extensive than the typical cash tender invitation unless the offeror publishes a summary prospectus pursuant to Rule 434a (17 C.F.R. § 230.434a) under the 1933 Act. *See also* Rule 434b (17 C.F.R. § 230.434b).

3. The information required by Rule 14d–1(c) promulgated pursuant to Section 14(d)(1) of the Securities Exchange Act of 1934.[2]

SECTION 1. *TERMS AND CONDITIONS OF THE OFFER*

A. THE OFFERING PRICE

The key element of the offer, which should be prominently displayed in the heading of the invitation, is the price at which the offeror stands ready to purchase the target's shares. Where the target has outstanding nonvoting securities convertible into its voting shares or more than one class of voting shares, the invitation may contain multiple offering prices reflecting the offeror's intention to purchase securities of each class.[3] The offering price is

[2] 17 C.F.R. § 240.14d–1, eff. July 30, 1968. Offers for the following types of securities are subject to the requirements of Section 14(d)(1) provided the offer contemplates that the offeror will own more than 5 percent of such securities after consummation of the offer:

(a) offers for any equity security which is registered pursuant to Section 12 of the 1934 Act;

(b) offers for any equity security of an insurance company which would have been required to be so registered except for the exemption contained in Section 12(g)(2)(G) of the 1934 Act; and

(c) offers for any equity security issued by a closed-end investment company registered under the Investment Company Act of 1940.

The provisions of Section 14(d) do not apply to the following types of offers:

(a) offers where the acquisition, together with all other acquisitions by the same person of securities of the same class during the preceding twelve months, would not exceed 2 per centum of that class;

(b) offers by the issuer of such security; and

(c) offers which the Commission may exempt as not entered into for the purpose of, and not having the effect of, influencing the control of the target company or otherwise as not comprehended within the purposes of Section 14(d).

Rule 14d–2 also exempts certain additional types of offers and communications from the provisions of Rule 14d–1(c), including the following: offers to purchase securities made in connection with a distribution of securities permitted by Rules 10b–6, 10b–7 and 10b–8; offers to purchase securities evidenced by a script certificate, order form or similar document which represents a fractional interest in a share of stock or similar security; offers to purchase securities pursuant to a statutory procedure for the purchase of dissenting shareholders' securities; offers for the call or redemption of any security in accordance with the terms and conditions of the governing instruments; and offers to purchase securities in transactions exempt from registration under the Securities Act of 1933 pursuant to Section 3(a)(10) thereof.

[3] *See, e.g.,* "Offer to Purchase Common Stock and 5 percent Convertible Subordinated Debentures of Electronic Specialty Co. by International Controls Corp. at $39 per share and $1,236 per $1,000 Debenture net (without brokerage

generally expressed as the net price to be received by tendering shareholders, and accordingly, transfer taxes, if any, which are paid by sellers of securities, are borne by the offeror. Other expenses of the offering such as brokerage commissions or solicitation fees are also paid by the offeror.

The invitation may also contain a table summarizing the price range of the target's stock during the last several years and the current market price. The inclusion of such information may be particularly effective where the tender price represents a substantial premium over the current market price or where the price range during the last several years has been substantially lower than the tender bid. The failure of the target to make any meaningful dividend payments may also be discussed.

B. The Number of Shares to Be Purchased

The invitation should specify the number of shares the offeror seeks to purchase as well as the terms pursuant to which the offeror will purchase if the number of shares tendered either exceeds or fails to equal the amount which the offeror seeks to obtain.[4]

The offeror will normally express its intent to purchase shares in one of the following forms:

1. The offeror will purchase all shares tendered; or
2. The offeror will purchase a specified number of shares if at

---

charge and free from transfer taxes) to the Seller," Wall Street Journal, Aug. 26, 1968, at 17; "General Host Corporation Offer to Purchase for Cash all Common and Preferred Stock of Cudahy Company at $22 per Common Share and $25 per Preferred Share," N.Y. Times, June 29, 1971, at 57. (The Cudahy Preferred Stock had both a conversion feature and voting rights.) *Cf.* provision in "Offer to Purchase for Cash Shares of Common Stock of J. J. Newberry Co. at $22 Per Share," N.Y. Times, Jan. 26, 1972, at 51, as follows: "Tenders of convertible securities of Newberry will not be accepted; any holder of such securities who wishes to accept this offer must first exercise his conversion privilege and then tender the shares of common stock received on conversion."

For an example of an extremely rare type of offer to purchase securities of more than one issuer, *see* "Thatcher Banking Partners Offer to Purchase Shares of Capital Stock and Certain Receipts Therefor of The First National Bank of Denver at $120.00 Per Share (and of Affiliated Banks at the prices set forth herein)," N.Y. Times, Aug. 6, 1968, at 49.

[4] *Cf.* the tender invitation of Thatcher Banking Partners, *supra* note 3, which failed to specify the number of shares sought by the offeror as well as other important details. Instead, the invitation provided that the complete terms of the offer were available "from the Depositary, the Dealer-Manager or your bank or broker."

least that number of shares is tendered. If the shares tendered do not equal the number of shares the offeror seeks to purchase, the offeror will invariably reserve the right to purchase all, a part, or none of the shares tendered. Similarly, where the shares tendered exceed the number of shares the offeror seeks to purchase, the offeror may purchase all, a part, or none of such excess shares; or

3. The offeror will purchase any and all shares tendered up to a specified maximum number of shares. If the shares tendered exceed the maximum number of shares the offeror commits itself to purchase, the offeror will reserve the right to purchase all, a part, or none of such excess shares.[5]

C. Pro Rata Purchases

If the offeror intends to purchase less than all outstanding shares, Section 14(d)(6) of the 1934 Act [6] requires that the shares be purchased on a pro rata basis, according to the number of shares deposited by each tenderor, where a greater number of securities than the offeror seeks to purchase is deposited within ten days after the invitation is first published.[7] If the shares tendered do not exceed the requested number during the first ten days of the offer, the offeror, at its option, may purchase any and all shares tendered on a first-come, first-served basis.

To evade the effect of pro rata purchases, the practice of short-tendering became popular. This practice, whereby brokers and others would tender a greater number of shares than they or their customers owned, resulted in a disproportionately large number of their securities being accepted in relation to the shares tendered by other persons. To eliminate this practice, the SEC

[5] The Hale Bros. Associates, Inc. invitation to purchase shares of Magnetics, Inc. contained a rather uncommon condition regarding the offeror's commitment to purchase. The offer provided that Hale Bros. would purchase all shares tendered up to 750,000 shares if at least 565,000 shares were tendered. The offer also provided that if less than 565,000 or more than 750,000 shares were tendered, Hale Bros. could purchase all but not less than all shares tendered, but would have no obligation to do so. Wall Street Journal, Nov. 5, 1968, at 24.

[6] 15 U.S.C. § 78n(d)(6).

[7] The NYSE guidelines on tender offers, which antedate the federal tender rules, also recommend pro rata purchases for a minimum ten-day period. *See* NYSE Company Manual, at A–179, 180.

adopted Rule 10b-4 which prohibits any person from tendering shares which he does not own.[8]

D. Return of Shares Not Purchased

Where an offer is made for less than all outstanding shares, the invitation must provide for the return of shares which are not accepted. Accordingly, provision is usually made for the return of unaccepted shares without expense to the shareholder promptly after the expiration of the offer. When the offeror accepts some but not all shares tendered by a stockholder, new certificates for the balance of shares returned may have to be issued. The shareholder may then expect some delay resulting from the transfer process. Similarly, delay can be expected where the shareholder requests, as permitted in some tender invitations, that shares not purchased be registered in a name other than that in which the tendered shares are registered.[9]

E. Date and Time of Expiration; Withdrawal Privileges

The date and time of expiration of the offer should be clearly indicated in the invitation. To be eligible for acceptance, most offers provide that tenders must actually be received by either the depositary or the forwarding agent on or before the date and time of expiration. However, the actual deposit of securities may take place after the expiration date. A number of offers provide for the acceptance of tenders without the concurrent deposit of shares where the tenderor obtains a guarantee from a securities dealer or a bank or trust company that the certificates will be deposited within a specified number of days after the expiration of the tender period.[10] The guarantee, however, must be received by the offeror's agent or depositary prior to the expiration date.

While the federal statutory provisions relating to tender offers do not expressly prescribe either the minimum or maximum

[8] 17 C.F.R. § 240.10b–4, eff. July 1, 1968. *See also* Bache & Co., Inc. v. International Controls Corp., 324 F. Supp. 998 (S.D.N.Y. 1971).

[9] A reasonable delay in returning shares not purchased apparently does not constitute a breach of contract nor does such delay violate Section 10(b) of the 1934 Act. *See* Salinger v. Ling-Temco-Vought, Inc., and Mellon National Bank and Trust Co., 324 F. Supp. 1006 (W.D. Pa. 1971), discussed in note 19, *infra*.

[10] *Cf.* Bache & Co., Inc. v. International Controls Corp., *supra* note 8.

length of the offering period, the combined effect of Sections 14(d)(5) and 14(d)(6) of the 1934 Act may create the same result.[11]

Section 14(d)(5) provides, *inter alia,* that a depositor (tendering shareholder) may withdraw his shares ". . . at any time after sixty days from the date of the original tender offer. . . ."[12] While the opportunity to withdraw does not preclude the offeror from continuing the bid for a longer period, it normally will be impractical to do so unless the offeror has received substantially fewer shares than it seeks to purchase as the risk of withdrawals must necessarily constitute a threat to the ultimate success of the offer.

Section 14(d)(5) also provides for withdrawal ". . . at any time

[11] *See* Hayes and Taussig, *Tactics of Cash Takeover Bids,* 45 HARV. BUS. REV. 135, at 141 (March–April 1967), a study of cash tender offers for the period 1956–1966 which found that the median time for contested cash tenders between announcement of the offer and the expiration date was seventeen days with the range being 4 to 82 days (excluding extensions of offers).

The NYSE recommends an offering period of approximately thirty days but in no event less than ten days. *See* NYSE COMPANY MANUAL, at A–180.

[12] The intent of this particular provision is to ". . . prevent tendered securities from being tied up indefinitely awaiting a decision by the person making the offer as to whether or not he will purchase them." *Report of Committee on Interstate & Foreign Commerce, "Disclosure of Corporate Equity Ownership,"* H.R. REP. No. 1711, 90th Cong., 2d Sess. 10 (1968). Unfortunately the language of the statute gives no clue as to the substance of the right to withdraw. E.g., if the offeror agrees to purchase all shares tendered, does this cut off the shareholder's right to withdraw if the offer continues for more than sixty days? Must the shareholder receive payment within sixty days? Must he receive notice of acceptance within sixty days? *Cf.* "Invitation for Tenders of 1,000,000 common shares of Metro-Goldwyn-Mayer, Inc. at $35 per share net," which provides that "All tendering stockholders waive any right to receive any notice of the acceptance of their tender." The offer also provides that "Shareholders who tender their shares . . . may withdraw such shares after September 21, 1969 [60 days], unless theretofore purchased by the undersigned. Payment for all shares duly tendered and purchased pursuant thereto will be made . . . not later than a reasonable time following the expiration of the right to tender hereunder." N. Y. Times, July 23, 1969, at 62. *See also* "Offer to Purchase 1,500,000 Shares of Capital Stock of Western Air Lines, Inc. by Kirk Kerkorian at $45 per share net," providing that, "Unless shares tendered have been paid for on or prior to February 6, 1969 [60 days] they may also be withdrawn after such date." N. Y. Times, Dec. 13, 1968, at 79.

There have been no cases interpreting this provision and the Commission has not exercised its rule-making power to clarify the problem. In the absence of any judicial or administrative expression on the subject, in the authors' opinion, the better rule would provide that the shareholder may withdraw his shares at any time after sixty days unless, prior thereto, he receives either payment for shares tendered or a notice of acceptance of the tender and a commitment to pay for such shares within a reasonable period.

until the expiration of seven days after the time definitive copies of the offer or request or invitation are first published. . . ."[13] This clause, however, does not appear to require the offeror to purchase shares for at least seven days if it does not choose to do so.

On the other hand, Section 14(d)(6), which provides that tendered shares must be purchased on a pro rata basis where the shares tendered exceed the number of shares to be purchased during the first 10 days of the offer, may require the offeror to continue to purchase shares for at least ten days.[14] However, where an offer is made for all outstanding shares, Section 14(d)(6) becomes inoperative and the offeror is not required to continue the bid for any minimum period of time.

F. Extension of the Offering Period

To increase the offeror's flexibility without adding to the risks of exposure to changing business and market conditions, most invitations provide that the offeror reserves the right to extend the length of the offering period.[15] If the invitation fails to provide for this possibility and the offering period is in fact extended, the extension may be considered a new offer which will require the offeror to create additional pro rata purchase and withdrawal privileges. In addition, an unauthorized extension may create withdrawal rights for all tendered shares which are not purchased by the original expiration date.[16] An unauthorized extension may also give

[13] In addition to the withdrawal rights created by Section 14(d)(5) of the 1934 Act, the tendering shareholder may have additional withdrawal rights as a matter of basic contract law. See subsection (f) of this section, *Extension of the Offering Period*. *Cf.* Levenburg v. Merrill Lynch, Pierce, Fenner & Beane, 334 Mich. 508, 54 N.W.2d 626 (1952).

[14] *See* Metro-Goldwyn-Mayer Inc. v. Transamerica Corp., 303 F. Supp. 1354 (S.D.N.Y. 1969). *But see* subsection (G) of this section, *The "Out" Clause*.

[15] From the offeror's viewpoint, the essence of a properly structured tender offer is one which creates maximum flexibility while at the same time granting potential tenderors some reasonable assurance that their shares will be accepted. If the offer is qualified by too many conditions and the invitation reads something like, "I'll buy all shares tendered—maybe," potential tenderors will be less likely to develop any interest in the offer. *See* Whitman, *The Strategy of Tender Solicitations*, Blair & Co., Inc., N.Y. (April 1967). For an example of an offer qualified by some unusual conditions, *see* "Contingent Offer to Purchase All the Outstanding Class A Common and Common Stock of the Automobile Banking Corporation," N.Y. Times, Aug. 2, 1968, at 51.

[16] *See* 5 Williston on Contracts (3d ed. 1961) §§ 663–666A, § 735 at 476–77; 8 Williston on Contracts (3d ed. 1964) § 952B.

rise to a cause of action for rescission or damages if payment for shares purchased pursuant to the original offer is not made promptly after the original expiration date.[17]

G. The "Out" Clause

The offeror determines the price to be paid for the target's shares based upon conditions existing shortly before the offer is made. During the offering period, however, any number of events may occur which the offeror can neither foresee nor control. An adverse change in the business or capitalization of the target, a national emergency or a physical disaster such as a hurricane or earthquake, to name but a few possibilities, may prove equally disastrous to the offeror if it proceeds with the offer or purchases shares already tendered. To reduce the risks of uncertainty the invitation should provide that the offeror may, at its option, withdraw the bid without any obligation to purchase any shares tendered if certain unforeseen developments occur.

A provision of this type might provide that:

> The offeror may withdraw this invitation at any time, at its option, and shall not be obligated to purchase any of the shares tendered pursuant to the offer if any state of war or national emergency or banking moratorium or suspension of trading on the New York Stock Exchange shall have been declared or if any act of sabotage or any natural disaster shall effect any material change in the business or operations of the target, or if any other material change in the capitalization or business of the target is proposed or occurs.[18]

[17] *Cf.* Salinger v. Ling-Temco-Vought, Inc. and Mellon National Bank and Trust Co., *supra* note 9. *See also* 6 Williston on Contracts (3d ed. 1962) §§ 845–857; 8 Williston on Contracts (3d ed. 1964) § 948.

[18] Surprisingly, a number of offers have not contained such clauses, thereby raising fundamental questions of contract law. Absent such a clause, can the offeror immediately terminate the offer? Even if the offer may be revoked at any time, is the offeror obligated to purchase those shares already tendered where a sufficient number of shares have been tendered to trigger the offeror's obligation to purchase (e.g., where the offeror agrees to purchase "X" number of shares if at least "X" number are tendered and such shares are in fact tendered or where the offeror agrees to take all shares tendered)? *See* 1 Williston on Contracts (3d ed. 1957) §§ 50–61D; 8 Williston on Contracts (3d ed.) § 947B at 69–70, § 948C at 152. *See also* Levenburg v. Merrill Lynch, Pierce, Fenner & Beane, 334 Mich. 508, 54 N.W.2d 626 (1952). If the offer may be revoked at any time and the con-

H. Payment of the Purchase Price

The time of payment of the purchase price will generally depend upon the alternatives which the offeror has with regard to its obligations to purchase shares. Where the offeror agrees to purchase all shares tendered, payment may be made shortly after delivery of the shares to the depositary. Thus the tendering shareholder may receive payment prior to the expiration of the offer. Where the offeror has the option of taking down less than all shares tendered, the invitation will normally provide that payment for shares tendered will be made promptly or within a reasonable period of time after the expiration of the offer. In practice, a short delay in payment can be expected to enable the offeror to prorate and process the shares tendered.[19]

I. Dividends and Distributions

Adequate provision must be made in the invitation for the possibility of the declaration and payment of dividends or distribu-

---

ditions binding the offeror to purchase shares have not been met at the time the offer is terminated, is the offeror nevertheless obligated to purchase shares already tendered since the inability to fulfill the conditions has been caused by the offeror's termination of the bid? *See* 5 Williston on Contracts (3d ed. 1961) § 677; 8 Williston on Contracts (3d ed. 1964) § 948C at 156.

[19] *See* Salinger v. Ling-Temco-Vought, Inc. and Mellon National Bank and Trust Co., 324 F. Supp. 1006 (W.D. Pa. 1971), where the plaintiff asserted a claim for damages pursuant to Section 10(b) of the 1934 Act for delays in payment for tendered shares purchased by the offeror and the return of tendered shares not purchased. LTV's tender invitation provided that the offer would expire on June 6, 1968, and that "Payment for shares tendered on or prior to June 6, 1968, will be made promptly thereafter." Plaintiff received payment for the shares accepted by the offeror on June 20, 1968, and on July 3, 1968, received a certificate representing the shares not purchased. Defendant's motion for summary judgment was granted upon findings that: (a) LTV committed no fraudulent act or omission under Section 10(b); and (b) Section 10(b) was not applicable to Mellon Bank, which served as the offeror's tender agent, since it was not a party to any representations concerning the stock of the target company.

The court went on to note that plaintiff's cause of action, if any, would be for breach of contract. In commenting on such an action the court stated that the commitment to pay "promptly" should be interpreted as meaning "without undue delay" rather than "instantly" and that a finding of a breach upon the facts of this case, where the delay in processing large amounts of tendered shares was unavoidable, would be "grossly unwarranted."

tions by the target company during the course of or in anticipation of the tender offer.[20] While the offeror may believe that its bid will be more attractive where the tendering shareholder retains the dividend or distribution, the failure to provide for the retention or recapture of a dividend or distribution which substantially alters the capital structure or financial position of the target company could seriously undermine the offeror's prospects for success as well as the contemplated economic benefits to be derived from the takeover.

Where the target company regularly pays a relatively modest cash dividend at or about the same time each year and the declaration, payment and/or record dates fall within or near the proposed tender offering period, the invitation may provide that the tendering shareholder will be entitled to retain the dividend without any corresponding reduction in the stated price which the offeror is willing to pay for the shares. On the other hand, the offeror must provide for the possibility that the target company, in an effort to undermine the takeover attempt, may significantly reduce its cash position by declaring a special and substantial cash dividend. To neutralize the potentially adverse effects of such action, the invitation can be expected to provide that the price paid for shares tendered will be reduced by the amount of such special dividend.

The offeror, however, may not be adequately protected simply by reducing the purchase price if the distribution takes the form of a stock dividend or rights offering because the resulting dilution of the offeror's proportionate interest in the target occasioned by the distribution must necessarily undermine its attempt to acquire control. Accordingly, many offers, in an attempt to counteract the target's defensive declaration of stock dividends or rights offerings, require the shareholder to remit such distribution to the depositary or the forwarding agent. Pending

[20] Where the record date for any dividend or distribution occurs prior to acceptance by the offeror of the tendered shares, payment will be made to the tendering shareholder. Even where the record date occurs after acceptance of the shares, payment may still be made to the tendering shareholder if the offeror's name has not yet been recorded, as transferee, on the books of the target company.

receipt of the distribution, the offeror will withhold payment of the purchase price.[21]

To deal with these contingencies many invitations contain provisions similar to the following:

> If the target company should declare any dividends or distributions or issue any rights which are payable to stockholders of record on a date occurring prior to the transfer to the offeror's name of any shares of common stock purchased under this offer, then (i) the purchase price per share payable by the offeror will be reduced by the amount of any cash dividend, and (ii) any other dividend, distribution, or rights shall be required to be remitted by the tendering stockholder to the depositary for the account of the offeror; and pending such remittance or appropriate assurance thereof, the offeror may withhold the purchase price or deduct from the purchase price the amount or value of such other dividend, distribution, or rights as to any shares of common stock purchased by the offeror but not transferred to the offeror's name by the record date therefor.

If the offeror had purchased securities in the open market, it would be entitled to the above described dividends or distributions only if the actual purchase took place before the ex-date. Provisions of the type noted above, however, have apparently created rights entitling the offeror to dividends or distributions even where the purchase takes place after the record date.

J. Brokerage Commissions and Solicitation Fees

The success or failure of a tender offer often depends upon the efforts of broker-dealers in soliciting shares of the target. The offeror who discounts the importance of the broker-dealer or the selection of an effective dealer-manager, because he believes that the premium offered over market will provide sufficient incentive

[21] In one instance, the offeror conditioned delivery of securities to be issued in an exchange offer on receipt of payment of a cash dividend. While the offeror may have found it necessary to proceed in this manner in order to avoid numerous adjustments in the exchange ratio, the target company emphasized this point in advertisements designed to discourage stockholders from tendering their shares. *See* B. F. Goodrich Statement to Stockholders, "Additional Reasons Why Northwest's Offer Will Fail," N.Y. Times, Aug. 7, 1969, at 53.

to encourage shareholders to tender, may be rudely surprised when the tendered shares are counted.[22]

The offeror will normally retain a brokerage firm as "dealer-manager" to direct and coordinate the solicitation effort. For its services, the dealer-manager may receive an override on all shares purchased, a fixed cash fee, stock, warrants or a combination thereof. Soliciting dealers receive a fee per share generally ranging from 1½ percent to 3 percent of the tender price on securities tendered through their respective firms and purchased by the offeror.[23] There is generally no limit on the maximum fees which will be paid to any one dealer for soliciting shares.[24]

The invitation for tenders will usually specify the amount of the solicitation fee to be received by soliciting dealers and will describe the class of eligible persons entitled to receive such fee. The offeror generally will seek the broadest possible solicitation effort. Nevertheless, a number of invitations have inexplicably limited the class of persons who may receive fees to members of the NASD or of a national securities exchange. Other offers have included banks and trust companies as well as foreign dealers (ineligible for membership in the NASD) which agree to comply with Section 25 (a) and (b) of the NASD Rules of Fair Practice.[25] Only a handful of offers seek to encourage truly comprehensive solicita-

[22] The importance to the offeror of broker-dealer participation was not always appreciated. *See* NYSE Member Firm Educational Circular No. 161 (June 15, 1962) and No. 216 (Nov. 18, 1966).

The role of the arbitrageur, i.e., the professional trader, must also be considered in evaluating the prospects for success. See Chapter 6, *infra*, "The Role of Professional Risk Arbitrageurs in Tender Offers."

[23] The New York Stock Exchange ban on customer-directed give-ups, effective December 8, 1968, would appear to bar such reciprocal arrangements with regard to tender solicitation fees. *See* NYSE CONSTITUTION, Art. XV, § 1. *See also, In the Matter of* Provident Management Corp., SEC Securities Act Release No. 5115 (Dec. 1, 1970), CCH FED. SEC. L. REP. ¶ 77,937, discussed in Chapter 2, note 54.

[24] *But see* the invitation of the Pyrites Co., Inc., for common stock of U.S. Borax & Chemical Corp. providing for a soliciting dealer's fee of .75 per share with a maximum to any one solictor of $2,500 in respect of all shares tendered on behalf of any one beneficial owner. Wall Street Journal, Dec. 9, 1968, at 27.

[25] Where the invitation does not include a particular class of solicitor, payment of the fee may be withheld. Foreign banks, which often function as securities dealers and have been named by customers as solicitors in connection with substantial numbers of shares tendered during the last several years, have experienced difficulties in this regard. To avoid problems of this nature, a nonspecified solicitor should contact the offeror prior to soliciting shares in order to obtain a commitment on the fee.

tion by providing for the payment of solicitation fees "to any securities dealer or to a bank or trust company."

This diversity in approach may result from differing interpretations of Section 25(a) of the NASD Rules, which provides: "No member shall deal with any nonmember broker or dealer except at the same prices, for the same commissions or fees, and on the same terms and conditions as are by such member accorded to the general public."

The applicability of Section 25(a) to solicitation fees generated in connection with a cash tender offer seems questionable.[26] Dealers engaged in the solicitation of tenders are not dealing or engaging in securities transactions with each other but rather are independently soliciting tenders of shares to be transmitted directly to the offeror's forwarding agent or depositary.[27] On the other hand, there may be some justification for applying Section 25(a) where all solicitation fees are paid to an NASD dealer-manager which then reallows a portion of such fees to soliciting

[26] With regard to exchange offers, however, the NASD Rules may prohibit equal participation in fees by members and nonmembers. Section 25(b)(2) provides that no NASD member shall "join with any nonmember broker or dealer in any syndicate or group contemplating the distribution to the public of any issue of securities or any part thereof." *But see In the Matter of* the National Association of Securities Dealers, Inc., SEC Adm. Proc. File No. 3-2428 (May 28, 1971) where the Hearing Examiner held, *inter alia*, that "The NASD's construction and application of its Rule 25 as precluding participation by its members as principal underwriters in parallel distributions is not legally justified under its Rule 25 or Section 15A(i) of the 1934 Act inasmuch as such parallel distributions involve no dealing with or 'joining with' the nonmember." CCH FED. SEC. L. REP. ¶ 78,098, at 80,386–87. The Commission found that the NASD has no authority under Section 15(A)(i) of the 1934 Act to restrict its members from receiving concessions in their dealings with non-member broker-dealers and can only prohibit its members, pursuant to Rule 25, from giving non-members concessions not available to the general public. *See In the Matter of the* National Association of Securities Dealers, Inc., SEC Securities Exchange Act Rel. No. 9362 (June 7, 1972), CCH FED. SEC. L. REP. ¶ 78,831.

[27] *See In the Matter of* the National Association of Securities Dealers, *supra* note 25. Even if Section 25(a) were applicable, invitations which have participation in fees limited to members of the NASD and of a national securities exchange, would not be in compliance because there is no exemption for over-the-counter dealings between NASD members and exchange members which are not NASD members. On the other hand, cash tender invitations which have been limited to NASD members and banks and trust companies would not contravene § 25(a) as Art. 1, § 3 of the NASD By-Laws excludes banks (defined to include trust companies) from the definition of a broker or dealer. However, an NASD member participating in the issue of securities as an underwriter or in a selling group may not allow any selling commission to any bank or trust company.

dealers. It is customary practice, however, for the offeror to pay the solicitation fee directly to the soliciting dealer.

SECTION 2. *MECHANICS OF TENDERING SHARES*

The process by which shares are actually tendered pursuant to the offer must be clearly specified in the invitation in order to facilitate the prompt transfer of shares to the offeror.

The shareholder who desires to tender must deliver his shares together with a properly executed "Letter of Transmittal" to the offeror's depositary or forwarding agent. The transmittal letter, which is drafted by the offeror, has become a rather standardized document and serves as the basic instrument for effecting the transfer of shares.[28] In addition to requiring the tendering shareholder to represent that he may lawfully sell the shares and that the offeror will acquire clear and unrestricted title,[29] the letter of transmittal will usually require the shareholder to provide the following:

[28] Since the letter of transmittal authorizes the transfer of the tendered shares to the offeror, stock certificates generally need not be endorsed or accompanied by stock powers unless payment for the shares is to be made to or stock certificates for any unpurchased shares are to be registered in the name of a person other than the registered owner.

[29] It is essential that the language regarding the tenderor's representations be precisely worded to insure that the offeror does not become obligated to purchase restricted shares which cannot be identified as such because the share certificates do not contain appropriate restrictive legends. *See* SEC Securities Act Release No. 5121 (Dec. 30, 1970), CCH FED. SEC. L. REP. ¶ 77,943. If the offeror subsequently decides to sell any tendered shares in the open market, he may be precluded from doing so without registration if he accepted any restricted shares during the course of the tender offer. *But see* "Notice of Adoption of Rule 144 Relating to the Definition of the Terms 'Underwriter,' in Sections 4(1) and 2(11) and 'Brokers Transactions,' in Section 4(4) of the Securities Act of 1933, Adoption of Form 144, and Rescission of Rules 154 and 155 Under That Act," SEC Securities Act Release No. 5223 (Jan. 11, 1972), CCH FED. SEC. L. REP. ¶ 78,487, stating as follows: "For the purpose of the rule, the doctrine of 'fungibility' will not apply. That is, the acquisition during the two-year period of other securities of the same issuer, whether restricted or nonrestricted will not start the holding period running anew."

Query, however, whether Rule 144 eliminates fungibility to the extent that unrestricted shares may be sold at any time and without regard to the two-year holding period by a person owning both restricted and unrestricted shares? For background on the fungibility rule, *see Disclosure to Investors; A Reappraisal of Federal Administrative Policies Under the '33 and '34 Acts; The Wheat Report,* at 172 (1969); *Fungibility,* 4 REV. OF SEC. REG. 905 (June 22, 1971). *See also* Wander, *Rule 144 Revised,* 4 REV. OF SEC. REG. 853,861 (Oct. 21, 1971); Wander, *Rule 144 Adopted,* 5 REV. OF SEC. REG. 957,959 (March 8, 1972).

(a) identification of the shares tendered (by certificate number);
(b) name, address and delivery instructions for payment of the purchase price or return of shares not accepted;
(c) signature of registered owner; and
(d) signature of authorized guarantor.[30]

As a convenience to shareholders, some invitations incorporate a detachable letter of transmittal. Other offers merely advise that the form may be obtained from the offeror's depositary, forwarding agent, or dealer-manager or from the shareholder's broker or bank.

SECTION 3. *INFORMATION REQUIRED BY STATUTE AND REGULATION [SECTION 14(d)(1), RULE 14d-1(c)]*

Section 14(d)(1) of the 1934 Act [31] grants the SEC rule-making authority regarding, *inter alia*, information to be included in any tender invitation or announcement. Pursuant thereto, the Commission adopted Rule 14d-1(c) [32] which requires the tender invitation to contain the following information:

(i) The name of the person making the tender offer or invitation;
(ii) Provision for the depositor's withdrawal of shares [Section 14(d)(5)];
(iii) Date of expiration of period during which securities will be taken up pro rata [Section 14(d)(6)];
(iv) The information required by Items 2(a), (c) and (e), 3, 4, 5, and 6 of Schedule 13D, or a fair and adequate summary thereof.

a. Name and business address of the person filing Schedule 13D [Item 2(a)];

[30] A guarantee of delivery is normally required where there has been a tender without a concurrent deposit of share certificates. A signature guarantee may be required where the tenderor requests that payment be made or stock certificates be registered for shares not purchased to a person other than the registered owner. To afford the offeror some measure of protection, the invitation may provide that the guarantor must be a member of the NASD or of a national securities exchange or a United States bank or trust company.

[31] 15 U.S.C. § 78n(d)(1). [32] 17 C.F.R. § 240.14d–1(c).

b. Present principal occupation, and the name and address of any company where such occupation is carried on for person filing [Item 2(c)];
c. Criminal convictions, if any, within last ten years for person filing [Item 2(e)];
d. Source and amount of funds or other consideration in making purchases [Item 3];
e. Purpose(s) of transaction and if purpose is to acquire control, a description of any plans to make any major change in the target's business or corporate structure [Item 4];
f. Number of shares of target owned (including shares where there is a right to acquire) by the offering group and information as to all transactions effected during the past 60 days by person filing (and if a corporation, its subsidiaries, officers, directors and affiliated persons) [Item 5];
g. Description of arrangements, if any, with any person, with respect to any securities of the issuer [Item 6].[33]

SECTION 4. *OTHER INFORMATION*

(a) If the offeror does not intend to comply with any state securities law, the invitation should provide that tenders will not be accepted from stockholders in those states. Many invitations also provide that in states where tender offers must be made through licensed dealers unless the offeror registers as a broker-

[33] The above outline of the provisions of Schedule 13D is not intended to be definitive. A careful review should be made of the instructions contained within said Schedule 13D prior to drafting the required information. *See* SEC Securities Exchange Act Release No. 8370 (July 30, 1968), CCH FED. SEC. L. REP. ¶ 77,581. The failure to provide complete and thoroughly accurate information regarding these items may result, *inter alia*, in the issuance of a court order compelling the offeror to make a recission offer to tendering shareholders. *Cf.* Electronic Specialty Co. v. International Controls Corp., 409 F.2d 937 (2d Cir. 1969), *rev'g in part* 295 F. Supp. 1063 (S.D.N.Y. 1968). For supplemental opinion *see* 296 F. Supp. 462 (S.D.N.Y. 1968).

Eight copies of the material required by Rule 14d–1(c) must be filed with the SEC. *See* SEC Securities Exchange Act Release No. 8556 (March 24, 1969), CCH FED. SEC. L REP. ¶ 77,678.

dealer, the offer will be deemed to be made on behalf of the offeror by the dealer-manager or by soliciting dealers.[34]

(b) To eliminate any uncertainty regarding the expiration of the tendering shareholders withdrawal privileges pursuant to Section 14(d)(5) of the 1934 Act, the invitation may also contain the date on which the offer became or becomes effective as well as the specific dates and times when withdrawal can be made.

(c) Where one of the immediate objectives of a tender offer is to vote the tendered shares at a stockholders' meeting scheduled either during the course of the offer or shortly after the expiration of the offering period, the offer may provide that: (i) only those shares which are eligible to vote at the meeting will be accepted; and (ii) the person tendering shares execute an irrevocable proxy for all shares purchased by the offeror pursuant to the offer. The inclusion of such an irrevocable proxy provision has been held not to constitute a solicitation of proxies in violation of Section 14(a) of the 1934 Act.[35] However, where a tender offer is structured so that the proxies may be voted prior to the time the shares are purchased, it will be necessary for the offeror to comply with the proxy rules.[36] Along these same lines, a tender offer for shares of a friendly merger partner made prior to the requisite approval of shareholders (perhaps for the purpose of reducing the number of shares to be issued in the merger or to help assure approval of the merger) may constitute a solicitation within the meaning of the proxy rules. If the offeror is not required to comply with the proxy rules in such circumstances, the shareholders would in essence be required to evaluate the tender offer against the merger proposal without all the information concerning the merger which they would receive in the proxy statement.[37]

[34] See Chapter 5, Section 2, Statutes Regulating Tender Offerors as Dealers in Securities.

[35] *See* U.S. Smelting, Refining & Mining Co. v. Clevite Corp., Civ. Action Nos. C68–210; C68–345 (N.D. Ohio 1968), CCH FED. SEC. L. REP. ¶ 92,691; Mills v. Sarjem Corp., 113 F. Supp. 753 (D.N.J. 1955). *See also* analysis in Fleischer and Mundheim, *Corporate Acquisition by Tender Offer,* 115 U. PA. L. REV. 317, 368–70 (1967); Griffin and Tucker, *The Williams Act, Public Law 90–439—Growing Pains? Some Interpretations with Respect to the Williams Act,* 16 HOWARD L. J. 654, 702 (1971).

[36] See note 35, *supra.*

[37] See Griffin and Tucker, *supra* note 35, at 701–2.

(d) Inevitably some potential tenderors will have questions concerning details of the offer the answers to which do not appear in the invitation or which may be overlooked in a hurried reading. To encourage communication between the parties, the invitation may provide a toll-free telephone number for information and assistance.

Chapter 4. FEDERAL SECURITIES REGULATION OF TENDER OFFERS

Section 1. *BACKGROUND AND HISTORY OF FEDERAL REGULATION* [1]

Federal regulation of cash tender offers was originally proposed in October 1965 by Senator Harrison Williams of New Jersey for the ostensible purpose of protecting incumbent managements from "industrial sabotage" resulting from what were deemed to be reckless corporate raids on "proud old companies." [2] Such regulation, unique in that it represented perhaps the first attempt to enact securities regulation designed primarily for the benefit of the issuer rather than the investor, was inspired by the conglomerate merger mania of the early and mid 1960s. During this period, the cash tender offer, which had previously been resorted to only on infrequent occasions in the

[1] Leading articles on tender offers in general and federal regulation of such offers include the following: Bromberg, *Tender Offers: Safeguards and Restraints—An Interest Analysis*, 21 CASE WEST RES. L. REV. 613 (1970); Brown, *The Scope of the Williams Act and Its 1970 Amendments*, 26 BUS. LAW 1637 (July 1971); Fleischer and Mundheim, *Corporate Acquisition by Tender Offer*, 115 U. PA. L. REV. 317 (1967); Griffin and Tucker, *The Williams Act, Public Law 90–439—Growing Pains? Some Interpretations with Respect to the Williams Act*, 16 HOWARD L. J. 654 (1971); Hamilton, *Reflections on Cash Tender Offer Legislation*, 15 N.Y.L.F. 269 (1969), reprinted in N.Y.L.J. (Jan. 7–9, 1970); Robinson and Mahoney, *Schedule 13D: Wild Card in the Takeover Deck*, 27 BUS. LAW 1107 (July 1972). *See also*, Practising Law Institute, Corporate Law and Practice Handbook No. 82 *The Tender Offer* (1972); Sommer, *Tender Offers*, *P-H* SEC. REG. REP. ¶ 1101 (Jan. 27, 1971) (Reprint).

[2] 111 CONG. REC. 28256–60 (Oct. 22, 1965) (remarks of Senator Williams on S. 2731).

United States, emerged with frenetic abandon.[3] The following have been suggested as some of the underlying reasons for the rapid growth of the tender offer phenomenon in this country: [4]

1. Increased corporate liquidity and readily available credit;
2. Comparatively depressed price/earnings ratios, book values, and cash or quick assets ratios, making acquisition via the tender offer more attractive;
3. Greater recognition, sophistication, and knowledge with respect to the takeover via tender technique;
4. Lack of extensive federal or state regulation of tender offers;
5. Quicker and more successful results when compared with a full-dress proxy contest;
6. Greater flexibility—the ability to hedge by reserving certain options against a final and irrevocable commitment;
7. Psychology—the appeal to shareholders in straight dollars and cents language, eliminating the need, as in a proxy contest, to convince the shareholder that the insurgent can do a more efficient job;

[3] In 1960 there were only eight cash tender offers involving companies with securities listed on national securities exchanges as compared to 107 in 1966. In 1960 there were tender offers for $200 million of listed securities as compared to approximately $1 billion in 1965. *See* 111 CONG. REC. 24662–64 (Aug. 30, 1967). *Cf.* AUSTIN AND FISHMAN, CORPORATIONS IN CONFLICT—THE TENDER OFFER (Masterco 1970) at 10. For a compilation of tender offers for companies other than banks and insurance companies during the period January 1, 1965–July 31, 1968 which apparently would have been within the scope of the Williams Act if the Act had been in effect at that time, *see Senate Hearings on S. 336 and S. 3431, infra.* note 13, at 18–24.

For an excellent comparative analysis of the English and American approach to tender offer regulation *see* Branson, *Some Suggestions From A Comparison Of British And American Tender Offer Regulation,* 56 CORNELL L. REV. 685 (1971) and authorities cited therein. With regard to the Australian, Canadian, British and South African experience regulating takeover bids, *see also* Butler, et al, *Take-over Bids,* 27 BUS. LAW 243 (Nov. 1971); Golbert, *Taking It Over in Australia and South Africa, Reflections on Corporate Take-Overs, Amalgamations and Mergers Down Under,* 27 BUS. LAW 281 (Nov. 1971); Ross-Skinner, *Stock Tenders—British Style,* 90 Duns Review 32–5 (Sept. 1967); Fleischer and Mundheim, *Corporate Acquisition by Tender Offer,* 115 U. PA. L. REV. 317, 323–28 (1967); 6 LOSS, SECURITIES REGULATION 3665–69 (2d ed. 1969); Georgeson & Co., *Trends in Management–Stockholder Relations,* No. 96, Jan. 1961; 111 CONG. REC. 28256–57 (1965).

[4] *See* Whitman, *The Strategy of Tender Solicitation,* published by Blair & Co., Inc., New York City (April 1967); Hayes and Taussig, *Tactics Of Cash Takeover Bids,* 45 HARV. BUS. REV. 135,136 (March–April 1967); AUSTIN AND FISHMAN, *supra* note 3, at 8–9.

8. Notwithstanding the actual capital investment, the reduced costs of effecting a tender offer when compared with a proxy contest;
9. A new "respectability" for cash tender offers.

While no hearings were held on the original Williams Bill, many of its proposals formed the basis for a second bill introduced by Senator Williams in 1967.[5] By the time this second bill was introduced, however, there was a greater recognition of the desirability of providing investors confronted with a tender offer with certain basic substantive protections together with full disclosure of the terms, conditions, and financing of the offer as well as the identity and pertinent background information regarding the offeror. In addition, there was a growing recognition that tender offers might in some cases promote the best interests of society by providing an effective method of removing entrenched but inefficient management. Nonetheless, the view persisted that the motives behind many tender offers did not reflect a desire to improve the management of companies and were but disguised forms of industrial sabotage. References by a co-sponsor of the legislation to attempted takeovers by undisclosed principals financed by Swiss banks, to the "corporate raider," and to the "takeover pirate" helped to generate hearty Congressional support for the second Williams Bill.[6]

While the bill was embraced by the SEC and supported by several managements that had recently fought off cash takeover bids,[7] there were others who opposed such regulation.[8] Opposition to the bill was based primarily on the contention that the legislation was weighted so as to give incumbent management an

[5] 113 CONG. REC. 854–56 (Jan. 18, 1967) (remarks of Senator Williams on S. 510).

[6] *See* 113 CONG. REC. 854 (Jan. 18, 1967) (remarks of Senator Kuchel on S. 510). *See also* 113 CONG. REC. 24662–66 (Aug. 30, 1967).

[7] *See Hearings on S. 510 Before the Subcomm. on Sec. of the Senate Comm. on Banking and Currency*, 90th Cong., 1st Sess. at 15,175,244 (1967); H.R. REP. No. 1711, 90th Cong., 2d Sess. 12 (1968).

[8] *See Senate Hearings on S. 510, supra* note 7, at 114; Mundheim, *Why the Bill on Tender Offers Should Not Be Passed*, INSTITUTIONAL INVESTOR at 24 (May 1967); Manne, *Why Cash Tender Offers Should Remain Unregulated*, COMMERCIAL & FINANCIAL CHRONICLE § 2, at 12 (May 23, 1968). *Cf.* Brudney, *A Note on Chilling Cash Tender Solicitations*, 21 RUTGERS L. REV. 609 (1967).

unfair advantage in defending against a cash takeover bid and would therefore help to promote inefficient management. One commentator went so far as to suggest that the purpose of the legislation was to enhance the powers of the SEC rather than to protect the legitimate interests of the investing public. In addition, it was argued that a tender offer was in essence an open-market transaction and that traditional market forces, powered by individual self-interest, would best promote the interests of investors and our corporate system as a whole.

These objections notwithstanding, the final version of the second Williams Bill, which took the form of amendments to the Securities Exchange Act of 1934, became law on July 29, 1968 [9] and was ostensibly designed to provide investors with full disclosure and other substantive protections within a statutory framework favoring neither the tender offeror nor the management of the target company.[10] To insure adequate disclosure as well as the continued integrity of the securities markets in connection with acquisitions of securities which might cause or affect changes in control of public corporations, the bill also granted the SEC authority to regulate corporate repurchases of their own securities and imposed detailed disclosure requirements on persons acquiring more than 10 percent of certain equity securities other than pursuant to a tender offer. The Commission immediately adopted "temporary regulations" to effectuate those sections of the statute which were not self-operative.[11] These regulations were amended a month later and are still in effect.[12]

In 1970, the Williams Act was amended, primarily to expand SEC rule-making authority and to extend the coverage of the law

[9] Act of July 29, 1968, Pub. L. No. 90–439, 82 Stat. 454 (codified as 15 U.S.C. §§ 78m(d)–(e), 78n(d)–(f) (1970)). For legislative history, *see Senate Hearings on* S. 510, *supra* note 7; *Hearings on H.R. 14475*, S. 510, *Before the Subcomm. on Commerce and Finance of the House Comm. on Interstate and Foreign Commerce*, 90th Cong., 2d Sess. (1968); H.R. Rep. No. 1711, 90th Cong., 2d Sess. (1968); S. Rep. no. 550, 90th Cong., 1st Sess. (1967).

[10] *See* H.R. Rep. No. 1711, 90th Cong., 2d Sess. (1968); S. Rep. No. 550, 90th Cong., 1st Sess. (1967).

[11] *See* SEC Securities Exchange Act Release No. 8370 (July 30, 1968) CCH Fed. Sec. L. Rep. ¶ 77,581.

[12] *See* SEC Securities Exchange Act Release No. 8392 (Aug. 30, 1968) CCH Fed. Sec. L. Rep. ¶ 77,715.

to certain types of offers previously exempt from regulation.[13] These amendments, designed for the benefit of the public investor and referred to as "consumer protection" [14] legislation, provided for the following:

1. Reduction of the percentage of stock ownership needed to trigger the disclosure requirements of the Act from 10 percent to 5 percent in an effort to provide public disclosure at a more meaningful level;
2. Extension of the Act to cover exchange tender offers in order to provide investors subject to such offers with the substantive protections of the Act;
3. Extension of the Act to cover tender offers for insurance companies; [15]
4. Rule-making power for the SEC under the anti-fraud provision of the Act to enable it to deal more effectively with fraudulent practices; and
5. Rule-making power for the SEC to create flexibility in regulation of persons in a control relationship with the issuer.[16]

Little more than four years have now elapsed since the passage of the Williams Act. To historians, four years would hardly qualify as a "history" from which one can draw any valid conclusions in evaluating the impact of the Williams Act on the future of the tender offer as a viable acquisition technique. Nevertheless, the experience to date has demonstrated that the tender offer will continue as a practical method of acquiring control of public corporations. Those who viewed the Act with alarm as sounding the

[13] Act of Dec. 22, 1970, Pub. L. No. 91–567, 84 Stat. 1497. *See also* 116 CONG. REC., 3023–24 (Feb. 10, 1970) (remarks of Senator Williams on S. 3431); *Hearings on S. 336 and S. 3431 Before the Subcomm. on Sec. of the Senate Comm. on Banking and Currency*, 91st Cong., 2d Sess. (1970); *Hearings on H.R. 4285*, S. 3431 *and* S. 336 *Before the Subcomm. on Commerce and Finance of the House Comm. on Interstate and Foreign Commerce*, 91st Cong., 2d Sess. (1970); H.R. REP. No. 91–1655, 91st Cong., 2d Sess. (1970); S. REP. No. 91–1125, 91st Cong., 2d Sess. (1970).

[14] *See* S. REP. No. 91–1125, 91st Cong. 2d Sess. (1970), entitled *Additional Consumer Protection In Corporate Equity Ownership And In Corporate Takeover Bids.*

[15] For a compilation of tender offers for insurance companies during the period 1965–70 which apparently would have been within the scope of the Williams Act if the 1970 amendments had been in effect at that time, *see House Hearings on H.R. 4285, S. 3431 and S. 336, supra* note 13, at 19.

[16] For a succinct and thorough analysis of the Williams Act, *see* Brown, *The Scope of The Williams Act And Its 1970 Amendments*, 26 BUS. LAW. 1637 (1971).

death knell for cash tender offers need only note the substantial number of such offers since the effective date of the Act to allay their fears.[17] Equally significant is the fact that the Williams Act has had a salutary impact on the market place and has enabled investors to make more informed investment decisions. The Williams Act has thus advanced not only investor protection but investor confidence as well, within a statutory framework which preserves the required flexibility of private enterprise in our market economy.

SECTION 2. *WHAT IS A TENDER OFFER FOR PURPOSES OF THE FEDERAL SECURITIES LAWS?*[18]

Neither the Williams Act nor the rules adopted by the Commission pursuant thereto attempt to define a "tender offer."

[17] From July 29, 1968 through June 1970 there were over 100 cash tender offers which were subject to the filing and disclosure requirements of the Williams Act and the SEC rules thereunder. *See Senate Hearings on S. 336 and S. 3431, supra,* note 13, at 91–99 (July 29, 1968–Feb. 28, 1970); *House Hearings on H.R. 4285,* S. *3431 and* S. *336, supra,* note 13, at 17 (March 1, 1970–June 30, 1970.) [Note: The House Hearings report reproduces the same list of tender offers as the Senate Hearings report for the period July 29, 1968–February 28, 1970 but inadvertently omits 10 tender offers which appear in the Senate Hearings report. The House Hearings report, however, contains the approximate total assets of the target company. These figures do not appear in the Senate Hearings report.] *See also* Metz, *Marketplace: Raiders Poised to Strike Anew?* N.Y. Times, Dec. 8, 1971, at 96.

[18] The status of tender offers under contract law also deserves some comment. In most instances, tender offers are conditional offers to purchase securities. The acceptance takes place when the shareholder commits himself to tendering his shares. Many cash tender offers are not specifically identified as such but instead are represented as "invitations for tenders." While the use of the term "invitation for tenders" implies that the person seeking to purchase the securities is requesting the shareholder to make an offer, the terms and conditions of the invitation normally suggest otherwise. Thus, whether called an "offer to purchase" or an "invitation for tenders," it is the purchaser who is actually making the offer and not the shareholder and a binding contract is created when the shareholder tenders his securities in accordance with the terms of the offer. *See* Levenburg v. Merrill Lynch, Pierce. Fenner & Beane, 334 Mich. 508, 54 N.W.2d 626 (1952). See also Chapter 3, note 18. In contrast, an "invitation for tenders" requested by a governmental authority for bids on a construction contract or by a toll highway commission to purchase bonds for cancellation are in most instances requests to contractors or bondholders to make an offer. In such circumstances, the tender must be accepted by the authority or commission before there is a binding contract. *See, e.g.,* "Invitation for tenders by the treasurer of the Illinois State Toll Highway Commission," Wall Street Journal, Nov. 1, 1968, at 24; "Invitation for tenders of the government of Abu Dhabi," N.Y. Times, Feb. 21, 1972, at 42.

However, the failure of both the Congress and the Commission to define the term reflects neither oversight nor a tacit acknowledgment that the term has acquired a generic meaning which is universally recognized. Instead, the absence of a definition apparently derives from the fact that the Congress and the Commission were of the view that a tender offer for purposes of the federal regulatory scheme may well encompass transactions yet unborn which are not considered tender offers in general custom and usage. Thus the question of just what is encompassed by the term tender offer has been intentionally left open, in an ostensible effort to preserve the flexibility of both the Commission and the courts in making a determination on a case-by-case basis.

In attempting to determine the types of transactions which may be deemed to be tender offers, it is appropriate to fashion a definition which sets forth the generally accepted or acknowledged meaning of the term. Thus, a tender offer may be generally defined as:

> A public offer or solicitation by a company, an individual or a group of persons to purchase during a fixed period of time all or a portion of a class or classes of securities of a publicly held corporation at a specified price or upon specified terms for cash and /or securities.

This definition would, in essence, encompass *public* offers to purchase securities directly from security holders (either with or without the assistance of a broker-dealer) as opposed to purchases effected *privately* or open-market purchases effected through the facilities of an organized securities exchange or in the over-the-counter market. In addition, public offers to purchase securities in exchange for securities of other issuers held by the offeror would also constitute a tender offer as that term is generally defined.

To date, the position of the courts and the SEC on just what is a tender offer has not been fully developed. The Commission, however, has taken the position that a "special bid" to purchase equity securities through the facilities of a national securities exchange would ordinarily constitute a tender offer within the meaning of the Williams Act.[19] A "special bid" may be described as an offer to purchase a block of securities on a national securities exchange during a fixed period of time and at a specified price but at not less than the higher of the current bid or the last sale.[20] Generally speaking, it is substantially higher. Although the stock exchange regulations governing the use of the special bid are quite restrictive, the technique could be most useful to those desiring to acquire a large block of stock in a short period of time under the cloak of relative secrecy. In essence, the special bid is simply a tender offer effected as an exchange transaction. However, the Commission, by deeming special bids to be tender offers under the Williams Act, has virtually eliminated the special bid as a practical technique, because it would be well nigh impossible for an offeror to comply with the withdrawal and proration provisions [Sections 14(d)(5) and (6)] of the Williams Act in a special bid transaction effected on a securities exchange. The extent to which the special bid may still be a viable technique would therefore appear to be limited to those tender offers which are not subject to the Williams Act.

If a special bid is deemed to be a tender offer, what then is the status of privately negotiated purchases or regular market transactions effected on an exchange or in the over-the-counter market? In *Cattlemen's Investment Company v. Fears*[21] the U.S. District Court for the Western District of Oklahoma held that an active and widespread solicitation of shareholders by use of the mails, telephone calls and personal visits (although not by general newspaper advertising) for the purpose of purchasing their shares constituted a tender offer subject to the Williams Act. The defendant, who had failed to comply with Section 14(d) of the Williams Act was enjoined from voting all stock acquired by him without prior compliance with the statute.

[19] *See* SEC Securities Exchange Act Release No. 8392 (Aug. 30, 1968), CCH FED. SEC. L. REP. ¶ 77,715.

[20] *See* New York Stock Exchange Rule 391; American Stock Exchange Rule 560.

[21] Civ. 72–152 (W.D. Okla., May 3, 1972), CCH FED. SEC. L. REP. ¶ 93,487. The SEC, in a memorandum submitted to the court, *amicus curiae,* concluded that the defendant's conduct constituted a tender offer subject to the Williams Act. *See also* response of SEC Div. of Corp. Fin., Jan. 4, 1972 to letter of Frederic H. Wright, re: Cattlemen's Investment Co., CCH FED. SEC. L. REP. ¶ 78,775.

The Cattlemen's case, however, cannot be expected to constitute authority for the general proposition that privately negotiated offers to purchase shares constitute tender offers within the meaning of the Williams Act. Instead, the opinion appears to reflect only what has previously been recognized as good law, i.e., private offers to purchase or sell securities must truly be private. On the other hand, a "private" solicitation of a large number of persons would appear to constitute a "public" tender offer for purposes of the Williams Act.[22]

A more puzzling expression of views with regard to whether open-market purchases constitute tender offers appears in a response by the staff of the SEC to a no-action request by a company which sought to increase its holdings in another issuer from 37.1 percent to 50 percent.[23] Counsel for the acquiring company advised the staff that the proposed purchases would be made in the open-market or in private transactions but that such purchases would be limited to accepting or declining offers of shares made to it as opposed to making offers for shares either directly or by placing bids through brokers. In addition, the staff was advised that in order to avoid any questions regarding full disclosure under Rule 10b–5 of the 1934 Act, the acquiring company would issue a release, prior to effecting any purchases, advising of its intention to make such purchases. While the staff granted the no-action request, it stated, without explanation, that "the question of whether the proposed transactions constitute a tender offer under Section 14(d) of the Securities Exchange Act of 1934 is not free from doubt." [24]

[22] The SEC release announcing adoption of temporary rules and regulations under §§ 13(d), (e) and 14(d) described Rule 14d–2 as containing exclusions which provide that Regulation 14D (17 C.F.R. §§ 240.14d–1 et seq.) does not apply to certain communications which in the absence of such a rule would be deemed to be tender offers. One exclusion was stated to be for "offers to no more than ten security holders during any period of twelve months." However, no such exclusion appears in Rule 14d-2 or in any other rule adopted by the Commission to date. *See* SEC Securities Exchange Act Release No. 8392 (Aug. 30, 1968), CCH Fed. Sec. L. Rep. ¶ 77,715.

See also SEC v. Ralston Purina Co., 346 U.S. 119 (1953); Lively v. Hirschfield, 440 F. 2d 631 (10th Cir. 1971); Hill York Corp. v. American International Franchises, Inc., 448 F. 2d 680, at 687–88 (5th Cir. 1971). *Cf.* Katz v. Amos Treat & Co., 411 F.2d 1046, 1053–54 (2d Cir. 1969).

[23] *See In re* American General Insurance Co., Dec. 17, 1971, CCH Fed. Sec. L. Rep. ¶ 78,588 (correspondence in full text).

[24] *Id.*, at p. 81, 262.

Along these same lines, however, a leading article on the Williams Act suggests that a public announcement by a prospective purchaser of its intention to acquire shares in the open market at prevailing prices, in an amount which would result in the ownership of more than 5 percent of such shares, "appears to involve an invitation to the shareholders to tender at such prices as may prevail" and would appear to be "equivalent to" a tender offer.[25]

If the essential element in transforming open-market purchases into tender offers is considered to be a public announcement of the prospective purchaser's intentions, it is obvious that one must determine whether the anti-fraud provisions require such disclosure. Simply stated, the anti-fraud provisions of the federal securities laws do not require a public announcement of a prospective purchaser's intentions to acquire securities, provided, of course, that the purchases do not involve any type of overreaching. The law could hardly be otherwise unless one would be willing to accept the ludicrous result of requiring every investor who intended to make substantial purchases of a security to disclose such intention prior to its initial purchase.[26]

On the other hand, it must be recognized that there may be instances where a person seeking to obtain control by means of open-market purchases of the target's securities either may be required or will voluntarily decide to make a public announcement of its intentions. While the economic realities of the market place often make a public announcement of an intention to make open-market purchases incompatible with the objective of purchasing securities at the most favorable prices, there may be situations where the prospective purchaser will believe that such an announcement will encourage security holders to dispose of their shares at prices below that at which the securities could be purchased pursuant to a conventional tender offer. In addition, the prospective purchaser may choose the open-market route in an

[25] *See* Griffin and Tucker, supra note 1, at 700–1.

[26] See also text accompanying notes 38–44, Chapter 2.

While this discussion suggests that open-market or privately negotiated purchases will not be considered tender offers if no public announcement of the prospective purchasers intentions are made, it must be noted that even without such an announcement, there have been suggestions that in some circumstances open-market or privately negotiated purchases may be tender offers. *See* Griffin and Tucker, *supra* note 1, at 701.

effort to circumvent the withdrawal, proration and best price provisions of Sections 14(d)(5), (6), and (7) of the 1934 Act.[27]

It is the authors' opinion that open-market and privately negotiated purchases are not and should not be deemed to be tender offers and therefore should not be regulated as such. This view is based upon the following:

(a) The Williams Act clearly distinguishes between tender offers and other forms of acquisition. While the distinction which the Act makes does not necessarily mean that open-market and privately negotiated purchases cannot be tender offers, the legislative history is sufficiently clear to justify this conclusion.[28] In this regard, it should be observed that the distinctions which the Williams Act makes between tender offers and other forms of acquisition are based primarily upon protecting the investor from the potential economic disadvantage resulting from a tender of

[27] With regard to Sections 14(d)(5), (6), and (7), see text accompanying notes 177–185, *infra*.

[28] *See* H.R. REP. No. 90–1711, 90th Cong., 2d Sess. 2 (1968):

"S. 510 amends the Securities Exchange Act of 1934 by requiring the disclosure of pertinent information and would afford other protections to stockholders (1) when a person or group of persons seeks to acquire a substantial block of equity securities of a corporation by a cash tender offer, alternatively called a 'take-over bid', or through open-market or privately negotiated purchases. . . ."

See also statement of Hon. Manuel F. Cohen, Chairman, SEC, *Hearings Before the Subcomm. on Commerce and Finance of the House Comm. on Interstate and Foreign Commerce*, 90th Cong., 2d Sess. (July 1, 1968) at 11, 14:

"A tender offer is quite different from the ordinary market transaction with which the average investor is familiar. In so far as it is an offer at all it is subject to complex and sometimes deceptive conditions. Rather it is an invitation to the public security holder who 'tenders' his security to give the other party an option—to be exercised only if certain minimum shares are tendered within a specified time and perhaps specifying a maximum which the original 'offeror' is prepared to take—but giving him discretion to accept a lesser or larger amount or to extend the time limits. Tendering in response to such an offer involves deposit of the public security holder's shares or obtaining a guarantee from a stock exchange member or other financially responsible person that they will be deposited. . . .

"Not all acquisitions of substantial blocks of securities are made by means of tender offers. A corporation or individual—or a group of corporations or individuals—can acquire a substantial block of stock of a company through a program of purchases in the open market, or through privately-negotiated purchases from substantial stockholders, and thus achieve the power to influence the management and control of the corporation, without the other stockholders even becoming aware of this development."

See also GAF v. Milstein, 453 F.2d 709, 722n. 22 (2d Cir. 1971) *cert. denied*, 406 U.S. 910 (1972).

his shares *as compared with* the sale of those shares in the open market;[29]

(b) The underlying purpose of the Williams Act is to advise investors of the facts surrounding substantial acquisitions of securities which may lead to changes in control. While the Williams Act distinguishes between tender offers and other forms of acquisition for purposes of substantive regulation, the disclosures required by the Act does not vary with the method of acquisition; if the Act applies, all acquisitions must be disclosed on a Schedule 13D statement. Full disclosure of both open-market and privately negotiated purchases is therefore assured without regulation of such purchases as tender offers;[30] and

(c) Regulation of open-market purchases as tender offers would effectively preclude acquisitions other than by means of a traditional tender offer because it would not be possible to make open-market purchases which comply with the withdrawal, proration, and best-price provisions of Sections 14(d)(5), (6), and (7) of the 1934 Act. Similarly, there is no useful purpose served by compelling a purchaser in a private transaction to comply with Sections 14(d)(5), (6), and (7).

Accordingly, there appears to be little, if any, public policy basis for transforming the generally acknowledged meaning of a tender offer into an amorphous concept which will vary with the facts and circumstances of the individual case. The case by case approach to the question of just what is a tender offer leaves a great deal to be desired, particularly when one recognizes that the true touchstone of any effective system of jurisprudence is the promulgation of laws upon which men can reasonably plan their affairs. In addition to creating an unsettling legal environment,

[29] *See also* SEC Securities Exchange Act Release No. 8712 (Oct. 8, 1969) announcing adoption of Rule 10b–13 under the 1934 Act. This rule prohibits purchases by an offeror during the course of its tender offer otherwise than pursuant to the offer itself. The inference drawn from both the rule and the release announcing adoption of the rule is that open-market purchases should not be treated as tender offers.

[30] The fact that a Schedule 14D statement must be filed no later than the time a tender offer is made public, [*see* § 14(d)(1)], while the 13D statement can be filed up to ten days after 5 percent acquisitions made other than pursuant to a tender offer [*see* § 13(d)(1)] does not justify regulating open-market or privately negotiated purchases as tender offers.

such an approach also obscures the statutory distinction which the Williams Act makes between tender offers and other forms of acquisition, while contributing little to the principle of full disclosure.

It is the authors' view that Congress, by amendment to the statute, or the SEC, pursuant to its rulemaking authority, should define the term "tender offer." In light of the experience to date, the Commission has had sufficient time and opportunity to develop an appropriate definition. Both the statutory purpose of the Williams Act and the interests of public policy would be better served by this approach and would eliminate the uncertainties which presently exist.

It should also be noted that the question of just what constitutes a tender offer may not be limited to resolving the issues of whether privately negotiated and open market purchases can ever be deemed to be tender offers. For example, uncertainties have arisen regarding the question of whether an exchange of securities pursuant to a statutory merger or consolidation submitted for shareholder approval constitutes a tender offer. While an "exchange offer" is clearly a tender offer, an exchange of securities pursuant to a merger has not customarily been considered to be an exchange offer. An exchange offer is essentially an offer to purchase securities of one issuer for a consideration other than cash: normally securities of the offeror. On the other hand, an exchange of securities pursuant to a merger is not an offer to purchase securities in connection with a contest for control, but rather a part of the mechanics of the merger process itself. The staff of the Commission, to date, has not required compliance with Section 14(d) of the 1934 Act as a prerequisite to effecting a statutory merger or consolidation.[31]

[31] *See also* Smallwood v. Southdown, Inc., No. 3-3632-B (N.D. Tex. 1972), CCH Fed. Sec. L. Rep. ¶ 93,435; Dyer v. Eastern Trust and Banking Co., 336 F. Supp. 890 (D. Me. 1971), to the effect that an exchange of securities pursuant to a merger is not a tender offer. (Note that while the facts giving rise to these cases occurred at a time when exchange offers were exempt from Section 14(d) of the 1934 Act (i.e., prior to the 1970 amendments to the Williams Act), the holdings to the effect that Section 14(e) was inapplicable to the transactions in question constitutes on-point authority for the proposition that an exchange of securities pursuant to a merger is not a tender offer.) *Cf.* text and accompanying note 176, *infra.*

Section 3. *TYPES OF DISCLOSURE STATEMENTS REQUIRED TO BE FILED PURSUANT TO THE WILLIAMS ACT*

A. Schedule 13D—Disclosure by Persons Acquiring More Than 5 Percent of Certain Classes of Equity Securities

(1) Class of Persons Subject to Filing Requirements; Persons Entitled to Receive Copies of Filing; Time of Filing; Number of Copies; Filing Fees

Schedule 13D,[32] promulgated pursuant to the rulemaking authority granted the SEC under Section 13(d)(1),[33] can be generally described as the basic disclosure statement which must be filed when: (a) a person or group of persons acquires more than 5 percent of certain equity securities other than pursuant to a tender offer; or (b) a person or group of persons makes a tender offer which could result in the offeror owning more than 5 percent of certain equity securities.

Section 13(d)(1) and Rule 13d–1 [34] thereunder require a Schedule 13D report to be filed by any person directly or indirectly acquiring beneficial ownership [35] of more than 5 percent of the securities of any of the following classes: [36]

[32] 17 C.F.R. § 240.13d–101 (eff. July 30, 1968).

[33] 15 U.S.C. § 78m(d)(1). The statutory provisions of the Williams Act, which constitute amendments to the Securities Exchange Act of 1934, are codified as 15 U.S.C. §§ 78m(d)–(e), 78n(d)–(f). *E.g.*, § 13(d)(1) and § 13(e)(1) of the 1934 Act are cited respectively as 15 U.S.C. § 78m(d)(1) and 15 U.S.C. § 78m(e)(1). Similarly, §§ 14(d), (e) and (f) and subsections thereof of the 1934 Act are cited respectively as 15 U.S.C. § 78n(d), 15 U.S.C. § 78n(e) and 15 U.S.C. § 78n(f). Thus, where reference is made in the text or footnotes of this treatise to specific sections of the Williams Act without a corresponding U.S. Code citation, such citation may be obtained as indicated above.

[34] 17 C.F.R. § 240.13d–1. Rules promulgated pursuant to the Williams Act are designated in the U.S. Code of Federal Regulations as 17 C.F.R. § 240 followed by a decimal point and the specific rule number. E.g., Rule 14d–1 is cited as 17 C.F.R. § 240.14d–1. Where reference is made in the text or footnotes to a specific rule promulgated pursuant to the Williams Act without a corresponding "C.F.R." citation, such citation may be obtained as indicated above.

[35] For a discussion of the definition of the term "acquiring" in the Section 13(d)(1) context, see subsection (2) *infra.* A person who has a controlling influence over the voting of securities has a beneficial interest for purposes of the Williams Act. *See* Bath Industries v. Blot, 427 F.2d 97, 112 (7th Cir. 1970), *aff'd,* 305 F. Supp. 526, 537 (E.D. Wis. 1969), Ozark Air Lines, Inc. v. Cox, 326 F. Supp. 1113, 1117–18 (E. D. Mo. 1971). See also SEC Securities Exchange Act Release No. 7793 (Jan. 19, 1966).

[36] As originally enacted, Section 13(d)(1) required a Schedule 13D report to be filed by any person owning more than 10 percent of certain equity securities. A

(a) any equity security of a class which is registered pursuant to Section 12 of the 1934 Act;

(b) any equity security of an insurance company which would have been required to be so registered except for the exemption contained in section 12(g)(2)(G) of the 1934 Act; or

(c) any equity security issued by a closed-end investment company registered under the Investment Company Act of 1940.

The Schedule 13D statement, containing the information required thereby, must be filed by the purchaser(s) with the SEC within ten days after such acquisition.[37] Section 13(d)(1) and Rule 13d–1 also require that the Schedule 13D statement be sent by the purchaser(s), within ten days after the acquisition, to each exchange where the security is traded and to the issuer of the security, by registered or certified mail, at its principal executive office.

Pursuant to Section 14(d)(1) and Rule 14d–1(a) thereunder, a statement containing the information required by Schedule 13D

---

person who owned, prior to the effective date of the original Williams Act, more than 10 percent of a class of equity security described above and who had not acquired any additional securities of the same class subsequent to July 29, 1968 would not appear to be required to file a Schedule 13D statement until such time as his acquisitions in any twelve month period exceeded 2 percent of the class of equity security. *See* § 13(d)(6)(B), discussed in § 3A(2) of this chapter and in text accompanying notes 98–102, *infra.*

The 1970 amendments to the Williams Act, which became effective on December 22, 1970, reduced the required holdings needed to trigger the Schedule 13D filing requirement from 10 percent to 5 percent. These amendments do not operate retroactively, however. Thus, a person who owned, prior to December 22, 1970, more than 5 percent but not more than 10 percent of a class of equity security described above and who had not acquired any additional shares of the class after the amendment to the Act, would not appear to be required to file until such time as his acquisitions exceeded the 2 percent exemption provided for in § 13(d)(6)(B). *See* response of SEC Div. of Corp. Finance dated Jan. 18, 1971 to request for interpretative opinion by Ralph L. Halpern, Esq. (pub. availability date, Feb. 17, 1971); GAF Corp. v. Milstein, 453 F.2d, at 718, n.17; Nicholson File Co. v. H.K. Porter Co., 341 F. Supp. 508 (D.R.I. 1972); for a later development of this case involving Section 14(e), *see* H. K. Porter Co. v. Nicholson File Co. (Nov. 30, 1972), discussed in BNA, SEC. REG. & L. REP., No. 182 at A-4 *et. seq.*

[37] But see subsection (3), *infra. See also* response of SEC Div. of Corp. Finance re: American Pepsi Cola Bottlers, Inc., March 23, 1972, CCH FED. SEC. L. REP. ¶ 78,765, wherein the staff of the commission took the position that a corporation acquiring more than 5 percent of the outstanding stock of another issuer was required to file a Schedule 13D statement within ten days after the acquisition despite the fact that a public offering by the other issuer eight days after the acquisition reduced the percentage of the holdings of the acquiring corporation in the other issuer below 5 percent.

must also be filed by any person owning less than 5 percent of the securities of any of the classes noted above where the person proposes to make a tender offer, which, after consummation thereof, would result in the offeror owning more than 5 percent of such securities. The Schedule 13D report must be filed with the Commission and transmitted to the target company no later than the time copies of the offer or request or invitation for tenders are first published or sent to security holders.[38]

At the time of filing the Schedule 13D statement pursuant to Section 13(d) or Section 14(d), the person making the filing must pay a $100 non-refundable filing fee to the Commission.[39]

Rule 13d–1 and Rule 14d–1(e) require that 8 copies of the Schedule 13D statement be filed with the Commission.

(2) Exemptions from Filing a Schedule 13D Statement

Both the Williams Act and the rules thereunder provide a number of exemptions from the Section 13(d) and Section 14(d) filing requirements. Section 13(d)(6) provides as follows:

> The provisions of this subsection shall not apply to—
>
> (A) any acquisition or offer to acquire securities made or proposed to be made by means of a registration statement under the Securities Act of 1933;
>
> (B) any acquisition of the beneficial ownership of a security which, together with all other acquisitions by the same person of securities of the same class during the preceding twelve months, does not exceed 2 per centum of that class;
>
> (C) any acquisition of an equity security by the issuer of such security;
>
> (D) any acquisition or proposed acquisition of a security which the Commission, by rules or regulations or by order, shall exempt from the provisions of this subsection as not entered into for the purpose of, and not having the effect of, changing or influencing the con-

[38] Section 14(d)(1) and Rule 14d–1(a), unlike Section 13(d)(1) and Rule 13d–1, do not require the tender offeror to send the Schedule 13D statement to each exchange where the security is traded; it need only file such schedule with the Commission and transmit a copy to the issuer. However, once the offeror acquires more than 5 percent of the target's securities it will be compelled to send the Schedule 13D statement to the exchange(s) pursuant to the requirements of Section 13(d)(1) and Rule 13d–1.

[39] *See* Rule 13d–1; SEC Securities Exchange Act Release No. 9465 (Jan. 25, 1972), CCH Fed. Sec. L. Rep. ¶ 78,496.

trol of the issuer or otherwise as not comprehended within the purposes of this subsection.

Section 13(d)(6)(A), which exempts registered exchange offers, eliminates the unnecessary burden of duplicate filings since the exchange offeror's 1933 Act registration statement will furnish investors with adequate disclosure concerning the offer. Disclosure was also deemed to be unnecessary in the case of casual accumulations of securities as defined in Section 13(d)(6)(B) since such purchase patterns are not likely to result in corporate control contests. While disclosure of corporate purchases of their own securities, which is often resorted to as a means of defending against a takeover attempt, was considered necessary to protect investors, it was apparently concluded that purchases by the incumbents on behalf of the target company may involve very different regulatory considerations than purchases by insurgents. Accordingly, regulation of repurchases by an issuer has been separately provided for pursuant to a delegation of rule-making authority in Section 13(e).

Rule 13d–4 provides an additional exemption which has a somewhat more limited impact. This Rule provides that:

Acquisitions of securities of an issuer by a security holder who prior to such acquisition was the beneficial owner of more than 5 percent of the outstanding securities of the same class as those acquired shall be exempt from section 13(d) of the Act if the following conditions are met:

(a) The acquisition is made pursuant to pre-emptive subscription rights in an offering made to all holders of securities of the class to which the pre-emptive subscription rights pertain;

(b) The purchaser does not, through the exercise of such pre-emptive subscription rights, acquire more than his or its pro rata share of the securities offered; and

(c) The acquisition is duly reported pursuant to Section 16(a) of the Act and the rule and regulations thereunder.[40]

[40] Subsection (c) of Rule 13d–4 refers to acquisitions reported pursuant to Section 16(a) of the 1934 Act, i.e., more than 10 percent holdings. The rule, however, speaks in terms of acquisitions of more than 5 percent of the outstanding securities of an issuer. The failure to amend subsection (c) after the Williams Act was amended to reduce the required reported holdings from 10 percent to 5 percent appears to be inadvertent.

As specified, the Rule only exempts purchases by a person already owning more than 5 percent of an issuer's securities. This proviso would therefore appear to limit the availability of this exemption to situations where a purchaser became more than a 5 percent owner prior to passage of the Williams Bill or where an amendment of a previously filed 13D statement would have been required by virtue of the acquisition.

In addition to the Section 13(d)(6) and Rule 13d–4 exemptions, Section 14(d)(8) and Rule 14d–2 exempt certain types of tender offers and communications which might otherwise have been deemed to be tender offers subject to the provisions of Section 14(d). Section 14(d)(8) provides as follows:

> The provisions of this subsection shall not apply to any offer for, or request or invitation for tenders of, any security—
>
> (A) if the acquisition of such security, together with all other acquisitions by the same person of securities of the same class during the preceding twelve months, would not exceed 2 per centum of that class;
>
> (B) by the issuer of such security; or
>
> (C) which the Commission, by rules or regulations or by order, shall exempt from the provisions of this subsection as not entered into for the purpose of, and not having the effect of, changing or influencing the control of the issuer or otherwise as not comprehended within the purposes of this subsection.

A comparison of Section 13(d)(6) and Section 14(d)(8) reveals that these two provisions are identical with the exception that Section 14(d)(8) does not contain an exemption for "any acquisition or offer to acquire securities made or proposed to be made by means of a registration statement under the Securities Act of 1933." As originally enacted, Section 14(d)(8) contained such an exemption. However, the 1970 Amendments to the Williams Act [41] deleted the exemption for the purpose of extending the substantive protections of Sections 14(d)(5), (6), and (7) to investors to whom exchange offers are made.[42] Since the legislative history clearly indicates that the exemption was eliminated for the purpose stated above,[43] there has been some uncertainty cre-

[41] Act of Dec. 22, 1970 Pub. L. 91–567, 84 Stat. 1497.

[42] H.R. Rep. No. 91–1655, 91st Cong. 2d Sess. 4 (1970); S. Rep. No. 91–1125, 91st Cong., 2d Sess. 4 (1970).

[43] *Id.*

ated as to whether an exchange offer should be required to file a Schedule 13D statement. Thus it has been argued that the rationale underlying the exemption for registered exchange offers in Section 13(d)(6)(A) should apply equally to tender offers subject to Section 14(d), i.e., a Schedule 13D statement is unnecessary in connection with a registered exchange offer since the 1933 Act registration statement will provide investors with adequate disclosure.[44]

To date, however, there has not been any official expression of views on this matter by the Commission or its staff. Absent such views, it would appear to be necessary for an exchange offeror to file a Schedule 13D statement since the clear language of the statute indicates that the filing requirement is triggered by the provisions of Section 14(d) which does not contain an exemption for exchange tender offers.

Rule 14d–2, which contains additional exemptions from the requirements of Section 14(d) and the rules thereunder, provides as follows:

The rules contained in this regulation do not apply to the following communications:

(a) offers to purchase securities made in connection with a distribution of securities permitted by Rule 10b–6, 10b–7 or 10b–8.

(b) the call or redemption of any security in accordance with the terms and conditions of the governing instruments.

(c) offers to purchase securities evidenced by a script certificate, order form or similar document which represents a fractional interest in a share of stock or similar security.

(d) offers to purchase securities pursuant to a statutory procedure for the purchase of dissenting shareholders' securities.

(e) the furnishing of information and advice regarding a tender offer to customers or clients by attorneys, banks, brokers, fiduciaries or investment advisers, who are not otherwise participating in the tender offer or solicitation, on the unsolicited request of a person or pursuant to a general contract for advice to the person to whom the information or advice is given.

(f) a communication from an issuer to its security holders which does no more than (1) identify a tender offer or request or invitation for tenders made by another person, (2) state that the management

[44] *See also* discussion of Rule 434B under the 1933 Act, discussed in subsection 9 of this chapter.

of the issuer is studying the matter and will, on or before a specified date (which shall be not later than 10 days prior to the date specified in the offer, request or invitation, as the last date on which tenders will be accepted, or such shorter period as the Commission may authorize) advise security holders as to the management's recommendation to accept or reject the offer, request or invitation, and (3) request security holders to defer making a determination as to whether or not they should accept or reject the offer, request or invitation until they have received the management's recommendation with respect thereto.

(g) offers to purchase securities in transactions exempt from registration under the Securities Act of 1933 pursuant to Section 3(a)(10) thereof.

(3) The Special Problem of the "Group" as a "Person" for Purposes of Filing a Schedule 13D Statement

The most difficult question of statutory construction which has been posed to date under the Williams Act derives from the interrelationship of Section 13(d)(3), defining a "group" as a "person" and Section 13(d)(1) and Rule 13d–1 thereunder, which require a Schedule 13D statement to be filed by any "person" acquiring more than 5 percent of a class of certain specified equity securities. While the difficulties in construction arise in connection with acquisitions made other than pursuant to a tender offer, the issue assumes importance where a "group" of potential tender offerors choose to accumulate a position in the target's securities prior to making the offer.

Section 13(d)(3) [45] provides as follows:

When two or more persons act as a partnership, limited partnership, syndicate, or other group for the purpose of acquiring, holding, or disposing of securities of an issuer, such syndicate or group shall be deemed a "person" for the purposes of this subsection.

Section 13(d)(1) and Rule 13d–1 thereunder provide in relevant part:

Any person, who after acquiring directly or indirectly the beneficial ownership of any equity security of a class [specified therein] . . . is

[45] A "group" of two or more persons making a tender offer is deemed a "person" for purposes of § 14(d) of the 1934 Act. *See* § 14(d)(2). As noted above (see text accompanying note 38 *supra*), a person making a tender offer must file a Schedule 13D statement no later than the time the tender offer is made public.

directly or indirectly the beneficial owner of more than 5% of such class shall, within ten days after such acquisition . . . file with the Commission a [Schedule 13D statement]. . . .

The threshold issue presented by the interrelationship of these statutory provisions may be stated as follows: When must the 13D statement be filed by a group owning more than 5 percent of a class of equity securities specified in Section 13(d)(1)? More specifically, the question has become one of whether the filing requirement is triggered when the group is formed, when the members of the group agree to act in concert to acquire additional shares, or when the 5 percent group, once formed, make additional acquisitions which exceed the exemption provision of Section 13(d)(6)(B).[46] The courts which have had occasion to consider this issue have expressed decidedly different views. A review of these cases follows.[47]

In *Bath Industries, Inc., v. Blot,*[48] the facts of which occurred prior to reduction of the required reported holdings from 10 percent to 5 percent, the Seventh Circuit Court of Appeals held that a Schedule 13D statement must be filed "when, but only when, any group of stockholders owning more than 10 percent of the outstanding shares of the corporation agree to act in concert *to acquire additional shares.*"[49] The court based its decision on the legislative history of Section 13(d)(3) as expressed in both the House and Senate committee reports of the original Williams Bill:

[46] § 13(d)(6)(B) provides that the provisions of § 13(d) shall not apply to: "any acquisition of the beneficial ownership of a security which, together with all other acquisitions by the same person of securities of the same class during the preceding twelve months, does not exceed 2 per centum of that class; . . ."

[47] *See also* Griffin and Tucker, *The Williams Act, Public Law 90–439—Growing Pains? Some Interpretations with Respect to the Williams Act,* HOWARD L.J. 654, 680–86 (1971); Comment, *Section 13(d) and Disclosure of Corporate Equity Ownership,* 119 U. PA. L. REV. 853 (1971). Stanton, *Acquisition by a Group,* 5 REV. OF SEC. REG. 985 (Jan. 21, 1972).

[48] 427 F.2d 97 (7th Cir. 1970), *aff'g* 305 F. Supp. 526 (E.D. Wis. 1969). For supplemental decisions, *see* Nos. 18044 and 18097 (7th Cir. 1970), CCH FED. SEC. L. REP. ¶ 92,635; No. 69–C–453 (E.D. Wis. 1970), CCH FED. SEC. L. REP. ¶ 92,868. *See also Recent Developments–An Informal Shareholder Group Must Meet Williams Act Disclosure Requirements Within Ten Days after the Group Has Decided to Acquire Additional Shares in Furtherance of a Plan to Seek Corporate Control,* 71 COLUM. L. REV. 466 (1971).

[49] *Id.* at 109.

[Section 13(d) (3)] would prevent a group of persons who seek to pool their voting or other interests in the securities of an issuer from evading the provisions of the statute because no one individual owns more than 10 percent of the securities. The group would be deemed to have become the beneficial owner, directly or indirectly, of more than 10 percent of a class of securities at the time they agreed to act in concert. Consequently, the group would be required to file the information called for in section 13(d)(1) within 10 days after they agree to act together, whether or not any member of the group had acquired any securities at that time. This provision is designed to obtain full disclosure of the identity of any person or group obtaining the benefits of ownership of securities by reason of any contract, understanding, relationship, agreement or other arrangement.[50]

The court turned next to the practical difficulties of determining when a group to acquire additional shares is actually formed. In this regard, it recognized that in view of "the unlikely execution of a formal agreement," the court would be confronted with the unholy dilemma of splitting the hairs which separate informal discussion and cooperation from an unwritten "agreement" to acquire additional shares. In an effort to eliminate the necessity of making such fine distinctions, the court stated the following rule:

[50] S. REP. No. 550, 90th Cong., 1st Sess. 8 (1967); H.R. REP. No. 1711, 90th Cong., 2d Sess. 8–9 (1968). It is important to note the distinction between the committee reports which provide that the group must file within ten days after they agree to act in concert and the *Bath* holding requiring the group to file when its members agree to act in concert *to acquire additional shares*. Section 13(d)(3), as noted, deems a "group" a "person" when they act together "for the purpose of acquiring, holding or disposing of securities. . . ." Accordingly, it appears that the holding in *Bath* would not require a "group" to file if it agreed to act in concert for the purpose of "holding" shares. Thus, under the *Bath* doctrine, a group which agreed to act in concert to attempt a takeover and did not purchase additional shares before it undertook a proxy solicitation or tender offer would not be required to file.

Professor Loss, in his treatise, interpreted the filing requirement of Section 13(d)(1) exactly as it is expressed in the committee reports. See 6 Loss, SECURITIES REGULATION 3664 (1969 Supp.). Professor Loss had apparently changed his opinion in this matter as noted in GAF Corp. v. Milstein, 324 F. Supp. 1062, 1067 (S.D.N.Y. 1971). Appearing as co-counsel for the defendants in that case, Professor Loss advised the court that the reports do not appropriately reflect the law as it was enacted. The district court agreed with the revised opinion expressed by Professor Loss. However, on appeal, the Second Circuit Court of Appeals held in effect that the position originally expressed in Professor Loss' treatise was correct i.e., that the filing requirement is triggered by virtue of the formation of the group and not by further acquisitions. *See* GAF Corp. v. Milstein, 453F.2d 709,715–18 (2d Cir. 1971), *cert. denied* 406 U.S. 910 (1972). For a discussion of the GAF case, see text accompanying notes 53–58, *infra*.

. . . once it is shown that such a group has agreed to pursue a common objective, and once it is further shown that a member of the group has *thereafter* purchased additional shares of the corporation's stock, then a *rebuttable presumption* arises that such purchase was made pursuant to an agreement of the group as of that date to acquire shares in furtherance of its objectives. Compliance with the Act's disclosure provisions would be required within ten days of such purchase.[51]

In addition, the court found that the exemption provided in Section 13(d)(6)(B) required the additional shares purchased to exceed 2 percent of the same class during the preceding twelve months before the filing requirement would apply.[52]

The holding in the *Bath* case has not been followed by other courts which have had occasion to consider the issue. In *GAF Corp. v. Milstein,*[53] the U.S. District Court for the Southern District of New York held that the formation of a group for the purpose of seeking control does not constitute a "constructive purchase" or acquisition by the group of the shares held by its individual members and that in the absence of any subsequent purchases which exceed 2 percent of the class during the preceding twelve months, a Schedule 13D statement need not be filed. While recognizing that the committee reports indicated that a filing is necessary upon formation of the group, the court held that such reports "should not be resorted to here since the specific statutory language is clear and compels the construction that the reportable event is the acquisition of the requisite amount of shares and not the mere formation of a group with a view to control." [54] In distinguishing the *Bath* case, the court

[51] *Id.* at 110. Presumably the court was of the view that it would be easier to determine when a group has a common objective than to determine when a group agreed to purchase additional shares.

[52] *Id.* at 111, n. 7.

[53] 324 F. Supp. 1062 (S.D.N.Y. 1971), *rev'd in part,* 453 F.2d 709 (2d Cir. 1971), *cert. denied,* 406 U.S. 910 (1972).

[54] *Id.* at 1067. *But see* Second Circuit opinion in this case at 716:

"We are well aware of the first catechism of statutory construction which teaches that we should begin the process of interpretation with "the language of the statute itself," *see* Jones v. Alfred H. Mayer Co., 392 U.S. 409, 420, 88 S.Ct. 2186, 20 L.Ed.2d 1189 (1968); that, however, is *toto caelo* from saying that the process must end there or that we are required to blind ourselves to other relevant aids to construction, particularly when dealing with a statute as complex as the one before us. The wisdom of Learned Hand guides us again: "it is one of

noted that purchases in excess of the 2 percent exemption were made after formation of the *Bath* group and that the mention of the 2 percent exemption evidenced the court's reliance on such purchases rather than the formation of the group.[55]

The holding of the district court in *GAF*, to the effect that GAF failed to state a claim under Section 13(d), was reversed on appeal.[56] The Second Circuit Court of Appeals held that a filing is necessary upon formation of the 5 percent group and that no further acquisitions are necessary to trigger the filing requirements.[57] The rationale of the court was clearly and concisely stated:

> In light of the statutory purpose as we view it, we find ourselves in disagreement with the interpretation of Bath Industries, supra, that the group owning more than 10%, despite its agreement to seize control, in addition, must agree to acquire more shares before the filing requirement of section 13(d) is triggered. The history and language of

---

the surest indexes of a mature and developed jurisprudence . . . to remember that statutes always have some purpose or object to accomplish, whose sympathetic and imaginative discovery is the surest guide to their meaning." Cabell v. Markham, *supra*, 148 F.2d at 739. *See also* United States v. Dickerson, 310 U.S. 554, 562, 60 S.Ct. 1034, 84 L.Ed. 1356 (1940). We are, therefore, totally puzzled by the experienced trial judge's conclusion that "the legislative reports should not be resorted to here since the specific statutory language is clear. . . ." 324 F.Supp. at 1067. Indeed, the statute before us is anything but a model of clarity and the ritualistic approach to statutory interpretation which the district judge suggests would close off the only light available to illumine the statute."

[55] *Id.* at 1071. While it is questionable whether the *Bath* case can be read so narrowly, it is important to note that even a broad interpretation of *Bath* may in many instances produce the same result reached by the district court in *GAF*. In *Bath* the court held that in the absence of a formal agreement by the group to acquire additional shares, it would be presumed that a filing was required if it could be shown that the group agreed to a common objective and further that a member of the group had "thereafter" purchased additional shares. Thus, the filing would be required within ten days of the purchase of additional shares and not within ten days of the time the group agrees to act in concert to acquire additional shares. Assuming the plaintiff is unable to overcome the obvious difficulties in proving a group agreement to acquire additional shares, the *Bath* holding should produce the same result expressed by the district court in *GAF*, namely, that the Schedule 13D filing will be required only after the requisite amount of purchases have been made subsequent to the formation of the group.

[56] GAF Corp. v. Milstein, 453 F.2d 709 (2d Cir. 1971). The court did not decide the question of whether the Milsteins had in fact violated Section 13(d), or, if they had, what relief would be appropriate. *Id.* at 722.

[57] This interpretation of the Schedule 13D filing requirement was urged in two law review articles submitted for publication prior to the Second Circuit opinion. See Griffin and Tucker, *supra* note 47, at 682–83; Comment, *supra* note 47, at 876.

section 13(d) make it clear that the statute was primarily concerned with disclosure of potential changes in control resulting from new aggregations of stockholdings and was not intended to be restricted to only individual stockholders who made future purchases and whose actions were, therefore, more apparent. . . . It hardly can be questioned that a group holding sufficient shares can effect a takeover without purchasing a single additional share of stock.[58]

The holdings of the Second and Seventh Circuits in *GAF* and *Bath* have not been the only judicial responses to the problem of when a Schedule 13D statement must be filed. The reasoning of the district court in *GAF*, for example, was relied upon by the U.S. District Court for the Eastern District of Missouri in *Ozark Air Lines, Inc. v. Cox*,[59] a case decided prior to the Second Circuit opinion in *GAF*. In that case, a decedent left more than 10 percent of the airline's stock to a non-profit medical center. The directors of the center passed a resolution authorizing its chairman, as trustee and executor under the will, to vote all such shares in accordance with a written agreement made by the chairman with other persons to gain control of Ozark. The airline then sought a temporary restraining order enjoining the stockholder group from soliciting proxies or voting its shares based on allegations that the group failed to file a Schedule 13D statement. In denying the plaintiff the requested relief, the court held that neither the inheritance by the trust of more than 10 percent of the airline's stock nor the formation of a group to acquire control triggered the filing requirement of Section 13(d)(1) "absent *further acquisitions*" which exceed the 2 percent rule.[60]

The text of the court's opinion is particularly important with regard to the scope of the term "acquisition" as used in Section 13(d):

The inheritance by the trust, and beneficial interest under the residuary clause of the will, is not such an "acquisition" as the section is designed to include. This subsection of the act clearly is designed to regulate filings regarding purposeful acquisitions, holdings or disposals which have the effect of changing or influencing the control of the issuer or affecting the market. The Cox Medical Center became a

[58] GAF Corp. v. Milstein, *supra* note 56, at 718.

[59] 326 F. Supp. 1113 (E.D. Mo. 1971). *See also* Nicholson File Co. v. H. K. Porter Co.. Inc., *supra* note 36.

[60] *Id.* at 1118.

holder without motive or purpose by inheritance of a beneficial interest, and a filing under Subsection 13d(1) on that basis does not advance the purpose of the act because it is irrelevant to the maintenance of fair and honest markets. Indeed, information to be furnished in a 13(d) filing expressly relates to purchases, as distinguished from the kind of interest acquired by Cox Medical Center.[61]

The court's finding that it is inappropriate to read the word "acquisition" more broadly than to mean "purchase" to advance the purposes of the Williams Act must be regarded as a setback for those who view such interpretation as creating a loophole in the protections afforded by the Act.[62] The loophole, it is contended, derives from the fact that under this interpretation a shareholder owning less than 5 percent of the target's shares could accumulate sufficient voting power to change or influence control without any disclosure by forming a group of persons, each owning less than 5 percent of the target's outstanding shares.[63] However, the Second Circuit's interpretation of the term "acquisition" in the *GAF* case stands in stark contrast to the findings of the district courts in both *GAF* and *Ozark:*

The Act nowhere explicitly defines the concept of "acquisition" as used in section 13(d). Although we are aware of Learned Hand's warning "not to make a fortress out of the dictionary" Cabell v. Markham, 148 F. 2d 737,739 (2d. Cir.) aff'd, 326 U.S. 404 (1945), some light, although dim, is shed by Webster's Third International Dictionary. It tells us that "to acquire" means "to come into possession [or] control." If the allegations in the complaint are true, then the group, which must be treated as an entity separate and distinct from its members, could have gained "beneficial control" of the voting rights of the preferred stock only after its formation, which we must assume occurred after the effective date of the Williams Act. Manifestly, according to the complaint, the group when formed acquired a beneficial interest in the individual holdings of its members. We find our-

[61] *Id.* at 1117–18.

[62] *Cf.* Griffin and Tucker, *supra* note 1, at 682–83:

"The authors' position is that the formation of the group involves an acquisition. If the members of the group in the aggregate own in excess of 5 percent, then the formation of the group exhausts the 2 percent exemption and the 5 percent exclusion and the group should file a Schedule 13D within ten days of the formation of such group. Under such circumstances, it is unnecessary for any of the members of such group, after its formation, to purchase additional shares in order to make Section 13(d)(1) applicable to the group and to require filing of a statement pursuant to Rule 13d–1."

[63] *Id.* at 683–84.

selves in agreement with the statement of the Court of Appeals for the Seventh Circuit in Bath Industries, Inc. v. Blot, 427 F. 2d 97, 112 (7th Cir. 1970), that in the context of the Williams Act, where the principal concern is focused on the battle for corporate control, "voting control of stock is the only relevant element of beneficial ownership." Thus, we hardly can agree with Judge Pollack that the language of the statute compels the conclusion that individual members must acquire shares before the group can be required to file.[64]

The court went on to note that:

> Specifically, we were told, "the purpose of section 13(d) is to require disclosure of information by persons who have acquired a substantial interest, or increased their interest in the equity securities of a company by a substantial amount, within a relatively short period of time." S. Rep. No. 550 at 7; H.R. Rep. No. 1711 at 8. Otherwise, investors cannot assess the potential for changes in corporate control and adequately evaluate the company's worth. . . .
>
> That the purpose of section 13(d) is to alert the marketplace to every large, rapid aggregation or accumulation of securities, regardless of technique employed, which might represent a potential shift in corporate control is amply reflected in the enacted provisions.[65]

It should also be noted that the *Ozark* findings are in direct conflict with those of the U.S. District Court for the Southern District of New York in *Sisak v. Wings & Wheels Express, Inc.*[66] In this case the plaintiff claimed that upon passage of a decedent's 31 percent interest in Wings & Wheels to his estate, the estate, the executor, and the principal beneficiary, as beneficial owners of more than 10 percent of a class of equity securities of Wings & Wheels failed to file the required Schedule 13D statement. The defendants argued "that since 'the Estate acquired its Wings stock not by purchase or by any business transaction but by operation of law upon the death of Mr. Richter,' they were not required to file under §13(d)." [67] The court rendered judgment for the plaintiffs based on findings that the statute was not limited "to any particular mode of 'acquisition' nor has the SEC so limited its operation by regulation" and further that the purpose of the filing provision was "to disclose 'material facts con-

[64] GAF Corp. v. Milstein, *supra* note 56, at 715.
[65] *Id.* at 717. *See also* Bath Industries v. Blot. *supra* note 48, at 109.
[66] 70 Civ. 2817 (S.D.N.Y. 1970), CCH FED. SEC. L. REP. ¶ 92,991.
[67] *Id.* at p. 90,668.

cerning the identity, background, and plans of the person' . . . acquiring a substantial amount of securities. . . ." [68]

In summary, it should be noted that the strict construction approach of the district courts in both *GAF* and *Ozark* does not reflect the law in the Second and Seventh Circuits. The unsettled nature of the law in other jurisdictions coupled with the more liberal interpretations which many courts have given to the federal securities laws in an effort to insure the protection of the investing public suggests that prudent counsel would be well advised to consider recommending to their clients, wherever located, that they minimize the risks of potential liability by filing a Schedule 13D statement at the time the group is formed.[69]

While the question of when a "group" must file a Schedule 13D statement has been thoroughly reviewed by several courts, as noted above, the question of just what types of arrangements between investors will create a "group" for purposes of the Schedule 13D filing requirements has received little exposure to date. In the *GAF* case, the Second Circuit Court of Appeals discussed the question of whether management groups which control companies with registered securities and whose members collectively own more than 5 percent of a class of a company stock must file a 13D statement. The court stated:

> Although this problem is not part of the narrow issue we must decide, we cannot close our eyes to the implication of our decision. . . . Management groups *per se*, are not customarily formed for the purpose of "acquiring, holding, or disposing of securities of [the] issuer" and would not be required to file unless the members conspired to pool their securities interests for one of the stated purposes.[70]
>
> The more difficult question, and a question we need not decide on this appeal, is whether management groups which expressly agree to pool their interests to fight a potential takeover are subject to section 13(d). Nor do we intimate any view on whether an insurgent group which has filed under section 13(d) and subsequently is successful in its takeover bid remains subject to the section. In any event, as we

[68] *Id.*

[69] With regard to the consequences of a failure to file by a group, *see Committee for the New Management of Butler Aviation v. Widmark,* No. 71C 1528 (S.D.N.Y. 1971), CCH Fed. Sec. L. Rep. ¶ 93,332. See also Chapter 10, *infra.*

[70] *See* GAF v. Milstein, *supra* note 56, at 719.

have already indicated, the Commission can forestall any untoward effects under the exemptive power conferred upon it by section 13(d)(6)(D).[71]

To date, the staff of the Commission has taken the most expansive view of "what is a group." The staff had occasion to express its position in response to a letter of special counsel to twelve institutional lenders which had loaned an aggregate of $30 million to the Budd Company.[72] The company had entered into twelve separate loan agreements pursuant to which the lenders received warrants to purchase Budd common stock, which, if exercised in the aggregate, would result in the lenders receiving approximately 14 percent of the company's outstanding stock. Upon the opinion of special counsel, no Schedule 13D filing was made on behalf of the lenders as a group. Counsel's opinion letter was based in large measure on the fact that the loan agreements were separate and distinct from each other, did not require the consent of the other lenders and further that there was no agreement or understanding between any of the lenders to participate in making the loans or to take any action with regard to the exercise ot the warrants. The only common tie among the lenders, other than the similarity of the form of the agreements and the concurrent timing of the closings, appeared to be that each lender was "concerned" that the aggregate borrowing equal $30 million. However, the borrowing was effected at two closings and the lenders at the later closing were not committed to consummate the transaction if they felt that there had been any adverse change in conditions.[73] On the basis of these facts counsel concluded that there was no agreement by the lenders to act in concert to acquire additional shares or for that matter no agreement to act in concert for any purpose. As noted previously, Section 13(d)(3) requires concerted action or agreement for the purpose of acquiring, holding, or disposing of securities for a "group" to be deemed a "person."

[71] *Id.* at 719, n. 20.

[72] For the correspondence in full text, *see* The Budd Company, CCH Fed. Sec. L. Rep. ¶ 78115. *See also* 102 BNA Sec. Reg. L. Rep. C–1 (May 19, 1971). For other examples of "what is a group," *see* Griffin and Tucker, *supra* note 47, at 685–86.

[73] Counsel's letter does not specify whether the lenders at the earlier closing could rescind their transactions if the borrowings did not aggregate $30 million.

Without setting forth its reasons, the staff advised counsel that a Schedule 13D filing would be required of the group. While the staff's expansive reading of section 13(d)(3) cannot be considered as a guideline which will necessarily be followed by the Commission in the future, it does serve to give some indication of the present administrative position regarding the applicability of the Section 13(d) filing requirements.[74] Accordingly, counsel, even where it does not consider the arrangement between investors to constitute a group, should nevertheless file a Schedule 13D with a disclaimer denying the existence of a group.[75] Similarly, where institutional investors engage in arrangements similar to the Budd Company transaction described above, counsel may find it appropriate to file a Schedule 13D and state therein that the group was terminated by the consummation of the transaction and that no further reports would be filed.[76]

(4) THE SIGNIFICANCE OF THE "GROUP" IN PROXY CONTESTS

While this treatise deals with the use of tender offers in effecting corporate control, the "group" problem has had, at this writing, its most critical impact on proxy contests. Starting with the *Bath* case discussed above, [77] the rules for SEC regulated proxy contests have undergone a radical and unexpected change. Now, any group of insurgents having more than 5 percent of an issuer's equity securities, in addition to the requirement of filing Schedule 14B's under the proxy rules, must also file Schedule 13D's with the SEC.

It should be observed that the cases discussed in part (3) of this section, i.e., *Bath, Sisak, GAF,* and *Ozark,*[78] all involved proxy contests subject to Section 14 of the 1934 Act and the proxy rules promulgated thereunder. The authors believe that the requirement of filing Schedule 13D's in addition to Schedule 14B's,[79] as first enunciated in the *Bath* case, must have come as a great surprise to Senator Williams as well as to the Commission.[80]

[74] Still to be answered are such interesting questions as whether a broker-dealer managing discretionary accounts which own in the aggregate more than 5 percent of the issuers' equity securities must file a Schedule 13D statement.

[75] *See* Griffin and Tucker, *supra* note 1. at 684.

[76] *Id.*

[77] See text accompanying notes 48–52, *supra.*

[78] See text accompanying notes 48–71, *supra.*

[79] 17 C.F.R. ¶ 240.14a–102.

[80] In the early winter of 1970, the authors were on the threshold of two proxy contests in which they represented opposition groups. Having become aware of

Despite its first surprise at this turn of events and notwithstanding the added burden of administration resulting from the additional filing requirement, the staff of the Commission has been quick to accept and process these filings. Likewise, as the authors well know from their own experience, the members of the bar usually active in proxy contests have been equally quick to adjust to this added filing requirement and are evolving acceptable techniques in respect thereto.

While, for a period of time the viability of the "group doctrine" as enunciated in the *Bath* case was questioned by many attorneys, since the *GAF* case, there remains little doubt in the minds of those knowledgeable in the ground rules of proxy contests that this doctrine must now be reckoned with. Accordingly, as of this writing, experienced and knowledgeable attorneys cautiously advise the filing of Schedule 13D's within ten days after a 5 percent group has been formed for the purpose of undertaking a proxy contest.[81]

(5) Percentage of Class of Security Computation

In determining, for purposes of Sections 13(d) and 14(d), whether a person is the beneficial owner of more than 5 percent of any class of equity security, provision has been made for the same type of computation applied to determine whether a person owns more than 10 percent of any class of equity security for purposes of the filing and short-swing profits liability provisions of Section 16 of the 1934 Act.[82] In calculating the percentage of a class of equity security owned by any person, Sections 13(d)(4) and 14(d)(3) provide that:

---

the *Bath* decision, it was thought prudent to file Schedule 13D's along with the required Schedule 14B's. When this was done, it was a matter of some surprise at the Commission, apparently because the *Bath* case had not been thoroughly circulated to staff members of the Division of Corporation Finance. They raised their own questions as to whether it was necessary, and the authors suggested that the schedules be filed and that there be final comment after the Staff had an opportunity to analyze the *Bath* case. It is only a matter of history to relate that the Commission has fully accepted the "group doctrine" enunciated in that decision.

[81] *See* Griffin and Tucker, *The Williams Act, Public Law 90–439—Growing Pains? Some Interpretations with Respect to the Williams Act,* 16 Howard L.J 654, 682–683 (1971). With regard to the time schedule for filing Schedule 14B's, *see* Rule 14a–11(c), 17 C.F.R. ¶ 240.14a–11(c).

[82] *See* Rule 16a–2, 17 C.F.R. ¶ 240.16a–2.

Such class shall be deemed to consist of the amount of the outstanding securities of such class, exclusive of any securities of such class held by or for the account of the issuer or a subsidiary of the issuer.

Rule 13d–3 provides additional guidelines for determining whether a person is more than a 5 percent owner: [83]

In determining, for the purposes of Section 13(d) or Section 14(d) [of the Act], whether a person is directly or indirectly the beneficial owner of securities of any class, such person shall be deemed to be the beneficial owner of securities of such class which such person has the right to acquire through the exercise of presently exercisable options, warrants or rights or through the conversion of presently convertible securities, or otherwise. The securities subject to such options, warrants, rights or conversion privileges held by a person shall be deemed to be outstanding for the purpose of computing the percentage of outstanding securities of the class owned by such person but shall not be deemed to be outstanding for the purpose of computing the percentage of the class owned by any other person.[84]

In determining the aggregate amount of securities outstanding, a question may arise regarding the source to be used for obtaining such information. For purposes of Section 16(a), Rule 16a–2(a) provides that "[a] person acting in good faith may rely on the information contained in the latest consolidated financial statement in a registration statement or annual report filed with the Commission under the Act . . . ." The absence of such a statement in Sections 14(d)(3), 13(d)(4) and Rule 13d–3 thereunder, which are obviously patterned after Rule 16a–2, perhaps suggests that specific reference sources do not lend themselves to

[83] One must note with some discomfort the disorganized draftsmanship evidenced by three separate provisions relating to the manner in which the computation is made for purposes of Sections 13(d) and 14(d). *Cf.* the computation under Section 16, which succinctly sets forth the manner in which the computation is to be made in two paragraphs of a single rule.

[84] For example, assume a target company has outstanding 1,000,000 common shares, $1 million of debentures convertible into 100,000 shares of common and 100,000 warrants to purchase 100,000 common shares. The person seeking to acquire control is the beneficial owner of the following amounts of the target's securities: 50,000 common shares; $50,000 principal amount of debentures presently convertible into 5,000 shares of common; and 5,000 presently exercisable warrants to purchase 5,000 common shares.

For purposes of Rule 13d–3, the person seeking to acquire control would divide 1,010,000 shares outstanding by 60,000 shares and would be deemed to own 5.9 percent of the target's outstanding common shares.

a meaningful generalization regarding good faith reliance where a person acquires or proposes to acquire a substantial block of securities for the purpose of acquiring control. Thus, for example, it is doubtful whether a potential tender offeror seeking to acquire control can or should rely upon a ten-month-old annual report to determine the amount of shares which the target company has outstanding. Accordingly, for purposes of Sections 13(d) and 14(d), any person close to the 5 percent figure would be well advised to base its calculation on the latest public document of the target which contains such information.[85]

(6) INFORMATION REQUIRED BY SCHEDULE 13D

The full text of the disclosures required by Schedule 13D is reproduced below. If the statement is filed by a group such as a partnership or syndicate, the information required by Items 2 to 6 must be given with respect to each member of the group and each person controlling such member. If a corporation is part of the group or the statement is filed by a corporation, the information required by Items 2 to 6 must be given with respect to each officer and director of the corporation and each person controlling the corporation.[86] In preparing Schedule 13D, the item numbers and captions of the items are to be included, but the instructions specifying how the item is to be answered are to be omitted. If an item is inapplicable or the answer is in the negative, the response should so state.[87]

SCHEDULE 13D

ITEM 1. SECURITY AND ISSUER.

State the title of the class of equity securities to which this statement relates and the name and address of the issuer of such securities.

ITEM 2. IDENTITY AND BACKGROUND.

State the following with respect to the person filing this statement:

[85] This might be a proxy statement or a quarterly financial report which contains figures showing the average number of shares outstanding for the most recent three-month period.

[86] Schedule 13D, Note B.

[87] Schedule 13D, Note A.

(a) Name and business address;

(b) Residence address;

(c) Present principal occupation or employment and the name, principal business and address of any corporation or other organization in which such employment is carried on;

(d) Material occupations, positions, offices or employments during the last 10 years, giving the starting and ending dates of each and the name, principal business and address of any business corporation or other organization in which such occupation, position, office or employment was carried on; and

(e) Whether or not, during the last 10 years, such person has been convicted in a criminal proceeding (excluding traffic violations or similar misdemeanors) and, if so, give the dates, nature of conviction, name and location of court, and penalty imposed, or other disposition of the case. A negative answer to this sub-item need not be furnished to security holders.

ITEM 3. SOURCE AND AMOUNT OF FUNDS OR OTHER CONSIDERATION.

State the source and amount of funds or other consideration used or to be used in making the purchases, and if any part of the purchase price or proposed purchase price is represented or is to be represented by funds or other consideration borrowed or otherwise obtained for the purpose of acquiring holding, or trading the securities, a description of the transaction and the names of the parties thereto.[88]

ITEM 4. PURPOSE OF TRANSACTION.

If the purpose of the purchases or prospective purchases is to acquire control of the business of the issuer of the securi-

[88] Section 13(d)(1)(B) provides "that where a source of funds is a loan made in the ordinary course of business by a bank, as defined in section 3(a)(6) of this title, if the person filing such statement so requests, the name of the bank shall not be made available to the public." This provision would appear to permit purchasers to omit the names of lender(s) in tender offer soliciting materials [see Rule 14d–1(c)(4)] and in the Schedule 13D statement sent to the issuer.

Strict confidentiality of the purchaser's source of financing is generally conceded to be of the essence in order to limit the possibility that the target company or its friends will be able to persuade the lender to withdraw its financial support. The above-quoted provision is one of but a few accommodations which the Williams Act affords to the insurgents.

ties, describe any plans or proposals which such persons may have to liquidate such issuer, to sell its assets to or merge it with any other persons, or to make any other major change in its business or corporate structure.

ITEM 5. INTEREST IN SECURITIES OF THE ISSUER.

State the number of shares of the security which are beneficially owned, and the number of shares concerning which there is a right to acquire, directly or indirectly, by (i) such person, and (ii) each associate of such person, giving the name and address of each such associate.

ITEM 6. CONTRACTS, ARRANGEMENTS, OR UNDERSTANDINGS WITH RESPECT TO SECURITIES OF THE ISSUER.

Furnish information as to any contracts, arrangements, or understandings with any person with respect to any securities of the issuer, including but not limited to transfer of any of the securities, joint ventures, loan or option arrangements, puts or calls, guaranties of loans, guaranties against loss or guaranties of profits, division of losses or profits, or the giving or withholding of proxies, naming the persons with whom such contracts, arrangements, or understandings have been entered into, and giving the details thereof.

ITEM 7. PERSONS RETAINED, EMPLOYED OR TO BE COMPENSATED.

Where the Schedule 13D relates to a tender offer, or request or invitation for tenders, identify all persons and classes of persons employed, retained or to be compensated by the person filing this Schedule 13D, or by any person on his behalf, to make solicitations or recommendations to security holders and describe briefly the terms of such employment, retainer or arrangement for compensation.

ITEM 8. MATERIAL TO BE FILED AS EXHIBITS.

Copies of all requests or invitations for tenders or advertisements making a tender offer requesting or inviting tenders, additional material soliciting or requesting such tender offers, solicitations or recommendations to the holders of the security to accept or reject a tender offer or request or invitation for tenders shall be filed as an exhibit.[89]

SIGNATURE

I certify that to the best of my knowledge and belief the information set forth in this statement is true, complete and correct.

____________________	______________________________
(Date)	*(Signature)*

If the statement is signed on behalf of a person by an authorized representative, evidence of the representative's authority to sign on behalf of such person shall be filed with the statement.

While the instructions specifying how each item of Schedule 13D should be answered are for the most part self-explanatory, difficulties in interpretation have arisen under Item 4 regarding the requirement that the person filing "describe any plans or proposals which such persons may have" to make a major change in the target's business or corporate structure.

In *Susquehanna Corp. v. Pan American Sulphur Co.*,[90] the response to Item 4 by the tender offeror, Susquehanna, provided in relevant part:

Pan American had 4,751,342 shares of common stock issued and outstanding as of October 31, 1968. Susquehanna through its offer intends to purchase 1,800,000 shares at $40 per share, which, if acquired, should, in the opinion of Susquehanna's Management, give Susquehanna working control of Pan American. If control is achieved, it is contemplated that the business of Pan American will be conducted as a subsidiary of Susquehanna serving as its natural resources arm.

Susquehanna does not plan or propose to liquidate Pan American, to sell its assets to, or merge it with, any other person, or to make any other major change in its business or corporate structure. However, if, at some subsequent time, it should appear the interests of the Pan American stockholders would be better served by any of the

[89] For the information required to be included in: (a) additional material soliciting tender offers; and (b) solicitations or recommendations to security holders to accept or reject a tender offer, *see* Rule 14d–1(d) and Rule 14d–4(c).

[90] 423 F.2d 1075 (5th Cir. 1970), *rev'g* No. SA–69–CA–67 (W.D. Tex. 1969), CCH FED. SEC. REP. ¶ 92,473.

foregoing courses of action, Susquehanna may propose or adopt such course.

Pan American Sulphur Company (PASCO) sought to enjoin Susquehanna from voting its shares, alleging *inter alia,* violations of Sections 13(d)(1) and 14(d)(1) in that Susquehanna failed to disclose in its Schedule 13D statements that: (a) it was trying to obtain control of PASCO by electing a majority of Susquehanna's representatives to the PASCO board of directors and that (b) it intended to merge PASCO with American Smelting & Refining Co. (ASARCO). PASCO's claim regarding the alleged merger intentions of Susquehanna was based in large measure on a telegram sent by the president of Susquehanna to the president of ASARCO proposing to negotiate a merger which would be subject to the approval of the boards of PASCO and ASARCO and stating possible terms for such a merger. The telegram was sent several days after Susquehannas's President discussed the matter with PASCO's President and one day after Susquehanna filed an amended Schedule 13D statement which failed to disclose its merger intentions.

The Court of Appeals reversed the lower court's grant of injunctive relief and directed dismissal of the suit. In finding that Susquehanna's response to Item 4 clearly indicated that control of PASCO was the object of the tender offer, the court concluded that shareholders and public investors were fully advised of the offeror's intention to obtain control.[91] With regard to Susque-

[91] The court also found that PASCO could not have been misled into an "understanding," within the meaning of Item 6 of Schedule 13D, that Susquehanna would not seek control and attempt to elect a majority of PASCO's board.

Susquehanna filed the following as its Item 6:

"Neither Susquehanna, nor its officers or directors, or any of their associates has any contracts, arrangements or understandings with respect to the securities of Pan American. However, Pan American's Certificate of Incorporation does not provide for cumulative voting, and accordingly ownership of 1,800,000 shares will not insure any representation on the Board of Directors of Pan American. If, however, Susquehanna acquires 1,800,000 shares pursuant to this Offer, it expects to request Pan American's Board of Directors to fill the two vacancies now existing on its Board of Directors with persons designated by Susquehanna. The designees of Susquehanna will be selected from its directors and officers listed herein. It is possible that representatives of Pan American will be invited to occupy any vacant seats on Susquehanna's Board."

With regard to the adequacy of an Item 6 response, *see also* Sisak v. Wings and Wheels Express, Inc., 70 Civ. 2817 (S.D.N.Y. 1970), CCH FED. SEC. L. REP. ¶ 92,991 at pp. 90, 668–69.

hanna's merger intentions, the court found that Susquehanna's disclosures were fair and complete and that it would have been misleading for Susquehanna to have indicated that there was a merger plan or proposal since Susquehanna's interest in merging "never got off the ground," having been repudiated by PASCO and not even acknowledged by ASARCO.[92]

The court's holding that an offeror need not disclose its desire or intention to merge where meaningful steps to accomplish such intention have not taken place may appear to be somewhat at odds with a broad reading of the Item 4 requirement that the purchaser disclose "plans or proposals which such persons may have to . . . merge [the issuer] with any other persons." Nevertheless this holding seeks to establish a fundamentally workable judicial guideline for future cases of this nature—namely, that something more than the state of mind of the offeror need be shown before an "intention" to make a major change in the target's business or corporate structure will constitute a plan or proposal within the meaning of Item 4.

The findings of the court of appeals regarding the "plans or proposals" language of Item 4 is in marked contrast with the SEC's analysis of the same facts. The Commission's review of these events resulted from an unrelated administrative proceeding in which the staff alleged that Susquehanna's Schedule 13D statement was false and misleading in failing to disclose Susquehanna's plans to use PASCO's cash assets to merge it with or to acquire another corporation.[93]

[92] In reaching this result, the court stressed its conclusion that "[i]t should be obvious to even the uninitiated that when a corporation takes over control of another corporation having $60,000,000 in cash assets, some kind of change in the latter's business or corporate structure will likely occur some time in the future." In this regard the court also emphasized that Susquehanna had provided for this possibility by providing in Item 4 that "if, at some subsequent time, it should appear the interests of the Pan American stockholders would be better served by . . . [a merger], Susquehanna may propose or adopt such course." *Supra* note 90, at 1083, 1085.

[93] *In the Matter of Reports of The Susquehanna Corp.*, SEC Securities Exchange Act Release No. 8933 (July 17, 1970), CCH Fed. Sec. L. Rep. ¶ 77,842.

The Commission's hearings in this matter were instituted pursuant to Section 15(c)(4) of the 1934 Act, which provides that:

"If the Commission finds, after notice and opportunity for hearing, that any person subject to the provisions of section 12, 13, or subsection (d) of section 15 of this title or any rule or regulation thereunder has failed to comply with any

In concluding that Susquehanna's Schedule 13D statement failed to comply in material respects with Sections 13(d)(1) and Rule 13d–1 thereunder, the Commission succinctly set forth its findings:

> In our opinion, however, in the words of the examiner, "the energy, aggressiveness and persistence of the Korholz efforts to bring to fruition his intentions to put the cash assets to use by acquisition or merger give to his intentions the substance, quality and character of a plan, as the term is used in the statute." The significant consideration is not whether an acquisition or merger was planned with ASARCO or any other specific company, but whether, as found by the examiner, there was a plan to use the cash assets to acquire or merge with any company upon securing control of PASCO. A tender offeror normally is not able to make definite arrangements for an acquisition by or merger of the target company with a third company before control has been obtained. It is therefore not important that ASARCO did not respond to Susquehanna's proposed merger terms or that no specific proposal to acquire another company was made to or accepted by any such company.[94]

In *Electronic Specialty Co. v. International Controls Corp.*,[95] the first appellate decision dealing with the Williams Act, the target company (Electronic Specialty Co.) sought to enjoin the defendant from voting the stock acquired pursuant to a tender offer, claiming, *inter alia,* that the offeror failed to disclose that it had "a fixed and definite plan to merge the target and the offeror on a so-called 'share-for-share' basis." While there was testimony at the trial that ICC proposed a share-for-share merger as a "basis for negotiation" there was no evidence to indicate that ICC had a fixed commitment to merge the two companies on that basis. In denying the plaintiff the requested relief, both the District Court and the Court of Appeals found, on the facts pre-

---

such provision, rule, or regulation in any material respect, the Commission may publish its findings and issue an order requiring such person to comply with such provision or such rule or regulation thereunder upon such terms and conditions and within such time as the Commission may specify in such order."

[94] Susquehanna conceded that negotiations did not have to reach the stage of an agreement in principle for a "plan" to exist and that a plan need not be in writing. However, it contended that a plan should be more definite than Susquehanna's which offered but "a mere possibility or hope" of consummation.

[95] 409 F.2d 937 (2d Cir. 1969), *aff'g in part* 295 F. Supp. 1063 (S.D.N.Y. 1968). For prior opinion *see* 296 F. Supp. 462 (S.D.N.Y. 1968).

sented, that the offeror's statement that it would "give consideration" to a merger if the tender offer was successful constituted adequate disclosure.[96]

The Commission's view of the "plans and proposals" language of Item 4 is not easily reconciled with that of the Second and Fifth Circuits. The disclosures in both the ICC and Susquehanna 13D statements would appear to have clearly alerted even the most unsophisticated investor that an eventual merger of the respective target companies with other corporations was a possibility if the offers succeeded.[97] The Commission's apparent desire to get offerors to commit themselves to a more definite statement of their intentions, which in certain instances might later be challenged as a fraudulent attempt to manipulate the market if the offerors subsequently changed their minds, would appear to add little to the continued integrity of the securities markets or the protection of investors.

The view that an offeror be firmly committed to making a major change in the business or corporate structure of the target before it is required to make definite statements regarding such plans appears to be based upon a sound approach to the realities of the market place. While it is possible that the reluctance of an offeror to commit itself to a more definite statement may be motivated by the fear that such disclosure would discourage shareholders from tendering, it is more likely that such a statement would have the opposite effect. Thus, if the offeror disclosed that it planned to merge the target with the offeror or perhaps an unnamed third company if the tender offer is successful, shareholders may be stampeded into tendering their shares to eliminate

[96] ICC's disclosure regarding merger possibilities which appeared in its published tender invitation provided as follows:

"The Company [ICC] intends through this Offer to acquire control of Specialty. It does not presently have any plans or proposals to liquidate Specialty, to sell its assets or merge it with any persons (other than the Company or its subsidiaries), or to make any other change in its business or corporate structure, except that it intends to continue Specialty's stated plans to sell its Space Conditioning Division and will consider the possible liquidation or sale of any other unprofitable divisions. Upon completion of this Offer the Company will give consideration to a merger between itself or a subsidiary and Specialty."

295 F. Supp. 1063, 1079–1080. The district court also rejected plaintiff's claim that ICC's response to Items 3 and 6 of Schedule 13D were false. *Id.* at 1080.

[97] See note 92, *supra*.

the uncertainties of investment in a newly structured company which would have an uncertain market value and business future. It may well be questioned whether either Congress or the Commission intended such an end result in the statute or the rules thereunder.

(7) Amendments of Schedule 13D Statements

Rule 13d–2,[98] promulgated pursuant to the rule-making authority granted the Commission in Section 13(d)(2), requires an amendment to the Schedule 13D statement to be filed if any "material change" takes place in the facts set forth therein. The amendment must be filed "promptly" with the Commission and sent to the issuer and each exchange where the security is traded.

Neither the statute nor the rule affords any guidelines on just what is a "material change," which in most instances must necessarily depend upon the specific facts and circumstances of the particular case. Perhaps the most frequent problem which has arisen regarding amendments concerns the question of when a disposition or additional acquisition of securities subsequent to the original filing will constitute a "material change" for purposes of Rule 13d–2. A conservative guideline which has been suggested with regard to the acquisition of shares provides that the 13D statement need not be amended until such additional purchases aggregate more than 2 percent of the class of securities to which the 13D statement relates.[99] Thereafter, each subsequent acquisition of more than 2 percent of the class would require an additional amendment. Similarly, dispositions of more than 2 percent of the class might also be considered a material change which should be disclosed to investors although Section 13(d)(1) (unlike the filing requirements in connection with trading by insiders, which require reports on both purchases and sales [100]) deals only with purchases.[101]

[98] 17 C.F.R. § 240.13d–2.

[99] *See* Brown, *The Scope of the Williams Act and Its 1970 Amendments,* 26 Bus. Law 1637, 1640 (July 1971); Schmults and Kelly, *Disclosure in Connection with Cash Take-Over Bids: The New Regulations,* 24 Bus. Law 19, 22 (Nov. 1968).

[100] *See* Section 16(a) of the 1934 Act.

[101] The underlying purpose of the Williams Act is to advise investors of sub-

This approach relies for support on the Schedule 13D filing exemption contained in Section 13(d)(6)(B) for acquisitions which do not exceed 2 percent of the class during the preceding twelve months. While neither the statute nor the rules suggest any interrelationship between this exemption and the material change test, the 2 percent rule as applied to amendments would appear to be a fundamentally sound rule of thumb.[102]

B. SCHEDULE 13D—SHORT FORM FILING

The 1970 Williams Act amendment, which reduced the requisite percentage of securities owned to trigger the filing requirements from 10 percent to 5 percent, increased the likelihood that persons acquiring relatively large blocks of securities in the ordinary course of business and not for the purpose of participating in contests for control would also be required to file a Schedule 13D statement. In an effort to eliminate the unnecessary burden of requiring persons such as exchange specialists, over-the-counter market makers and investment companies to comply with extensive reporting requirements which might not be necessary to protect the interests of investors, the House Committee on Interstate and Foreign Commerce proposed an amendment which would enable the Commission to permit a simplified filing for such persons.[103] The committee amendment, which was eventually adopted as Section 13(d)(5), provides that the Commission, by rule, regulation or order, may permit a short form filing in lieu of a statement under 13(d)(1) by any person, "if it appears to the Commission that such securities were acquired by such person in the ordinary course of his business and were not acquired for the

---

stantial block acquisitions which may eventually lead to changes in control. Query whether disclosure of sales of such securities, which may evidence the fact that control is not being sought, furthers this purpose.

Cf. GAF Corp. v. Milstein, 324 F. Supp. 1062, 1070 (S.D.N.Y. 1971): "The inapplicability of the 2% exemption to sales indicates that Congress felt that sales at crucial times may be even more important than purchases when a tender offer is made, and therefore the holder must report any material changes in his holdings caused by disposing of securities."

[102] The SEC, however, has not expressed its views of the applicability of the 2 percent rule to amendments. In this regard it is recommended that the SEC consider an appropriate release outlining its position on what constitutes a "material change."

[103] H.R. REP. No. 91–1655, 91st Cong., 2d Sess. 4 (1970).

purpose of and do not have the effect of changing or influencing the control of the issuer nor in connection with or as a participant in any transaction having such purpose or effect." Section 13(d)(5) also provides that the simplified filing disclose the name of the purchaser, the number of shares subject to Section 13(d)(1) which are owned by him, the dates of purchase and such other information as the Commission may specify.

Section 13(d)(5) thus creates an alternative to the Commission's choosing between a full exemption under Section 13(d)(6)(D) [104] and a full Schedule 13D filing. While such a provision would help to eliminate what might be termed the inherent administrative reluctance to grant exemptions, the Commission has yet to propose any rules pursuant to Section 13(d)(5).[105] The delay in doing so, coupled with the obvious interest of Congress to reduce the filing burdens on persons whose normal activities clearly do not fall within the regulatory purpose of Section 13(d), suggests that Congress by statute, should have provided appropriate exemptions or permitted short form filing for such persons.

c. Disclosure by Issuers Repurchasing Their Own Securities (Section 13(e) and Rule 13e–1)

Section 13(e)(1) is the basic statutory provision providing for disclosure in connection with purchases by an issuer of its own securities. This provision states as follows:

> It shall be unlawful for an issuer which has a class of equity securities registered pursuant to section 12 of this title, or which is a closed-end investment company registered under the Investment Company Act of 1940, to purchase any equity security issued by it if such purchase is in contravention of such rules and regulations as the Commission, in the public interest or for the protection of investors, may adopt (A) to define acts and practices which are fraudulent, deceptive, or manipu-

[104] Section 13(d)(6)(D) provides that the provisions of Section 13(d) do not apply to: "any acquisition or proposed acquisition of a security which the Commission, by rules or regulations or by order, shall exempt from the provisions of this subsection as not entered into for the purpose of, and not having the effect of, changing or influencing the control of the issuer or otherwise as not comprehended within the purposes of this subsection."

[105] While there have been no rules proposed to date, a purchaser may apply to the Commission requesting an order permitting a simplified filing or granting a complete exemption.

lative, and (B) to prescribe means reasonably designed to prevent such acts and practices. Such rules and regulations may require such issuer to provide holders of equity securities of such class with such information relating to the reasons for such purchase, the source of funds, the number of shares to be purchased, the price to be paid for such securities, the method of purchase, and such additional information, as the Commission deems necessary or appropriate in the public interest or for the protection of investors, or which the Commission deems to be material to a determination whether such security should be sold.

Rule 13e–1 prohibits an issuer from reacquiring any of its equity securities (of a class specified in Section 13(e)(1)) during the course of a tender offer made by any other person unless the issuer has filed an information statement with the SEC and has within the preceding six months transmitted the substance of this information to its shareholders.[106] The statement filed with the Commission must contain the following information:

(1) The title and amount of securities to be purchased, the names of the persons or classes of persons from whom, and the market in which, the securities are to be purchased, including the name of any exchange on which the purchase is to be made;
(2) The purpose for which the purchase is to be made and whether the securities are to be retired, held in the treasury of the issuer or otherwise disposed of, indicating such disposition; and
(3) The source and amount of funds or other consideration used or to be used in making the purchases, and if any part of the purchase price or proposed purchase price is represented by funds or other consideration borrowed or otherwise obtained for the purpose of acquiring, holding, or trading the securities, a description of the transaction and the names of the parties thereto.

While the information required by Rule 13e–1 appears self-explanatory, some confusion may result with regard to the specific disclosures required by paragraph (3). As noted earlier in this chapter in connection with the disclosures required pursuant to Schedule 13D, Section 13(d)(1)(B) provides "that where a source of funds is a loan made in the ordinary course of business by a

[106] Rule 13e–1 requires an issuer repurchasing its shares during the course of a tender offer to file only if the offeror has filed a statement pursuant to Rule 14d–1 and the issuer has received notice thereof. Presumably, the issuer need not comply with Rule 13e–1 if the offeror fails to comply with Rule 14d–1.

bank, as defined in Section 3(a)(6) of this title, if the person filing such statement so requests, the name of the bank shall not be made available to the public." [107] Paragraph (3) above is identical with Item 3 of Schedule 13D, but neither Section 13(e)(1) nor Rule 13e–1 thereunder makes any provision for nonpublic treatment of the name of any bank which will finance the issuer's purchases; nor is there any provision enabling the Commission, upon its own motion or by order upon application, to permit nonpublic treatment of such information. Thus, issuers repurchasing their own securities must disclose the specific source of any financing while tender offerors and potential tender offerors are permitted to obtain nonpublic treatment if the source of financing is a bank as defined in Section 3(a)(6) of the 1934 Act. There appear to be no persuasive reasons for making any such distinction. Furthermore, public disclosure of the name of a regulated bank will do little, if anything, to advance the legitimate interests of investors while confidentiality of such information is generally recognized as a prudent business policy. Accordingly, the Commission would be well advised to amend Rule 13e–1 to provide for nonpublic treatment of such information.

Another source of potential difficulty regarding the disclosure provisions of Section 13(e) derives from the rather nonspecific wording of Section 13(e)(2), which provides, for purposes of Section 13(e)(1), that "purchases by or for the issuer, or any person controlling, controlled by, or under the common control with the issuer, or a purchase subject to control of the issuer or any such person, shall be deemed to be a purchase by the issuer."

While there is some evidence in the legislative history to indicate that Section 13(e)(2) is limited to purchases by a parent or subsidiary of the issuer, or by a welfare or pension fund subject to the influence of the issuer's management,[108] there has been continued concern that the provision will be interpreted to apply to purchases by institutions or other unaffiliated third parties arranged by or made at the request or suggestion of the issuer.[109] If

[107] See note 88, *supra*.

[108] *See* statement of Manuel F. Cohen, *Hearings on H.R. 14475, S. 510, Before the Subcomm. on Commerce and Finance of the House Comm. on Interstate and Foreign Commerce*, 90th Cong., 2d Sess. 15 (July 1, 1968).

[109] Rule 12b–2 governing all reports filed pursuant to ¶ 13 defines the term

in fact this provision is broadly interpreted to include purchases by such third parties, it would appear that the better rule would restrict its application to those purchases where the issuer has a clearly identifiable interest (such as through guarantees or buy-back arrangements) in the securities.

In an apparent effort to avoid interpretative problems of this nature, the 1970 amendments added a sentence to Section 13(e)(2) to give the SEC rule-making authority to define and delimit the scope of this provision. There have been no such rules promulgated to date.[110]

D. Schedule 14D—Disclosure by Persons Making a Solicitation or Recommendation to Accept Or Reject a Tender Offer

(1) Class of Persons Required to File; Time of Filing

Pursuant to the rule-making authority granted the Commission

"control" (including the terms "controlling," "controlled by" and "under common control with") as "the possession directly or indirectly, of the power to direct or cause the direction of the management and policies of a person whether through the ownership of voting securities, by contract or otherwise."

[110] The Commission has proposed to adopt Rule 13e–2, which provides for comprehensive regulation of the prices, amounts, and circumstances under which an issuer may repurchase its securities. Unlike Rule 13e–1, which relates only to repurchases during the course of a tender offer, proposed Rule 13e–2 is applicable to repurchases made at any time by an issuer. Subsection (c) of proposed Rule 13e–2 provides that:

"For the purpose of this rule, a purchase by or on behalf of any bonus, profit-sharing, pension, retirement, thrift, savings, incentive, stock purchase, or similar plan of the issuer or its employees shall be deemed to be a purchase by the issuer, unless the plan is operated and purchases are made by a trustee who is independent of the issuer. A trustee shall not be deemed independent of the issuer if the trustee or the issuer, or an affiliate of either, directly or indirectly controls, is controlled by, or is under common control with the other (provided that a common directorship shall not alone affect the trustee's independence), or if the issuer directly or indirectly has any control or influence over the time when or the price at which securities may be purchased, the amount of securities to be purchased, or the selection of the broker or dealer through or from whom they are to be purchased."

As expressly stated, the description of purchases which are deemed to be purchases by an issuer is applicable only for purposes of Rule 13e–2. However, in the absence of any rules defining purchases deemed to be made by the issuer for purposes of Rule 13e–1, subsection (c) should furnish a useful guideline to the extent that purchases are made by or on behalf of a pension, profit-sharing or similar plan.

in Section 14(d)(4), Rule 14d–4(a)[111] thereunder requires a Schedule 14D[112] statement to be filed by any person (other than an exempt person) making a solicitation or recommendation to security holders to accept or reject a tender offer subject to Section 14(d) of the 1934 Act.[113] The person making the solicitation or recommendation must file the Schedule 14D statement with the Commission no later than the time copies are first published or sent or given to security holders.[114] If any material change occurs in the facts set forth in the statement, the person filing is required to "promptly" file an appropriate amendment.[115]

To avoid the unnecessary burden of duplicate filings, the Rule exempts tender offerors who are required by Rule 14d–1(a) to file a Schedule 13D statement[116] and persons, other than the issuer or the management of the issuer, who make no written solicitations or recommendations other than to transmit solicitations or recommendations, copies of which have been filed with the Commission pursuant to Rule 14d–1. This latter exemption is designed primarily to enable brokers and dealers to transmit copies of any solicitations or recommendations on behalf of the offeror without the necessity of filing a Schedule 14D statement. In addition, a Schedule 14D statement need not be filed by attorneys, banks, brokers, fiduciaries, and investment advisers who are not otherwise participating in the tender offer or solicitation and who

[111] 17 C.F.R. ¶ 240.14d–4, eff. July 30, 1968.

[112] 17 C.F.R. ¶ 240.14d–101, eff. July 30, 1968.

[113] Section 14(d) applies to tender offers which contemplate that the offeror will own more than 5 percent of the outstanding securities of any class of equity security which is registered pursuant to Section 12 of the 1934 Act or an equity security of an insurance company which would have been required to register except for the exemption in Section 12(g)(2)(G) of the 1934 Act or any equity security issued by a closed-end investment company registered under the Investment Company Act of 1940. A limited number of exemptions from Section 14(d) are provided for in Section 14(d)(8) and Rule 14d–2.

[114] Rule 14d–4(a), 17 C.F.R. § 240.14d–4(a). The Rule does not specify the number of copies which must be filed. Rules 13d–1, 13d–2, 13e–1, 14d–1, and 14f–1 require 8 copies of the statements filed thereunder to be submitted to the Commission. *See* SEC Securities Exchange Act Release No. 8556 (March 24, 1969), CCH FED. SEC. L. REP. ¶ 77,678.

[115] Rule 14d–4(b), 17 C.F.R. § 240.14d–4(b). With regard to what constitutes a "material change," see text accompanying notes 98–102, *supra*.

[116] A tender offeror subject to Rule 14d–1(a) is required to file copies of all solicitations or recommendations to security holders as an exhibit to its Schedule 13D statement. *See* Rule 14d–1(a), (d) and (e); Item 8, Schedule 13D.

furnish information and advice regarding a tender offer to their customers and clients, provided such information or advice is furnished on an unsolicited basis (i.e., upon request) or pursuant to a general contract for advice.[117]

While the nature of the exemptions appears to limit the applicability of Rule 14d-4 to solicitations or recommendations made by the target company or its management, the Rule, in fact, has a broader application. For example, a prospective competing tender offeror will be required to file a Schedule 14D statement before it may lawfully issue a press release which could have the effect of discouraging security holders from tendering their shares pursuant to an existing offer.[118]

(2) Information Required by Schedule 14D

The full text of the disclosure required by Schedule 14D is as follows: [119]

Schedule 14D

Item 1. Security and Issuer.

(a) State the title of the class of equity securities to which this statement relates and the name and address of the issuer of such securities.

(b) Identify the tender offer or request or invitation for tenders to which this statement relates and state the reasons for the solicitation or recommendation to security holders to accept or reject such tender offer, request, or invitation for tenders.

[117] Rule 14d–2(e), 17 C.F.R. § 240.14d–2(e).

[118] *See* SEC v. Madison Square Garden Corp., No. 69 Civ. 4364 (S.D.N.Y. 1970), CCH Fed. Sec. L. Rep. ¶ 92,649, discussed in text accompanying note 122, *infra*.

[119] The release announcing adoption of Schedules 13D and 14D contained instructions on the preparation and form of a Schedule 13D statement but did not provide similar instructions in connection with Schedule 14D. Presumably, the instructions to Schedule 13D apply equally to Schedule 14D. *See* SEC Securities Exchange Act Release No. 8370 (July 30, 1968), CCH Fed. Sec. L. Rep. ¶ 77,581. See also text accompanying notes 86–87, *supra*.

With regard to the information required to be included in any solicitation to accept or reject a tender offer, see Section 8 of this chapter, *infra*.

ITEM 2. IDENTITY AND BACKGROUND

(a) State the name and business address of the person filing this statement.

(b) Describe any arrangement or understanding in regard to the solicitation with (i) the issuer or the management of the issuer or (ii) the maker of the tender offer or request or invitation for tender of securities of the class to which this statement relates.

ITEM 3. PERSONS RETAINED, EMPLOYED OR TO BE COMPENSATED.

Identify any person or class of persons employed, retained or to be compensated, by the person filing this Schedule 14D, or by any person on his behalf, to make solicitations or recommendations to security holders and describe briefly the terms of such employment, retainer or arrangement for compensation.

ITEM 4. MATERIAL TO BE FILED AS EXHIBITS.

Copies of all solicitations or recommendations to accept or to reject a tender offer or request or invitation for tenders of the securities specified in Item 1 shall be filed as an exhibit.

SIGNATURE

I certify that to the best of my knowledge and belief the information set forth in this statement is true, complete and correct.

________________ ________________________

(*Date*) (*Signature*)

(3) WHAT CONSTITUTES A SOLICITATION OR RECOMMENDATION TO ACCEPT OR REJECT A TENDER OFFER FOR PURPOSES OF RULE 14d–4?

Since the Schedule 14D statement must be filed no later than the time copies of any solicitation or recommendation to accept or reject a tender offer are first published or sent or given to security holders, it is essential to determine what types of statements will constitute a solicitation or recommendation for purposes of Rule 14d–4. The only guideline furnished by the statute and rules appears in Rule 14d–2(f).[120] This Rule provides that Section 14(d) and the rules thereunder shall not apply to a communication from an issuer to its security holders which does no more than provide the following information:

(1) identify a tender offer or request or invitation for tenders made by another person. (2) state that the management of the issuer is studying the matter and will, on or before a specified date (which shall be not later than 10 days prior to the date specified in the offer, request or invitation, as the last date on which tenders will be accepted, or such shorter period as the Commission may authorize) advise security holders as to the management's recommendation to accept or reject the offer, request or invitation, and (3) request security holders to defer making a determination as to whether or not they should accept or reject the offer, request or invitation until they have received the management's recommendation with respect thereto.[121]

While prudent judgment would suggest that any statement made prior to filing a Schedule 14D statement should not exceed the guidelines of Rule 14d–2(f), it should be noted that the Rule does not make it unlawful *per se* to issue additional information. Thus a target company or a prospective offeror would not be precluded from making any statements which are not intended and do not have the effect of influencing security holders to accept or reject the offer. It is important to emphasize, however, that a solicitation or recommendation to accept or reject an offer may be inferred from the surrounding facts and circumstances although the statement makes no direct attempt to influence security holders. In *SEC v. Madison Square Garden Corp.*,[122] the Commission alleged that a press release by a prospective tender offeror reaffirming its previously revealed plans to acquire a target corporation, constituted a solicitation and recommendation to the target's security holders to reject a competing tender offer which had been announced the previous day. An injunction by consent

[120] 17 C.F.R. § 240.14d–2(f), eff. July 30, 1968.

[121] While the obvious thrust of Rule 14d–2(f) is directed toward statements made by a target company, the wording of the Rule could conceivably be interpreted to apply to prospective competing exchange offerors commenting on an existing offer.

[122] No. 69 Civ. 4364 (S.D.N.Y. 1970), CCH Fed. Sec. L. Rep. ¶ 92,649. For a summary of the complaint, see 19 BNA Sec. Reg. & L. Rep., A–2, A–3 (Oct. 8, 1969).

was entered against the prospective offeror and persons acting in concert with the offeror for failure to file a Schedule 14D statement.

E. Disclosure in Connection with Arrangements for Election of Directors Without a Meeting (Section 14(f) and Rule 14f–1 Thereunder)

Section 14(f) and Rule 14f-1 [123] represent an attempt by Congress and the Commission to eliminate the disclosure vacuum which existed in connection with voluntary transfers of corporate control which were effected without shareholder knowledge.[124] In the tender offer context, these provisions will have particular importance where management of the target approves of a takeover attempt and agrees to facilitate the transfer of control.

In the typical situation arising out of such transfers, one or more holders of a controlling block of stock privately sell their shares at a premium over the current market price and arrange for the nominees of the purchaser to immediately replace at least a majority of the board of directors.[125] By compelling disclosure

[123] 17 C.F.R. § 240.14f–1, eff. July 30, 1968.

[124] For a succinct and thorough analysis of Section 14(f), see Ratner, *Section 14(f): A New Approach to Transfers of Corporate Control,* 54 Cornell L. Rev. 65 (1968).

[125] The fundamental issues involving the sale of a controlling block of stock at a premium and the replacement of a board of directors without a shareholders' vote are well defined. The answers, however, are not, and have perplexed the courts and commentators for many years. The leading cases are Essex Universal Corp. v. Yates, 305 F.2d 572 (2d Cir. 1962); Perlman v. Feldmann, 219 F.2d 173 (2d Cir. 1955), *cert. denied,* 349 U.S. 952 (1955). *See also* McClure v. Law, 161 N.Y. 78, 55 N.E. 388 (1899); Gerdes v. Reynolds, 28 N.Y.S.2d 622 (N.Y. Co. Sup. Ct. 1941); Manacher v. Reynolds, 39 Del. Ch. 401, 165 A.2d 741 (1960); Tyron v. Smith, 191 Or. 172, 229 P.2d 251 (1951); Goode v. Powers, 97 Ariz. 75, 397 P.2d 56 (1964); McCord v. Martin, 47 Cal. App. 717, 191 P. 89 (1920); Porter v. Healy, 244 Pa. 427, 91A. 428 (1914); Christophides v. Porco, 289 F. Supp. 403 (S.D.N.Y. 1968).

For a landmark case involving the sale of control of a mutual fund management company, *see* Rosenfeld v. Black, 445 F.2d 1337 (2d Cir. 1971), *rev'g* 319 F. Supp. 891 (S.D.N.Y. 1970). For an analysis of this case, *see* 18 Rev. of Sec. Reg. 853 (Oct. 21, 1971); 108 BNA Sec. Reg. & L. Rep. A–1 (June 30, 1971). *See also* Sec. Reg. and Transfer Rep. (Oct. 4, 1971) at 3. *Cf.* SEC v. Insurance Securities, Inc., 254 F.2d 642 (9th Cir. 1958) *cert. denied,* 358 U.S. 823 (1958); Krieger v. Anderson, 173 A.2d 626 (Del. Ch. 1961).

Frequently cited articles on the sale of corporate control include Jennings, *Trading in Corporate Control* 44 Calif. L. Rev. 1 (1956); Leech, *Transactions in Corporate Control,* 104 U. Pa. L. Rev. 725 (1956); Hill, *The Sale of Controlling*

of information on the transactions effecting the transfer of control and on the new directors, in advance of their taking office, Section 14(f) and Rule 14f-1 afford shareholders a greater opportunity to block transactions which may have an adverse impact on the corporation and its security holders. In large measure, such leverage derives from the fact that the courts can be expected to be more receptive to a motion seeking to enjoin a proposed transfer of control than one seeking to set aside a consummated transfer.[126] Prior to the passage of the Williams Act, such information normally was not given to shareholders until there was a subsequent proxy solicitation following installation of the new directors.[127]

Section 14(f) provides as follows:

> If, pursuant to any arrangement or understanding with the person or persons acquiring securities in a transaction subject to subsection (d) of this section or subsection (d) of section 13 of this title, any persons are to be elected or designated as directors of the issuer, otherwise than at a meeting of security holders, and the persons so elected or designated will constitute a majority of the directors of the issuer, then, prior to the time any such person takes office as a director, and in accordance with rules and regulations prescribed by the Commission, the issuer shall file with the Commission, and transmit to all holders of record of securities of the issuer who would be entitled to vote at a meeting for election of directors, information substantially equivalent to the information which would be required by subsection (a) or (c) of this section to be transmitted if such person or persons were nominees for election as directors at a meeting of such security holders.

Rule 14f–1 requires the issuer to file with the Commission and transmit to all holders of record of securities of the issuer who would be entitled to vote at a meeting for election of directors, information substantially equivalent to that which would be required to be transmitted by Items 5(a), (d), (e) and (f), 6 and 7 of

---

Shares, 70 HARV. L. REV. 986 (1957); Berle, *The Price of Power: Sale of Corporate Control*, 50 CORNELL L. Q. 628 (1965). *See also* FLETCHER, CYC. OF CORPS. § 5805 (rev. vol. 1970); Bromberg, Sales of Control, *Bootstrapping*, 5 REV. OF SEC. REG. 879 (July 17, 1972); Bromberg, *Bootstrapping*, 5 REV. OF SEC. REG. 885 (Aug. 16, 1972); Bromberg, *Integration*, 5 REV. OF SEC. REG. 877 (Sept. 6, 1972).

[126] *See* Ratner, *supra* note 124, at 70.

[127] *See* Item 5(e), Schedule 14A, 17 C.F.R. § 240.14a–101.

Schedule 14A [128] of Regulation 14A [129] if such persons were nominees for election as directors at a meeting of such security holders. Pursuant to Section 14(f) the information must be filed with the Commission and transmitted to security holders not less than ten days prior to the date any such person takes office as a director or such shorter period prior to that date as the Commission may authorize upon a showing of good cause.

SECTION 4. *FRAUD AND MISREPRESENTATION IN CONNECTION WITH TENDER OFFERS [SECTION 14(e)]*

Section 14(e) is the basic statutory fraud provision prohibiting material misstatements and fraudulent, deceptive, and manipulative acts and practices "in connection with any tender offer or request or invitation for tenders, or any solicitation of security holders in opposition to or in favor of any such offer, request or invitation." Although Section 14(e) is patterned after Section 10(b) and Rule 10b-5 thereunder as well as Rule 14a-9 under the proxy rules, it differs from these provisions in two noteworthy respects: first, Section 14(e) is self-operative while Section 10(b) did not become effective until the SEC promulgated rules thereunder; and second, Section 14(e) applies to fraudulent conduct in connection with any tender offer while Rule 14a–9 is more limited in scope and relates only to proxy solicitations which contain materially misleading representation.[130] Moreover,

[128] 17 C.F.R. § 240.14a–101, eff., as amended Feb. 15, 1968. For an analysis of the information required by Schedule 14A, *see* ARANOW AND EINHORN, PROXY CONTESTS FOR CORPORATE CONTROL, 182–227 (2d ed. 1968).

[129] 17 C.F.R. § 240.14a–1 et seq., eff., as amended Feb. 15, 1968.

Regulation 14A requires that every person solicited for a proxy be furnished with a written proxy statement containing the information specified in Schedule 14A, provided such solicitation is subject to the proxy rules.

[130] Although Section 14(e) is self-operative, the 1970 Williams Act amendments granted the SEC rule-making authority to "define, and prescribe means reasonably designed to prevent, such acts and practices as are fraudulent, deceptive or manipulative."

For examples of some of the problem areas which the Commission may deal with pursuant to its rule-making authority under Section 14(e), *see Hearings on S. 336 and S. 3431 Before the Subcomm. on Securities of the Senate Comm. on Banking and Currency*, 91st Cong., 2d Sess. at 12 (1970). *See* also Brown, *The*

Section 10(b) and Rule 10b–5 thereunder prohibit fraudulent conduct "in connection with the purchase or sale of any security." As more fully discussed below, the deletion in Section 14(e) of the purchaser-seller limitation in Section 10(b) has enabled persons who might be denied standing to sue under Section 10(b) (e.g., offerors, target companies, and nontendering shareholders) to challenge fraudulent conduct in connection with tender offers.

Section 14(e) provides in full text as follows:

It shall be unlawful for any person to make any untrue statement of a material fact or omit to state any material fact necessary in order to make the statements made, in the light of the circumstances under which they are made, not misleading, or to engage in any fraudulent, deceptive, or manipulative acts or practices, in connection with any tender offer or request or invitation for tenders, or any solicitation of security holders in opposition to or in favor of any such offer, request, or invitation. The Commission shall, for the purposes of this subsection, by rules and regulations define, and prescribe means reasonably designed to prevent, such acts and practices as are fraudulent, deceptive, or manipulative.[131]

(1) Standing to Sue under Section 14(e)

(a) Background and Development of Section 14(e)

The purpose of Section 14(e) was expressed as follows in the Senate and House Committee Reports accompanying S. 510:

This provision would affirm the fact that persons engaged in making or opposing tender offers or otherwise seeking to influence the deci-

---

Scope of the Williams Act and Its 1970 Amendments, 26 Bus. Law 1637, 1647 (July 1971).

Section 14(e) applies to all tender offers, without regard to the class or kind of security involved or to whether the tender offer is subject to Section 14(d)(1) and Rule 14d–1 thereunder. *See, e.g.*, Dyer v. Eastern Trust and Banking Co., 336 F. Supp. 890 (D. Me. 1971); response of SEC Div. of Corp. Finance, May 1, 1972, to request for no-action letter re: Henry Heide, Inc., CCH Fed. Sec. L. Rep. ¶ 78, 838.

[131] The absence in Section 14(e) of any reference to the facilities of interstate commerce has prompted one distinguished commentator to question the constitutionality of this provision. *See* 6 Loss 3661 (Supp. 1969). *Cf.* Section 17(a) of the Securities Act of 1933, 15 U.S.C. § 77q(a) and Section 10 of the Securities Exchange Act of 1934, 15 U.S.C. § 78j. As a practical matter, litigants should allege and be prepared to prove the use of interstate facilities. 6 Loss 3661 (Supp. 1969).

sion of investors or the outcome of the tender offer are under an obligation to make full disclosure of material information to those with whom they deal.[132]

Based on this expression of the legislative intent coupled with a broad reading of the phrase "in connection with the purchase or sale of any security" in Section 10(b), one might expect that the passage of Section 14(e) would be duplicative of Section 10(b) and provide little, if anything, in the way of additional investor protection.[133] This might well be so were it not for the fact that a number of courts have taken narrower views of Section 10(b) and have required that the plaintiff be a defrauded purchaser or seller in order to have standing to challenge fraudulent conduct under Section 10(b).[134]

Thus, in some jurisdictions a target company might not have standing under Section 10(b) to maintain an action for either damages or an injunction based upon alleged fraudulent conduct by the offeror.[135] In other jurisdictions where the courts have taken a somewhat broader view of Section 10(b), an issuer would apparently be able to enjoin the offeror from manipulating its

[132] S. Rep. No. 550, 90th Cong., 1st Sess. 10–11 (1967); H.R. Rep. No. 1711, 90th Cong., 2d Sess. 11 (1968).

[133] Section 14(e) "[i]n effect—applies Rule 10b–5 both to the offeror and to the opposition—very likely, except perhaps for any bearing it may have on the issue of standing, only a codification of existing case law." Electronic Specialty Co. v. International Controls Corp, 409 F.2d 937, 940–41 (2d Cir. 1969).

[134] *See* Birnbaum v. Newport Steel Corp., 193 F.2d 461 (2d Cir. 1952), *cert. denied,* 343 U.S. 956 (1952); Iroquois Industries, Inc. v. Syracuse China Corp., 417 F.2d 963 (2d Cir. 1969), *cert. denied,* 399 U.S. 909 (1970), *aff'g* Civ. No. 67–310 (W.D.N.Y. 1968), CCH Fed. Sec. L. Rep. ¶ 92,301; Greater Iowa Corp. v. McLendon, 378 F.2d 783 (8th Cir. 1967); Herpich v. Wallace, 430 F.2d 792 (5th Cir. 1970); Coffee v. Permian Corp., 306 F. Supp. 1371 (N.D. Tex. 1969); Jachimiec v. Schenley Industries Inc., No. 15024 (7th Cir. 1965), *cert. denied,* 382 U.S. 841 (1965). *Cf.* Crane Co. v. Westinghouse Air Brake Co., 419 F.2d 787 (2d Cir. 1969), *cert. denied,* 400 U.S. 822 (1970); Mutual Shares Corp. v. Genesco, Inc., 384 F.2d 540 (2d Cir. 1967); Britt v. Cyril Bath Co., 417 F.2d 433 (6th Cir. 1969); Kahan v. Rosenstiel, 424 F.2d 161 (3d Cir. 1970); Vine v. Beneficial Finance Co., 374 F.2d 627 (2d Cir. 1967), *cert. denied,* 389 U.S. 970 (1967); Entel v. Allen, 270 F. Supp. 60 (S.D.N.Y. 1967); Butler Aviation International, Inc. v. Comprehensive Designers, Inc., 307 F. Supp. 910 (S.D.N.Y. 1969), *aff'd,* 425 F.2d 842 (2d Cir. 1970); Superintendent of Insurance of New York v. Bankers Life & Casualty Co., 404 U.S. 6 (1971).

[135] *See* Greater Iowa Corp. v. McLendon, *id.;* Herpich v. Wallace, *id.;* Jachimiec v. Schenley Industries, Inc., *id.;* GAF Corp. v. Milstein 453 F.2d 709, 721–22 (2d Cir. 1971), *cert. denied,* 406 U.S. 910 (1972); Nicholson File Co. v. H.K. Porter Co., Inc., Civ. No. 4876 (D. R.I. 1972), CCH Fed. Sec. L. Rep. ¶ 93,452. *See also* CCH Fed. Sec. L. Rep. ¶ 93,713.

stock or engaging in other fraudulent conduct in connection with the offer [136] but would be denied standing in an action for damages.[137] Similarly, nontendering shareholders who were fraudulently dissuaded from selling their shares would be denied standing under Section 10(b) in an action for damages [138] although nontendering shareholders could maintain an action for an injunction.[139] Likewise, in an action for damages, a tender offeror, although a purchaser, was denied standing under Section 10(b) since it could not claim to be a defrauded purchaser or a purchaser who relied upon alleged fraudulent conduct by the management of the target company.[140]

As a result of the patchwork application of Section 10(b) by the courts, the Commission apparently pressed for the passage of Section 14(e), not to "affirm" the principles of full disclosure, but rather to assure that all forms of fraudulent conduct in connection with tender offers could be challenged by private litigants.

(b) Case Law Developments

In *Neuman v. Electronic Specialty Co.*, [141] the plaintiffs, who were nontendering shareholders of the target company, instituted an action for damages against the target based upon allegations that the target fraudulently discouraged them from tendering their shares pursuant to a tender offer made by International Controls Corp. Plaintiffs claimed that such conduct constituted violations of Section 10(b) and Section 14(e) and Rule 10b–5. The defendant moved to dismiss the complaint on the ground that a

[136] *See* Crane Co. v. Westinghouse Air Brake Co., *supra* note 134; General Time Corp. v. Talley Industries, Inc., 403 F.2d 159, (2d Cir. 1968), *cert. denied*, 393 U.S. 1026 (1969); Britt v. Cyril Bath Co., *supra* note 134; Mutual Shares Corp. v. Genesco Inc., *supra* note 134.

[137] *Cf.* Iroquois Industries, Inc. v. Syracuse China Corp., *supra* note 134; Birnbaum v. Newport Steel Corp., *supra* note 134.

[138] *See* Birnbaum v. Newport Steel Corp. *supra* note 134; Stull v. Greene, Civ. No. 69-440 (S.D.N.Y. 1970) CCH Fed. Sec. L. Rep. ¶ 92,657.

Query, whether there is any meaningful rationale for denying standing to nontendering shareholders who were fraudulently dissuaded from selling their shares while granting standing to shareholders who were fraudulently enticed into selling? Such a result appears to represent the ultimate perversion of Section 10(b).

[139] *Cf.* Mutual Shares Corp. v. Genesco, Inc., *supra* note 134; Moore v. Great American Corp., 274 F. Supp. 490 (N.D. Ohio 1967).

[140] *See* Iroquois Industries, Inc. v. Syracuse China Corp., *supra* note 134.

[141] No. 68C 1817 (N.D. Ill. E.D. 1969), CCH Fed. Sec. L. Rep. ¶ 92,591.

plaintiff must actually purchase or sell the subject securities in order to maintain a private action under Rule 10b–5 or Section 14(e).

In holding that the plaintiffs had standing under both Rule 10b–5 and Section 14(e), the court noted that although it viewed the coverage of Rule 10b–5 to be as broad as that of Section 14(e), standing under 14(e) existed even if Rule 10b–5 required the plaintiff to be a purchaser or seller:

> Moreover, it may be noted that, if the difference in the language of 10b–5 and 14e is relied upon to insist that 10b–5 may be invoked only by a plaintiff who consummates an actual purchase or sale while 14e relates specially to tender offers and protecting stockholders apart from any purchase and sale, then though the instant 10b–5 claim would have to be dismissed, the claim under 14e would nevertheless stand.[142]

The Eastern and Southern Districts of New York, which have generally required a plaintiff to be a purchaser or seller to maintain standing under Rule 10b–5, have granted standing under Section 14(e) where the plaintiff is neither a purchaser nor a seller of securities.[143] Thus a nontendering shareholder has been found to have standing to maintain a derivative action on behalf of the target corporation for damages against a tender offeror [144] and a target company has been held to have standing to enjoin alleged fraudulent conduct by a tender offeror.[145] The dicta in other opinions likewise suggest that tender offerors, nontender-

142 *Id.*, at p. 98,705. *Cf.* GAF Corp. v. Milstein, *supra* note 135; Nicholson File Co. v. H.K. Porter Co., Inc., *supra* note 135; Iroquois Industries, Inc., v. Syracuse China Corp., *supra* note 134.

143 The converse is perhaps more significant, i.e., no case has been found where a court denied standing under Section 14(e) because the plaintiff was neither a defrauded purchaser nor a seller.

144 Fabrikant v. Jacobellis, No. 69–C–880 (E.D.N.Y. 1970), CCH FED. SEC. L. REP. ¶ 92,686.

145 Butler Aviation International, Inc. v. Comprehensive Designers, Inc., 307 F. Supp. 910 (S.D.N.Y. 1969), *aff'd*, 425 F.2d 842 (2d Cir. 1970). The district court in the *Butler* case found that plaintiffs had standing to sue under Rule 10b–5 as well as Section 14(3). The Court of Appeals found, however, that in view of the fact that standing existed under Section 14(e) it would not pass on the standing question under Rule 10b–5.

ing shareholders, and target companies have standing to enjoin fraudulent conduct under Section 14(e).[146]

In considering the implications of the standing issue in an action for damages under Section 14(e), it must also be emphasized that standing, alone, will have little practical significance unless the plaintiff can prove a causal connection between its loss and the alleged wrong as well as actual damages. Thus, for example, a nontendering shareholder will be required to prove that reliance on an alleged misrepresentation was the actual cause of his refusal to tender and that he suffered calculable damages.[147] Sustaining the burden of proof of actual damages may be particularly difficult for a target company even where it can prove that the offeror's misrepresentations enabled it to obtain control of the target. In a situation of this type, however, the target company can be expected to seek appropriate equitable relief to prevent the transfer of control.

(2) The Scope of the Phrase "in Connection with Any Tender Offer"

As noted earlier in this chapter, Section 14(e) applies to fraudulent conduct "in connection with any tender offer or request or invitation for tenders, or any solicitation of security holders in opposition or in favor to any such offer, request or invitation."

One of the more difficult questions of statutory construction still to be resolved under the Williams Act involves the applicability of Section 14(e) to fraudulent conduct that takes place prior to the actual commencement of any tender offer. More specifically, the issue is one of whether fraudulent conduct that takes place in connection with a *proposed* tender offer which is

[146] *See* Electronic Specialty Co. v. International Controls Corp., 409 F.2d 937 (2d Cir. 1969) recognizing standing to sue by nontendering shareholders and target companies, and by implication, tender offerors, under Sections 14(d) and (e); Crane Co. v. Westinghouse Air Brake Co., 419 F.2d 787 (2d Cir. 1969), *cert. denied*, 400 U.S. 822 (1970); MGM v. Transamerica Corp., 303 F. Supp. 1354 (S.D.N.Y. 1969).

[147] See Neuman v. Electronic Specialty Co., *supra* note 141. For a discussion of the existence of private rights of action, standing to sue and establishing a cause of action under the Williams Act amendments to the 1934 Act, see text accompanying notes 32–76, Chapter 10.

never "actually made" can be considered to be "in connection with any tender offer" as that phrase is used in Section 14(e). This specific issue must be distinguished from the question of whether fraudulent conduct that takes place prior to commencement of a tender offer which, in fact, is actually made, falls within the scope of Section 14(e). While no court has as yet had occasion to consider this latter question, there can be little doubt that fraudulent conduct that takes place prior to commencement of a tender offer which is actually made will violate Section 14(e) provided the fraud relates in some way to the offer itself. Any other interpretation would completely thwart the purpose of the statute because market manipulations and other fraudulent conduct in connection with tender offers would often be most effective prior to the actual commencement of the offer.[148]

The issue regarding the applicability of Section 14(e) to proposed tender offers that are never made will normally have limited significance in the contested tender offer context since most offerors attempt to take the opposition by surprise and do not make announcements of their intentions prior to making the offer itself. This issue, however, will assume importance in the following types of situations:

(a) A potential target company announces a proposed tender offer for its own shares that it never intends to make in an effort to discourage a potential offeror;

(b) A person announces a proposed tender offer that he never intends to make in an effort to persuade the management of the target company to consider a merger proposal or take some other action in connection with the target's affairs;

(c) A person announces a proposed tender offer that he never intends to make in order to dispose of securities of the issuer at artificially inflated prices; and

(d) A prospective offeror makes misleading statements in connection with a proposed offer that it intends to make

[148] *Cf.* SEC v. Okin, 132 F.2d 784 (2d Cir. 1943) involving the applicability of the proxy rules to communications preliminary to the actual solicitation of proxies, discussed in ARANOW AND EINHORN, PROXY CONTESTS FOR CORPORATE CONTROL at 102–3 (2d ed. 1968). *See also* Note, *Cash Tender Offers*, 83 HARV. L. REV. 377, 397 (1969).

but because of other legitimate considerations decides not to proceed.

The only case which considered the applicability of Section 14(e) to a proposed tender offer which was never actually made has left the issue in doubt. In *Levine v. Seilon Inc.*,[149] a former preferred shareholder of the defendant corporation brought an action for damages under Sections 14(e) and 10(b), alleging, *inter alia,* that the corporation never intended to effect a previously announced invitation to preferred shareholders to exchange their shares for common stock of the corporation and that such action had the effect of:

(1) artificially inflating the market price of the preferred shares; (2) misleading the preferred shareholders into retaining their holdings when they could have sold them on the market at a higher price, (3) misleading the public into buying preferred shares and inducing the preferred shareholders to consent to new credit arrangements which they had previously refused to approve.

In dismissing the complaint, the district court held that: Section 14(e) of the Act did not apply because "no tender offer was made in this case" and Section 14(e) "appear[s] to have been intended to prevent misrepresentations with respect to tender offers or invitations for tenders that are actually made." [150]

On appeal, the SEC (as amicus) contended that Section 14(e) "does not require that the fraud be in connection with tender offers, requests or invitations for tenders that are 'actually made' as distinguished from those which have not as yet commenced." [151] The court of appeals affirmed dismissal of the complaint on other grounds without reaching the Section 14(e) issue but noted that "we are not sure we would agree with the district court's rather restrictive reading of this provision. . . ." [152]

[149] 439 F.2d 328 (2d Cir. 1971).

[150] *See* SEC amicus brief in Levine v. Seilon, Inc., reproduced in 85 BNA Sec. Reg. & L. Rep. E–1, E–2 (Jan. 20, 1971).

The district court dismissed the Section 10(b) claim on the ground that the alleged fraud was not in connection with the purchase or sale of any security.

[151] *See* SEC amicus brief in Levine v. Seilon, Inc., *id.*

[152] Levine v. Seilon, Inc., *supra* note 150, at 335.

The *Seilon* case involves a tender offer by an issuer for its own securities. While such offers, as well as other types of offers enumerated in the Williams Act and the rules thereunder, are exempt from the disclosure provisions of Section

While the ultimate resolution of this issue must await further judicial consideration and analysis, there is some basis for suggesting that the district court's interpretation of Section 14(e) was correct despite the fact that the result in *Seilon* seems quite harsh. As noted previously, the legislative history indicates that the purpose of Section 14(e) was to "affirm the fact that persons engaged in making or opposing tenders or otherwise seeking to influence the decision of investors or the outcome of the tender offer are under an obligation to make full disclosure of material information to those with whom they deal." [153]

The obvious thrust of this expression of the legislative intent coupled with the statutory language itself appears to indicate that the statute was directed to tender offers which are actually made as distinguished from plans or proposals to make tender offers which are never carried out.[154] In this regard it is important to note that the courts may justifiably read statutory provisions in the light of what Congress actually did rather than what was best for Congress to do or what the SEC might have intended.[155]

On the other hand, it may be argued that a narrow reading of Section 14(e) will permit a person fraudulently to represent that he intends to make a tender offer where such mispresentation enables the person to accomplish his ultimate objective without ever having to make the offer. Given the fact that Section 14(e) clearly falls within the category of remedial legislation and that such legislation should be broadly construed to effectuate its purposes,[156] it would not be inappropriate to read the phrase "in connection with any tender offer" to include proposed tender offers (whether or not they are subsequently effected) as well as

14(d), they are nevertheless subject to Section 14(e) which prohibits, without exception, fraudulent conduct in connection with any tender offer.

[153] See text accompanying note 132, *supra*.

[154] Pursuant to this interpretation, fraudulent conduct prior to commencement of a tender offer would still be proscribed by Section 14(e), provided the offer was actually made and the fraud related to the offer.

[155] For two examples of the strict construction approach to the tender rules, *see* GAF Corp. v. Milstein, 324 F. Supp. 1062 (S.D.N.Y. 1971); Ozark Air Lines Inc. v. Cox, 326 F. Supp. 1113 (E.D. Mo. 1971).

[156] For the more liberal approach to statutory construction of the federal securities laws, *see* Tcherepnin v. Knight, 389 U.S. 332, 336 (1967); J. I. Case Co. v. Borak, 377 U.S. 426 (1964); Superintendent of Insurance of New York v. Bankers Life & Casualty Co., 404 U.S. 6 (1971).

tender offers which are "actually made." Absent a Congressional amendment, however, the ultimate determination regarding the scope of Section 14(e) must await further judicial development.[157]

SECTION 5. *SHORT-TENDERS* [*RULE 10b–4*]

Where the terms of a tender offer provide that the offeror may purchase less than all shares tendered, the shareholder has no assurance that the shares which he tenders will be accepted even if he tenders within hours of publication of the request or invitation for tenders. If the acceptance of shares is contingent upon the offeror receiving a specified minimum number of shares and the offeror does not receive such minimum, all shares tendered may of course be returned. Even where the minimum number of shares is tendered, the shareholder may still have only a portion of his shares accepted if the offeror either chooses to make purchases on a pro rata basis or is required to do so pursuant to Section 14(d)(6).

To evade the impact of pro rata purchases, the practice of short-tendering became popular. This practice, whereby brokers and others would tender a greater number of shares than they or their customers owned, resulted in a disproportionately large number of their securities being accepted in relation to the shares tendered by other persons.[158] Thus, if a broker estimated

[157] It has not been uncommon for federal agencies, including the SEC, to effectively expand the scope of a statutory provision by the promulgation of administrative rules and regulations. Generally speaking, such rules and regulations go unchallenged although substantial questions are often raised as to whether they were enacted pursuant to a valid exercise of administrative authority. While there has been no indication to date that the Commission proposes to adopt a rule under Section 14(e) which will directly or indirectly prohibit fraudulent conduct in connection with any proposed tender offer, it should be noted that such a rule will not obviate the need for an ultimate judicial determination of the scope of Section 14(e).

[158] One arbitrageur has concluded that Rule 10b–4 has worked to the detriment of the investing public by creating wider spreads between market and tender prices in prorated cash offers. Where a cash offer is prorated, the arbitrageur's ability to short-tender enables him to hedge against the risk of a market price decline once the offer expires. *See* Wyser-Pratte, "Risk Arbitrage," *The Bulletin*, NYU Graduate School of Bus. Admin., Nos. 74–75 (May 1971) at 57–61.

While the spreads between market and tender prices may in fact be wider,

that only one-half of all shares tendered would be accepted, he might tender twice as many shares as his tendering customers owned in an effort to insure that all the shares actually owned would be accepted.[159] The short-tender was made possible because many tender offers provided that the stock certificates did not have to be physically deposited at the time of tender if a bank or an exchange member guaranteed that if the shares were accepted delivery of the certificates would be made on demand or at a specified time. This procedure was originally introduced to encourage tenders on behalf of shareholders who were out of town or who were otherwise not in a position to deposit their certificates.[160]

The development of the short-tendering abuse from a practice which served a legitimate and lawful purpose resulted in the Commission adopting Rule 10b-4.[161] This Rule prohibits any person from either tendering shares which he does not own or guaranteeing the tender of shares where there is reason to believe that the shares tendered are not on hand and immediately available for delivery.[162] The Rule provides in full as follows:

(a) It shall constitute a "manipulative or deceptive device or contrivance" as used in Section 10(b) of the Act for any person, in response

---

Rule 10b–4 will nevertheless benefit the average investor by increasing the proportion of his shares which are accepted in prorated cash offers. For a more detailed discussion of the role of the arbitrageur in tender offers, see Chapter 6.

[159] If the estimate proved erroneous and the broker was obligated to deliver more shares than his tendering customers owned, he would be compelled to purchase additional shares to fulfill the contractual commitment. If the market price of the target's shares was equal to or even slightly higher than the tender price, the broker might still be able to profit on the transaction where the soliciting dealer's fee exceeded the added incremental cost of "covering" the short tender. On the other hand, if a more attractive competing offer was made subsequent to the tender, the tendering broker might be required to cover at substantially higher prices.

[160] *See* SEC Securities Exchange Act Release Nos. 8224 (Jan. 3, 1968) and 8321 (May 28, 1968), CCH FED. SEC. L. REP. ¶¶ 77,515 and 77,558; S. REP. No. 550, 90th Cong., 1st Sess. 5 (1967).

[161] 17 C.F.R. § 240.10b–4, eff. July 1, 1968. *See* SEC Securities Exchange Act Release No. 8321 (May 28, 1968), CCH FED. SEC. L. REP. ¶ 77,558.

[162] A broker's short-tender of 148 shares out of a tender of over 30,000 shares was found not to be a violation of Rule 10b–4 where the short tender was caused by an error in duplicate customer instructions and the broker, upon discovering its error, immediately purchased additional shares to cover the short. The court held that Rule 10b–4 is not properly applied to a situation where the error is of minor proportions and there is no specific intent to defraud. *See* Bache & Co., Inc. v. International Controls Corp., 324 F. Supp. 998 (S.D.N.Y. 1971).

to an offer for, or to a request or invitation for tenders of, any security,

(1) to tender any security for his own account unless (A) he owns the security or, (B) he owns a security convertible into or exchangeable for, or owns an option, warrant or right to purchase the tendered security, intends to acquire the tendered security, by conversion, exchange, or exercise of such option, warrant or right to the extent necessary to deliver the tendered security, and, upon the acceptance of his tender, he does convert, exchange, or exercise such option, warrant or right to the extent necessary to deliver the tendered security. *Provided, however,* that if he tenders a security on the basis of his ownership of an option to purchase such security, he shall have reason to believe that the maker or writer of the option has title to and possession of such security and will promptly deliver it upon exercise of the option; or,

(2) to tender or guarantee the tender of any security on behalf of another person, unless (A) such security is in the possession of the person making the tender or giving the guarantee, or (B) the person making the tender or giving the guarantee, upon information furnished by the person on whose behalf the tender or guarantee is made, has reason to believe that such person owns the security tendered and, as soon as possible, without undue inconvenience or expense, will deliver the security for the purpose of the tender to the person making the tender or giving the guarantee, or (C) the person on whose behalf the tender or guarantee is made owns a security convertible into, or exchangeable for, or owns an option, warrant or right to purchase the tendered security and the person making the tender has reason to believe that such other person intends to acquire the tendered security, by the conversion, exchange or exercise of such option, warrant or right to the extent necessary to deliver the tendered security. *Provided, however,* that if the tender or guarantee of the tender of a security is made on the basis of the ownership of an option to purchase such security, the person making the tender or guarantee shall have reason to believe that the maker or writer of the option has title to and possession of such security and will promptly deliver it upon exercise of the option.

(b) For the purposes of this section, a person shall be deemed to own a security if (1) he or his agent has title to it; or (2) he has purchased, or has entered into an unconditional contract, binding on both parties thereto, to purchase it but has not yet received it; or (3) he owns a security convertible into or exchangeable for it and has tendered such security for conversion or exchange; or (4) he has an option to purchase or acquire it and has exercised such option; or (5) he has rights or warrants to subscribe to it and has exercised such rights or warrants. *Provided, however,* that a person shall be deemed to own securities only to the extent that he has a net long position in such securities.

SECTION 6. *OUTSIDE PURCHASES BY A TENDER OFFEROR DURING THE OFFERING PERIOD [RULE 10b–13]*

Rule 10b–13 [163] prohibits a tender offeror, from the time the offer is publicly announced until the expiration of the offering period, from directly or indirectly purchasing equity securities of the same class which are the subject of the offer other than pursuant to the offer itself. Any arrangements or understandings made during the course of the offer to purchase the securities after termination of the offer are also prohibited. The rule applies to purchases of securities immediately convertible into securities of the same class sought under the offer but does not prohibit an offeror from converting securities owned at the time of the commencement of the offer.[164] Exemptions from Rule 10b–13 are permitted for certain stock option plans as well as for transactions which the Commission may exempt as not contemplated by the Rule.[165] The Rule in full text provides as follows:

[163] 17 C.F.R. § 240.10b–13, eff. Nov. 10, 1969.

[164] Although Rule 10b–13 applies to offers by an issuer for its own securities, the rule does not prohibit an exchange offeror from making outside purchases of a class of its own nonconvertible securities which are to be issued in exchange for its securities of another class. However, Rule 10b–6 may prohibit the offeror from making such purchases. See text accompanying notes 168–171 *infra*. *See also* SEC Securities Exchange Act Release No. 8712 (Oct. 8, 1969), CCH FED. SEC. L. REP. ¶ 77,745.

[165] Open-market purchases of securities during the course of a tender offer by arbitrageurs who subsequently tender such shares and receive soliciting dealer's fees for such tenders, are not subject to the prohibitions of Rule 10b–13 provided the payment of the soliciting dealer's fees is adequately disclosed. *See* SEC Securities Exchange Act Release No. 9395 (Nov. 24, 1971), CCH FED. SEC. L. REP. ¶ 78,417.

Prior to adoption of this interpretative release, the Division of Trading and Markets of the SEC viewed purchases of the target's securities during the course of a tender offer by persons who received soliciting dealer's fees for tendering such securities, as purchases indirectly made or arranged for by the person making the tender offer. Such purchases were deemed to violate Rule 10b–13 and the soliciting dealer making such purchases was considered to be an aider and abettor. The staff's position applied to purchases made at prices in excess of the tender price as well as to purchases made below the tender price. Purchases and subsequent tenders made in anticipation of receiving the soliciting dealer's fee, but prior to the actual signing of the soliciting dealer's agreement were also viewed by the

(a) No person who makes a cash tender offer or exchange offer for any equity security shall, directly or indirectly, purchase, or make any arrangement to purchase, any such security (or any other security which is immediately convertible into or exchangeable for such security), otherwise than pursuant to such tender offer or exchange offer, from the time such tender offer or exchange offer is publicly announced or otherwise made known by such person to holders of the security to be acquired until the expiration of the period, including any extensions thereof, during which securities tendered pursuant to such tender offer or exchange offer may by the terms of such offer be accepted or rejected; *provided, however,* that if such person is the owner of another security which is immediately convertible into or exchangeable for the security which is the subject of the offer, his subsequent exercise of his right of conversion or exchange with respect to such other security shall not be prohibited by this rule.

(b) The term "exchange offer" as used in this rule shall include a tender offer for, or request or invitation for tenders of, any security in exchange for any consideration other than for all cash.

(c) The provisions of this rule shall not apply to a purchase of a security of the same class as that which is the subject of a cash tender offer or exchange offer (or of any other security which is immediately convertible into or exchangeable for such security) if such purchase is made by the issuer, by participating employees of the issuer or the employees of its subsidiaries, or by the trustee or other persons acquiring such security for the account of such employees, pursuant to (1) a stock option plan involving only "qualified stock options," or qualifying as an "employee stock purchase plan" as those terms are defined in Sections 422 and 423 of the Internal Revenue Code of 1954, as amended, or "restricted stock options" as defined in Section 424(b)

---

staff as violative of Rule 10b–13. *See* response of the Division of Trading and Markets, SEC, to request for interpretative opinion, MSL industries, Inc., CCH FED. SEC. L. REP. ¶ 78,320 (correspondence in full text) and discussed in 120 BNA SEC. REG. & L. REP. C–1 (Sept. 29, 1971).

Release No. 9395 represents a clear recognition by the Commission of the public interest value of arbitrage activities in tender offers. Such activities help to produce narrower spreads between market and tender prices, thereby enabling shareholders to make advantageous open-market sales. Shareholders are thus presented with an attractive alternative to the possible risks and uncertainties that tendered shares will not be accepted or will be prorated. While the rationale underlying Release No. 9395 is fundamentally sound, it must be noted that it conflicts with one of the ostensible purposes of Rule 10b–13. The Commission's release announcing adoption of Rule 10b–13 advised that the rule would eliminate outside purchases which could aid the offeror by driving the market price to a level where public investors are enticed into selling their shares in the open market to arbitrageurs, who in turn would tender the shares. *See* SEC Securities Exchange Act Release No. 8712 (Oct. 8, 1969), CCH FED. SEC. L. REP. ¶ 77,745, discussed in note 167, *infra*.

of the Internal Revenue Code of 1954, as amended; *provided, however*, that for the purposes of this paragraph an option which meets all of the conditions of that section other than the date of issuance shall be deemed to be "restricted stock options"; or (2) a savings, investment, pension or other stock purchase plan providing for both (A) periodic payments (or payroll deductions) for acquisition of securities by or on behalf of participating employees and (B) periodic purchases of the securities by participating employees, or the person acquiring them for the account of such employees.

(d) This rule shall not prohibit any transaction or transactions if the Commission, upon written request or upon its own motion, exempts such transaction or transactions, either unconditionally or on specified terms or conditions, as not constituting a manipulative or deceptive device or contrivance or a fraudulent, or deceptive or manipulative act or practice comprehended within the purpose of this rule.

The Commission's primary objective in adopting this rule was to insure that tendering shareholders received the highest price paid by the offeror for the subject securities as well as to protect tendering shareholders from the possible adverse impact of outside purchases which were effected below the tender price.[166] Where the offeror made outside purchases above the tender

[166] As originally proposed, the rule would have required the offeror to purchase all shares *tendered* at the highest price paid during the offering period or the tender price, whichever was higher. The rule was revised as a result of comments submitted to the Commission which pointed out that: (a) a single outside purchase would obligate the offeror to purchase all the tendered shares, notwithstanding the fact that such purchases might exceed the number of shares requested as well as the offeror's ability to pay for such shares; and (b) a purchase by a third person who might be deemed a member of a "group" within the meaning of Section 14(d)(3) might compel the offeror to purchase all shares tendered even when the offeror, in good faith, did not consider that it had control over or any interest in the purchased securities. Several comment letters, including one from a co-author of this treatise, criticized the original proposal as providing for an unnecessary "over-kill." *See* SEC Securities Exchange Act Release No. 8595 (May 5, 1969), CCH FED. SEC. L. REP. ¶ 77,706; SEC Securities Exchange Act Release No. 8391 (Aug. 30, 1968), CCH FED. SEC. L. REP. ¶ 77,593.

The release announcing adoption of Rule 10b–13 (SEC Securities Exchange Act Release No. 8595) stated that the Rule was adopted "pursuant to the provisions of the Securities Exchange Act of 1934, and particularly Sections 10(b), 13(e), 14(e) and 23(a) thereof, . . ." Query whether the adoption of Rule 10b–13 pursuant to Section 14(e) represents an indirect attempt by the Commission to avoid the *Birnbaum* doctrine in connection with cases alleging violations of this rule? If so, why didn't this rule become Rule 14e–1 rather than Rule 10b–13? For a discussion of the issue of standing to sue under Section 14(e), see text accompanying notes 132–147, *supra*.

price, the tendering shareholders might be unable to withdraw their shares to take advantage of higher market prices. Thus, if the offeror was willing to pay more than the tender price, the Commission felt that tendering shareholders should also be given the opportunity to sell at higher prices. On the other hand, outside purchases effected below the market price might result in the rejection of some and perhaps all shares tendered if the offeror obtained a sufficient number of shares at lower prices. It should be added, however, that while the rule eliminates any opportunity the offeror may have to purchase securities at more favorable prices, it also serves to protect the offeror by preventing large stockholders from lawfully extracting a greater consideration for their shares than that granted to public investors pursuant to the terms of the offer.[167]

The adoption of Rule 10b–13 has also eliminated some of the controversy resulting from existing interpretations of Rule 10b–6 [168] which, *inter alia,* prohibits a person making a distribution from bidding for or purchasing the security which is the subject of the distribution or any right to acquire that security.[169] The apparent purpose of Rule 10b–6 was to prohibit a person engaged in a distribution from inflating the market value of the security to be distributed since such activity would have the effect of facilitating the distribution of the securities at artificially high prices.[170] In an exchange offer context, the offeror's purchase of

[167] The Commission's release announcing adoption of Rule 10b–13 stated that outside purchases by the offeror during the course of the offering were often fraudulent or manipulative in nature and served to deceive investors "as to the true state of affairs." As support for its position, the release advised that outside purchases could defeat the offer by driving the market price above the tender price or by otherwise reducing the number of tendered shares below the number of shares the offeror seeks to obtain. Alternatively, it was noted that outside purchases could aid the offeror by driving the market price to a level where public investors are enticed into selling their shares in the open market to arbitrageurs, who in turn tender the shares. *See* SEC Securities Exchange Act Release No. 8712 (Oct. 8, 1969), CCH FED. SEC. L. REP. ¶ 77,745.

[168] 17 C.F.R. § 240.10b–6, eff. Nov. 20, 1964. But see also text accompanying notes 28–31, Chapter 10.

[169] The Commission has described the application of Rule 10b–13 to exchange offers as "essentially a codification of existing interpretations under Rule 10b–6." *See* SEC Securities Exchange Act Release No. 8712 (Oct. 8, 1969). But see text accompanying notes 28–31, Chapter 10.

[70] *See* SEC v. Scott Taylor & Co., 183 F. Supp. 904 (S.D.N.Y. 1959); SEC v. Electronics Security Corp., 217 F. Supp. 831 (D. Minn. 1963); *In the Matter of*

its own securities during the course of a distribution of the very same securities could have the effect of reducing the number of shares which it would be required to issue pursuant to the offer.[171]

The Commission, however, has viewed Rule 10b–6 more broadly and has taken the position that the securities to be acquired by an offeror in an exchange offer (i.e., the target's securities) are, in substance, rights to acquire the securities being distributed.[172] Under this interpretation, Rule 10b–6 would prohibit (absent an exemption [173]) outside purchases of the target's securities despite the fact that such purchases might increase rather than decrease the market price of such securities thereby making the offeror's exchange package less attractive.[174] This paradoxical result has been approved by the Second Court of Appeals but has led other courts and commentators to question whether such purchases of a target's securities involve the type of manipulation which Rule 10b–6 was designed to prevent and has accordingly cast doubt on the soundness of the Commission's position. The adoption of Rule 10b–13, prohibiting outside purchases of the target's securities by the offeror during the course of the offer, has for the most part rendered resolution of this issue academic.[175]

Bruns, Nordeman & Co., 40 S.E.C. 652 (1961); R. A. Holman & Co. v. SEC, 366 F.2d 446 (2d Cir. 1966), amended on other grounds, 377 F.2d 665 (2d Cir. 1967), *cert. denied,* 389 U.S. 991 (1967).

[171] *See* SEC v. Georgia-Pacific Corp., 66 Civ. No. 1215 (S.D.N.Y. 1966), CCH FED. SEC. L. REP. ¶ 91,692. For excerpts of complaint, *see* CCH FED. SEC. L. REP. ¶ 91,680. *See also* Prospectus, Genesco, Inc., May 10, 1966, reprinted in relevant part in CCH FED. SEC. L. REP. ¶ 77,354.

Where the value of the securities to be distributed is "pegged" for purposes of the exchange offer, purchases by the offeror would not have such a manipulative effect.

[172] *See* SEC Securities Exchange Act Release No. 8712 (Oct. 8, 1969); SEC Securities Exchange Act Release No. 8595 (May 5, 1969).

[173] Subsection (a)(3) of Rule 10b–6 provides for a number of exemptions from the prohibitions of the Rule including "(2) unsolicited privately negotiated purchases . . . effected neither on a securities exchange nor from or through a broker or dealer" and "(5) brokerage transactions not involving solicitation of the customer's order."

[174] Purchases of the target's securities by the target itself or by persons acting in concert with the target may also raise problems under Rule 10b–6. See text accompanying notes 72–76, 85, Chapter 9.

[175] *See* Chris-Craft Industries, Inc. v. Piper Aircraft Corp., 303 F. Supp. 191,198 (S.D.N.Y. 1969), *rev'd in part, sub nom.,* Chris-Craft Industries, Inc., v. Bangor

Perhaps the most difficult interpretative problem arising out of Rule 10b–13 concerns the application of this provision to purchases of a target's stock during the pendency of statutory merger or consolidation proceedings. More specifically, the issue is one of whether an exchange of securities pursuant to a merger can be considered an exchange offer for purposes of Rule 10b–13. The issue may assume importance in the contested tender offer context where a competing tender offer is made and the target's proposed merger partner considers purchasing the target's stock in an effort to insure that it has enough votes to carry the merger.

Rule 10b–13(b) defines an exchange offer as follows: "The term 'exchange offer' as used in this rule shall include a tender offer for, or request or invitation for tenders of, any security in exchange for any consideration other than for all cash."

Applying this definition in the merger context, it is clear that if the merger is approved there will be thereafter an exchange of securities. However, the proposed merger partner, by virtue of its interest in consummating the merger may be deemed, in effect, to be offering to exchange its securities for those of the target company. Thus, while the term "exchange offer" has not customarily been considered to include an exchange of securities pursuant to a merger, the definition in Rule 10b–13(b) conceivably could be so applied.[176]

Assuming Rule 10b–13 could be so applied, it would be neces-

Punta Corp., 426 F.2d 569 (2d Cir. 1970); Armour & Co. v. General Host Corp., 296 F. Supp. 470 (S.D.N.Y. 1969). *See also* Chris-Craft Industries, Inc. v. Piper Aircraft Corp., 337 F. Supp. 1128, 1140–43 (S.D.N.Y. 1971). For a well reasoned criticism of the SEC's position, *see* Lowenfels, *Rule 10b–13, Rule 10b–6 and Purchases of Target Company Securities during an Exchange Offer,* 69 COLUM. L. REV. 1392 (1969). *See also* Weitzen v. Kearns, 271 F. Supp. 616 (S.D.N.Y. 1967). *Cf.* Miller v. Steinbach, 268 F. Supp 255 (S.D.N.Y. 1967). But see text accompanying notes 28–31, Chapter 6.

[176] If Rule 10b–13 is not so applied, the perplexing issues previously discussed in connection with Rule 10b–6 would be resurrected, i.e., would the purchase of the target's stock by the proposed merger partner violate Rule 10b–6 by creating a right to purchase securities which are the subject of a distribution? Since the distribution would only be made if the shareholders approved the merger, it could be argued that the purchase of the target's shares only creates a right to vote on the merger agreement as opposed to a right to purchase securities which are the subject of a distribution. For an excellent discussion of this issue as well as Rule 10b–6 and Rule 10b–13 in general, see Goolrick, *Purchases on The Market of Target Company Stock,* 26 BUS. LAW 457 (Nov. 1970).

sary to determine the period of time during which the proposed merger partner would not be able to purchase the target's shares. As previously noted, the rule prohibits purchases by an offeror from the time the offer is publicly announced or made known to security holders until the expiration of the offering period. While the scope of the phrase "from the time such . . . offer is publicly announced" has not yet been reviewed by the courts, it would seem clear that it refers to public announcements of proposals to make an offer as well as to public statements advising that the offer has in fact become effective. So interpreted, the rule may well prohibit purchases of the target's securities from the time the merger negotiations are publicly announced.

SECTION 7. *REGULATION OF THE TERMS, CONDITIONS, AND DISCLOSURES IN THE REQUEST OR INVITATION FOR TENDERS*

(1) WITHDRAWAL PRIVILEGES (SEC. 14(d)(5))

Section 14(d)(5) provides that persons who have deposited their shares pursuant to a tender offer may withdraw such shares at any time within seven days after the time copies of the offer are first published or at any time after sixty days from the date of the original offer. The provision has been interpreted to require a withdrawal period of seven 24-hour days after the date on which the tender offer is first made. Similarly, the sixty-day withdrawal provision apparently does not become effective until the sixty-first day after the date on which the tender offer is first made.[177]

The purpose of the seven-day withdrawal provision is to enable shareholders who tender their shares immediately after announcement of the offer to reconsider their decision.[178] The statute thereby effectively creates an absolute right of rescission during the first seven days of the offer. On the other hand, the right to withdraw after sixty days does not create an absolute withdrawal right for tendering shareholders. This provision was designed to prevent the offeror from tying up the tendered

[177] *See* Griffin and Tucker, *supra* note 1, at 709–10.

[178] H.R. REP. No. 1711, 90th Cong., 2d Sess. at 10 (1968).

shares for an indefinite period of time.[179] Thus Section 14(d)(5) would not appear to permit a shareholder to demand the return of tendered shares if within sixty days from the date of the original tender he receives either payment for shares tendered or a notice of acceptance of the tender and a commitment to pay for such shares within a reasonable period.

Section 14(d)(5) also permits the SEC, pursuant to rule, regulation or order, to vary the length of either withdrawal period if such variance is necessary or appropriate in the public interest or for the protection of investors. For example, the Commission might consider extending the seven-day withdrawal period where the offeror circulates revised disclosures to correct previously distributed solicitation materials. The Commission might also grant an offeror's request for an order extending the sixty-day withdrawal provision for a reasonable period where consummation of the offer is subject to regulatory approval and such approval might not be obtainable within sixty days.[180]

(2) Increased Consideration to Be Paid to Tendering Security Holders (Sec. 14(d)(7))

Section 14(d)(7) provides that where a tender offeror increases the consideration to be paid for tendered securities during the course of the offer, it must also pay the increased consideration for securities purchased to those security holders who tendered prior to announcement of the increase, regardless of whether the securities previously tendered were actually purchased before or after the announcement. Since Section 14(d)(7) applies only to increases in consideration prior to the expiration of the offer, one of the obvious methods of avoiding the effect of this provision is for the offeror to let its offer expire without increasing the consideration and shortly thereafter make a second offer for securities of the same class at an increased consideration. Although this approach may have some surface appeal, an offeror would be well advised to resist any temptation to proceed in this manner. Such an approach smacks of an attempt to exploit investors and may well tarnish the offeror's reputation in the investment community as well as compromise its ability to successfully consum-

[179] *Id.* [180] *Id.*

mate future takeover attempts. An equally important consideration is the possibility that the second offer may be viewed as an extension of the offering period of the initial offer for purposes of Section 14(d)(7). Thus, if it can be shown that but for the requirement of Section 14(d)(7), the offeror would have simply extended its initial offer, the offeror might be required to pay the increased consideration to all shareholders who tendered pursuant to the initial offer.[181]

Any discussion of Section 14(d)(7) would perhaps be incomplete without some comment on the objective of Congress in incorporating this particular provision in the Williams Act. The express purpose of Section 14(d)(7), as specified in the committee reports, is to "assure fair treatment of those persons who tender their shares at the beginning of the tender period, and to assure equality of treatment among all shareholders who tender their shares." [182] It may be questioned, however, whether principles of fairness and equality really require the offeror to pay an additional premium to shareholders who were willing to sell their shares at the original tender price and who received a premium above market on such sale. There has been no serious claim, for example, that the interests of fairness and equality require a purchaser accumulating a large block of stock in the open market to pay all sellers the highest price paid during the course of the accumulation. Nor is there any meaningful basis for requiring a tender offeror to do so. The net effect of the two forms of accumulation is essentially the same. Only the form or structure of purchase differs—the open-market purchaser enjoying the anonymity of the auction market in accumulating shares while the purchases by the tender offeror are segregated and distinguishable from other purchases of the same security. To require the latter to pay all sellers the highest price paid during the course of the accumulation exalts form over substance.

In essence, it would appear that Section 14(d)(7) must realistically be viewed as permitting a form of "free-riding," whereby

[181] Query, whether a second offer undertaken solely to cut off the rights of certain shareholders to the increased consideration would constitute fraud within the meaning of Section 14(e) or Rule 10b–5?

[182] H.R. Rep. No. 1711, 90th Cong., 2d Sess. at 11 (1968); S. Rep. No. 550, 90th Cong., 1st Sess. at 10 (1967).

tendering shareholders are able to reap unanticipated benefits resulting from advantageous market developments which take place after they have committed themselves to selling their shares at a lower price. This approach must be regarded as fundamentally inconsistent with basic principles of contract law in that, absent fraud or manipulation by the purchaser, a rise in the market price of a security or the opportunity to obtain more favorable terms *after* a binding agreement has been reached has never been a sufficient justification for permitting the seller to rescind or modify the terms of the original agreement. Viewed in this light, one may question whether Section 14(d)(7) has the effect of compromising, rather than advancing, the continued integrity of the market place.

(3) Pro Rata Purchases (Sec. 14(d)(6))

In order to give all shareholders an equal opportunity to participate in a tender offer, Section 14(d)(6) provides:

> Where any person makes a tender offer, or request or invitation for tenders, for less than all the outstanding equity securities of a class, and where a greater number of securities is deposited pursuant thereto within ten days after copies of the offer or request or invitation are first published or sent or given to security holders than such person is bound or willing to take up and pay for, the securities taken up shall be taken up as nearly as may be pro rata, disregarding fractions, according to the number of securities deposited by each depositor. The provisions of this subsection shall also apply to securities deposited within ten days after notice of an increase in the consideration offered to security holders, as described in paragraph (7), is first published or sent or given to security holders.

As stated, Section 14(d)(6) applies only where the shares tendered during the first ten days of the offer exceed the number of shares which the offeror seeks to obtain.[183] If the shares tendered

[183] The NYSE guidelines on tender offers, which antedate the federal tender rules, also recommend pro rata purchases for a minimum ten-day period. *See* NYSE Company Manual, at A-179, 180.

The companion House Bill (H.R. 14475), in contrast to the Williams Bill (S. 510), required the offeror to purchase shares on a pro rata basis for the full offering period. The NYSE objected to this provision on the ground that it would tend to tie up large blocks of securities for extended periods, thereby producing abnormal price fluctuations as well as creating uncertainties for both offerors and tendering shareholders. *See* Statement of Donald L. Calvin, *Hearings on H.R. 14475*,

do not exceed the requested number during the first ten days of the offer, the offeror, at its option, may purchase any and all shares ultimately tendered on a first-come, first-served basis.

The second sentence of Section 14(d)(6), relating to the applicability of this provision where an offer to increase the consideration paid for tendered shares is made during the offering period, has raised difficult questions of statutory interpretation. Two examples illustrate the scope of the problem:

(1) A tender offer is made to acquire 500,000 shares of an issuer. During the first 10 days of the offer only 250,000 shares are tendered. To bolster its prospects for success, the offeror increases the consideration which will be paid for tendered shares and during the next ten days an additional 750,000 shares are tendered. Query whether the offeror is required to purchase the 250,000 shares tendered prior to the increased consideration while pro-rating only the additional shares tendered of which only 250,000 shares will be accepted; or is the offeror required to prorate all shares tendered?;

(2) A tender offer is made to acquire 500,000 shares of an issuer. During the first 10 days of the offer 750,000 shares are tendered. The offeror then decides that it would like to purchase up to 1 million shares and in order to induce shareholders to tender, it increases the consideration which it will pay for tendered shares. Within 10 days after the notice to acquire additional shares, 750,000 shares are tendered. Query whether the offeror is required to purchase all 750,000 shares tendered prior to the increase in consideration while pro-rating the additional shares tendered of which only 250,000 shares will be accepted; or is the offeror required to separately pro-rate the shares tendered before and after the notice of the increase in consideration, accepting 500,000 shares from each; or is the offeror required to pro-rate all shares tendered?

The 1968 Williams Act report of the House Committee on Interstate and Foreign Commerce describes the mechanics of the increased consideration provision of Section 14(d)(6) as follows:

S. 510 *Before the Subcomm. on Commerce and Finance of the House Comm. on Interstate and Foreign Commerce*, 90th Cong., 2d Sess. at 49–50 (1968).

If the person making the tender offer increases the consideration, a new 10-day pro rata period would be required allowing all shareholders a fair opportunity to participate in the offer. In the event that the consideration is increased, all shares deposited before the increase would be required to be taken up before any shares deposited thereafter, unless all shares deposited pursuant to the tender offer were taken up on a pro rata basis.[184]

It would therefore appear that if the offeror represents in its original invitation for tenders that it will purchase shares on a pro rata basis only if the shares tendered during the first ten days of the offer exceed the number of shares requested, it will be required to accept all shares tendered prior to the notice of increased consideration while pro rating only those shares subsequently tendered.[185] On the other hand, if the offeror agrees to accept shares on a pro rata basis, whether or not it is required to do so by virtue of Section 14(d)(6), it would be required to prorate all shares accepted without making any distinction as to when the shares were tendered.

(4) Information Required to Be Included in the Tender Offer [Rule 14d–1(c)]

Rule 14d–1(c) requires all tender offers or requests or invitations for tenders to include the following information:

(1) The name of the person making the tender offer, request or invitation;

(2) The exact dates prior to which, and after which, security holders who deposit their securities will have the right to withdraw their securities pursuant to Section 14(d)(5) of the Act, or otherwise;

(3) If the tender offer or request or invitation for tenders is for less than all of the outstanding securities of the class and the person making the offer, request or invitation is not obligated to purchase all of the securities tendered, the date of expiration of the period during which the securities will be taken up pro rata pursuant to Section 14(d)(6) (§ 240.14d–1 et seq.), or otherwise; and

(4) The information required by Items 2(a), (c) and (e), 3, 4, 5, and 6 of Schedule 13D, or a fair and adequate summary thereof.

[184] H.R. Rep. No. 1711, 90th Cong., 2d Sess. at 11 (1968).

[185] A change made in the basis for accepting shares at the time the notice of the increased consideration is published might be deemed to work a fraud upon security holders who tendered prior to the notice of the increase.

Any additional material soliciting tenders subsequent to the initial solicitation must contain the name of the person making the solicitation together with the information required by Items 2(a), (c) and (e), 3, 4, 5 and 6 of Schedule 13D; however, such material may omit any of the information previously furnished to the persons solicited.[186] Copies of the additional soliciting materials must be filed with the Commission as an amendment to the Schedule 13D statement [187] no later than the time copies of such material are first published or sent or given to security holders.[188] Copies of the original tender offer or request or invitation for tenders must be filed as an exhibit to the original Schedule 13D statement.[189]

(5) Exemptions from Regulation (Sec. 14(d)(8); Rule 14d–2)

Section 14(d)(8) provides that the provisions of Section 14(d) do not apply to tender offers or requests or invitations for tenders of any security:

> (A) if the acquisition of such security, together with all other acquisitions by the same person of securities of the same class during the preceding twelve months, would not exceed 2 per centum of that class;
> (B) by the issuer of such security; or
> (C) which the Commission, by rules or regulations or by order, shall exempt from the provisions of this subsection as not entered into for the purpose of, and not having the effect of, changing or influencing the control of the issuer or otherwise as not comprehended within the purposes of this subsection.

Rule 14d–2 [190] contains additional exemptions for the following types of offers:

(1) Offers to purchase securities made in connection with a distribution permitted by Rules 10b–6, 10b–7, or 10b–8; [191]

(2) The call or redemption of any security in accordance with the terms and conditions of the governing instruments; [192]

[186] Rule 14d–1(d), 17 C.F.R. § 240.14d–1(d).
[187] *See* Item 8, Schedule 13D.
[188] Rule 14d–1(d), 17 C.F.R. §240.14d–1(d).
[189] *See* Rule 14d–1(a); Item 8, Schedule 13D.
[190] 17 C.F.R. § 240.14d–2.
[191] Rule 14d–2(a).
[192] Rule 14d–2(b).

(3) Offers to purchase securities evidenced by a script certificate, order form or similar document which represents a fractional interest in a share of stock or similar security; [193]

(4) Offers to purchase securities pursuant to a statutory procedure for the purchase of dissenting shareholders' securities; [194] and

(5) Offers to purchase securities in transactions exempt from registration under Section 3(a)(10) of the 1933 Act.[195]

SECTION 8. *INFORMATION REQUIRED TO BE INCLUDED IN ANY SOLICITATION OR RECOMMENDATION TO ACCEPT OR REJECT A TENDER OFFER* [*RULE 14d–4(c)*]

Rule 14d–4(c) [196] requires any written solicitation or recommendation to security holders to accept or reject a tender offer subject to Section 14(d) to include the name of the person making such statement together with the information required by Items 1(b) and 2(b) of Schedule 14D or a summary thereof. Any written solicitation or recommendation may omit any of such information previously furnished to security holders.

It is important to note that Rule 14d–4(c) applies whether or not the person making such solicitation is required to file a Schedule 14D statement. Thus, for example, any such solicitation made by a tender offeror must include the information required by Rule 14d–4(c). Since a further solicitation by a tender offeror to accept the offer may well be considered additional tender soliciting material pursuant to Rule 14d–1(c), the offeror should also include the information required by this latter rule in any written solicitations. Copies of solicitations and recommendations to accept or reject an offer made by management of the target and others required to file a Schedule 14D statement must be filed as an exhibit to that schedule. Copies of all such solicitations by a tender offeror must be filed as an exhibit to its Schedule 13D statement.

[193] Rule 14d–2(c). [194] Rule 14d–2(d). [195] Rule 14d–2(g).
[196] 17 C.F.R. § 240.14d–4(c).

SECTION 9. *INFORMATION REQUIRED TO BE INCLUDED IN PROSPECTUSES RELATING TO EXCHANGE TENDER OFFERS [RULE 434B—SECURITIES ACT OF 1933]*

Rule 434B was adopted by the Commission to insure that prospectuses issued in connection with tender offers subject to Section 14(d) of the 1934 Act and made pursuant to a 1933 Act registration statement contain the specific disclosures required to be included in any tender offer or request or invitation for tenders. By requiring any prospectus to include the information required by Rule 14d–1(c) under the 1934 Act, Rule 434B helps to eliminate the uncertainties which existed in attempting to interpret the 1933 Act disclosure requirements in a tender offer context. The full text of the Rule is as follows:

Notwithstanding the provisions of any form for the registration of securities under the Act, any prospectus relating to securities to be offered in connection with a tender offer for, or a request or invitation for tenders of, securities which is subject to Section 14(d) of the Securities Exchange Act of 1934 shall, if used after January 28, 1971, include all of the information, not otherwise required to be included therein, required by Rule 14d–1(c) under such Act to be included in all such tender offers, requests or invitations, published, sent or given to the holders of such securities.

The prospectus containing the information required by Rule 434B must be filed as an exhibit to the tender offeror's Schedule 13D statement.[197]

SECTION 10. *PREREGISTRATION PUBLICITY IN AN EXCHANGE TENDER OFFER (GUN-JUMPING)*

Where an offer involving an exchange of securities pursuant to a 1933 Act registration statement is contemplated, it becomes necessary to consider the scope of permissible preregistration publicity in connection with such an offer. Section 5(c) of the 1933 Act [198] prohibits any sale or offer to sell prior to the filing of a registration statement and provides in full as follows:

[197] Rule 14d–1(f), 17 C.F.R. § 240.14d–1(f).

[198] 15 U.S.C. § 77e(c).

It shall be unlawful for any person, directly or indirectly, to make use of any means or instruments of transportation or communication in interstate commerce or of the mails to offer to sell or offer to buy through the use or medium of any prospectus or otherwise any security, unless a registration statement has been filed as to such security, or while the registration statement is the subject of a refusal order or stop order or (prior to the effective date of the registration statement) any public proceeding of examination under section 8.

In an effort to establish some meaningful guidelines regarding the types of statements which may or may not be considered as "offers to sell" during the preregistration period, the Commission adopted Rule 135 under the 1933 Act,[199] which sets forth the parameters of permissible preregistration publicity. This rule provides as follows:

For the purpose only of Section 5 of the Act, a notice given by an issuer that it proposes to make a public offering of securities to be registered under the Act shall not be deemed to offer any securities for sale if such notice states that the offering will be made only by means of a prospectus and contains no more than the following additional information:

(1) The name of the issuer;

(2) The title, amount and basic terms of the securities proposed to be offered, the amount of the offering, if any, to be made by selling security holders, the anticipated time of the offering and a brief statement of the manner and purpose of the offering without naming the underwriters;

(3) In the case of a rights offering to security holders of the issuer, the class of securities the holders of which will be entitled to subscribe to the securities proposed to be offered, the subscription ratio, the proposed record date, the approximate date upon which the rights are proposed to be issued, the proposed term or expiration date of the rights and the approximate subscription price, or any of the foregoing;

(4) In the case of an offering of securities in exchange for other securities of the issuer or of another issuer, the name of the issuer and the title of the securities to be surrendered in exchange for the securities to be offered, the basis upon which the exchange may be made, or any of the foregoing;

(5) In the case of an offering to employees of the issuer or to employees of any affiliate of the issuer, the name of the employer and class or classes of employees to whom the securities are proposed to

[199] 17 C.F.R. § 230.135, as amended (1970).

be offered, the offering price or basis of the offering and the period during which the offering is to be made, or any of the foregoing; and

(6) Any statement or legend required by State law or administrative authority.

(b) Any notice contemplated by this rule may take the form of a news release or a written communication directed to security holders or employees, as the case may be, or other published statement.

In view of the fact that the provisions of Rule 135 are relatively specific, the practical application of the rule would appear to be largely mechanical. In the exchange tender offer context, however, difficulties in interpretation have arisen in connection with the scope of the phrase "the basis upon which the exchange may be made" in subsection (4) of the rule.

In *Chris-Craft Industries, Inc. v. Piper Aircraft Corp.*,[200] a contender for control of a target corporation (Piper) alleged that press releases issued by both a competing offeror and the target company prior to the filing of a registration statement pursuant to which the competing offeror would make an exchange offer for the target's shares constituted violations of Section 5(c) and Rule 135. The allegations were based upon a portion of the press releases which stated that the competing offeror's exchange package would consist of securities "to be valued in the judgment of The First Boston Corporation at not less than $80 per Piper share."[201]

In denying Chris-Craft's request for an injunction and other equitable relief, the district court concluded that the reference to the $80 valuation in the press release constituted permissible disclosure since it related to "the basis" upon which the exchange was to be made.

While the Second Circuit Court of Appeals affirmed the denial of injunctive relief (primarily upon a finding that no irreparable

[200] 303 F. Supp. 191 (S.D.N.Y. 1969), *aff'd in part, sub. nom.*, Chris-Craft Industries, Inc. v. Bangor Punta Corp., No. 33983 (2d Cir. 1969), CCH FED. SEC. L. REP. ¶ 92,510, *aff'd on rehearing*, 426 F.2d 569 (2d Cir. 1970) (*en banc*).

[201] 303 F. Supp. 191, 196. While the 1970 amendments to Rule 135 modified, *inter alia*, that portion of the Rule which was at issue in the *Chris-Craft* case, the nature of the amendment would not have effected the result in this case. *See* SEC Securities Act Release No. 5101 (Nov. 19, 1970), CCH FED. SEC. L. REP. ¶ 77,927. *See also* SEC Securities Act Release No. 5180 (Aug. 16, 1971), CCH FED. SEC. L. REP. ¶ 78,912.

harm would result if the injunction was denied), the majority of the court disagreed with the lower court's interpretation of Section 5(c) and Rule 135. In a decision in which four separate opinions were rendered, the majority held that Rule 135 set forth "exclusive" categories of information not deemed to be an offer to sell and that the press release reference to the $80 valuation did not fall within its scope.[202] The court then remanded the case for a determination of an appropriate remedy in light of the court's findings.[203]

While the Second Circuit Court's opinion cannot be faulted on a strict reading of Section 5(c) and Rule 135, the implications of the result in this case merit further reflection. The underlying purpose of the 1933 Act is to insure full disclosure to investors of all relevant facts and circumstances pertaining to an offering of securities. Conceivably, however, the interrelationship of Section 5(c) and Rule 135 on one hand and both the anti-fraud rules and the disclosure requirements of Section 13(d) on the other could well lead to the anomalous result where disclosure will be prohibited by the former and required by the latter. For example, the district court in the *Chris-Craft* case emphasized the fact that the $80 valuation was substantially in excess of the market value at the time the press release was issued and that pursuant to "the directives of Securities and Exchange Commission v. Texas Gulf Sulphur Co." such valuation constituted material information which should be disclosed.[204]

On the other hand the circuit court found that:

[202] 426 F.2d 569, 574. Prior to the Chris-Craft suit, the SEC obtained a consent injunction against Bangor Punta Corp. and Piper Aircraft Corp. for alleged gun-jumping. *See* SEC v. Bangor Punta Corp., No. 1388-69 (D.D.C. 1969), CCH FED. SEC. L. REP. ¶ 92,428. The Commission appeared as *amicus* in the private suit brought by Chris-Craft.

[203] After the decision on appeal, Chris-Craft abandoned its claim for injunctive relief and instead instituted an action for damages alleging, *inter alia*, a violation of Section 5. Recovery of damages was denied. *See* Christ-Craft Industries, Inc. v. Piper Aircraft Corp., 337 F. Supp. 1128, 1136–38 (S.D.N.Y. 1971). For a related case in which the court dismissed an action for damages by Bangor Punta Corp. alleging that certain wrongful acts of Chris-Craft Industries, Inc. caused Bangor Punta to pay more than it would have otherwise been required to pay for control of Piper Aircraft Corp., *see* Bangor Punta Corp. v. Chris-Craft Industries, Inc., 337 F. Supp. 1147 (S.D.N.Y. 1971). *See also* SEC v. Bangor Punta Corp., 331 F. Supp. 1154 (S.D.N.Y. 1971).

[204] 303 F. Supp. 191, 195.

The only material fact in this case within the meaning of Texas Gulf Sulphur was Bangor Punta's commitment to offer its securities for Piper Aircraft shares. Rule 135 provides adequately for the announcement of a material fact such as this; further disclosure would, as stated above, thwart other policies of the securities laws. Had Bangor Punta observed Rule 135 by revealing immediately its intention to make an exchange offer and by later revealing the titles of the securities it proposed to offer and the basis or ratio on which the exchange was proposed to be made as soon as these matters were decided, adequate information concerning the proposed transaction would have been placed before the public and the potentially misleading estimate of value would have been avoided. Even if we assume that knowledge of the value figure involved here might conceivably have conferred some benefit on insiders had it not been revealed, we feel that this risk of unfair advantage is outweighed by the danger that substantial numbers of investors were misled by the figure's publication. The fact that a few additional sophisticated investors could have discovered the $80 value guarantee in the description of the transaction which Bangor Punta filed with the SEC pursuant to Section 13(d) of the 1934 Act is of no moment. Such investors would almost certainly be small in number and any arguable danger of permitting them an unfair advantage is outweighed by the stronger probability that the press release misled a large number of unsophisticated investors.[205]

Whether the view enunciated by the circuit court in *Chris-Craft* is likely to withstand the test of further judicial review is a subject on which reasonable men presently differ.[206]

SECTION 11. *FEDERAL REGULATION OF TENDER OFFERS OTHER THAN PURSUANT TO THE SECURITIES ACT OF 1934 AND THE SECURITIES ACT OF 1933*

A. FEDERAL REGULATION OF TENDER OFFERS IN "REGULATED INDUSTRIES"

Regulation of tender offers pursuant to the federal securities laws constitutes but a part of the total federal regulatory scheme affecting such offers. In addition, there are a number of federal

[205] 426 F.2d 569, 575–76.

[206] *See, e.g.*, Comment, *Preregistration Publicity in an Exchange Offer*, 119 U. PA. L. REV. 174 (1970). *See also* THE WHEAT REPORT, DISCLOSURE TO INVESTORS: A REAPPRAISAL OF FEDERAL ADMINISTRATIVE POLICIES UNDER THE '33 AND '34 ACTS, at 132–33 (1969).

statutes and regulations which may be applicable where either the offeror or the target company is engaged in activities within the jurisdiction of certain federal agencies. A number of federal statutes presently require federal agency approval before any changes of control can be effected in companies subject to their respective jurisdictions.[207] The Federal Aviation Act of 1958,[208] for example, makes it unlawful for any person to acquire control of an air carrier unless such acquisition of control has first been approved by an order of the Civil Aeronautics Board.[209] Any person owning 10 percent or more of the voting securities or capital of an air carrier will be presumed to be in control unless the Board finds otherwise.[210] Similarly, the Federal Communications Act of 1934 [211] requires prior approval from the Federal Communications Commission before there can be any transfer of control of any corporation holding a radio or television construction permit or station license.[212] The Federal Communications Act also prohibits any alien or any corporation controlled by an alien from holding a station license.[213]

In addition to requiring agency approval prior to a change in control, other federal agencies have asserted their jurisdiction in connection with tender offers by adopting regulations similar to the disclosure and reporting requirements under the federal securities laws.[214] The anti-trust laws must also be carefully considered before a prospective tender offeror can proceed with any confidence.[215]

207 Prospective offerors engaged in regulated industries or which seek to acquire companies in such industries must also consider the implications of state regulation of regulated industries prior to attempting a takeover attempt.

208 49 U.S.C. § 1301 et seq.

209 49 U.S.C. § 1378(a)(5) (as amended Pub. L. 91–62 [1969]).

210 49 U.S.C. § 1378(f). *See also* § 1377(b) Federal Aviation Act requiring any person owning more than 5 percent of any class of the capital stock or capital of a regulated air carrier to file ownership reports with the board.

211 47 U.S.C. § 151 et seq.

212 47 U.S.C. § 310(b).

213 47 U.S.C. § 310(a). *See also* Federal Shipping Act, 46 U.S.C. § 808; Interstate Commerce Act, 49 U.S.C. §§ 1, 5, 312, 912, and 1011.

214 *See, e.g.*, regulations of the: (a) Comptroller of the Currency, Parts 11 and 12 (12 C.F.R. § 11.3, 11.4); (b) Federal Reserve System, Part 206 (12 C.F.R. § 206.1); (c) Federal Deposit Insurance Corp., Part 335.5 (12 C.F.R. § 335.5(l), (m), and (n)).

215 *See, e.g.*, § 7 of the Clayton Act, 15 U.S.C. § 18; §§ 1 and 2 of the Sherman Act, 15 U.S.C. § 1, 2.

For tender offer cases involving federal regulation other than pursuant to the federal securities laws, see Chapter 9, *infra*, notes 150–152, 154.

B. Regulation Of Tender Offers Under The Public Utility Holding Company Act Of 1935

While regulation of public utilities by the Securities and Exchange Commission pursuant to the Public Utility Holding Company Act of 1935 [216] is deemed to be "securities regulation," the nature of such regulation within the tender offer context is similar to that affecting other regulated industries where prior federal agency approval is required before a change in control can be effected. Section 9(a)(1) of the 1935 Act makes it unlawful for a registered holding company [217] or subsidiary company thereof to acquire any securities or utility assets or any other interest in any business unless approved by the SEC or except as an exemption may be applicable. A holding company is defined in Section 2(a)(7) of the Act as follows:

> (A) any company which directly or indirectly owns, controls, or holds with power to vote, 10 per centum or more of the outstanding voting securities of a public-utility company or of a company which is a holding company by virtue of this clause or clause (B), unless the Commission, as hereinafter provided, by order declares such company not to be a holding company; and
>
> (B) any person which the Commission determines, after notice and opportunity for hearing, directly or indirectly to exercise (either alone or pursuant to an arrangement or understanding with one or more other persons) such a controlling influence over the management or policies of any public-utility or holding company as to make it necessary or appropriate in the public interest or for the protection of investors or consumers that such person be subject to the obligations duties, and liabilities imposed in this title upon holding companies.[218]

[216] 15 U.S.C. § 79 *et seq*. A bill to provide for the transfer to the Federal Power Commission of certain regulatory functions presently exercised by the SEC under the Public Utility Holding Act has recently been introduced in the Senate. *See* S. Bill 3866 (SEC letter of transmittal and explanatory statement of the draft bill reproduced at CCH Fed. Sec. L. Rep. ¶ 78,928).

[217] Section 4 of the 1935 Act makes it unlawful for any holding company to engage, directly or through subsidiary companies, in any business in interstate commerce unless registered under the Act.

[218] Section 2(a)(5) of the 1935 Act defines the term "public utility company" as an electric utility company or a gas utility company. Section 2(a)(3) defines "electric utility company" as "any company which owns or operates facilities used for the generation, transmission, or distribution of electric energy for sale, other than sale to tenants or employees of the company operating such facilities for their own use and not for resale". Section 2(a)(4) defines "gas utility company" as "any

Section 9(a)(2) of the Act makes it unlawful, unless the acquisition is approved by the Commission, for *any person* to acquire any security of any public utility company, if such person is deemed an affiliate (pursuant to Section 2(a)(11)(A) of the Act) of such company and of any other public utility company, or will by virtue of such acquisition become such an affiliate. Section 2(a)(11)(A) defines an affiliate as: "(A) any person that directly or indirectly owns, controls, or holds with power to vote, 5 per centum or more of the outstanding voting securities of such specified company."

Section 10(a) of the Act describes the procedure to be followed in applying for approval of acquisitions and sets forth the information to be included in such application. Sections 10(b) and (c) enumerate the guidelines upon which the Commission shall determine whether to approve the acquisition.

In addition, Section 11 of the 1935 Act requires the Commission to scrutinize the corporate structure of each registered holding company and its subsidiaries for the express purpose of determining "the extent to which the corporate structure of such holding-company system and the companies therein may be simplified, unnecessary complexities therein eliminated, voting power fairly and equitably distributed among the holders of securities thereof, and the properties and business thereof confined to those necessary or appropriate to the operations of an integrated public-utility system." [219]

---

company which owns or operates facilities used for the distribution at retail (other than distribution only in enclosed portable containers, or distribution to tenants or employees of the company operating such facilities for their own use and not for resale) of natural or manufactured gas for heat, light or power." Where the amount of electric energy sold or natural or manufactured gas distributed at retail is relatively small, the Commission may by order declare that a company operating any such facilities is not a public utility if it finds that the company is primarily engaged in a nonpublic utility business.

[219] In late 1965, the Pennzoil Co. made a cash tender offer to purchase a minimum of one million common shares of United Gas Corp., a "gas utility company" within the meaning of the 1935 Act. If all the shares tendered pursuant to the offer were purchased, Pennzoil would have owned substantially more than 10 percent of United's stock and would as a practical matter control United. Under Section 2(a)(7) of the Act, Pennzoil would then have apparently been required to register as a public utility holding company. United sought an injunction against Pennzoil from acquiring 10 percent or more of its outstanding shares or, in the alternative, from voting such shares if acquired, claiming, *inter alia*, that if Penn-

Where a proposed acquisition is subject to Federal agency approval, the potential acquirer is confronted with the problem of what steps, if any, it may take toward achieving its objective in advance of such approval. As an apparent result of two tender offer cases involving public utility companies,[220] the Commission attempted to clarify the issue by adopting Rule 51 under the 1935 Act.[221] The rule makes it unlawful for a person subject to Section 9(a) of the Act, i.e., the proposed acquirer, to take any action in connection with the acquisition unless all of the following conditions are satisfied:

(a) The transaction contemplated by the Preliminary Agreement is expressly conditioned on Commission approval and the application for such approval is filed with the Commission as soon as practicable.
(b) No standby, option or similar fee is paid or payable by or on behalf of the Proposed Acquirer as consideration for the Preliminary Agreement.
(c) The Proposed Acquirer does not indemnify or agree to indemnify any person against any market or investment risk in connection with such person's acquisition, retention or disposition of the subject matter of the proposed acquisition.
(d) The Proposed Acquirer does not transfer to any person (other than a subsidiary or successor in interest by merger or consolidation), by way of assignment or otherwise, any of its rights or interest in respect of the subject matter of the proposed acquisition unless such transfer is conditioned upon consummation of the Preliminary Agreement following its approval by the Commission.
(e) In case a proposed transaction includes an acquisition of secur-

zoil became a holding company, United as a subsidiary company might be required to divest itself of certain valuable non-utility subsidiaries and that such divestiture would result in irreparable damage and loss to United, thereby breaching Pennzoil's fiduciary obligations, as controlling shareholder, to United and its remaining shareholders. In denying United's motion, the court found that regulation of United under the 1935 Act did not by itself constitute a breach of Pennzoil's fiduciary obligations and that even if divestiture was required, experience under the Act indicated that it would not result in damages or a loss in values. *See* United Gas Corp. v. Pennzoil Co., 248 F. Supp. 449 (S.D.N.Y. 1965), *aff'd per curiam*, 354 F. 2d 1002 (2d Cir. 1965).

220 *See In the Matter of* Northeast Utilities, SEC Holding Co. Act Release No. 15825, Aug. 18, 1967, CCH Fed. Sec. L. Rep. ¶ 77,467; *In the Matter of* Eastern Gas and Fuel Associates, SEC Holding Co. Act Release No. 15887, Nov. 3, 1967, CCH Fed. Sec. L. Rep. ¶ 77,481.

221 17 C.F.R. § 250.51, eff. July 15, 1968. See SEC Holding Co. Act Release No. 16081 (June 7, 1968), CCH Fed. Sec. L. Rep. ¶ 77,562. While the Williams Act is acknowledged as the initial attempt at regulation of tender offers on the Federal level, Rule 51 actually antedates its enactment by fifteen days.

ities pursuant to an invitation for tenders to be made prior to the approval of such acquisition, provision shall be made that any person tendering such securities (the Tenderer) may demand in writing the return of any deposited securities at any time after 60 days from the initial mailing or publication of the invitation for tenders unless prior to the receipt of such demand either (1) the proposed acquisition has been approved by the Commission and the Proposed Acquirer is obligated to consummate the transaction or (2) the Tenderer has been issued a transferable certificate of deposit which meets the conditions specified in paragraph (f) of this section.

(f) A transferable certificate of deposit for purposes of paragraph (e) of this section may be issued in exchange for tendered securities subject to the following conditions:

(1) The terms of the certificate of deposit as proposed to be issued are specified in the invitations for tenders, including equitable provision for return of the tendered securities in the event the proposed transaction is not approved by the Commission or otherwise fails of consummation, for exercise of voting rights and for receipt of dividends or interest by the Tenderer during the deposit period.

(2) The Proposed Acquirer files with the Commission an application-declaration proposing the issuance of such certificates of deposit in exchange for tendered securities.

(3) Upon notice and after a hearing which shall be limited to the fairness of the terms and conditions of such issuance and exchange and to compliance with the conditions of this Rule, the Commission in its discretion may by order permit such issuance and exchange on such terms and conditions as it shall approve. Any person to whom it is proposed to issue a certificate of deposit shall be entitled to appear at such hearing.

(4) If the terms and conditions specified in the certificates of deposit to be issued pursuant to order of the Commission differ from those specified in the invitation for tenders previously published by the Proposed Acquirer, the Commission may in such order require the Proposed Acquirer to give notice thereof by mail (and publication if deemed appropriate) to all persons who have tendered their securities and to provide up to 20 days after mailing of such notice for any such person to elect, in a manner prescribed by the Commission, either to continue or to revoke his tender. The terms and conditions specified in the certificates of deposit may be modified only pursuant to order of the Commission.[222]

[222] The explanatory statement contained in the release adopting Rule 51 (*see* note 221, *supra*) described the rule as follows:

"In general the rule permits only such preliminaries as will not substantially affect the public interest or the interest of investors or consumers in the event the Commission finds that a proposed transaction does not conform to the applicable statutory standards. The rule also takes into account the possibility that an application for approval of an acquisition under Section 10, particularly a contested one, may take a substantial period of time for disposition, and contemplates the possible issuance of certificates of deposit. Pending further experience the Commission has not attempted advance prescription of appropriate terms of the certificate of deposit. It will be necessary, on a case-by-case basis, to give consideration to such matters as provision for voting rights and dividends, possible adjustments of the proposed tender price in the light of contingencies after invitation for tenders and other matters. The provision for a preliminary hearing on the fairness of the exchange for certificates of deposit has the purpose among others of meeting the requirements for exemption of the issuance of the certificates of deposit under Section 3(a)(10) of the Securities Act of 1933.

Several of the comments received on the published proposal expressed concern that the rule as proposed would prohibit usual indemnification of depositaries and others participating as agents in the solicitation of tenders against expenses and liabilities incurred in that capacity. There was also concern that a proposed acquirer could not agree to bear its share of legal, engineering, accounting or similar incidental fees and expenses arising from execution of a preliminary agreement and permissible preliminary steps in the planning stages. To meet these problems, paragraph (c) of the adopted rule has been revised to prohibit only indemnification against market or investment risk extended to a person who acquires, retains or disposes of the securities or assets subject to a preliminary agreement in contemplation of their ultimate acquisition by the proposed acquirer."

CHAPTER 5. STATE SECURITIES REGULATION OF TENDER OFFERS

State regulation of securities transactions has generally tended to follow the philosophy of the Securities Act of 1933 [1] and the Securities Exchange Act of 1934 [2] by requiring issuers to make full disclosure to investors and regulating the activities of those persons through whom securities are purchased and sold. In recent years many states have gone further in attempting to provide additional investor protection by adopting review procedures designed to screen out offerings which are deemed to be unfair or inequitable.

The response of some states to the tender offer phenomenon, however, has been unique in that for the first time the impetus for regulation was apparently inspired by the legislature's concern for the issuer rather than the investor. Fears that established local concerns might be taken over by outside interests which in turn would close down plants and leave local residents jobless apparently prompted several legislatures to consider bills which would have effectively precluded tender offers for companies located within their states.[3] To date, Ohio, Virginia, and Nevada

[1] 15 U.S.C. §§ 77a et seq. [2] 15 U.S.C. §§ 78a et seq.

[3] The bills were not academic exercises in the legislative process. In Ohio, Northwest Industries, Inc. had begun what turned into a hotly contested battle for Ohio-based B. F. Goodrich & Co. One commentator who played a major role in the legislation is reported to have remarked that as far as Ohio corporations are concerned, "the corporate takeover as a form of corporate warfare is a thing of the past; acquisitions will hereafter be negotiated." *See* 23 BNA SEC. REG. & L. REP. A–3, A–6 (Nov. 5, 1969).

In Pennsylvania, attempted takeovers of Sharon Steel Corp., Piper Aircraft Corp., and Westinghouse Air Brake Co. may have influenced the legislature to consider a bill requiring an offeror for shares of a company incorporated in Pennsylvania or having its principal office in the state to obtain approval of either the

have adopted local interest legislation.[4] A number of other states, however, have passed statutes regulating tender offers for domestic insurance companies and at least two states regulate tender offerors as dealers in securities. In addition, other states, though not enacting new legislation, have regulated exchange tender offers pursuant to their existing blue-sky statutes.

SECTION 1. *LOCAL INTEREST STATUTES*

A. OFFERS SUBJECT TO REGULATION

The Ohio Takeover Act [5] applies to tender offers for equity securities of any company incorporated in Ohio *or* having its principal place of business and substantial assets within the state.[6] The Nevada Takeover Bid Disclosure Act [7] is more restricted in

---

target's directors, the majority of its shareholders, or the Secretary of the Commonwealth of Pennsylvania. Pa. H.B. 841 (1969 Sess.). This bill was not passed. *See also* Metz, "Market Place: States Defiant on Take-Overs," N.Y. Times, June 3, 1969, at 62.

In Illinois a bill patterned after the Pennsylvania bill was the apparent response to Ling-Temco-Vought's acquisition of Wilson & Co. and General Host's takeover of Armour & Co. The bill, however, was eventually defeated. *See* 5 BNA SEC. REG. & L. REP. A–9 (July 2, 1969).

[4] State regulation in the form of local interest statutes, particularly the Ohio legislation, has been severely criticized as "special interest" legislation designed to protect incumbent management "under the fiction of requiring fair disclosure to shareholders." *See* Sommer, *The Ohio Takeover Act: What Is It?*, 21 CASE W. RES. L. REV. 681, 720 (1970). The Ohio Act has also drawn the fire of the New York Stock Exchange and the Investment Bankers Association of America. *See* 1 BNA SEC. REG. & L. REP. A–11, 12 (June 4, 1969); Metz, "Market Place: States Defiant on Take-Overs," *supra* note 3. On the other hand, this form of state regulation has been defended on the ground that a takeover bid "is in essence an internal affairs transaction which a state having legislative jurisdiction over the corporation's internal affairs may reasonably regulate." *See* Shipman, *Some Thoughts About the Role of State Takeover Legislation: The Ohio Takeover Act*, 21 CASE W. RES. L. REV. 722, 724 (1970). *See also* Freeman, *Business Associations, The Fifteenth Annual Survey of Virginia Law*, 56 VA. L. REV. 1536 (1970); Gibson and Freeman, *Business Associations, The Thirteenth Annual Survey of Virginia Law*, 54 VA. L. REV. 1225, 1235–43 (1968).

The State of Wisconsin recently enacted a local interest statute. *See* WIS. STAT. §§ 552.01 et seq., effective July 1, 1972. The Wisconsin statute was enacted after this treatise went to press and accordingly is not discussed herein.

[5] OHIO REV. CODE ANN. § 1707.041 (Page Supp. 1970). This act took effect on October 9, 1969. For two excellent analyses of the Ohio act, *see* Sommer, *supra* note 4; Shipman, *supra* note 4. *See also The Ohio Takeover Act*, 3 REV. SEC. REG. 896 (July 15, 1970).

[6] OHIO REV. CODE ANN. § 1707.041(A)(1).

[7] NEV. REV. STAT. § 78.376–.3778 (1969). This act took effect on March 4, 1969.

its application in that it applies only to offers for the equity securities of companies incorporated in the state.[8] The Virginia Take-Over Bid Disclosure Act,[9] on the other hand, applies only to offers for equity securities of companies incorporated under the laws of Virginia which do business in the state.[10] Offers which do not contemplate that the offeror will own more than 10 percent of any class of the target's outstanding equity securities upon completion of the offer are not subject to regulation under these statutes.[11] Exemptions from regulation are provided for in each of the statutes as follows:

(a) exchange offers registered pursuant to the Securities Act of 1933 (Nevada); [12]
(b) isolated offers not made to stockholders generally (Nevada and Virginia) and offers made to not more than fifty persons (Ohio); [13]
(c) offers by an issuer to purchase its own shares or shares of a subsidiary of which the issuer owns at least two-thirds of the voting stock (Nevada and Virginia); [14]
(d) offers to purchase shares of a class not registered pursuant to Section 12 of the Securities Exchange Act of 1934 (Nevada and Virginia); [15]
(e) offers to purchase shares by a registered broker-dealer in the ordinary course of its business and neither the principal nor the broker solicits orders to sell shares of the target company (Nevada and Virginia) and bids made by a dealer for its own account in the ordinary course of its business (Ohio); [16]

[8] NEV. REV. STAT. § 78.3765.

[9] VA. CODE ANN. §§ 13.1–528 to –541 (Supp. 1970). This act took effect on March 5, 1968, approximately four months prior to the passage of the Williams Act. For a good discussion of the Virginia statute prior to the 1970 amendment of that statute and the justification for this form of state regulation, *see* Gibson and Freeman, *supra* note 4. *See also* Freeman, *supra* note 4; Statutory Comments, *Take-Over Bids in Virginia*, 26 WASH. & LEE L. REV. 323 (1969).

[10] VA. CODE ANN. § 13.1–529(e).

[11] NEV. REV. STAT. § 78.377(1); OHIO REV. CODE ANN. § 1707.041(A)(1); VA. CODE ANN. § 13.1–529(i).

[12] NEV. REV. STAT. § 78.377(2)(b).

[13] NEV. REV. STAT. § 78.377(2)(a); VA. CODE ANN § 13.1–529(b)(i).

[14] NEV. REV. STAT. § 78.377(2)(c); VA. CODE ANN. § 13.1–529(b)(ii).

[15] NEV. REV. STAT. § 78.377(2)(e); VA. CODE ANN. § 13.1–529(b)(iv).

[16] NEV. REV. STAT. § 78.377(2)(d); VA. CODE ANN. § 13.1–529(b)(iii); OHIO REV. CODE ANN. § 1707.04(A)(1)(A).

(f) offers to which the target company's board of directors consents, if the board has recommended acceptance to shareholders and the terms of the offer have been furnished to shareholders (Ohio) and offers which the target company's board recommends to shareholders if at least two-thirds of such shareholders consent after a solicitation of proxies pursuant to Section 14 of the Securities & Exchange Act of 1934 (Virginia); [17]

(g) offers which by administrative rule, regulation or order are exempted as not entered into for the purpose of effecting, changing or influencing the control of the target company, or otherwise not comprehended within the purposes of the statute (Virginia and Ohio); [18]

(h) exchange offers not involving any public offering within the meaning of Section 4 of the Securities Act of 1933 (Ohio); [19]

(i) offers where the offeror or the target company is a public utility or a public utility holding company, or a bank or bank holding company, or a savings and loan holding company and the bid is subject to approval by the appropriate federal agency (Ohio); [20] and

(j) offers where the offeror and the target company are banks and the offer is part of a merger transaction subject to approval by appropriate federal supervisory authorities.[21]

Purportedly, any tender offers (other than the above exempted offers) to purchase equity securities of any corporation within the scope of the Ohio, Virginia, and Nevada statutes, even those made exclusively outside the state and to nonresidents, are subject to the requirements of the acts.[22] In this sense, these statutes

[17] OHIO REV. CODE ANN. § 1707.041(A)(1)(D); VA. CODE ANN. § 13.1–529(b)(v).

[18] VA. CODE ANN. § 13.1–529(b)(vi); OHIO REV. CODE ANN. § 1707.041(F)(2).

[19] OHIO REV. CODE ANN. § 1707.041(A)(1)(B).

[20] OHIO REV. CODE ANN. § 1707.041(H)(1),(2),(3).

[21] OHIO REV. CODE ANN. § 1707.041(H)(4).

[22] The Ohio act prohibits exclusively out-of-state offers for equity securities of an Ohio corporation. *See* OHIO REV. CODE ANN. § 1707.041(C).

The Ohio act also requires that tender offers for equity securities of an Ohio corporation be made to Ohio shareholders on the same terms as such offer is made to nonresident shareholders. *See* OHIO REV. CODE ANN. § 1707.041(C). This particular provision, however, appears to have little practical significance as tender offerors have not been known to vary the terms of their offers based upon

are perhaps the boldest attempts by any states to give extraterritorial effect to their securities laws and would appear to raise serious questions as to their constitutionality.[23]

It is obvious, however, that if the traditional blue-sky approach had been followed, the effect of state regulation, as a practical matter, would have been minimal. If the state were to regulate all tender offers to its residents for their stock in all corporations wherever located, offerors could simply avoid soliciting in those states. Shareholders in those states who wished to take advantage of an attractive offer, however, could sell their shares in the open market where the price of the target's shares will normally be trading at only a fraction less than the consideration offered by the tender bid.[24] Since the differential, albeit small, between the

---

the residency of shareholders. *But see* Sparton Corp. v. Ward, No. 243,230 (C. P. Ct., Franklin County, Ohio, Jan. 8, 1971); Sparton Corp. v. Ward, No. 71–8 (Ct. App., Franklin County, Ohio, Jan. 12, 1971), discussed in text accompanying notes 39–43, *infra*.

[23] "Although the criteria for determining the validity of state statutes affecting interstate commerce have been variously stated, the general rule that emerges can be phrased as follows: Where the statute regulates even-handedly to effectuate a legitimate local public interest, and its effects on interstate commerce are only incidental, it will be upheld unless the burden imposed on such commerce is clearly excessive in relation to the putative local benefits. Huron Cement Co. v. Detroit, 362 U.S. 440, 443 (1960). If a legitimate local purpose is found, then the question becomes one of degree. And the extent of the burden that will be tolerated will of course depend on the nature of the local interest involved, and on whether it can be promoted as well with a lesser impact on interstate activities." Pike v. Bruce Church Inc., 397 U.S. 137, 142 (1970).

"For the [Supreme] Court has viewed with particular suspicion state statutes requiring business operations to be performed in the home State which could more efficiently be performed elsewhere. Even where the State is pursuing a clearly legitimate local interest, this particular burden on commerce has been declared to be virtually *per se* illegal." *Id.* at 145.

Cf. Shipman, *supra* note 4, at 740–55, for a very thorough analysis of the constitutional issues raised by the Ohio Act and the view that the statute should withstand constitutional challenge. *See also* Statutory Comments, *Take-Over Bids in Virginia, supra* note 9.

[24] The extent of the market price discount will be influenced primarily by the contingencies affecting the offeror's commitment to purchase the tendered shares. However, where there is some expectation that the offeror will increase the consideration or that a competing tender will be made or simply a revised market evaluation of the worth of the target's shares, the market price of the target's shares may exceed that of the existing offer.

Where the market price of the target's shares is substantially less than the consideration offered by the tender, the local shareholder might attempt to tender his shares through an out-of-state broker, using an out-of-state address. Brokers that knowingly violated the law, however, would be subject to revocation of their

market price and the tender price will offer the open-market purchaser (generally a professional arbitrageur) [25] an opportunity for a trading profit, the shares would inevitably find their way to the tender offeror.[26] Thus, the only accomplishment of state regulation would have been to deny local shareholders the full premium price.[27]

Nevertheless, the extraterritorial impact of the state takeover statutes cannot be justified on the ground that the traditional blue-sky approach would be ineffective. Instead, the issue must be framed in terms of whether the local benefits which are derived from regulation of securities transactions that take place outside the state between nonresident investors justify the burdens imposed on interstate commerce by this type of regulation.[28] Phrased in these terms, it is difficult to see how the statutes can withstand constitutional challenge. If the purpose of state takeover regulation is found to be the prevention of relocation of local industry, the statutes may be held to be "virtually *per se* illegal." [29] If the benefit sought is the protection of all shareholders of local corporations, the burden on interstate commerce would still appear to be excessive, particularly in view of the protections afforded investors by the extensive federal tender rules.

B. Disclosure and Waiting Period Requirements

Both the Ohio and Virginia acts impose detailed disclosure requirements on the offeror which go substantially beyond the re-

---

broker-dealer licenses in those states as well as civil and criminal liabilities. *See, e.g.*, Va. Code Ann. § 13.1–506, § 13.1–519, § 13.1–520, § 13.1–521, § 13.1–522, § 13.1–535, § 13.1–536, § 13.1–537, § 13.1–539. Acceptance of shares tendered by a stockholder residing in a state where the offer could not lawfully be made would also subject the offeror to civil and criminal liabilities. *See, e.g.*, Va. Code Ann. § 13.1–535, § 13.1–536, § 13.1–537, § 13.1–539.

[25] See Chapter 6, *infra*, "The Role of Professional Risk Arbitrageurs in Tender Offers."

[26] Rule 10b–13 (17 C.F.R. § 240.10b–13), promulgated pursuant to the Securities Exchange Act of 1934, prohibits the offeror from making open-market purchases during the course of the tender offer. For a more detailed discussion of Rule 10b–13, see Chapter 4, Section 2(B).

[27] In addition to the spread between the market price and the tender price, the sale of shares in the open market will require payment of brokerage commissions and possibly transfer taxes, further reducing the net proceeds of sale. Brokerage commissions and transfer taxes, if any, are normally borne by the offeror when shares are disposed of pursuant to a tender offer.

[28] *See* Pike v. Bruce Church Inc., *supra* note 23.

[29] *Id.* at 145.

quirements of Schedule 13D of the Williams Act and require such information to be filed with the state regulatory authorities and transmitted to the target company not less than twenty days prior to the effective date of the offer.[30] The extent of these disclosures is substantially equivalent to the combined information of Schedule 13D[31] of the Williams Act and registration form S-1[32] promulgated pursuant to the Securities Act of 1933. Thus, in line with the S-1 requirements, the offeror is required to disclose complete information on its organization and operations, including, among other items, financial statements for the current period and for the three most recent annual accounting periods, a brief description of the location and general character of its principal physical properties, a description of all but routine litigation, a brief description of the general business development of the offeror and its subsidiaries during the past five years (as well as projected future developments), and biographical summaries of all directors and officers together with disclosure of any material interest of any director or officer in any material transaction during the preceding three years or in any proposed material transaction to which the offeror or any of its subsidiaries was or is to be a party.[33] While the Ohio statute does not require the information filed with the Ohio Division of Securities and the target company to be transmitted to security holders, it does compel the offeror to make a public announcement of the terms of the proposed offer at least twenty days prior to the date of the offer. On the other hand, the Virginia statute provides that where a take-over bid is sent by mail to offerees, it must be accompanied by a copy of the statement filed with the State Corporation Commission.[34]

[30] OHIO REV. CODE ANN. § 1707.041(B)(1), (3); VA. CODE ANN. § 13.1–531(a), (b). The Virginia statute also provides that all written solicitation material used by the offeror in connection with the bid must be filed with the State Corporation Commission and the target company not less than ten days prior to publication. *Id.* § 13.1–531(c). Once a tender offer has been properly made, any written solicitations or recommendations to shareholders to accept or reject a tender offer for a Virginia corporation must be filed with the State Corporation Commission not later than the first publication date. *Id.* § 13.1–532.

[31] 17 C.F.R. § 240.13d–101. [32] 17 C.F.R. § 239.11.

[33] OHIO REV. CODE ANN. § 1707.041(B)(3)(g); VA. CODE ANN. § 13.1–531(b)(vii). Query, whether such information is truly material in a cash tender offer?

[34] OHIO REV. CODE ANN. § 1707.041(B)(1). The Ohio act goes even further in constructing roadblocks in the path of the offeror. § 1707.041(B)(2) of that act provides as follows:

In addition to the requirement that the offeror file a detailed disclosure statement with the state and the target company not less than twenty days prior to the effective date of the offer, both statutes contemplate the possibility of additional delay to give the regulatory authorities, upon their own initiative or at the request of the target company, an opportunity to hold hearings to determine whether adequate disclosure has been made and whether any violations of the acts have occurred.[35]

The disclosure provisions of the Nevada act closely parallel Schedule 13D. Nevada accordingly does not require, as do Ohio and Virginia, detailed information on the organization and operations of the offeror. In addition, the Nevada statute contains no provision for hearings regarding the proposed offer, and the required information need only be filed with the resident agent of the target company at least *ten* days prior to the effective date of the offer.[36]

"No offeror shall make a take-over bid if he owns five per cent or more of the issued and outstanding equity securities of any class of the target company, any of which were purchased within one year before the proposed take-over bid, and the offeror, before making any such purchase, or before the thirtieth day following the effective date of this section, whichever is later, failed to publicly announce his intention to gain control of the target company, or otherwise failed to make fair, full, and effective disclosure of such intention to the persons from whom he acquired such securities."

Thus, quite unlike the federal statute, which only requires disclosure of a potential offeror's intention to acquire control once it has obtained more than 5 per cent of the target's stock, the Ohio act may require a public announcement of the offeror's intention (if in fact its intention is to obtain control) up to a year prior to its acquisition of 5 per cent or more of the target's stock. The offeror, however, may avoid such disclosure by not accumulating 5 per cent or more of the target's stock prior to the offer. For a critical analysis of this particular provision, *see* Sommer, *supra* note 4, at 711–14.

VA. CODE ANN. § 13.1–530(e).

[35] OHIO REV. CODE ANN. § 1707.041(B)(1), (4); VA. CODE ANN. § 13.1–531(a).

[36] NEV. REV. STAT. § 78.3771(1). The Nevada statute also requires that any written solicitations or recommendations to shareholders must be filed with the target company not later than the time copies of such solicitations or recommendations are first published or transmitted to shareholders. *Id.* §§ 78.3771(2), 78.3773.

In addition, the Nevada statute contains a provision similar to § 14(f) of the 1934 Act, 15 U.S.C. § 78n(f), and providing in substance that if a majority of the directors of the target company are to be replaced without a meeting of stockholders, pursuant to an arrangement with the offeror, then, before the new directors take office, the offeror must furnish the target company and its shareholders with information substantially equivalent to that which would be required by Sections 14(a) or 14(c) of the 1934 Act if the new directors were being elected at a meeting of shareholders. NEV. REV. STAT. § 78.3771(3). The Virginia statute

The waiting period requirement, which has no counterpart in the federal statute, effectively eliminates one of the major advantages of the tender offer technique—that of surprise. In addition, the waiting period requirement has also drawn criticism as increasing the probability of disruptive and irregular price movements.[37] The Ohio disclosure provision requiring the offeror to make a public announcement of the proposed terms of the offer at least twenty days before the effective date may also conflict with the federal rules relating to publicity given to exchange offers prior to the effective date of the registration statement.[38]

To date, there has been only one reported instance of an offeror commencing a tender offer prior to the expiration of the waiting period. In that case, a New York corporation made an offer outside Ohio for securities of an Ohio corporation prior to the expiration of the twenty-day waiting period. The offer provided that it would not become effective as to Ohio residents until the expiration of the waiting period.[39] The target company

---

contains a similar provision, but requires the relevant information to be furnished to the State Corporation Commission rather than to the target company. VA. CODE ANN. § 13.1–531(d).

[37] In commenting on the Ohio act, the New York Stock Exchange advised that the impact of the waiting period requirement on market prices might compel the Exchange to stop trading in the target company's stock for the full twenty-day period. *See* Statement by the NYSE on Amend. Sub. S.B. No. 138, File No. 90 (Reg. Sess. 1969), May 9, 1969, reported in 1 BNA SEC. REG. & L. REP. A–11 (June 4, 1969). Conceivably any trading halt might be extended for an additional forty days if a hearing is ordered on the proposed offer.

[38] *See* § 5 of the Securities Act of 1933 and Rules 134, 135, 433, 434A, and 435B promulgated pursuant to the 1933 Act; SEC Securities Act Release No. 4697 (May 28, 1964); Sommer, *supra* note 4, at 699–700. *See also* Chris-Craft Industries Inc. v. Bangor Punta Corp., 426 F.2d 569 (2d Cir. 1970) (*en banc*), *aff'g sub nom.* Chris-Craft Industries, Inc. v. Piper Aircraft Corp., 303 F. Supp. 191 (S.D.N.Y. 1969). *Cf.* SEC v. Bangor Punta Corp., No. 1388–69 (D. D.C. 1969), CCH FED. SEC. L. REP. § 92,428. *See also* Comment, *Preregistration Publicity in an Exchange Offer,* 119 U. PA. L. REV. 174 (1970).

[39] *See* Wall Street Journal, Dec. 16, 1970, at 27, col. 5. The offer provided in relevant part as follows:

"This Offer is not being made to, nor will tenders be accepted from, stockholders residing in Ohio until such time the Offer may be made to residents of Ohio in accordance with the Law of Ohio. Information has been filed with the Ohio Securities Division in compliance with that law. This Offer will become effective as to Ohio residents at 10:00 A.M., Eastern Standard Time, Monday, January 4, 1971, unless delayed by reasons of appropriate action by the Ohio Securities Division, and will remain effective until 5:00 P.M., Eastern Standard Time, Friday, January 15, 1971, unless extended upon notice to the Depositary."

then sued the acting commissioner of the Ohio Division of Securities alleging, *inter alia,* that: (1) the offeror failed to make a public announcement of the terms of the proposed offer and it failed to file copies of the information required by the Ohio statute at least twenty days prior to the commencement of the offer; (2) the offeror failed to make the offer to Ohio residents on the same terms as it made to shareholders residing outside the state; and (3) the acting commissioner had wrongfully failed to enforce the express provisions of the Ohio securities laws.[40] On the basis of these alleged facts, the target company requested that the court issue temporary and permanent restraining orders and injunctions compelling rescission of all illegal tenders and prohibiting the offeror from continuing to accept tenders. The target company also requested that the court take any further action necessary to preclude the offeror from violating Ohio law, including a hearing to determine additional facts.[41]

After a hearing, the Court of Common Pleas of Franklin County, Ohio, found that the tender offer raised substantial questions under the Ohio securities laws. It therefore ordered the defendant (the acting commissioner of the Ohio Division of Securities) to hold hearings on the matter. However, all other relief requested was denied.[42] On appeal, plaintiff's motion for a temporary injunction enjoining further solicitations and compelling rescission of previously tendered shares was granted pending final disposition of the matter.[43] Shortly thereafter, the tender offer was withdrawn. Plaintiff's motion to dismiss the action because of mootness still remains before the Court of Common Pleas. Thus, while the allegations involved in this case have not been fully adjudicated, the effect of the appellate court's decision to grant the form of injunctive relief described above may well be to dampen the enthusiasm of potential offerors to do battle on the waiting period issue.

[40] *See* Complaint, Sparton Corp. v. Ward, No. 243,230 (C.P. Ct., Franklin City, Ohio, Jan. 8, 1971).

[41] *Id.*

[42] Sparton Corp. v. Ward, No. 243,230 (C.P. Ct., Franklin City, Ohio, Jan. 8, 1971).

[43] Sparton Corp. v. Ward, No. 71–8 (Ct. App., Franklin City, Ohio, Jan. 12, 1971).

C. Substantive Provisions

In large measure, the substantive provisions of the state statutes trace the federal legislation, although each of the states has added a few new wrinkles of its own. Section 14(d)(6) of the 1934 Act,[44] which requires the offeror to make pro rata purchases when the shares tendered during the first ten days of the offer exceed the number of shares requested, is incorporated almost verbatim in the Ohio act.[45] The Nevada and Virginia acts contain the same basic provision but delete the ten-day limitation.[46] Each of the statutes also incorporates the substance of Section 14(d)(7) of the 1934 Act [47] which provides that where the terms of the tender offer are changed prior to its expiration by increasing the consideration offered for shares purchased, the offeror must pay the increased consideration for all shares purchased pursuant to the offer, regardless of when tendered or accepted.[48]

The Nevada and Virginia acts also provide that the shareholder may withdraw shares deposited pursuant to a tender offer at any time within twenty-one days from the date of the first invitation to deposit shares.[49] Shareholders are not given this initial extended period of withdrawal by federal statute. Section 14(d)(5) of the 1934 Act limits the withdrawal period to the first seven days of the offer, but also provides an additional withdrawal period after sixty days.[50]

The Nevada and Virginia statutes also require that offers made for shares of Nevada and Virginia corporations must be kept open for acceptance at least twenty-one days and not more than thirty-five days from the date of the first invitation to deposit shares.[51] The federal statute contains no similar provision, but Section 14(d)(6) of the 1934 Act [52] has been interpreted so as to

[44] 15 U.S.C. § 78n(d)(6). [45] Ohio Rev. Code Ann. § 1707.041(C).

[46] Nev. Rev. Stat. § 78.3772(3); Va. Code Ann. § 13–1–530(c).

[47] 15 U.S.C. § 78n(d)(7).

[48] Nev. Rev. Stat. § 78.3772(4); Ohio Rev. Code Ann. § 1707.041(C); Va. Code Ann. § 13.1–530(d).

[49] Nev. Rev. Stat. § 78.3772(2); Va. Code Ann. § 13.1–530(b).

[50] 15 U.S.C. § 78n(d)(5) (1970).

[51] Nev. Rev. Stat. § 78.3772(1); Va. Code Ann. § 13.1–530(a).

[52] 15 U.S.C. § 78n(d)(6) (1970):

"Where any person makes a tender offer, or request or invitation for tenders,

require the offeror to continue its offer for at least ten days if the offer is for less than all the outstanding shares.[53]

The Ohio statute has one provision that is not repeated in either the federal, Virginia, or Nevada laws by requiring that any takeover bid made for an Ohio corporation must be made by an Ohio-licensed securities dealer.[54] Thus, either the offeror must become registered as a dealer or must retain the services of an Ohio-licensed dealer to undertake the offer on its behalf in Ohio.

D. Enforcement and Remedial Provisions

The Virginia statute authorizes the State Corporation Commission to issue injunctions [55] and impose fines,[56] and grants offerees civil remedies in the form of rescission or the equivalent in damages where the offeror fails to comply with the act or makes a materially false or misleading offer.[57] In addition, the Virginia statute specifically provides for criminal penalties for violations of the act.[58] The Nevada statute, which is incorporated as part of the Nevada General Corporation Law rather than as part of the securities law, also provides for civil liabilities [59] and makes violations of the act a criminal offense,[60] but does not grant any administrative enforcement powers. The Ohio takeover statute does not contain any provisions providing for administrative enforcement, civil remedies or criminal penalties, but instead incorporates the compliance and remedial sections of the general

---

for less than all the outstanding equity securities of a class, and where a greater number of securities is deposited pursuant thereto within ten days after copies of the offer or request or invitation are first published or sent or given to security holders than such person is bound or willing to take up and pay for, the securities taken up shall be taken up as nearly as may be pro rata, disregarding fractions, according to the number of securities deposited by each depositor. The provisions of this subsection shall also apply to securities deposited within ten days after notice of an increase in the consideration offered to security holders, as described in paragraph (7), is first published or sent or given to security holders."

[53] Metro-Goldwyn-Mayer, Inc. v. Transamerica Corp., 303 F. Supp. 1354, 1359 (S.D.N.Y. 1969). If an offer is made for all outstanding shares, § 14(d)(6) becomes inoperative and the offeror is not required to continue the bid for any minimum period of time.

[54] Ohio Rev. Code Ann. § 1707.041(C). See also text accompanying notes 64–71 *infra.*

[55] Va. Code Ann. § 13.1–535. [56] *Id.* § 13.1–537. [57] *Id.* § 13.1–539.

[58] *Id.* § 13.1–536. [59] Nev. Rev. Stat. § 78.3774. [60] *Id.* § 78.3778.

blue-sky law by reference.[61] Both the Nevada and Virginia statutes contain long-arm provisions,[62] while the Ohio act does not require the offeror to consent to service of process.[63]

SECTION 2. *STATUTES REGULATING TENDER OFFERORS AS DEALERS IN SECURITIES*

At least two states—Ohio by specific statutory provision and Pennsylvania by administrative interpretation—presently regulate tender offerors as dealers in securities or, alternatively, require state-licensed securities dealers to make the bid on behalf of the offeror.[64]

Section 1707.041(C) of the Ohio statute provides in relevant part that "[n]o takeover bid shall be made [for an Ohio corporation] unless division (B) of Section 1707.14 of the Revised Code has been complied with." Section 1707.14(B) of the Ohio Revised Code provides in part that "[n]o person shall . . . engage in the business of buying, selling, or dealing in securities otherwise than in transactions through or with a licensed dealer, unless such person is licensed as a dealer by the division."

Pursuant to an interpretative release by the Pennsylvania Securities Commission,[65] a corporation making a cash or exchange tender offer in Pennsylvania to stockholders of another corpora-

[61] *But see* Sommer, *supra* note 4, at 718–19, questioning whether the general liability and penalty provisions of the Ohio securities law are validly incorporated within the takover statute. OHIO REV. CODE ANN. § 1707.041(E) provides that "[a]n offeror is subject to the liabilities and penalties applicable to a seller, and an offeree is entitled to the remedies applicable to a purchaser, as set forth in §§ 1707.041–1707.44, inclusive, of the Revised Code." The reference to § 1707–041 is a misprint in the official version of the statute. The reference should be to § 1707.41. *See* Sommer, *supra* note 4, at 718.

[62] NEV. REV. STAT. § 78.3775; VA. CODE ANN. § 13.1–540.

[63] An exchange offeror, however, may be required to file a consent to service of process to cover possible actions for fraud committed in connection with the sale of securities in Ohio. *See* OHIO REV. CODE ANN. § 1707.11.

[64] Proposed revisions of the Pa. Securities Act presently being considered by the state legislature include a provision specifically exempting tender offerors as dealers in securities.

[65] *See* Pennsylvania Securities Commission Bulletin, *Warnings on Corporate Takeovers, Mutual Fund Registrations,* June 1, 1969, CCH BLUE SKY L. REP. ¶ 41,336.

tion is considered a dealer in securities and is required to register as such.[66] The Securities Commission, however, has not required the offeror to register where a Pennsylvania-licensed securities dealer makes the bid on its behalf.[67]

Thus, offerors in both Pennsylvania and Ohio may avoid both the burdens of registration and the delays occasioned by the registration process by providing that the bid will be deemed to be made by the dealer-manager or by soliciting dealers.[68]

While the Pennsylvania and Ohio approach permitting licensed securities dealers to make a bid on behalf of an offeror fairly preserves the legitimate interests of the state in the transaction without unduly burdening the offeror, it also serves to obscure the more fundamental issue of whether a tender offeror is properly viewed as a dealer in securities. In this connection, it should be noted that neither Pennsylvania nor Ohio gives effect to statutory exceptions to the definitions of the term "dealer" which would appear to exempt tender offerors from regulation as such.

Section 1707.14(B) of the Ohio Revised Code provides an exception from the definition of a "dealer" where the securities are the subject matter of a transaction enumerated in section 1707.03(B) of the code. This section provides in relevant part that:

[66] Section 2(f) of the Pennsylvania Securities Act, 70 PA. STAT. ANN. § 32(f) (Purdon), defines the term dealer to include "any person . . . in the business of buying securities directly from individuals who are not registered hereunder." Section 3 of the Act makes it unlawful for a dealer to engage in the securities business in Pennsylvania unless registered as such. 70 PA. STAT. ANN. § 33 (Purdon). While the interpretative release refers only to tender offers made by a corporation, it is presumably meant to apply to offers made by individuals as well. Section 2(c) of the Act defines the term "person" to mean an individual or a company. 70 PA. STAT. ANN. § 32(c) (Purdon).

[67] Presumably the bidder is not considered to be buying shares "directly" from individuals. See the definition of the term "dealer" in note 66 *supra*. Query whether an unregistered offeror may lawfully accept shares tendered directly by shareholders who do not choose to use the facilities of a securities dealer? Query whether shareholders may be personally solicited by an unregistered offeror?

[68] Normally, the offeror will provide in the invitation for tenders that the bid will be deemed to be made by the dealer-manager or by soliciting dealers "in any states which require tender offers to be made by licensed dealers." This language is used as an attempt to avoid any inadvertent violations in states which broadly define the term "dealer" and have not expressed opinions as to the necessity of dealer registration by tender offers.

> A sale of securities made by or on behalf of a bona fide owner, neither the issuer nor a dealer, is exempt, if such sale is made in good faith and not for the purpose of avoiding Sections 1707.01 to 1707.45, inclusive, of the Revised Code, and is not made in the course of repeated and successive transactions of a similar character.[69]

Since the phrase "repeated and successive transactions" apparently refers to the seller of the securities, it is questionable whether the legislative intent of the Ohio statute has been properly effectuated.

Section 2(f) of the Pennsylvania Securities Act contains a very similar provision which also appears to exempt tender offerors from the definition of "dealer." This section provides:

> None of the following transactions shall constitute the person engaging therein a "dealer" within the meaning of this act, that is to say:
>
> * * * *
>
> (3) Isolated transactions in which securities are sold by the owner thereof or by his agent for the owner's account, such sales not being made in the course of repeated and successive transactions of a like character by such owner, or on his account by such agent, and such owner or agent not being the underwriter of such securities.[70]

It would therefore appear that regulation of tender offerors as dealers in both Ohio and Pennsylvania may be invalid until the legislatures enact specific statutory provisions requiring tender offers to be made by licensed securities dealers. Such regulation is likely to go unchallenged, however, since most tender offerors choose to employ the services of soliciting dealers and others can be expected to do so rather than possibly risk their offer on an adverse ruling.[71]

[69] OHIO REV. CODE ANN. § 1707.03(B).

[70] 70 PA. STAT. ANN. § 32(f) (Purdon).

[71] Prior to the passage of the Ohio takeover statute, the Ohio Division of Securities interpreted § 1701.14 of the Ohio Revised Code to require a tender offer in that state to be made by an Ohio-licensed securities dealer. The issue was raised in connection with a tender offer made in Ohio for an Ohio target company. The Division ordered the offeror to discontinue its bid until the services of an Ohio dealer were employed. The offeror subsequently engaged Ohio dealers and recommenced its offer. *See* Order, Ohio Division of Securities, May 15, 1967, reported in Sommer, *supra* note 4, at 683.

An unreported decision of the Federal District Court for the Southern District of Ohio denying a motion for a preliminary injunction to enjoin a tender offer by Condec Corp. for shares of Lunkenheimer Co. described the Ohio Division of Se-

SECTION 3. *STATUTES REGULATING EXCHANGE OFFERS*

A number of states which have not enacted any new legislation regulating tender offers have nevertheless been able to regulate exchange tender offers pursuant to their general blue-sky registration provisions. These states empower their blue-sky commissioners to deny registration to any offering of securities which would be unfair or inequitable or which would work or operate as a fraud upon purchasers.[72] Statutes of this nature go substantially beyond the protection afforded by the disclosure provisions of federal law and in effect require an independent determination by the state as to the investment merit of the securities being offered.

In a bitterly contested takeover attempt, the State of Wisconsin denied the application of General Host Corporation for registration of its subordinated debentures and warrants which were to be issued in exchange for common stock and debentures of Armour & Co., when the state found that the exchange offer would be unfair and inequitable to Armour stockholders.[73] The Wisconsin Securities Commissioner based his decision upon calculations made by his office which indicated that the cash flow of General Host would be insufficient to cover the interest requirements on

---

curities position with regard to the registration of tender offerors as dealers as a "'one shot' Ohio administrative ex post facto interpretation." *See* Layritz v. Condec Corp., Civil No. 6439 (S.D. Ohio W. Div., 1967), noted in Sommer, *supra* note 4, at 683.

[72] *E.g.*, CAL. CORP. CODE § 25143 (West. Supp. 1971); ILL. REV. STAT. ch. 121½, § 137.11(B) (1969); KY. REV. STAT. § 292.390 (1962); WIS. STAT. § 551.28 (1967).

[73] Release of Wisconsin Office of Commissioner of Securities, Feb. 10, 1969, CCH BLUE SKY L. REP. ¶ 70,805. The New York Stock Exchange refused to list the debentures of General Host because its earnings appeared insufficient to cover interest charges on the debentures. *See* Wall Street Journal, April 18, 1969, at 3, col. 1. *See also* Monthly Bulletin, August 1967, Wisconsin Office of the Commissioner of Securities, describing the reasons for an order prohibiting Ling-Temco-Vought from making any further solicitations in Wisconsin in connection with an exchange offer which would normally have been exempt from registration, CCH BLUE SKY L. REP. ¶ 52,688. *See also* Wall Street Journal, Feb. 7, 1969, at 14, col. 2; Feb. 11, 1969, at 3, col. 2.

the outstanding debentures if the offer was successful.[74] The commissioner also found that the amount of outstanding debentures and warrants would be unreasonably large in proportion to other classes of General Host securities if the exchange offer was successful.[75]

Section 4. *STATUTES REGULATING TENDER OFFERS FOR INSURANCE COMPANIES*

State regulation of tender offers for insurance companies may have been encouraged by the failure of the original federal tender legislation to cover acquisitions of or offers for securities of insurance companies which were not registered pursuant to §12 of the 1934 Act.[76]

The state statutes [77] generally require an offeror for voting se-

[74] While the Wisconsin order prohibited General Host from making its offer in that state, Wisconsin shareholders or debenture holders were free to tender their Armour securities on an unsolicited basis. Release of Wisconsin Office of Commissioner of Securities, *supra* note 73.

[75] *See also In the Matter of* the Proposed Exchange Offer by Northwest Industries, Inc. of Certain Debentures, Preferred Stock and Warrants to Holders of Shares of Common Stock of the B. F. Goodrich Co., File No. 24040 (Ohio Dep't of Commerce, Div. of Sec., May 1, 1969), CCH Blue Sky L. Rep. ¶ 70,816. The Division of Securities issued a show cause order regarding a proposed denial of Northwest Industries' application to register warrants in connection with its attempted takeover of Goodrich. The Division found that it could not accurately evaluate the proposed offer because of a number of contingencies relating to the transaction and another exchange offer in which Northwest was then engaged. The Ohio statute requires a determination that the proposed offer will not be on grossly unfair terms and will not defraud purchasers before the Division can approve registration.

[76] 1970 amendments to the Williams Act extended the scope of the tender rules to include equity securities of an insurance company which would have been required to be registered under § 12, except for the exemption contained in § 12(g)(2)(G), 15 U.S.C. § 78 1(g)(2)(G) (1970).

Prior to the passage of the 1970 amendments, the Indiana legislature enacted extensive legislation regulating tender offers for domestic insurance companies and insurance holding companies which controlled one or more domestic insurers. This legislation was repealed in 1971. *See* Ind. Stat. Ann. §§ 39–3735, 3736 [Acts of 1969, ch. 214, §§ 2, 3, p. 786] (Burns Supp. 1970) (eff. March 13, 1969), repealed by Acts 1971, P.L. 387, § 2 (Burns Supp. 1971).

[77] *See, e.g.,* Conn. Gen. Stat. Ann. §§ 38–39b–e (Supp. 1971) (eff. June 11, 1969); Md. Ann. Code art. 48A, § 494 (Supp. 1971) (eff. July 1, 1969); N.H. Rev. Stat. Ann. § 401–B: 3 (Supp. 1971) (eff. Aug. 7, 1971), superseding N.H. Rev. Stat. Ann. § 401–A (Supp. 1970) (eff. June 30, 1969); 40 Pa. Stat. Ann. § 459.6 (Purdon) (eff. Nov. 25, 1968). *See also* 40 Pa. Stat. Ann. § 459.5

curities of a domestic insurance company (or an insurance holding company which controls a domestic insurer) to disclose all pertinent information regarding the offer to the state insurance commissioner and the target company, where the offeror will own in excess of a specified percentage of the voting securities or will be in control of such insurance company [78] upon completion of the offer.

In most instances, the statements which must be submitted to both the insurance commissioner and the target company are quite extensive and compel the offeror to disclose substantially the same information required by Schedule 13D of the Williams Act and/or registration form S-1 promulgated pursuant to the Securities Act of 1933.[79] Exemptions from regulation are provided for certain types of offers, including those which are undertaken for a purpose or having an effect other than to change or influence control.[80]

Unlike the federal rules which permit the offeror to make his bid once he has complied with the filing and disclosure requirements of the statute, the states prohibit the offeror from proceeding with his plan until approval has been granted by the state insurance commissioner. The offeror can expect substantial delays

---

(Purdon); WIS. STAT. ANN. § 617.12 (West's Special Pamphlet 1970) (eff. Feb. 25, 1970); CAL. ANN. CODE (Ins. Code) § 1215.2 (West's Supp. 1971) (added by Stats. 1969, c. 1275, p. 2487, § 1). *See also* N.Y. INS. LAW § 69–f (McKinney Supp. 1970) (eff. Sept. 1, 1969) ("No person, other than an authorized insurer, shall acquire control of any domestic insurer, . . . except (1) after 20 days' written notice to the insurer, . . . of its intention to acquire control, and (2) with the prior written approval of the superintendent.").

[78] *E.g.*, in Conn. and Pa. the requisite percentage is 10 per cent. *See* CONN. GEN. STAT. ANN. § 38–39b (a); 40 PA. STAT. ANN. § 459.6(b) (Purdon). In New Hampshire and Maryland control is presumed where the offeror will own, respectively, 10 per cent and 15 per cent or more of the target's stock. *See* N.H. REV. STAT. ANN. §§ 401–B: 1(III), 401–B: 3(I); MD. ANN. CODE art. 48A, §§ 492(c); 494(a). *See also* CAL. ANN. CODE (Ins. Code) §§ 1215(b), 1215.2(a) (control presumed upon ownership of more than 10 percent of the voting securities). The repealed Indiana statute applied only to offers whereby the offeror would own in excess of 40 percent of the target's stock. *See* note 76, *supra*.

[79] *See, e.g.*, N.H. REV. STAT. ANN. § 401–B: 3(II); CAL. ANN. CODE (Ins. Code) § 1215.2(a); 40 PA. STAT. ANN. § 459.6(c) (Purdon); CONN. GEN. STAT. ANN. § 38–39b(b). *See also* CAL. INS. CODE § 1215.2(c), permitting the filing of a Schedule 13D statement or an S-1 registration statement in lieu of the statutory filing requirement. Cf. CONN. GEN. STAT. ANN. § 38–39c.

[80] *See, e.g.*, 40 PA. STAT. ANN. § 459.6(1) (Purdon); N.H. REV. STAT. ANN. § 401–B: 3; CONN. GEN. STAT. ANN. § 38–39e.

in receiving approval,[81] particularly if the bid is contested by the target company, and must be prepared to participate in hearings on the proposed plan. The bases upon which an order granting or denying approval will be made are set forth in the statutes and normally go far beyond a simple determination of the fairness of the proposed offer to the shareholders of the target company. The effect of the proposed offer on competition, the intent to continue the prudent transaction of business, the financial stability of the offeror and the target, and the interests of policyholders and creditors as well as shareholders all may be considered before an order will issue.[82]

In an effort to insure that stockholders of insurance companies are fully apprised of all relevant facts regarding the offer, several state statutes require the target to mail copies of all initial filings, amendments, and notices of public hearings to its stockholders within a specified number of days after receipt of such information.[83] These statutes also provide that the expenses incurred by the target in distributing such information must be borne by the offeror, who is required to file an acceptable bond or other deposit in an amount specified by statute or to be determined by the insurance commissioner.[84]

[81] *See, e.g.,* CONN. GEN. STAT. ANN. § 38–39d (a) providing for delays of up to one year just in holding a hearing on the question of whether the commissioner shall grant approval.

[82] *See, e.g.,* CONN. GEN. STAT. ANN. § 38–39d (b); N.H. REV. STAT. ANN. § 401–B: 3(VI); CAL. INS. CODE § 1215.2(d).

State regulatory approval authorizing the offeror to proceed with the tender offer would not preclude the SEC from seeking injunctive relief against either the offeror or the target company for alleged violations of the federal tender rules. The McCarran-Ferguson Act, 15 U.S.C. §§ 1011–15, provides in relevant part that "no act of Congress shall be construed to invalidate, impair, or supersede any law enacted by any State for the purpose of regulating the business of insurance . . . unless such Act specifically relates to the business of insurance. . . ." *Id.* § 1012(b). The 1970 amendments to the Williams Act extended the scope of the tender rules to include tender offers for equity securities of an insurance company which would have been required to be registered under § 12 of the 1934 Act, except for the exemption contained in § 12(g)(2)(G). *See also* SEC v. National Securities, Inc., 393 U.S. 453 (1969), *rev'g* 387 F.2d 25 (9th Cir. 1967) where the Supreme Court held that the McCarran-Ferguson Act did not preclude the SEC from seeking injunctive relief for violations of Rule 10b–5 under the 1934 Act in connection with allegedly fraudulent proxy materials which were used to facilitate a merger previously approved by a state insurance director.

[83] *See, e.g.,* CONN. GEN. STAT. ANN. § 38–39b(a); N.H. REV. STAT. ANN. § 401–B: 3(VII).

[84] *Id.*

SECTION 5. *CONCLUSION*

State regulation of tender offers has once again focused attention on the necessity of developing a truly integrated framework of securities regulation whereby state law will provide a meaningful complement to federal regulation.[85] When viewed in light of the extensive federal regulation of tender offers and the broad anti-fraud provisions found in most state securities statutes, the present forms of state tender offer regulation would appear to fall short of this goal.

Of particular concern to the authors are the state local interest statutes. Thinly disguised as legislation for the protection of investors, these statutes cannot in any practical sense be viewed as anything more than attempts to protect incumbent management and local industry.[86] If the effect of the statutes were limited to securities transactions which take place within the state's borders, such legislation might still be justifiable as a valid exercise of state power. The assumed benefits derived from applying these statutes to transactions outside the state, however, cannot justify the adverse impact which such regulation has upon interstate commerce. The local interest statutes should thus be regarded as a step backward in the orderly development of the securities laws.

[85] For a persuasive article advocating federal preemption of securities regulation under the Securities Act of 1933, *see* Millonzi, *Concurrent Regulation of Interstate Securities Issues: The Need for Congressional Reappraisal,* 49 VA. L. REV. 1483 (1963). *See also* Armstrong, *The Blue Sky Laws,* 44 VA. L. REV. 713 (1958).

The SEC's Special Study of Securities Markets concluded that "There has not been and should not be Federal preemption in the field of securities regulation." *Report of Special Study of Securities Markets,* H.R. Doc. No. 95, 88th Cong., 1st Sess., pt. 4, at 734 (1963).

Section 18 of the Securities Act of 1933, 15 U.S.C. § 77r (1970), provides that "[n]othing in this subchapter shall affect the jurisdiction of the securities commission . . . of any State . . . over any security or any person." Section 28(a) of the Securities Exchange Act of 1934, 15 U.S.C. § 78bb(a) (1970), contains a similar provision but adds a proviso to the effect that preemption was not intended provided that state regulation does not conflict with the statute. The absence of a qualifying clause in the 1933 Act is of no consequence since federal law preempts state regulation only where a conflict between the two exists. *See* U.S. CONST. art. VI, cl. 2.

[86] The Ohio statute makes this conclusion patently obvious by providing an exemption from regulation for offers approved by the target's board of directors. See text accompanying note 17, *supra.*

CHAPTER 6. THE ROLE OF PROFESSIONAL RISK ARBITRAGEURS IN TENDER OFFERS [1]

While federal and state regulation of the securities industry is based essentially upon the principle of full public disclosure to insure the protection of the investing public, there are nevertheless various aspects of the "money game" which are just shadows to even the most sophisticated investors. There is perhaps no form of activity in the securities markets which has been more esoteric than that engaged in by professional risk arbitrageurs. Significantly, the unpublicized and often mysterious nature of their activities has served to obscure the importance of their role in tender offers.[2]

Professional arbitrage activities are conducted primarily by a small and tightly knit group of individuals who are associated with member firms of the New York Stock Exchange. These firms, which include several of the leading investment banking houses on Wall Street, commit substantial amounts of capital to the various forms of risk and riskless arbitrage. In the tender offer context, professional arbitrageurs often make substantial open-market purchases of the target's shares at prices somewhere between the market price of the target's shares prior to the offer and the tender price, for the purpose of subsequently tendering such shares at a profit. The price which arbitrageurs will pay for such shares will be determined primarily by their evaluation of

[1] The authors wish to give special acknowledgment to Robert Rubin, general partner of Goldman Sachs & Co., who has generously contributed his time to offer many helpful and creative suggestions in connection with the preparation of this chapter.

[2] It has been estimated, for example, that over 50 percent of all tenders in cash and exchange offers come from arbitrageurs. *See* O'Boyle, *Changing Tactics in Tender Offers*, 25 BUS. LAW. 863, 866 (Jan. 1970).

the risk that tendered shares will not be accepted. The willingness to assume the risk of nonacceptance coupled with competition among arbitrageurs will have the effect of driving the market price of the target's shares closer to the tender price. Arbitrage activities therefore provide a much-needed element of liquidity to the market place and enable public investors who are unprepared to assume the risks inherent in tendering to dispose of their shares at favorable prices in the open market.

This chapter explores some of the basic mechanics, functions, and regulatory problems of arbitrage activities in tender offers.[3]

SECTION 1. *BACKGROUND*

Arbitrage may be broadly defined as the purchase of property in one market and the simultaneous or near-simultaneous sale of the same property, or its equivalent, in either the same or a different market for the purpose of generating a profit resulting from the differential in price for such property or its equivalent. An arbitrageur in securities is therefore not an investor in the ordinary sense of the word in that he engages in such transactions in an effort to take advantage of price differentials rather than purchasing or selling securities on the basis of fundamental investment values.

In its classical form, arbitrage activities involve essentially riskless transactions. Such activities are said to have originated in the late medieval period when Venetian merchants bought and sold interchangeable currencies. This form of arbitrage activity is still practiced today in the international money markets. The development of organized securities markets and highly sophisticated communications networks led to another popular form of arbitrage activity whereby traders seek to generate profits resulting

[3] The leading treatises on arbitrage are EVANS, ARBITRAGE IN DOMESTIC SECURITIES IN THE UNITED STATES (Parker, 1965); Wyser-Pratte, "Risk Arbitrage," *The Bulletin*, NYU Grad. School of Bus. Admin., Nos. 74–75 (May 1971). *See also* Henry, *Activities of Arbitrageurs in Tender Offers*, 119 U. PA. L. REV. 466 (1971); O'Boyle, *supra* note 2; *Huge Profits Out of Tiny Margins*, BUSINESS WEEK (May 28, 1966) at 114; *A Feast for the Arbitrageurs*, FORTUNE (Feb. 1969), at 165; Williamson, *The ITT-Hartford File, Debacle or Profit Opportunity*, INVESTORS FORUM (July 1972) at 7.

from price differentials which arise in a security traded on more than one exchange or in different markets.

The increasing use and acceptance of convertible securities, particularly in the United States, has led to yet another application of the riskless arbitrage principle in the securities markets. The vast majority of arbitrage transactions in convertible securities involve bonds, preferred stocks, warrants or rights which are convertible or exchangeable into common stocks of the same issuer. Price differentials arising in connection with convertible securities, however, are not as readily identifiable as those which may be found simply by comparing prices of identical securities in various markets. Instead, the arbitrageur is required to compute the value of the convertible security in terms of the security into which it is convertible or exchangeable. Arbitrage in convertibles has been contrasted with arbitrage in identical securities in different markets in that the former does not involve

> . . . a wild scramble of buying X common in New York, then selling it in San Francisco in a matter of moments, like the international arbitrager who buys Shell trading in Amsterdam and sells it in London. Instead, it is chiefly concerned with the buying of a security at one price and the selling of its *equivalent* (security) at a *higher* price, *usually in the same market.*[4]

Two examples will illustrate the basic mechanics and limitations of this form of arbitrage:

(1) A debenture selling at $1,000 is convertible into 50 shares of a common stock selling at $21 per share. By simultaneously purchasing the debenture and selling short 50 shares of the common stock, the arbitrageur could realize a gross profit [5] of $50 per bond. The short sale would subsequently be covered by delivery of the common stock received by converting the debenture into the 50 shares of common stock.

(2) A debenture selling at $1,000 is convertible into 50 shares of a common stock selling at $19 per share. Unlike the first

[4] EVANS, *supra* note 3, at 21.

[5] I.e., before floor brokerage charges, transfer taxes, SEC fees and the cost of borrowed capital. In the case of private investors, brokerage commissions must be considered.

example, the trader will not be able to generate an arbitrage profit by selling the debentures short and going long the common stock because the common stock cannot be converted into the debentures. The opportunity for an arbitrage profit in convertibles therefore derives only from the one-way convertibility of the security which can be converted as compared with the fungibility or two-way convertibility of foreign exchange or of the security which is traded in different markets.

Developments in the late 1930s led to the evolution and application of the classical arbitrage concept to risk transactions, resulting in a distinctly different form of arbitrage activity. During this period, many railroad reorganization plans which were subject to the approval of certain classes of security holders provided for the issuance of new securities in exchange for certain outstanding classes of securities. The risks and uncertainties surrounding the ultimate consummation of the reorganization plans created a differential in price between the outstanding securities and the securities proposed to be issued, the latter being traded on a "when-issued" basis. Arbitrageurs willing to incur the risks would sell the new securities on a "when-issued" basis and purchase the outstanding securities in an attempt to profit on the differential.[6]

The passage of the Public Utility Holding Company Act of 1935, which required a number of public utilities to formulate divestiture plans, fostered similar "arbitrage at risk" activities in the securities of certain utilities and their subsidiaries. Thus, in order to have the opportunity to exploit the price differentials, arbitrageurs were required to assume the risks and uncertainties surrounding the consummation of the divestiture plans.[7]

The evolution and application of the classical arbitrage concept to risk transactions led to the application of the basic principles of arbitrage to cash and exchange tender offers and it is this development to which we now turn.

[6] Wyser-Pratte, *supra* note 3, at 8. [7] *Id.* at 8, 9.

SECTION 2. *ARBITRAGE IN CASH TENDER OFFERS*

Arbitrage in cash tender offers derives primarily from the differentials which arise between open market and tender prices for the target's shares. The arbitrageur thus attempts to purchase the target's shares at the lower open market price for the purpose of tendering such shares at the higher tender offer price. The differentials or spreads between open market and tender prices are caused essentially by the risk that some and perhaps all of the shares tendered will not be accepted.[8] In many instances, the risk of nonacceptance derives from the possibility that the offer will fail and that all shares tendered will be returned to stockholders. The failure of the offer may be caused simply by the fact that the offeror has not received a sufficient number of shares to achieve its objective. In other cases, legal action initiated by the target company, a stockholder or a regulatory authority, may effectively doom the offer. Even where the offer is successful the risk of nonacceptance may still be present if there are tenders in excess of the total number of shares which the offeror seeks to purchase. In such circumstances, the offeror may be required by law or may voluntarily agree to accept tendered shares on a prorated basis.[9] Similarly, if the offeror purchases tendered shares on a first-come, first-served basis, a tenderor may find that none of his shares are accepted where the tender is not made during the first few days of the offering period.

The risk of nonacceptance makes the arbitrageur vulnerable to a potential decline in the market price of the target's shares to a level below that at which the arbitrageur purchased the tendered shares. The arbitrageur is therefore confronted with the possibility that it will be unable to profitably dispose of the unaccepted

[8] Where the risk of nonacceptance appears to be minimal or nonexistent and there is no differential between the market and the tender price, arbitrageurs may still make open market purchases and subsequent tenders of such shares. In some instances, open market purchases may actually be effected at a price in excess of the tender price. The arbitrageur's profit in transactions of this nature is generated from the soliciting dealers fees received for tendered shares. See Section 5 of this chapter.

[9] *See* Section 14(d)(6) of the 1934 Act.

shares once the offer expires. Where the tender premium over market is substantial and the target's shares are generally conceded to be fully priced prior to the offering, a substantial decline in the price of the target's shares immediately upon the termination of the offering represents a very real possibility.

The extent to which the arbitrageur believes that the potential risk of nonacceptance will become reality obviously affects the price he is willing to pay for the target's shares. The greater the risks of uncertainty, the less the arbitrageur will be willing to pay and accordingly the greater the spread which can be expected between market and tender prices. As the offering progresses, the spread will increase or decrease depending upon the expectations of arbitrageurs regarding the likelihood of tendered shares being accepted.

Prior to adoption of Rule 10b–4 under the 1934 Act, arbitrageurs were able to hedge against the risk of nonacceptance resulting from prorated purchases by tendering a greater number of shares than they owned. This practice, known as "short-tendering,"[10] was made possible by virtue of the fact that many tender offers provided that the stock certificates did not have to be physically deposited at the time of tender if a bank or an exchange member guaranteed that if the shares were accepted, delivery of the certificates would be made on demand or at a specified time.[11]

The following example illustrates the potential benefit which accrued through the use of the short-tender technique:

> Assume that a tender offer of $75 per share is made for any and all shares of the target up to 20 percent of the target's outstanding voting shares. Prior to announcement of the tender offer, the target's shares were selling at $60.00. Upon announcement of the tender offer, the price of the target's shares in the open market immediately increased to $69.00.

[10] For a more detailed discussion of Rule 10b-4, see text accompanying notes 158–162, Chapter 4.

[11] Even where the certificates had to accompany the tender, arbitrageurs might still be able to short-tender if they could borrow the securities. This form of short-tendering involves additional risks, however, since the arbitrageur cannot be certain that he will be able profitably to replace the borrowed stock if the tender is accepted.

If the arbitrageur estimated that tenders would exceed the number of shares requested to the extent that only 25 percent of all shares tendered would be accepted, the arbitrageur might purchase 100 (x) shares at $69 per share but tender 400 (x) shares. If the estimate proved correct and only one quarter of all shares tendered were accepted, the arbitrageur could be assured of a gross profit of $6 per share since all shares which he actually owned would be accepted.

In contrast, an investor who purchased the full number of shares actually tendered would have a profit of $6 per share on 25 percent of the shares tendered but would be exposed to the risk of a substantial price decline on the remaining shares which were not accepted. If the open market price of the target's shares immediately dropped to its pre-offer level once the offer expired, the investor would find himself with a loss of $9 per share on 75 percent of all shares which he tendered. The net effect of this transaction would be a $6 per share gain on 25 percent of the shares tendered and a $9 per share loss on the remaining 75 percent of the shares, resulting in a loss of $5.25 on each share tendered.[12]

While the short tender substantially benefited the arbitrageur, the practice had an adverse impact on other tenderors by reducing the number of their shares which were accepted in prorated cash offers. The disproportionately large number of shares which were being accepted from arbitrageurs in relation to the shares tendered by others prompted the SEC to adopt Rule 10b-4, which prohibits short-tendering. The Rule, however, has been criticized by one arbitrageur as working to the detriment of the investing public by creating wider spreads between market and tender prices.[13] Wider spreads are said to result from the fact

[12] Although the short-tender enabled the arbitrageur to hedge against the market, the technique still involved a degree of risk. If the offeror accepted a greater number of shares than the arbitrageur estimated, a "short-squeeze" could develop as traders frantically tried to cover their short positions, thereby driving the price of the target's shares above the tender price. A competing tender offer at a higher price could prove equally disastrous to an arbitrageur who underestimated the number of shares which were accepted. For a graphic description of the effects of an underestimate by arbitrageurs in a tender offer for Columbia Pictures Corp., *see* Wyser-Pratte, *supra* note 3, at 60.

[13] *See* Wyser-Pratte, *supra* note 3, at 61.

that the Rule eliminates the arbitrageur's ability to hedge against a market decline, thereby increasing the risk factor. As the risk increases, the arbitrageur will presumably be compelled to pay less for the target's shares in the open market.

Assuming that spreads have in fact increased, the Rule nevertheless benefits the investing public by increasing the proportion of their tendered shares which are accepted by the offeror. This benefit far outweighs any possible impact which the Rule may have on investors who choose to sell in the open market rather than tender their shares.

SECTION 3. *ARBITRAGE IN EXCHANGE TENDER OFFERS*

Arbitrage in exchange tender offers is based upon the same one-way convertibility principle employed in connection with arbitrage activities in convertible securities. In convertible arbitrage, the arbitrageur will sell short the issuer's common stock and simultaneously purchase a security which is convertible into such common shares, where the proceeds of the short sale will exceed the cost of purchasing the convertible security. The short sale is then "covered" by converting the convertible security into the common shares. In an exchange offer, the arbitrageur purchases the target's shares and, in the simplest case, sells short an equivalent amount of the offeror's securities. The arbitrageur then tenders the target's shares and covers his short position with the securities of the offeror received pursuant to the exchange offer.[14] Thus, the risk of market fluctuations is for all practical purposes avoided. Unlike convertible arbitrage, however, the differentials in exchange offers between the package offered and the target's securities derive essentially from the risk that some and perhaps all of the tendered shares will not be accepted. In this regard, exchange offer arbitrage is similar to that in cash tender offers. If the tendered shares are not accepted, the arbitrageur may sustain losses on the sale of the target's shares once the offer expires. Arbitrageurs also face the added risk that they will be

[14] Where the securities offered are of a newly issued class, arbitrageurs will short these securities on a "when-issued" basis.

unable to cover the short sale of the offeror's shares at a price below that at which the short was effected.

The mechanics of exchange offer arbitrage can perhaps be best illustrated by means of the following example:

> Assume that the offeror will exchange two shares of its common stock for each share of the target's common stock. The offeror's shares are trading in the open market for $50 while the market price of the target's stock is $90.
>
> By shorting 2(x) of the offeror's shares and simultaneously purchasing 1(x) of the target's shares, the arbitrageur is able to lock himself into a gross spread or profit of $10 for each share tendered—provided, of course, that the tendered shares are accepted.

Where the exchange offering includes a newly issued class or classes of securities, the arbitrageur's potential profit is more difficult to calculate. The following example illustrates some of the basic valuation considerations in an exchange offer package which includes two new classes of securities:

> Assume that the offeror, for each share of the target's stock, will exchange:
>
> (i) one share of its presently outstanding common stock;
>
> (ii) one new ten-year warrant to purchase one share of common at $20; and
>
> (iii) $10 principal amount of a new 4 percent, 30-year debenture convertible into 40 shares of common per thousand dollars principal amount (i.e., .4 shares of the offeror's common for each share of the target's common stock).
>
> The offeror's common shares are presently trading at $20 while the market price of the target's common shares, after reacting to the announcement of the offer, is $30.

The valuation of the exchange offer package might be derived as follows:

> (i) one share of the offeror's common stock ($20);
>
> (ii) one ten-year warrant to purchase one share of the offeror's common stock at $20. The market value of warrants gener-

ally depends upon the length of time to maturity of the warrant, its exercise price, the price and volatility of the common stock and the issuer's growth potential. With the common selling at $20, the warrant exercisable at $20 and assuming the growth prospects of the offeror to be mediocre, the warrants might have a market value of 35 percent of the exercise price or $7; and

(iii) $10 principal amount of a 4 percent, 30-year debenture convertible into .4 shares of the offeror's common stock. The value of a nonconvertible debenture will be influenced primarily by the degree of the professional investment community's confidence in the ability of the offeror to pay the interest and redeem the debenture at maturity. The interest rate on the debenture as compared to prevailing interest rates on similar securities of comparable companies will also have an important influence on the debenture's market value. Valuation of a convertible debenture, however, normally begins with a determination of the stock equivalent value of the debenture or, as it is often referred to, the conversion parity. In this example, the conversion parity would be $8 (i.e., .4 shares of the offeror's common X the market price (20) of these shares). A premium over the conversion parity would then be calculated. The determination of the premium is essentially a subjective calculation based upon such factors as the offeror's credit worthiness, the yield, if any, on the offeror's common stock and the growth potential of the offeror.[15] Assuming the offeror's credit standing to be moderately speculative and the future growth prospects of the offeror to be uninspiring, an arbitrageur might assume a premium of 12½ percent which would add $1 to the present value of the debenture (.125 x $8).

The market value of the $10 principal amount of debentures would then be $9.

Based on these assumptions, arbitrageurs could purchase the target's shares at $30 while shorting the offeror's exchange pack-

[15] The conversion feature creates added present value to the debenture since it will enable debenture holders to participate in any future growth of the company.

age at $36. If the tendered shares are accepted, thereby enabling the arbitrageur to cover the short sale with the securities received in the exchange, a $6 gross profit would be assured. However, it must be noted that if the arbitrageur shorted the new debentures and warrants prior to the effective date of the registration statement, such short sales might constitute violations of Section 5 of the 1933 Act.[16] Prior thereto, he may purchase the target's shares and attempt to hedge such purchases by shorting the securities into which the debentures and the warrants are exchangeable, i.e., the offeror's outstanding common stock.

While the offeror can assume a rather extensive degree of sophistication on the part of the professional investment community in valuing its exchange package, it must be emphasized that an offer consisting of securities with intricate conversion or exercise privileges may nevertheless cause confusion and uncertainty with the result that arbitrageurs may be unwilling to risk their capital on the offering. In other instances, uncertainties regarding the fundamental nature and value of the securities being offered may chill investor interest in the offering, in which event the arbitrageur may be unable to participate in the offering due to the absence of purchasers for the securities which the arbitrageur would sell short. In one bitterly contested takeover attempt, involving several competing exchange offers, the failure of what appeared to be the most attractive offer may have been caused by the initial confusion which resulted from the unconventional nature of the security which was offered.[17]

SECTION 4. *EVALUATING THE RISK OF NONACCEPTANCE*

The arbitrageur's evaluation of the risk of nonacceptance becomes one of the most important factors affecting the open-

[16] *See also* discussion in Henry, *supra* note 3, at 474–75.

[17] In the multi-sided battle for control of the United Fruit Co. in 1969, Zapata-Norness Corp. offered a new $2 preferred stock convertible into 1.4 shares of its common stock after 90 days and into $120 worth of common stock after January 31, 1971, provided, however, that the preferred could not be converted into more than 2 common shares after the latter date. *See* Wyser-Pratte, *supra* note 3, at 56, 76–77.

market price of the target's shares during the course of the tender offer, for it is this risk which will ultimately determine the price he is willing to pay for substantial amounts of such shares.[18] In essence, the arbitrageur pits his evaluation of the probability that shares tendered will be accepted against other investors who are confronted with the same basic decision regarding the offer.[19] The professional arbitrageur, however, appears to enjoy one distinct and crucial advantage over the average investor—the expertise to quickly acquire and assess information regarding the major variables which affect the acceptance or nonacceptance of tendered shares. In some instances, such information is obtained through sources which are not available to the average investor.[20]

Some institutional investors, for example, may be willing to reveal their intentions regarding the offer to their prime brokers and other select members of the investment community. Similarly, major brokerage firms with arbitrage departments will be able to get some indication of the public's response to the offer by calculating the acceptance ratio of their own customers.

There are a number of factors which the arbitrageur must consider in evaluating the risks of nonacceptance. As the offer progresses and conditions change, these variables are continually reevaluated, resulting in appropriate adjustments in the price the arbitrageur is willing to pay for the target's shares. The following subsections outline some of the more basic factors which must be considered.

1) Legal and Other External Influences

Legal impediments to the successful consummation of a tender offer can evolve from a variety of sources. In recent years, for example, the potential threat of antitrust action has created considerable uncertainty regarding the status of any number of offers. Uncertainties may also arise where the acquisition is subject to the approval of a federal or state regulatory agency. Stockholders' suits as well as legal and other defensive action by the target it-

[18] Where the offer has little, if any, chance of success, arbitrageurs may avoid the offer completely.

[19] In this respect, arbitrage activities can be viewed essentially as a microcosm of securities trading in general.

[20] *See* Wyser-Pratte, *supra* note 3, at 58–59; Henry, *supra* note 3, at 470.

self will also have an unsettling influence on the ultimate success of the offer. Where the offer involves the issuance of additional shares requiring shareholder approval or is contingent on a favorable tax ruling, additional uncertainties may be presented. The arbitrageur must be quick to evaluate the probable impact of major upheavals in economic or monetary conditions on the offer. Similarly, significant changes in the business or capitalization of either the target or the offeror can be expected to affect the arbitrageur's delicate calculations.

(2) Terms and Conditions of the Offer

The terms and conditions of the offer have a fundamental impact on the risk of nonacceptance and, accordingly, affect the nature and extent of the arbitrageur's activities in connection with the offer. Where the offeror unconditionally agrees to purchase any and all shares tendered, the arbitrage risk is substantially reduced.[21] Assuming there are no apparent regulatory impediments to the offeror acquiring the target's shares, the spread between the market and the tender price will normally be small, with minimal open-market price fluctuations throughout the offering period. Where the risk is minimal, the market price may actually exceed the tender price. In such circumstances the source of the arbitrage profit will be the soliciting dealers' fee received by the arbitrageur for tendered shares. Although the differential will be small, the profits can nevertheless be huge if the volume of shares tendered by the arbitrageur is substantial.

Where the offer provides that the offeror may purchase less than all shares tendered, the arbitrageur's risk increases. In some tender invitations, for example, the offeror's obligation to purchase tendered shares has been conditioned as follows:

> The offeror will purchase a specified number of shares if at least that number of shares are tendered. If the shares tendered do not equal or exceed the number of shares sought, the

[21] It is the rare instance where a tender offer is truly unconditional. Even where the offeror agrees to purchase any and all shares tendered, the tender invitation can be expected to contain an "out" or "escape" clause providing that the offeror may withdraw the bid without any obligation to purchase any shares tendered, if, for example, an adverse change in the business or capitalization of the target should occur or a state of national emergency shall have been declared. See text accompanying note 18, Chapter 3.

offeror will reserve the right to purchase all, a part, or none of the shares tendered. Where the shares tendered exceed the number of shares sought, the offeror will reserve the right to purchase all, a part, or none of such excess shares.

Where the offer is so conditioned, the arbitrageur must make an assumption, based upon a number of variables including the offeror's cash position, lines of credit and the cost of money, that the offeror will accept more or less than the requested number of shares.[22]

The number of shares which the offeror seeks to obtain in relation to the total outstanding shares is another important factor which the arbitrageur will consider in evaluating the risk of nonacceptance. In this regard, it should be noted that the risk of nonacceptance generally can be expected to decrease as the percentage of the outstanding shares which the offeror seeks to obtain increases.

A conditional offer may also require the arbitrageur to consider the actual timing of his tender. The interrelationship of the timing of the tender and the risk of nonacceptance may assume critical importance where the offeror is not required to purchase shares on a prorated basis. With regard to tender offers subject to the Williams Act, Section 14(d)(6) of the 1934 Act provides that when more than the specified number of shares are tendered during the first ten days of the offer, all shares tendered must be accepted on a prorated basis. If less than the requested number are tendered during the first ten days, the offeror, at its option, may purchase tendered shares on a first-come, first-served basis. In many instances, the arbitrageur may prefer to wait until the last days of the offer before tendering to preserve his flexibility should a competing offer be made at a higher price. This may well be an advisable practice where the offer provides that tendered shares will be accepted on a prorated basis. However, where the offeror will purchase shares on a first-come, first-served basis if less than the requested number of shares are tendered during the first ten days of the offer, the arbitrageur may be compelled to tender during the first few days of the offer in order to increase the likelihood that the shares will be accepted.

[22] *See* Wyser-Pratte, *supra* note 3, at 59.

(3) SECURITIES OF THE TARGET HELD BY OTHERS

Any thorough analysis of the risk of nonacceptance where a minimum number of shares must be tendered in order to trigger the offeror's obligation to purchase any shares necessarily requires an evaluation of the probable reaction of other shareholders to the offer. In this regard it is important to bear in mind that while tenders by others will increase the probability of success of the offer, this will also decrease the percentage of tendered shares which will be accepted from each tenderor. Thus, the arbitrageur must attempt to determine the total number of shares which will be tendered in relation to both the total number of shares outstanding and the percentage of the outstanding shares which will be accepted by the offeror.

Initially, the arbitrageur will normally attempt to isolate the number of shares held by each of the following classes of shareholders at the inception of the offer: (a) insiders of the target company; (b) institutional investors; (c) the offeror; (d) other arbitrageurs; and (e) the public. Through his apparently extensive and reliable contacts within the investment community, the arbitrageur is able to obtain a fairly good indication of the total shares which are likely to be tendered pursuant to the offer.[23] With such information as a guideline, the arbitrageur can normally proceed with some confidence in determining the price it will pay for the target's shares in the open market.[24]

SECTION 5. *THE ARBITRAGEUR AS A SOLICITING DEALER*

In an effort to stimulate the solicitation of tenders by brokerage firms, banks, and trust companies, tender offerors generally pay a generous soliciting dealer's fee for shares tendered through such firms and accepted by the offeror. In most instances, soliciting dealers receive a fee per share ranging from 1½ percent to 3 percent of the tender price. Where arbitrage activities are con-

[23] *See* Wyser-Pratte, *supra* note 3, at 58–59.

[24] Some offerors publicly disclose the total number of shares tendered as the offer progresses. Such information enables arbitrageurs to evaluate the accuracy of their own projections.

ducted by a brokerage firm, the receipt of a soliciting dealer's fee for tendered shares becomes an important element in the determination of the price the arbitrageur will be willing to pay for the target's shares. Where the risk of nonacceptance of tendered shares is slight, for example, the compensation derived from the soliciting dealer's fee has enabled arbitrageurs to generate a profit on tenders of shares purchased on the open market at a price in excess of the tender price.

Prior to adoption of SEC Securities Exchange Act Release No. 9395,[25] the Division of Trading and Markets of the SEC viewed purchases of the target's securities during the course of a tender offer by persons who received soliciting dealer's fees for tendering such securities as purchases indirectly made or arranged for by the person making the tender offer.[26] Such purchases were deemed to violate Rule 10b–13 under the 1934 Act,[27] and the soliciting dealer making such purchases was considered to be an aider and abettor. The staff's position applied to purchases made at prices in excess of the tender price as well as to purchases made below the tender price. Purchases and subsequent tenders made in anticipation of receiving the soliciting dealer's fee, but prior to the actual signing of the soliciting dealer's agreement, were also viewed by the staff as violative of Rule 10b–13.

Exchange Act Release No. 9395 represents a clear recognition by the Commission of the public interest value of arbitrage activities in tender offers. This interpretative release provides that open-market purchases of the target securities during the course of a tender offer by arbitrageurs who subsequently tender such shares and receive soliciting dealer's fees for such tenders are not subject to the prohibition of Rule 10b–13 provided that the payment of the soliciting dealer's fees is adequately disclosed.

While arbitrageurs who obtain soliciting dealer's fees in connection with a cash or exchange tender offer will not be deemed to have violated Rule 10b–13, some uncertainty exists with regard to whether the receipt of such fees in connection

[25] Nov. 24, 1971, CCH FED. SEC. L. REP. ¶ 78,417.

[26] 17 CFR 240.10b–13, eff. Nov. 10, 1969.

[27] *See* response of Div. of Trad. and Mkts., SEC, to request for interpretative opinion, MSL Industries, Inc., CCH FED. SEC L. REP. ¶ 78,320 (correspondence in full text) and discussed in 120 BNA SEC. REG. & L. REP. C-1 (Sept. 29, 1971).

with an exchange offer may create liability for arbitrageurs under Rule 10b–6 of the 1934 Act.[28] This Rule prohibits an issuer, underwriter, prospective underwriter, broker, dealer, or any other person who has agreed to participate or is participating in a distribution from bidding for or purchasing any security which is the subject of a distribution. The ostensible purpose of Rule 10b–6 is to prohibit a person engaged in a distribution from inflating the market value of the security to be distributed, since such activity would have the effect of facilitating the distribution of these securities at artificially high prices. In an exchange offer context, the offeror's purchase of its own securities during the course of a distribution of the same securities could have the effect of reducing the number of shares which it would be required to issue pursuant to the offer. Both the Commission and the Second Circuit Court of Appeals have viewed Rule 10b–6 more broadly and have taken the position that the securities to be acquired by the offeror in an exchange offer (i.e., the target's securities) are, in substance, rights to acquire the securities being distributed.[29] Under this interpretation, Rule 10b–6 would prohibit (absent an exemption) outside purchases of the target's securities despite the fact that such purchases might increase rather than decrease the value of such securities, thereby making the offeror's exchange package less attractive.

In connection with arbitrage activities, the issue thus becomes one of whether the receipt of a soliciting dealer's fee makes an arbitrageur a person who has agreed to participate or is participating in a distribution within the meaning of Rule 10b–6. While the interests of arbitrageurs in exchange offers are presumably independent of the interests of offerors and derive only from their desire to generate a trading profit, it must be recognized

[28] 17 C.F.R. § 240.10b–6.

[29] *See* SEC Securities Exchange Act Release No. 8712 (Oct. 8, 1969) CCH FED. SEC. L. REP. ¶ 77,745; SEC Securities Exchange Act Release No. 8595 (May 5, 1969) CCH FED. SEC. L. REP. ¶ 77,706; Chris-Craft Industries, Inc. v. Bangor Punta Corp., 426 F.2d 569 (2d Cir. 1970), *rev'g in part, sub. nom.*, Christ-Craft Industries, Inc. v. Piper Aircraft Corp., 303 F. Supp. 191, 198 (S.D.N.Y. 1969). *Cf.* Armour & Co. v. General Host Corp., 296 F. Supp. 470 (S.D.N.Y. 1969); Lowenfels, *Rule 10b–13, Rule 10b–6 and Purchases of Target Company Securities During an Exchange Offer*, 69 COLUM. L. REV. 1392 (1969). *See also* Chris-Craft Industries, Inc. v. Piper Aircraft Corp., F. Supp. 1128, 1140–43 (S.D.N.Y. 1971).

that the success of the offer is essential to their generating a profit. The arbitrageur, therefore, seeks to promote the ultimate success of the offer. In fact, the very nature of arbitrage activities in an exchange offer serves to accomplish this end. Thus the arbitrageur's objectives and efforts are directed toward the same goal as that of the underwriter or selling syndicate member who actually engages in the distribution of the offeror's securities. Where the arbitrageur receives compensation from the issuer in the form of a soliciting dealer's fee for its efforts in promoting the success of the offer, there can be little basis for claiming that the arbitrageur is not "participating" in the offer. Assuming that one is willing to accept the Commission's and the Second Circuit's paradoxical view that Rule 10b–6 prohibits purchases of the target's securities during an exchange offer, the Rule, standing alone, would appear to bar arbitrageurs from receiving soliciting dealer's fees for tenders of the target's shares in an exchange offer.[30]

It is patently obvious, however, that such an interpretation would be squarely in conflict with Exchange Act Release No. 9395. As stated previously, this Release provides that open-market purchases of the target's securities during the course of a tender offer by arbitrageurs who subsequently tender such shares and receive soliciting dealer's fees for such tenders are not subject to the prohibition of Rule 10b–13 provided that the payment of the soliciting dealer's fees is adequately disclosed. While the Release speaks only in terms of Rule 10b–13, it is highly unlikely that the Commission would announce that it is lawful to engage in certain activities pursuant to one rule while failing to note that it is unlawful to do so under another rule. In this regard, it is also important to note that the Commission's release announcing adoption of Rule 10b–13 described the application of Rule 10b–13 to exchange offers as "essentially a codification of existing interpretations under Rule 10b–6." [31]

[30] Purchases and subsequent tenders made in anticipation of receiving the soliciting dealer's fee, but prior to the actual signing of the soliciting dealer's agreement, would also appear to be violative of Rule 10b–6.

[31] *See* SEC Securities Exchange Act Release No. 8712 (Oct. 8, 1969), CCH FED. SEC. L. REP. ¶ 77,745. As an indication of this assumption, *see* SEC's response to request for interpretative opinion, Henry Heide, Inc., CCH FED. SEC. L. REP. ¶ 78,838 (correspondence in full text available May 31, 1972).

The substance of Exchange Release No. 9395, which recognizes the public interest value of arbitrage activities in tender offers, clearly leads one to the conclusion that neither Rule 10b–13 nor Rule 10b–6 bars the acceptance of soliciting dealer's fees in connection with arbitrage activities in an exchange offer. However, in view of the uncertainty created in some quarters by this Release, it would appear incumbent upon the Commission to make some further public comment on the applicability of Rule 10b–6 to purchases of the target's shares by arbitrageurs who subsequently tender such shares pursuant to an exchange offer and receive soliciting dealer's fees for such tenders.

SECTION 6. *SUMMARY AND OBSERVATIONS OF THE AUTHORS*

If, as it is generally believed, and as the authors have experienced, the activities and participation of professional arbitrageurs can make or break a tender offer, what can the offeror do to encourage this activity so as to insure the success of the offer? The following have been suggested as some of the steps which may be taken to increase the likelihood of substantial participation by arbitrageurs:

1. Offer a good premium.
2. Limit the conditions of the offer.
3. Offer a generous soliciting dealers' fee.
4. Where feasible, disclose from time to time the quantity of tenders received.

The making of a tender offer, particularly where opposition can be anticipated, will prove to be an expensive undertaking.[32] It is therefore in the offeror's interest to take such steps as will enhance the chances of success. In taking the necessary steps to insure success, the prospective offeror must not overlook the significant role of the arbitrageur. In this regard, it is essential that the offeror carefully evaluate the variables which will encourage the arbitrageur's participation.

[32] See Section 1 of Chapter 2.

CHAPTER 7. THE TENDER OFFEROR AS AN INADVERTENT INVESTMENT COMPANY

Where the offeror neither seeks nor obtains a majority of the target's outstanding voting shares but nevertheless intends to retain the shares which were tendered, it should first determine whether retention of the shares will require it to register as an investment company pursuant to the provisions of the Investment Company Act of 1940 (hereinafter referred to in this chapter as "Act").[1] If registration is in fact required, the offeror that intends

[1] 15 U.S.C. § 80a–1 et seq.

Section 7 of the Act prohibits, *inter alia,* any investment company (other than an exempt company or transactions by an investment company incidental to its dissolution) from engaging in any business activity in interstate commerce unless registered under Section 8 of the Act. The Commission's remedies for violations of Section 7, as well as other provisions of the Act, are substantial. Section 42(e), authorizing the Commission to institute actions in any federal district court to enjoin violations of and enforce compliance with the Act, provides, in part, as follows:

"In any proceeding under this subsection to enforce compliance with Section 7, the court as a court of equity may, to the extent it deems necessary or appropriate, take exclusive jurisdiction and possession of the investment company or companies involved and the books, records, and assets thereof, wherever located; and the court shall have jurisdiction to appoint a trustee, who with the approval of the court shall have power to dispose of any or all of such assets, subject to such terms and conditions as the court may prescribe."

For cases involving alleged violations of Section 7 in proceedings pursuant to Section 42(e), *see* SEC v. S&P National Corp., 360 F.2d 741 (2d Cir. 1966), *aff'g* 265 F. Supp. 993 (S.D.N.Y. 1966). *For subsequent proceedings see* 267 F. Supp. 562 (S.D.N.Y. 1967), 273 F. Supp. 863 (S.D.N.Y. 1967), 285 F. Supp. 415 (S.D.N.Y. 1968); SEC v. Fifth Ave. Coach Lines, Inc., 289 F. Supp. 3 (S.D.N.Y. 1969), *aff'd* 435 F.2d 510 (2d Cir. 1970), *supp. opinion* 308 F. Supp. 947 (S.D.N.Y. 1970); SEC v. Townsend Corp of America, Civ. No. 336–61 (D.N.J. 1961). *See also In the Matter of* Townsend Corp. of America & Townsend Management Company, No. 4045 (Investment Company Act Release, Sept. 2, 1964), CCH FED. SEC. L. REP. ¶ 77,120. For a very thorough comparative analysis of

to continue actively to pursue its noninvestment activities will normally find that the sale of the target's stock will be preferable to the burdens of regulation under the Act. As a practical matter, if the offeror is a typical industrial corporation, it may be compelled to sell the target's shares because it will be unable to conform either its method of doing business or its capital structure to the requirements of the Act.[2]

---

these cases, *see* Kerr and Appelbaum, *Inadvertent Investment Companies—Ten Years After*, 25 Bus. Law 887, 889–905 (1970).

Section 42(e) also authorizes the Commission to refer alleged violations of the Act to the Justice Department for criminal prosecution. *See* Section 49 regarding penalties for willful violations. *See also* Section 47(b) regarding the invalidity of contracts made in violation of the Act or any rule, regulation, or order promulgated pursuant to the Act.

Private rights of action for violations of the 1940 Act have also been recognized. *See* Cogan v. Johnston, 162 F. Supp. 907 (S.D.N.Y. 1958); Brown v. Bullock, 294 F.2d 415 (2d Cir. 1961) (*en banc*); Taussig v. Wellington Fund, Inc., 313 F.2d 472 (3d Cir. 1963); Esplin v. Hirschi, 402 F.2d 94 (10th Cir. 1968). *Cf.* Brouck v. Managed Funds, Inc., 286 F. 2d 901 (8th Cir. 1961), *judg. vac. as moot* 369 U.S. 424 (1962); Greater Iowa Corp. v. McLendon, 378 F.2d 783 (8th Cir. 1967); Herpich v. Wallace, 430 F.2d 792 (5th Cir. 1970).

[2] Section 18 of the Act imposes, with certain very limited exceptions, substantive limitations on the capital structure of a registered investment company. Section 18(a) requires any outstanding senior securities (debt or equity) of a closed-end investment company (i.e., an issuer which does not issue redeemable securities) to meet certain prescribed asset coverage tests. Section 18(c) prohibits any registered closed-end investment company from issuing more than one class of a senior debt security or more than one class of a senior equity security. Section 18(d) makes it unlawful for any registered open-end or closed-end investment company to issue any warrants or rights to subscribe to a security.

In addition to the restrictions relating to an issuer's capital structure, the Act also imposes limitations in the following areas: the source of dividend payments (Section 19); the lending of money or property (Section 21); changes in the board of directors (Section 16); and transactions between affiliated persons and the issuer (Section 17). Once registered as an investment company, the issuer also becomes subject to extensive periodic reporting and filing requirements.

But see Section 6(c), granting the Commission broad discretionary power to exempt any person, security or transaction from any provision or provisions of the Act. *See also* "Cash Offer of General Host Corp. to Purchase all Common Stock and Preferred Stock of Cudahy Company," N.Y. Times, June 29, 1971, at 57, providing in part as follows: "General Host Corporation, a New York corporation, is primarily engaged in the manufacture and sale of bakery products, the operation of convenience food stores and also has interests in tourism operations. General Host Corporation is presently registered under the Investment Company Act of 1940 but disclaims the applicability of such Act and has applied for an order of the Securities and Exchange Commission declaring it not to be an investment company."

SECTION 1. *BACKGROUND AND GENERAL PRINCIPLES*

For purposes of determining the class of issuer subject to regulation under the Act, an investment company is defined in Section 3(a). This section proffers three separate definitions of an investment company, of which subsections (1) and (3) could conceivably apply to a tender offeror. Section 3(a)(1) defines an investment company as any issuer [3] which

> (1) is or holds itself out as being engaged primarily, or proposes to engage primarily, in the business of investing, reinvesting, or trading in securities.

Section 3(a)(3) defines the term as any issuer which

> (3) is engaged or proposes to engage in the business of investing, reinvesting, owning, holding, or trading in securities, and owns or proposes to acquire investment securities having a value exceeding 40 per centum of the value of such issuer's total assets (exclusive of Government securities and cash items) on an unconsolidated basis.

For purposes of Section 3(a), "investment securities" are defined to include all securities except the following:

> (A) Government securities [4]
> (B) Securities issued by employees' securities companies, and
> (C) *Securities issued by majority-owned subsidiaries of the owner which are not investment companies* [5]. (Emphasis added.)

Section 3(a)(1) has been said to describe the typical investment company, "i.e., a company that knows that it is an investment company and does not claim to be anything else, whereas Section 3(a)(3) 'catches the inadvertent investment company,' i.e., a com-

[3] Section 2(a)(21) of the Act defines "issuer" as "every person who issues or proposes to issue any security, or has outstanding any security which it has issued." Thus, an individual who makes a tender offer as distinguished from a corporate offeror will not be deemed to be an investment company under the Act.

[4] The only government securities excluded are the securities of the U.S. Government or its instrumentalities. *See* Electric Bond and Share Company, Investment Company Act Release No. 4590 (May 6, 1966).

[5] Section 2(a)(23) provides that a "'Majority-owned subsidiary' of a person means a company 50 per centum or more of the outstanding voting securities of which are owned by such person, or by a company which, within the meaning of this paragraph, is a majority-owned subsidiary of such person."

pany which does something else but suddenly comes up against the 40 per cent test." [6] While this distinction has been criticized as being somewhat artificial,[7] the typical corporate tender offeror which is actively engaged in an operating business or businesses can normally proceed with some confidence that it will not be deemed to be an investment company pursuant to Section 3(a)(1) if it cannot also be deemed to be an investment company pursuant to Section 3(a)(3).[8]

In determining whether a particular issuer falls within the definition expressed in Section 3(a)(3), the percentage of "investment securities" relative to the issuer's total assets (exclusive of government securities and cash items) assumes critical importance. Where the offeror acquires more than 50 percent of the target's voting stock, the target will be considered a "majority-owned subsidiary" of the offeror and since majority-owned subsidiaries are not considered "investment securities," the offeror would not fall within the Section 3(a)(3) definition of an investment company by virtue of its holdings in the target. On the other hand, where the offeror acquires less than a majority of the target's voting stock but the target's shares, together with any other investment securities, constitute more than 40 percent of the value of the offeror's total assets (exclusive of government securities and cash items),[9] the offeror will be required to register as an investment company if it is considered to be "engaged or proposes to engage in the business of investing, reinvesting, owning, holding or trading in securities."

[6] SEC v. Fifth Ave. Coach Lines, Inc., *supra* note 1, at 27. *See* Kerr, *The Inadvertent Investment Company: Section 3(a)(3) of the Investment Company Act*, 12 Stanford L. Rev. 29 (1959). *See also* Jaretski, *The Investment Company Act of 1940*, 26 Wash. U.L.Q. 303 (1941); Garrett, *When Is an Investment Company*, 37 U. Det. L.J. 355 (1960); Jennings and Marsh, Securities Regulation (2d ed. 1968) at 1111–14.

[7] SEC v. Fifth Ave. Coach Lines, Inc., *id.*

[8] However, tender offerors engaged in the business of taking controlling positions in other issuers for the primary purpose of generating capital gains rather than for actively operating and managing the companies may be considered "special situation" investment companies under Section 3(a)(1). *See In the Matter of* Bankers Securities Corp., 15 S.E.C. 695 (1944), *aff'd* 146 F.2d 88 (3d Cir. 1944); *In the Matter of* Forbisher Limited, 27 S.E.C. 944 (1948); Kerr and Appelbaum, *supra* note 1. *See also* SEC v. Fifth Ave. Coach Lines, Inc., *supra* note 1.

[9] *See* Section 2(a)(39) for the definition of "value" as used in Section 3 of the Act.

While Section 3(a)(3) appears to require that an issuer meet both the "investment company business" and "40 percent" tests before it will be considered an investment company, the section has been interpreted as effectively creating a presumption that an issuer is an investment company once investment securities exceed 40 percent of the value of such issuer's total assets (exclusive of government securities and cash items).[10] The fact that ownership of investment securities is simply the means by which an issuer's noninvestment activities are made possible will apparently not overcome the presumption.[11] However, the presumption can be rebutted if the issuer can demonstrate that its business activities fall within one of the exceptions provided in Section 3(b) of the Act.[12] Section 3(b)(1) excepts from the definition of an investment company those issuers "primarily engaged"

[10] *See* SEC v. S&P National Corp., *supra* note 1; *In the Matter of* International Mining Corp., 39 S.E.C. 86 (1959); *In the Matter of* International Bank, Investment Company Act Release No. 3986 (June 4, 1964), CCH FED. SEC. L. REP. ¶ 77,101. *See also* Kerr and Appelbaum, *supra* note 1. *But see In the Matter of* Gray Line Corp., Investment Company Act Release No. 6052 (May 14, 1970).

[11] *See In the Matter of* International Bank, *supra* note 10.

[12] *See* SEC v. S&P National Corp., *supra* note 1. Section 3(b) provides in full as follows:

"(b) Notwithstanding paragraph (3) of subsection (a), none of the following persons is an investment company within the meaning of this title:

(1) Any issuer primarily engaged, directly or through a wholly-owned subsidiary or subsidiaries, in a business or businesses other than that of investing, reinvesting, owning, holding, or trading in securities.

(2) Any issuer which the Commission, upon application by such issuer, finds and by order declares to be primarily engaged in a business or businesses other than that of investing, reinvesting, owning, holding, or trading in securities either directly or (A) through majority-owned subsidiaries or (B) through controlled companies conducting similar types of businesses. The filing of an application under this paragraph in good faith by an issuer in good faith other than a registered investment company shall exempt the applicant for a period of sixty days from all provisions of this title applicable to investment companies as such. For cause shown, the Commission by order may extend such period of exemption for an additional period or periods. Whenever the Commission, upon its own motion or upon application, finds that the circumstances which gave rise to the issuance of an order granting an application under this paragraph no longer exist, the Commission shall by order revoke such order.

(3) Any issuer all the outstanding securities of which (other than short-term paper and directors' qualifying shares) are directly or indirectly owned by a company excepted from the definition of investment company by paragraph (1) or (2) of this subsection."

See also Section 3(c) and Section 6 for exclusions from the definition of an investment company and exemptions from the provisions of the Act for certain investment companies.

in noninvestment company business directly or through wholly owned subsidiaries.[13] Section 3(b)(2) provides a procedure whereby the issuer can obtain an SEC order declaring that it is not an investment company if the SEC finds, pursuant to the issuer's application, that it is "primarily engaged" in a noninvestment company business either directly or through majority-owned subsidiaries or "controlled companies conducting similar types of businesses." [14] Section 3(b)(3) excepts any issuer whose outstanding securities are 100 percent owned, directly or indirectly, by a company excepted pursuant to Section 3(b)(1) or 3(b)(2). Thus, even though more than 40 percent of an issuer's assets consist of investment securities, it may nevertheless not be an investment company if it is "primarily engaged in a business or businesses other than that of investing, reinvesting, owning, holding, or trading in securities. . . ."

In determining whether an issuer is primarily engaged in a

[13] The exclusion provided in Section 3(b)(1) is self-operating, and an issuer meeting the conditions enumerated therein may rely on the exclusion without seeking an order from the SEC.

Section 2(a)(41) provides that a " 'Wholly-owned subsidiary' of a person means a company 95 per centum or more of the outstanding voting securities of which are owned by such person, or by a company which, within the meaning of this paragraph, is a wholly-owned subsidiary of such person."

[14] "In the usual case a company filing an application under Section 3(b)(2) is or has been engaged in an industrial enterprise but has acquired investment securities exceeding 40 per cent of its assets." *Report of the SEC on the Public Policy Implications of Investment Company Growth, Rep. of the Comm. on Interstate and Foreign Commerce,* H.R. REP. No. 2337, 89th Cong., 2d Sess. 327 (1966).

In addition to the Section 3(b)(2) procedure, an issuer in attempting to avoid the burdens of regulation under the Act may request an order pursuant to Section 6(c) exempting it from all provisions of the Act. *See, e.g.,* "Notice of filing of application by Great Northwest Industries Inc. for order pursuant to Section 3(b)(2) of the Act declaring that the company is not an investment company or in the alternative under Section 6(c) of the Act for an order exempting the company from all provisions of the Act." Investment Company Act Release No. 6508 (May 5, 1971). Conceivably, the Commission, for good cause shown, could exempt a company with 100 percent of its assets in investment securities pursuant to Section 6(c).

The phrase "controlled companies conducting similar types of businesses" requires similarity of businesses only between those controlled companies which will have a bearing on the determination of the primary business of the controlling company. Thus, the business of a particular controlled company can be dissimilar to both the businesses of the controlling company and controlled companies which affect the status of the controlling company. *See In the Matter of* American Manufacturing Co., Inc., 41 S.E.C. 415 (1963), CCH FED. SEC. L. REP. ¶ 76,902; *In the Matter of* International Bank, *supra* note 10.

noninvestment business, the courts and the Commission have generally been influenced by the following factors in considering the availability of an exception pursuant to Section 3(b)(1) or 3(b)(2):[15]

(a) Historical business development;
(b) Present business activities;
(c) Proposed plans for future business development;
(d) Public representations of business policy;
(e) Activities of directors and officers;
(f) Nature of present assets;
(g) Sources of present income.

While the weight given to each of these factors will vary with the facts and circumstances of the individual case, the income and asset tests have traditionally been considered the most important and provide some objective standards against which business activity can be measured.[16] In an effort to provide some broad guidelines in the tender offer context regarding the significance of the income and asset tests relative to the other factors noted above, it would appear necessary to first distinguish between tender offers where:

(1) The offeror fails to acquire either voting or working control but retains the target's shares for investment purposes;
(2) The offeror fails to acquire voting control but obtains working control; and
(3) The offeror acquires neither voting nor working control but retains the target's shares in a continuing effort to obtain either voting or working control.

[15] *See In the Matter of* The Tonapah Mining Co. of Nevada, 26 S.E.C. 426 (1947); *In the Matter of* Gray Line Corp., *supra* note 10; *In the Matter of* Great American Life Underwriters, Inc., 41 S.E.C. 1 (1960); *In the Matter of* International Bank, *supra* note 10; SEC v. S&P National Corp., *supra* note 1; *In the Matter of* The M. A. Hanna Co., 10 S.E.C. 581 (1941); *In the Matter of* United Stores Corp., 10 S.E.C. 1145 (1942).

"To determine whether a company is engaged primarily in the business of investing, its total activities of all sorts must be considered." SEC v. Fifth Ave. Coach Lines, Inc., *supra* note 1, at 28. *Cf. In the Matter of* American Manufacturing Co., Inc., *supra* note 14.

[16] *See In the Matter of* Tonapah Mining Co. of Nevada, *supra* note 15. *See also* Kerr and Appelbaum, *supra* note 1.

If the offeror retains the target's shares solely for investment purposes, and investment securities equal or exceed 50 percent [17] of its total assets (exclusive of government securities and cash items) and generate approximately the same percentage of its total net income,[18] the offeror's contention that it is "primarily engaged" in a noninvestment company business would be most difficult to sustain even where all the other factors support its position. On the other hand, where the percentage of the offeror's income generated from investment securities represents but a small portion of its income, the fact that investment securities exceed 50 percent of its total assets (exclusive of government securities and cash items) may not preclude a finding that it is not an investment company.

Where the offeror can present evidence that it has obtained working control for the purpose of actively operating and directing the business policies of the target, the fact that investment securities (consisting primarily of the target's shares) represent substantially more than 50 percent of the offeror's assets and income may not adversely affect its claim that it is not an investment company. Significantly, the Commission, in one instance, has viewed as support for its conclusion that an issuer was primarily engaged in a noninvestment company business, the fact that approximately two-thirds of the issuer's assets and over two-thirds of its total net income consisted of and was produced by subsidi-

[17] The 40 percent test of Section 3(a)(3) is inapplicable in determining whether a Section 3(b) exception is appropriate. As discussed above, the test under Section 3(b) is whether the issuer is "primarily engaged" in a noninvestment company business.

[18] Income derived from investment securities includes trading profits in securities as well as dividends and interest. *See In the Matter of* Tonapah Mining Co. of Nevada, *supra* note 15.

In determining the percentage of its income derived from investment securities, the issuer can be expected to claim that the computation should be based on pre-tax income since the 85 percent intercorporate dividend deduction will result in a much higher percentage of investment income after taxes. Although the Commission has referred to pre-tax income in computing the percentage of the issuer's income derived from investment securities, the after-tax picture would also appear worthy of examination in evaluating all factors affecting the issuer's status. *See In the Matter of* American Manufacturing Co., Inc., *supra* note 14; Kerr and Appelbaum, *Inadvertent Investment Companies—Ten Years After, supra* note 1, at 891, n. 33.

aries and controlled companies which it actively operated and managed.[19] On the other hand, where the offeror obtains working control of other companies for the primary purpose of subsequently disposing of their securities for a profit, it is doubtful whether a Section 3(b) exception would be appropriate if investment securities equal or exceed 50 percent of the offeror's assets and income.[20]

The relative importance of the income and asset tests where the offeror actively continues to seek control of the target may be substantially similar to the weight accorded these factors where the offeror retains the shares for investment purposes. While the offeror's intention to acquire control may be evidence of its plans for future noninvestment business development, the offeror will still be unable to claim that it is presently engaged primarily in noninvestment activities through a controlled company. Accordingly, if investment securities and investment income equal or exceed 50 percent of assets (exclusive of government securities and cash items) and income, respectively, the offeror will be hard pressed to justify an exception pursuant to Section 3(b)(1) or 3(b)(2).

Section 2. *THE SEC'S APPROACH REGARDING EXCHANGE TENDER OFFERS*

The exchange tender offer involves a public offering of securities and accordingly requires a 1933 Act registration statement to be filed with and declared effective by the SEC before the securities may lawfully be sold. In processing these registration statements, the staff of the Commission has in recent years required that the registrant take certain prescribed steps to insure that it will not incur liability as an unregistered investment company.[21]

[19] *In the Matter of* International Bank, *supra* note 10. *See also In the Matter of* The M. A. Hanna Co., *supra* note 15, where the Commission held that the applicant was not primarily engaged in the business of an investment company despite the fact that approximately 72 percent of the value of the applicant's total assets (exclusive of government securities and cash items) consisted of less than majority interests in other companies.

[20] See note 8, *supra*.

[21] The cash tender offeror is apparently on its own with regard to whether it will request a Section 3(b)(2) order or how and when it will dispose of a portion

Accordingly, where the purchase of any shares pursuant to the exchange offer is not contingent upon the offeror obtaining at least a majority of the target's outstanding voting shares, the staff has required the offeror to commit itself to an agreement or undertaking similar to the following:

> Where the shares acquired pursuant to the tender offer, together with any other investment securities held by the offeror, approach 40% of the value of the offeror's total assets (exclusive of government securities and cash items), the offeror will file an application for exemption under Section 3(b)(2) of the Act,[22] which will afford the offeror an automatic exemption from the Act for 60 days.[23] If the offeror has not acquired more than 50 percent of the target's outstanding voting stock at the end of the 60-day period [24] or has not at that time been granted an order pursuant to Section 3(b)(2) that it is primarily engaged in a noninvestment company business, and the value of investment securities then owned by the offeror approach 40% of its total assets (exclusive of government securities and cash items), the offeror will dispose of a portion of its invest-

---

of its investment securities should it independently determine that continued retention may create liability or compel registration under the Act.

For a discussion of the inadvertent investment company in an exchange tender offer context, *see* Kerr and Appelbaum, *supra* note 1. *See also* exchange offer prospectuses of: (a) The Slick Corp. for shares of Filtrol Corp., at 6–7 (February 7, 1969); (b) Northwest Industries Inc. for shares of B. F. Goodrich Co., at 7 (April 16, 1969); (c) Mite Corp. for shares of Heli-Coil Corp., at 12–13 (Sept. 15, 1969), reproduced in relevant part in Kerr and Appelbaum, at 896–99, nn. 50,52.

[22] *See, e.g., In the Matter of* The Slick Corporation, Notice of Filing of Application for Order Pursuant to Section 3(b)(2) of the Act Declaring That Company Is Not an Investment Company, Investment Company Act Release No. 5648 (April 4, 1969).

[23] This approach presumes that the offeror may be required to register as an investment company once its investment securities exceed 40 percent of total assets, notwithstanding the fact that Section 3(b)(1) excepts issuers "primarily engaged" in noninvestment company business. The staff in at least one instance has not required the offeror to file a Section 3(b)(2) application if it obtains an opinion of counsel that it will not become an investment company within the meaning of the Act by virtue of its acquisition of the target's securities. *See, e.g.,* Mite Corp. prospectus for shares of Heli-Coil Corp., *supra* note 21.

[24] When more than 50 percent of the outstanding voting shares are acquired, the Commission, upon application of the offeror, will permit withdrawal of the Section 3(b)(2) application. *See, e.g., In the Matter of* The Slick Corporation, Order Permitting Withdrawal of Application, Investment Company Act Release No. 5664 (April 28, 1969).

ment securities so that the value of investment securities after the disposition would not exceed the 40% limitation.[25] To facilitate the disposition of the investment securities, the offeror will agree to consent to an injunction against it by the SEC, including the appointment of a receiver for the purpose of disposing of the securities, if the Commission deems it appropriate to dispose of the offeror's holdings in that manner.

If the offeror is unwilling to dispose of a portion of its investment securities (perhaps because the sale will cause it to lose working control of the target), it may agree instead to register under the Act. The staff, however, has apparently not encouraged registration in the case of the typical industrial corporation because of the fact that the corporation will not be able to comply with the substantive provisions of the Act.[26]

The staff's approach in attempting to insure that the offeror does not inadvertently violate the Act is, for the most part, sound and workable. However, the staff's apparent insistence that the offeror consent to an injunction and the appointment of a receiver to dispose of the securities appears to suggest a degree of arbitrary or at least unreasonable administration of the federal securities laws. Compelling the offeror to consent to a finding of a federal securities law violation, with the attendant unfavorable publicity attached thereto, when the offeror, in the first instance, has stipulated that it will dispose of investment securities to insure that it will not violate the Act, would appear to provide little, if any, additional investor protection.

In addition, it should be added that the offeror may incur short-swing profit liability if investment securities are disposed of

[25] Query whether the offeror can lawfully dispose of any of the target's shares without a registration statement if it has acquired working control of the target? *Cf.* the issue of registration where the offeror has failed to acquire working control. See text accompanying notes 34–41, Chapter 8.

To reduce the risks of daily uncertainty resulting from fluctuating market values, some offerors have agreed to dispose of a sufficient amount of shares so that the value of investment securities after the sale will not exceed 35 percent of its total assets (exclusive of government securities and cash items). *See, e.g.*, Northwest Industries, Inc. and The Slick Corp. prospectuses, *supra* note 21.

[26] *See* Kerr and Appelbaum, *supra* note 1. See also text and accompanying note 2, *supra*.

by the receiver at a profit within six months of their purchase.[27] The failure of the staff to grant the offeror at least minimal flexibility regarding the timing of the sales so that it may avoid short-swing liability, would not appear to be justified as necessary for the protection of investors.[28] Accordingly, it would appear appropriate for the staff to reconsider its policy in this area.

[27] *See, e.g.*, The Slick Corp. prospectus, *supra* note 21, providing that ". . . the Company has agreed to consent to a court injunction against it by the Securities & Exchange Commission and to the appointment of a receiver for its Filtrol stock who will be required to dispose of the necessary amount of Filtrol stock within 60 days of his appointment. Any profit realizable by the Company from such sale would inure to and be recoverable by Filtrol Corporation under Section 16(b) of the Securities Exchange Act of 1934." *Cf.* Northwest Industries Inc. prospectus, *supra* note 21 providing that ". . . Industries has also agreed with the Commission to consent to court orders, including the appointment of a receiver for the purpose of disposing of investment securities within 60 days after his appointment, as the Commission may deem appropriate in order to implement the foregoing agreement. If by reason of the foregoing, Industries should be required to dispose of any shares of B. F. Goodrich Stock . . . and . . . should realize any profit . . . such profit may inure to and be recoverable by B. F. Goodrich under Section 16(b) of the Securities Exchange Act of 1934."

[28] If the offeror owns other investment securities, in addition to its holdings in the target, it presumably can choose the shares which will be sold to reduce its position below 40 percent. Where a receiver is appointed, the offeror's ability to determine which shares should be sold to reduce or eliminate any short-swing liability may be compromised.

See also discussion in Chapter 8, *infra*, generally on problems of disposing of shares acquired pursuant to a tender offer.

Chapter 8. CONSIDERATIONS IN DISPOSING OF SHARES ACQUIRED PURSUANT TO AN UNSUCCESSFUL TENDER OFFER

In undertaking a tender offer, the offeror generally seeks to obtain either voting or working control of the target company. In other instances it may attempt the offer as a preliminary step in an effort ultimately to acquire control through a proxy contest. When the offeror fails to receive a sufficient number of shares to achieve its objective,[1] it must determine what to do with the shares which were tendered. If the terms of the offer permit, the offeror may simply return the shares to the original tenderors. On the other hand, if the offeror committed itself to purchase the tendered shares, it must either sell the shares or retain them for investment purposes. This chapter explores some of the problems confronting the offeror in disposing of the target's shares.[2]

[1] A study of some 83 contested cash tender offers from 1956–1966 found that approximately 65 percent of the attempted takeovers were unsuccessful. *See* Hayes and Taussig, *Tactics of Cash Takeover Bids*, 45 Harv. Bus. Rev. 135, 137 (March–April 1967). *Cf.* the Austin-Fishman study of all tender offers involving NYSE-listed companies from 1956–1966 and all tender offers for which data were available for 1967, which revealed that only 22 percent of 191 cash offers and 15 percent of some 41 exchange offers were unsuccessful. *See* Austin and Fishman, *Corporations in Conflict—The Tender Offer* (Masterco, 1960), at 65. The variance in results is accounted for in part by the fact that the Austin-Fishman study includes uncontested tender offers.

In addition, success or the lack thereof apparently meant different things to each group of researchers. Although the Hayes-Taussig study does not define just when an offer is either successful or unsuccessful, the study apparently considers those tender offers as unsuccessful where no change in control has taken place. The Austin-Fishman study does not include as unsuccessful those offers in which the offeror receives tenders for fewer shares than requested but nevertheless purchases the shares and assumes a minority investment position. *See also Tender Offers—The Score Board*, Forbes, April 1, 1967, at 60.

[2] For an analysis of one of the potential problems confronting an unsuccessful offeror in retaining shares for investment purposes, see Chapter 7, "The Tender Offeror as an Inadvertent Investment Company."

SECTION 1. *THE IMPACT OF MARKET CONDITIONS*

In an effort to obtain the best price for the target's shares, the offeror can be expected to consider carefully the feasibility of open-market sales as well as the opportunities, if any, to consummate a private placement.[3] The method of disposition as well as the timing of the sale(s) will normally depend upon market conditions, the size of the offeror's holdings, and the various legal considerations involved.[4]

In effecting sales in the open market, the offeror may experience some difficulty in disposing of a large block of the target's shares at a profit shortly after the termination of the offering unless there is a significant change in market conditions or a revised evaluation of the worth of the target's shares. Once the tender period has expired, withdrawal of the price support created by the bid may cause the market price of the target's stock to decline rapidly to the trading range existing prior to the offer. Even where the market price does not decline to its former level, the offeror can expect at least a modest discount from the current market price if it is anxious to quickly dispose of the shares in a large block transaction.[5] Alternatively, consideration may be given to gradually disposing of the block in relatively small transactions. The ability of the auction market to absorb the shares at favorable prices in this manner will normally be limited to situations where the "float" and trading volume are both substantial.

The presence of a competing tender offer, however, may significantly enhance the offeror's ability to profitably dispose of the target's shares. While it is perhaps ironic that the opportunity to

[3] Another method of disposing of shares acquired in a tender offer is to make a withdrawal offer to the original tenderors. *See, e.g.*, "Withdrawal Offer of International Controls Corp. for Common Stock and Convertible Debentures of Electronic Specialty Co.," dated Sept. 16, 1968, discussed in Electronic Specialty Co. v. International Controls Corp., 409 F.2d 937, 944 (2d Cir. 1969). The tender offer (as revised) provided that International Controls would accept all Electronic Specialty common stock and convertible debentures tendered.

[4] In addition, the timing of the sale can, of course, be affected by the financial needs of the offeror.

[5] Where a large number of shares is involved, even a slight discount can result in substantial capital losses.

generate a profit from an unsuccessful tender offer should depend upon the cause of its failure, the existence of a more attractive competing bid will nevertheless enable the offeror to tender its shares or sell them in the open market at a favorable price. Similarly, if the target defeats the offer by announcing agreement on a proposed defensive merger, the offeror may be able to negotiate a profitable private placement where the shares obtained in the tender offer are needed to insure stockholder approval of the merger.[6]

SECTION 2. *SHORT-SWING PROFITS LIABILITY*

(1) THE DILEMMA IN PERSPECTIVE

Where profits are realized from purchases and sales within a six-month period, the percentage of the target's shares owned by the offeror may take on added significance. Section 16(b) of the 1934 Act [7] provides, *inter alia,* that any profits realized by a beneficial owner of more than 10 percent of any equity security registered pursuant to Section 12 of the 1934 Act [8] from a purchase and sale within any period of less than six months, are recoverable by the issuer, notwithstanding any intention on the part of the purchaser at the time he entered into the transaction of holding the security purchased for a period exceeding six months.[9]

[6] For a description of how two unsuccessful tender offerors (Loew's Theatres Inc. and Gulf and Western Industries Inc.) profited by losing, *see The Merger Movement Rides High,* FORTUNE, Feb. 1969, at 79, 158, 161.

[7] 15 U.S.C. § 78p. [8] 15 U.S.C. § 78e.

[9] In addition to 10 percent beneficial owners, Section 16(b) also applies to officers and directors of the issuer of the security. The express purpose of Section 16(b) is to prevent "the unfair use of information which may have been obtained by such beneficial owner, director, or officer by reason of his relationship to the issuer. . . ." By imposing strict liability for all short-swing profits, the statute presumes that the 10 percent stockholder is an "insider" and has access to material nondisclosed information. In short, Section 16(b) has been described as having a "prophylactic" effect on short-swing trading. *See* Blau v. Lehman, 368 U.S. 403, 413–14 (1962); Bershad v. McDonough, 428 F.2d 693, 696 (7th Cir. 1970).

Securities registered pursuant to Section 12 of the 1934 Act consist of (a) securities registered on any national securities exchange; and (b) securities of issuers with total assets exceeding $1,000,000 and a class of equity security (other than an exempted security) held of record by 500 or more persons.

Section 16(a) of the 1934 Act requires 10 percent stockholders and officers and

While the unsuccessful offeror may be well aware of Section 16(b) and have no intention of selling the target's shares within six months of acquisition, it may nevertheless be subject to short-swing profit liability because a sale may occur and a profit be realized, not as a result of any voluntary act of the offeror to dispose of the shares, but rather as a consequence of the target's consummation of a defensive merger. Thus, pursuant to a defensive merger agreement, an exchange of the target's shares for those of the merger partner by an unsuccessful tender offeror may constitute a "sale" for purposes of Section 16(b), which, when matched against the unsuccessful offeror's purchases, may create short-swing profit liability.

In determining whether the exchange of securities does in fact constitute a sale of the target's securities by the unsuccessful offeror within the meaning of Section 16(b), the issue has become one of whether an opportunity for speculative abuse exists. The principle generally adhered to has been stated in one leading case as follows: "Only when an opportunity for speculative abuse is present is it necessary to determine whether the transactions alleged to give rise to 16(b) liability may fairly be characterized as insider purchases and sales." [10]

In *Abrams v. Occidental Petroleum Corp.*[11] the Second Circuit Court of Appeals held that an exchange of securities pursuant to a defensive merger consummated within six months of the unsuccessful offeror's purchases and which the rejected offeror

---

directors of issuers of securities registered pursuant to Section 12 to file a statement with the SEC regarding the amount of all equity securities of such issuer beneficially owned by them. Any changes in ownership must be reported within ten days after the close of the calendar month in which the change occurred.

[10] Newmark v. RKO General, Inc., 425 F.2d 348, 351 (2d Cir. 1970), *cert. denied,* 400 U.S. 854 (1970). *See also* Abrams v. Occidental Petrolem Corp., 450 F.2d 157, 163 (2d Cir. 1971), *cert. granted,* U.S. (1972); American Standard Inc. v. Crane Co., No. 68 Civ. 2461 (S.D.N.Y. 1971), CCH FED. SEC. L. REP. ¶ 93,237 at 91, 472, discussed in note 15, *infra.*

[11] 450 F.2d 157 (2d Cir. 1971), *rev'g,* Nos. 67 Civ. 2858, 3291, 4042, and 4977 (S.D.N.Y. 1970), CCH FED. SEC. L. REP. ¶ 92,875, *cert. granted,* U.S. (1972). For supplemental district court opinions re: recovery of dividends, *see* CCH FED. SEC. L. REP. ¶ 92,930 (S.D.N.Y. 1971); stay of judgment pending appeal, 323 F. Supp. 570 (S.D.N.Y. 1971). For connected cases, *see* 600 California Corp. v. Harjean Co., 284 F. Supp. 843 (N.D. Tex. 1968); CMC Corp. v. Kern County Land Co., 290 F. Supp. 695 (N.D. Cal. 1968).

frantically, but unsuccessfully, tried to delay,[12] did not lend itself to the type of speculative abuse which Section 16(b) was designed to prevent. Accordingly, the exchange of securities was held not to constitute a sale for purposes of Section 16(b).[13] The court's finding that the transaction in question did not present an opportunity for speculative abuse was based upon the fact that the unsuccessful offeror had neither the ability to control nor advance knowledge of the defensive merger.[14] If the unsuccessful offeror had advance knowledge of the defensive merger, the possibility of speculative abuse might well have existed inasmuch as the tender offer could be viewed as an attempt to make a speculative profit from a defensive merger rather than as an attempt to

[12] Occidental, the unsuccessful offeror, proposed that the SEC adopt a new rule, Rule 16b–11, which would exempt Occidental from Section 16(b) liability. The Commission, however, declined to take any action on the proposed rule. Occidental apparently resolved that if the SEC failed to adopt the proposed rule its only alternative was "to commence every kind of litigation it could reasonably bring and attempt to stall the consummation of the Tenneco-[Old Kern] transaction for six months." Abrams v. Occidental Petroleum Corp., CCH Fed. Sec. L. Rep. ¶ 92,875 at 90,274–75. Thereafter, a number of stockholders suits were insituted to enjoin the consummation of the defensive merger. The target and the defensive merger partner then obtained an *ex parte* order enjoining Occidental, which was found to be the moving force behind the litigation, and the defendant who had initiated previous suits, from taking any further action in attempting to delay the transaction. *See* connected cases cited in note 11, *supra*.

[13] *Cf.* Newmark v. RKO General, Inc., *supra* note 10, at 351, 353–54.

[14] *Cf.* Newmark v. RKO General, Inc., *supra* note 10, at 353–54. The background and facts of the *Abrams* case were as follows: Pursuant to a tender offer, Occidental Petroleum Corp. purchased more than 20 percent of Kern County Land Co. Kern resisted the takeover attempt and effected a defensive merger with Tenneco Corp. The merger was consummated within six months of the purchases by Occidental pursuant to the tender offer. Tenneco therefore brought suit to recover the short-swing profits Occidental realized pursuant to an option agreement whereby Occidental agreed to sell the Tenneco securities received in exchange for its Kern shares.

While the terms of the option agreement provided that the option could not be exercised by Tenneco until six months after the expiration of the tender offer, the Federal District Court for the Southern District of New York nevertheless found that a "sale" had occurred when the option agreement was entered into and that a "profit was realized" when Occidental became irrevocably entitled to receive the new Tenneco shares upon the closing of the Kern-Tenneco agreement. In addition to the realized capital gains, the district court, in a separate opinion, held that the dividends received by Occidental were also recoverable under Section 16(b). The district court's findings resulted in a judgment of over $23 million against Occidental.

The Second Circuit reversed upon findings that neither the option agreement nor Occidental's involuntary acquisition of the Tenneco securities constituted a "sale" for purposes of Section 16(b).

acquire control. However, absent such knowledge, the *Abrams* case makes clear that the unsuccessful offeror is not required either to make a higher offer or attempt to block a transaction which it regards as beneficial to all stockholders, including itself.[15] Similarly, the inability to control the course of the defen-

[15] *Cf.* American Standard, Inc. v. Crane Co., No. 68 Civ. 2461 (S.D.N.Y. 1971), CCH FED. SEC. L. REP. ¶ 93,237, a case bearing striking similarities to *Abrams* and decided one day prior to the Court of Appeals opinion in that case, wherein the district court granted summary judgment in favor of a successful bidder which effected a defensive merger with the target company in an action for recovery of short-swing profits against an unsuccessful offeror:

"We hold that opportunities for speculative abuse did inhere in Crane's [the unsuccessful offeror's] transactions. . . . The record establishes that, in spite of the rejection by Air Brake [the target] of its original merger proposal, Crane voluntarily thereafter acquired the status of a 10 percent holder; that it was informed on March 4 of the proposed Air Brake-Standard merger and its ranking officer remarked that for Crane to be a stockholder of Standard would be an 'impossible situation'; that nevertheless Crane thereafter issued its tender offer, and that even after Standard's unexpected manipulative acts of April 19 it purchased over 490,000 shares of Air Brake—with the knowledge that either Standard would win the fight and Crane would be 'forced' to sell, or that it might reap a speculative harvest on the almost certain (and ultimately actual) rise in the price . . ." [CCH § 93,237 at p. 91,472]

Accordingly, we hold that the conversion of Crane's Air Brake stock into Standard stock constituted a sale of Air Brake to be matched against its cash purchases on that stock within a period of six months prior to the date of conversion. [CCH ¶ 93,237 at p. 91,474]

In light of the Second Circuit's opinion in *Abrams*, the district court in *American Standard* subsequently withdrew its opinion in order to consider the impact of the *Abrams* case. The district court thereafter reaffirmed its earlier opinion (*see* American Standard, Inc., v. Crane Co., 68 Civ. 2461 (S.D.N.Y. 1972), CCH FED. SEC. L. REP. ¶ 93,550) and in a supplemental opinion (*see* American Standard, Inc., v. Crane Co., 68 Civ. 2461 (S.D.N.Y. 1972), CCH FED. SEC. L. REP. ¶ 93,551) found that the Second Circuit's holding in *Abrams* required no change in its earlier opinion. In this regard, the district court found the compelling difference between *Abrams* and *American Standard* to be as follows:

. . . all of Occidental's cash purchases and its subsequent cash sales occurred more than six months apart (June 8-December 11), whereas Crane's acquisition and disposition of its shares *for cash* occurred within five months (January 25-June 7) of its becoming a 10% stockholder of Air Brake. Indeed, the *Occidental* plaintiffs made no claim based on Occidental's *cash* sales (because they occurred beyond the six-months statutory period), but complained rather that Occidental's receipt of the exchange stock on merger and its execution of a "call" option were "sales" as a matter of law. Standard's complaint against Crane, on the contrary, *is* based (Par. 9) on Crane's cash sales, matched against its acquisition of the Air Brake common. [CCH ¶ 93,551 at p. 92,626]

The district court's determination that the *Abrams* holding required no change in its earlier opinion was therefore based upon the fact that *Crane* had effected cash sales within six months of its purchases. It must be emphasized, however, that the Second Circuit's holding in *Abrams* for all practical purposes overrules *American Standard* to the extent that *American Standard* may be cited for the proposition that an involuntary exchange of securities by an unsuccessful offeror

sive merger, in which all stockholders would participate on an equal basis, eliminated the opportunity for speculative abuse since the unsuccessful offeror could not prevent the merger from taking place within six months of its purchases and accordingly could not avoid liability even though it attempted to do so.[16] Thus the ability of an unsuccessful offeror to avoid Section 16(b) liability under the *Abrams* rationale appears to be dependent upon the following conditions:

(a) The receipt by the unsuccessful offeror of securities of the merged company in exchange for its shares in the target company in a transaction which is not arranged or controlled by the unsuccessful offeror and in which all shareholders are entitled to participate on an equal basis; and

(b) The lack of privileged or inside information that the target

---

pursuant to a defensive merger constitutes a sale. Thus if *Crane* had not disposed of the *American Standard* shares (received pursuant to the defensive merger) for cash within six months of the purchase of the target's shares, there would appear to be little doubt that a finding by the district court that the exchange constituted a sale would be in error, in light of the Second Circuit's opinion in *Abrams*.

[16] *Cf.* Newmark v. RKO General, Inc., *supra*, note 10; American Standard, Inc. v. Crane Co., *supra* note 15, at CCH, p. 91,473.

Here Crane, although it did not possess the array of control powers exercisable by RKO, nevertheless knew that the probabilities were, from the time of Air Brake's rejection onward, that Air Brake would "seek another partner and that other partner" would "probably . . . make a slightly better offer." After March 4 it knew this to a certainty and, although it quite rightly points out that it could not have anticipated Standard's manipulation of April 19, it nevertheless purchased over 490,000 shares of Air Brake in a period of more than a month thereafter.

"Furthermore, aside from the fact that any party in Crane's position could reasonably have inferred from the dynamic pattern of take-over fights that it would either win control or be in a strong position to sell at a profit, there were also significant ways in which Crane could influence the course of events. For example, it could easily affect the exchange ratio of the merger by the terms of its own tender offer. It controlled the timing of its offer and had the opportunity to improve it with resultant effect on the ultimate terms of merger between Air Brake and Standard. Such power fits within the District Court's rationale in *Newmark* (294 F. Supp. 358, 365 (S. D. N. Y. 1968)) that an insider who "could influence the speed and timing of the merger, and possibly its outcome" may be liable under § 16(b). It must constantly be remembered that our search is not to determine whether Crane intended these results, but whether they were possibilities which inhered in the situation. We hold that they did, and that § 16(b) is applicable if Crane's transactions constituted purchases and sales within the meaning of the section."

company would arrange a defensive merger upon more favorable terms than the unsuccessful offeror's bid.[17]

While the Abrams case represents a departure from the strict prophylactic application of Section 16(b), which has characterized much of the previous litigation in this area, the court's approach appears to achieve an equitable result. In this regard it should be added that the courts now appear to be abandoning the more traditional approach to Section 16(b), whereby "automatic" liability was imposed whether or not there was any opportunity for speculative abuse. The relatively new approach to liability under Section 16(b) suggests a case by case inquiry into the question of whether the transactions at issue involve the type of speculative abuse which Section 16(b) was designed to prevent.[18] However, the Supreme Court's recent decision to review the *Abrams* case [19] leaves the ultimate rule of law in this area unsettled.

In addition, it should be noted that a finding by the U.S. Supreme Court that an exchange or conversion of securities pursuant to a defensive merger constitutes a "sale" will not create automatic liability for the unsuccessful offeror. As noted previously, Section 16(b) of the 1934 Act requires that there be "realized profits" from a purchase and sale within any period of less than six months. While the question of whether a profit is realized upon a conversion of securities pursuant to a merger has been answered in the affirmative by the Second Circuit,[20] the Third Circuit, in *Heli-Coil Corp. v. Webster*,[21] has held that no profits are realized in such a transaction, the rationale being that

[17] *See also* Note, *Stock Exchanges Pursuant to Corporate Consolidation: A Section 16(b) "Purchase or Sale,"* 117 U. PA. L. REV. 1034 (1969); Comment, *Securities Regulation—Exchange of Stock Pursuant to Merger is Sale by Insider under Section 16(b) of the Securities Exchange Act of* 1934, 84 HARV. L. REV. 1012 (1971); Hemmer, *Insider Liability for Short-Swing Profits Pursuant to Mergers and Related Transactions*, 22 VAND. L. REV. 1101 (1969); George, *The Application of Section 16(b) to Mergers: A Hidden Hazard*, 47 TEX. L. REV. 1417 (1969).

[18] *See* Katz, *Short-Swing Liability*, 2 REV. OF SEC. REG. 916 (April 16, 1969).

[19] *Cert. granted*, U.S. (1972).

[20] *See* Newmark v. RKO General, Inc., *supra* note 13; Blau v. Lamb, 363 F.2d 507 (2d Cir. 1966), *cert. denied*, 385 U.S. 1002 (1967).

[21] 352 F.2d 156 (3rd Cir. 1965).

profits are realized only when the securities received in the conversion are sold for cash.[22]

It must also be noted that the *Abrams* case leaves unanswered the important issue of whether an opportunity for speculative abuse exists where the unsuccessful offeror controls enough shares to block the defensive merger and either fails to vote such shares in opposition thereto or votes in favor of the merger. The dictum in the *Abrams* case suggests that even if the shares held by the unsuccessful offeror were essential to obtain the requisite shareholder approval of the defensive merger and the unsuccessful offeror voted the shares it held in favor of the merger, the court nevertheless would have found that no opportunity for speculative abuse existed on the ground that there should be no requirement as a condition precedent that the unsuccessful offeror attempt to block a transaction which would be beneficial to all stockholders.[23] The extent to which this dictum will find approval in other cases, however, is highly questionable, particularly when one recognizes that the court's dictum appears to contradict the holding of the case to the effect that the unsuccessful offeror's inability to control or prevent the merger was the essential element which eliminated the opportunity for speculative abuse.

(2) The Two-Step Sale as a Means of Limiting Section 16(b) Liability

The risks and uncertainties of potential 16(b) liability for the unsuccessful offeror in the defensive merger context have to some degree been minimized by the Supreme Court's findings in the case of *Reliance Electric Co. v. Emerson Electric Co.*[24] In

[22] *See also* Park & Tilford v. Schulte, 160 F.2d 984 (2d Cir. 1947), *cert. denied,* 332 U.S. 761 (1947); Ferraiolo v. Newman, 259 F.2d 342 (6th Cir. 1958), *cert. denied,* 359 U.S. 927 (1959); Blau v. Max Factor & Co., 342 F.2d 304 (9th Cir. 1965). *Cf.* B. T. Babbitt, Inc., v. Lachner, 332 F.2d 255 (2d Cir. 1964).

[23] The *Abrams* case involved an exchange of securities pursuant to a sale of the target's assets which, under state law, required approval of only a majority of the outstanding shares of the target and provided no appraisal rights for dissenters. Although the unsuccessful offeror did not oppose the sale because it did not regard the terms to be inequitable, it chose not to vote its stock. Nevertheless the necessary majority approval was readily obtained.

[24] 404 U. S. 418 (1972), *aff'g* 434 F.2d 918 (8th Cir. 1970). For district court opinion, *see* 306 F. Supp. 588 (D. Mo. 1969).

Reliance (the facts of which occurred prior to the Second Circuit's decision in *Abrams*), an unsuccessful tender offeror, confronted with a proposed defensive merger, limited its potential short-swing profit liability by disposing of its holdings in the target in two separate and independent sales—the first, reducing its holdings to just under 10 percent, and the second, disposing of the remaining shares.

The facts of the *Reliance* case are as follows: Pursuant to a tender offer, Emerson acquired 13.2 percent of the then outstanding shares of Dodge Manufacturing Corp. Dodge opposed the Emerson bid and agreed instead to merge with Reliance Electric Co. Prior to final approval of the merger, Emerson sold 37,000 shares of the target to reduce its holdings in Dodge to 9.96 percent. Two weeks later, Emerson disposed of its remaining 115,000 shares of Dodge in a sale to a buyer—entirely unrelated to the first buyer. Both sales resulted in profits for Emerson and occurred within six months of the tender offer purchases. After a demand by Reliance for the profits realized on both sales, Emerson sought a declaratory judgment as to its liability under Section 16(b). Reliance counterclaimed for the amount of the profits.

Emerson argued that Section 16(b), which exempts a transaction where the beneficial owner does not own more than 10 percent "both at the time of purchase and sale,"[25] was inapplicable because it did not own more than 10 percent of the Dodge stock at the time of the tender-offer purchases.[26] In finding liability for short-swing profits on the first sale, both the district court and the Eighth Circuit Court of Appeals rejected Emerson's interpretation of the language contained in the Section 16(b) exemption and held instead that the purchase by which a person becomes a 10 percent owner falls within the purview of Section 16(b).[27]

[25] The last sentence of Section 16(b) provides as follows: "This subsection shall not be construed to cover any transaction where such beneficial owner was not such both at the time of the purchase and sale, or the sale and purchase, of the security involved, or any transaction or transactions which the Commission by rules and regulations may exempt as not comprehended within the purpose of this subsection."

[26] In fact, Emerson owned no Dodge stock prior to the tender offer.

[27] To the contrary, *see* Arkansas-Louisiana Gas Co. v. W. R. Stephens Investment Co., 141 F. Supp. 841, 847 (W.D. Ark. 1956). *But see* Stella v. Graham–Paige Motors Corp., 232 F.2d 299 (2d Cir. 1956), *aff'g* 132 F. Supp. 100 (S.D.N.Y.

Emerson's efforts to limit its potential liability met with success on the second sale. In reversing the district court's judgment as to Emerson's liability on the second sale, the circuit court noted that Section 16(b) requires the seller to be a 10 percent stockholder at the time of purchase *and* sale. Since Emerson was no longer a 10 percent holder at the time of the second sale nor was the second sale the transaction by which it became a less than 10 percent owner, liability properly could not be imposed. The fact that the two sales were not legally tied to each other and were made at different times with two unrelated purchasers appears to have been the essential element which permitted the circuit court to treat the sales as independent transactions rather than as one continuous sale.[28]

The Supreme Court, in a 4–3 decision,[29] affirmed the judgment of the circuit court upon findings that Section 16(b) clearly contemplates that a statutory insider might have a pre-existing intent to "sell enough shares to bring his holdings below 10 percent, and later—but still within 6 months—sell additional shares free from liability under the statute." [30] Significantly, the Court's opinion stresses the congressional intent of predicating 16(b) liability on an "objective measure of proof." [31] In this regard the Court stated:

> If a "two-step" sale of a 10 percent owner's holdings within six months of purchase is thought to give rise to the kind of evil that Congress sought to correct through § 16(b), those transactions can be more effectively deterred by an amendment to the statute that preserves

---

1955), *cert. denied*, 352 U.S. 831 (1956). *See also* Note, *Purchase of Stock by Which Stockholder Becomes a 10% Beneficial Owner Is Covered by Section 16(b)*, 70 HARV. L. REV. 1312 (1957); Note, *Stockholder Acquiring 10% Ownership on Purchase Held Liable for Profits Under Section 16(b) of the Securities Exchange Act*, 57 COLUM. L. REV. 287 (1957).

[28] In fact, it would seem that once the offeror reduced his holdings below 10 percent, it would not be necessary for him to effect the second sale.

[29] The minority opinion, written by Justice Douglas, a former chairman of the SEC, termed the majority's judgment "a mutilation of the act." See *supra* note 24, at 428.

[30] *Supra* note 24, at 423.

The judgment of the court of appeals, affirming liability on the first sale, was not challenged by Emerson. Accordingly, the Supreme Court did not consider the question of liability on the first sale.

[31] *Supra* note 24, at 425.

its mechanical quality than by a judicial search for the will-o'-the wisp of an investor's "intent" in each litigated case.[32]

The future viability of the two-step sale as a means of limiting an unsuccessful offeror's short-swing profits liability can be expected to depend largely upon resolution of the question of whether an exchange of securities pursuant to a defensive merger constitutes a "sale" for purposes of Section 16(b)—for if such an exchange does not constitute a Section 16(b) "sale," there will be no need to effect a two-step transaction. The Supreme Court's recent grant of certiorari in the *Abrams* case should eliminate much of the present uncertainty in this area. The extent to which the two-step sale can be considered a practical method of limiting Section 16(b) liability in a situation where the *Abrams* case will not constitute a controlling authority, will depend upon the percentage of the target's outstanding shares owned by the unsuccessful offeror. In the *Reliance* case, for example, the unsuccessful offeror owned approximately 13 percent of the target's shares at the time it undertook the first part of the two-step sale. Thus its "first sale" short-swing liability on only slightly more than 3 percent of the target's shares was relatively limited. On the other hand, where an unsuccessful offeror owns substantially more than 10 percent of the target's shares, the two-step sale may prove to be an expensive alternative to the risks and uncertainties of litigation.[33]

SECTION 3. *SALES AND THE 1933 ACT REGISTRATION REQUIREMENTS*

If shares are to be disposed of in public transactions, the offeror must consider whether the sales will constitute a distribution which requires a registration statement to be filed under the Securities Act of 1933.

[32] *Id.*

[33] For some recent commentaries on Section 16(b), *see* Note, *Insider Trading: The Issuer's Disposition of an Alleged 16(b) Violation*, 1968 DUKE L.J. 94; Lowenfels, *Section 16(b): A New Trend in Regulating Insider Trading*, 54 CORNELL L. REV. 45 (1968); PAINTER, FEDERAL REGULATION OF INSIDER TRADING, Ch. III, at 24–52 (Michie, 1968); Goodman, *Expanding Short–Swing Liability*, 3 REV. OF SEC. REG. 891 (July 15, 1970); Katz, *supra* note 18.

Section 4(1) of the 1933 Act[34] exempts from registration "transactions by any person other than an issuer, underwriter or dealer." The term "underwriter" is defined in Section 2(11) of the 1933 Act[35] to include any person who purchases from an issuer with a view toward distribution. For purposes of determining who is an underwriter, the term "issuer" is defined to include any person directly or indirectly controlling the issuer. Thus, if the offeror can be considered to be controlling the issuer, it will be unlawful for any securities dealers to effect transactions in the shares of that company without a registration statement. While the term "control" is not defined for purposes of determining who is an issuer pursuant to Section 2(11), its meaning is generally understood to refer to the power of one person to direct the management or policies of any other person.[36] Since the offeror is disposing of its shares in the target because it has failed to obtain control, the act of sale itself will be evidence that control was not achieved and accordingly it would appear that the shares may be sold without a registration statement.[37]

Registration, however, may be required as a prerequisite to a public sale, even where the offeror has not obtained control of the target, if any unregistered shares were accepted pursuant to the tender offer or were otherwise acquired by the offeror. The theory underlying the possible necessity of registration is based upon the SEC's application of a "fungibility" principle to all shares of stock of an issuer. Although the principle has never been formalized in a rule or interpretative release, the staff of the Commission has taken the position that when a purchaser acquires unregistered shares he necessarily indicates the absence of any intent publicly to distribute any other shares of the same issuer which he then holds.[38] Accordingly, the staff's position re-

[34] 15 U.S.C. § 77d(i). [35] 15 U.S.C. § 77b(ii).

[36] *See, e.g.*, U.S. v. Re, 336 F.2d 306 (2d Cir. 1964), *cert. denied*, 379 U.S. 904 (1964). *See also* Rule 405(f) promulgated pursuant to the 1933 Act.

[37] Any attempt to apply a test of control on the basis of the percentage of the outstanding voting securities owned by the offeror as compared with incumbent management's holdings would not appear to be appropriate in the context of the unsuccessful tender offer.

[38] The theory underlying the fungibility concept is based on the fact that the economic effect of a sale of any shares would be the same as that of a sale of the shares most recently purchased. Even where registered shares are purchased sub-

quired that the tender offeror satisfy his original investment intent with regard to the unregistered shares before any registered shares could lawfully be sold.

In determining whether an investor has satisfied his investment intent, the staff of the Commission has traditionally placed emphasis on the length of time the person has held the securities and/or whether there has been an unforeseeable change in circumstances of the holder. Experience demonstrated, however, that reliance upon such factors not only failed to assure adequate disclosure of information to investors, but also has led to uncertainty in the application of the registration provisions of the 1933 Act. As a result, the Commission adopted Rule 144, which establishes objective guidelines regarding the sale of unregistered securities.[39] These guidelines include requirements that: (a) specified current information concerning the issuer be publicly available; (b) the person acquiring unregistered securities cannot distribute such securities for a minimum of two years; and (c) sales of unregistered securities will not exceed certain specified quantitative limitations.

The extent to which Rule 144 will affect the ability of the unsuccessful offeror to sell registered securities where he also owns unregistered securities of the target company is not entirely clear. The Commission's release announcing adoption of Rule 144 states that:

> For the purpose of the rule, the doctrine of "fungibility" will not apply. That is, the acquisition during the two-year period of other securities of the same issuer, whether restricted or nonrestricted, will not start the holding period running anew.[40]

---

sequent to the unregistered shares, the sale of the former without registration has been questioned. *See The Wheat Report,* Disclosure to Investors: A Reappraisal of Federal Administrative Policies under the '33 and '34 Acts, 172–73 (1969).

The prudent investor will normally seek a "no–action" letter from the staff of the Commission even where the shares to be sold are fully registered and have been acquired subsequent to the purchase of any unregistered shares. For some recent "no-action" letters involving the fungibility concept, *see* Roto American Corp., Feb. 19, 1971, CCH Fed. Sec. L. Rep. ¶ 78,026; Gino's, Inc., CCH Fed. Sec. L. Rep. ¶ 78,105, discussed in 99 BNA Sec. Reg. & L. Rep. C–4 (April 28, 1971), Sec. Reg. & Trans. Rep., May 15, 1971, at 4.

[39] SEC Securities Act Release No. 5223 (Jan. 11, 1972) eff. April 15, 1972.

[40] *Id.*

The above-quoted portion of Rule 144 appears to eliminate the effects of the fungibility concept. Thus, for example, it would appear that the sale of fully registered shares of the target company would be permitted by Rule 144 at any time within two years of the purchase of any unregistered securities. The rationale of the Commission in eliminating the fungibility concept was based upon the fact that fungibility bears little relationship to the needs of investors for disclosure.[41]

[41] For a comprehensive analysis of Rule 144, *see* Wander, *Rule 144 Adopted*, 5 REV. OF SEC. REG. 957 (March 8, 1972); Lipton, *Analysis of SEC Rule 144*, N.Y.L.J. (March 26, 1972), at 1, 6. *See also* Farquhar, *Interpreting Rule 144*, 5 REV. OF SEC. REG. 875 (Sept. 6, 1972).

Chapter 9. DEFENSIVE TACTICS TO THWART A TENDER OFFER

Section 1. *OBLIGATIONS, IF ANY, OF MANAGEMENT TO RESIST A TAKEOVER ATTEMPT*

Once a tender offer has been made, management of the target must decide whether it will contest the bid or if it does not choose to resist, whether it has any obligation to do so. Where an attractive offer is made by a well-managed, financially sound company whose operations are not incompatible with the target, management may recommend that its shareholders accept the bid or, at a minimum, not take any action opposing the bid. Not all offers, however, present such attractive possibilities. It has not been uncommon, for example, to find instances of attempted takeovers by offerors whose performance records were hardly designed to inspire confidence. Similarly, a number of exchange offers which relied heavily on the issuance of debt securities have cast serious doubts as to the ability of the offerors to meet their obligations under the terms of the instruments. Still other offerors have attempted to take over corporations to avail themselves of large cash reserves which were apparently needed to bail themselves out of previous mistakes. Nevertheless, management still may not be motivated to action. Indifference, inertia, or the failure to evaluate properly the offeror's prospects of success may well result in management doing nothing.

While the federal tender rules require the management of the target company to furnish certain specified information to both the SEC and the shareholders *if it chooses to make a recommen-*

dation regarding the offer,[1] the statute imposes no specific duty upon management to speak for or against the offer, or to take any other action regarding the offer.[2]

It must be noted, however, that the 1970 amendment to Section 14(e)[3] of the 1934 Act granted the SEC rule-making power to "define, and prescribe means reasonably designed to prevent, such acts and practices as are fraudulent, deceptive, or manipulative." During the course of the Senate Hearings regarding this amendment, the staff of the Commission advised that it might define the failure by incumbent management to disclose its position (pro or con) on the offer as a fraudulent practice under Section 14(e).[4] The staff's statement, however, appears to be inconsistent with both the legislative history and the statutory language of the Williams Act,[5] and it is questionable whether a broad rule promulgated pursuant to Section 14(e) compelling incumbent management to state its position on a tender offer would be upheld by the courts as a valid exercise of administrative rule-making power.[6]

A somewhat related but perhaps more fundamental issue

1 For a discussion of the federal rules pertaining to recommendations made by incumbent management, see text accompanying notes 169–174, *infra*.

2 The failure of the statute to require incumbent management to make a statement regarding the offer was not inadvertent. The legislative history of the Williams Bill clearly indicates that Congress was well aware of the importance of a statement by incumbent management setting forth its views regarding the offer: "As a practical matter, unless incumbent management explains its position publicly, the investor is severely limited in obtaining all of the facts on which to base a decision whether to accept or reject the tender offer." S. REP. No. 550, 90th Cong., 1st Sess. 2 (1967); H.R. REP. No. 1711, 90th Cong., 2d Sess. 2 (1968).

Cf. Section 14(c) of the 1934 Act and rules thereunder requiring issuers that do not solicit proxies in connection with an annual or other meeting of shareholders to furnish both the SEC and the shareholders information substantially equivalent to that which would be required if a proxy solicitation were made. *See also* Electronic Specialty Co. v. International Controls Corp., 409 F.2d 937, 945–46 (2d Cir. 1969), *aff'g in part*, 295 F. Supp. 1063 (S.D.N.Y. 1968).

3 15 U.S.C. § 78n(e), as amended (1970).

4 *See Hearings on S. 336 and S. 3431 Before the Subcomm. on Securities of the Senate Comm. on Banking and Currency*, 91st Cong., 2d Sess. 12 (1970). *See also* Brown, *The Scope of the Williams Act and Its 1970 Amendments*, 26 BUS. LAW 1637, 1647 (July 1971).

5 See note 2, *supra*.

6 One commentator has stated that because the statutory language and the legislative history indicate that a recommendation need not be made, a decision not to make one could not be a violation of Section 14(e). *See* Krasik, *Tender Offers: The Target Company's Duty of Disclosure*, 25 BUS. LAW 455, 460 (Nov. 1969).

which the courts have yet to consider is whether the anti-fraud provisions of the federal securities laws or common law principles of fiduciary responsibility require management to defend against a bid which may be inconsistent with the best interests of the corporation or its shareholders. The answer is by no means clear and may well depend upon the facts and circumstances of the individual case. For example, does management's obligation to prevent the misuse of corporate assets extend to a tender offer made by a corporation or by individuals which have had no experience in the operations of the target or where the bid represents some obvious evidence of a classical corporate rape? [7] If in fact there is a duty to resist, does management have an obligation to do more than just advise shareholders of the reasons it believes the offer is unacceptable? Does it make any difference if the bid is made at a substantial premium over market, and management honestly believes that the stock is fully priced at the current market? If management has nondisclosed material information which would lead one to believe that the market value of the target's stock does not reflect its true present value, will the failure to resist an offer made at an inadequate price create liability to those stockholders who tender their shares? [8] Will the failure of the target's management to disclose material adverse information regarding the offeror create similar liability? [9] What

[7] While the ultimate effects of a takeover on the target may not be known for several years, this fact alone will not preclude liability for culpable mismanagement.

[8] With regard to the obligations of management to make "voluntary" disclosures of material corporate developments, *see* SEC v. Texas Gulf Sulphur Co., 401 F.2d 833 (2d Cir. 1968) (*en banc*), *cert. denied, sub nom.* Kline v. SEC, 394 U.S. 976 (1969). For supplemental opinions, *see* No. 30882 (2d Cir. 1968) (*rehearing denied*), CCH FED. SEC. L. REP. ¶ 92,251; 312 F. Supp. 77 (S.D.N.Y. 1970), *aff'd in part*, No. 35143 (2d Cir. 1971), CCH FED. SEC. L. REP. ¶ 93,072; No. 65 Civ. 1182 (S.D.N.Y. 1971), CCH FED. SEC. L. REP. ¶ 93,211. For original lower court opinion, *see* 258 F. Supp. 262 (S.D.N.Y. 1966). *See also* Astor v. Texas Gulf Sulphur Co., 306 F. Supp. 1333 (S.D.N.Y. 1969).

See also speech of Herbert A. Einhorn, "Disclosure Problems of the Corporate Financial Executive," National Investor Relations Institute, May 24, 1971, N.Y.C.; Kennedy, *Tender Moment*, 23 BUS. LAW 1091, 1095 (July 1968).

For a good discussion of the underlying policy considerations supporting the view that management of the target should be required to make a recommendation (pro or con) regarding the tender offer, *see* Krasik, *supra* note 6, at 460–61.

[9] *Cf.* Boggess v. Hogan, No. 69C 2267 (N.D. Ill. 1971), CCH FED. SEC. L. REP. ¶ 93,075, where the court denied a motion to dismiss a class action suit brought by nontendering shareholders of the target company alleging violations of Rule

is the scope of potential liability for officers and directors who fail to resist a questionable offer because of some personal benefit to be derived if the offer succeeds? [10]

While the courts may be reluctant to impose an affirmative duty on management in an area which might properly be considered a matter of business judgment, there is evidence to indicate that this may not become the universal view. In *Northwest Industries, Inc. v. B. F. Goodrich Co.*,[11] a case which is discussed in detail below,[12] the court's persuasive dictum clearly states that management has a fiduciary responsibility to resist tender offers which, "in its best judgment, are detrimental to the company or its stockholders." [13] In light of the court's opinion in this case, efforts should therefore be made to minimize the risks of exposure to potential liability where management chooses not to oppose the offer. In this regard, management would be well advised to have some documentation setting forth the bases upon which it chose not to resist as evidence that it considered the matter and that it did not find the offer to be inconsistent with the best interests of the corporation or its stockholders.

10b-5 in that the offeror and certain of the directors of the target failed to disclose: (a) a secret agreement whereby the offeror would purchase the directors' shares at a premium price in exchange for their support of the offer; and (b) the offeror's plans to loot the target company.

In a companion case, the directors' suit specifically to enforce the secret agreement was dismissed. Hogan v. Teledyne, Inc., No. 69C 1941 (N.D. Ill. 1971), CCH FED. SEC. L. REP. ¶ 93,074. *See also* Rothschild v. Teledyne, Inc., No. 69C 2276 (N.D. Ill. 1971), CCH FED. SEC. L. REP. ¶ 93,076.

[10] *Id. See also* Broffe v. Horton, 172 F. 2d 489 (2d Cir. 1949); Klink, *Management's Role In Recommending For Or Against An Offer*, 39 ANTITRUST LAW JOURNAL (Section of Antitrust Law, American Bar Association) 325 (1970).

[11] 301 F. Supp. 706 (N.D. Ill. 1969).

[12] See text accompanying notes 109–11.

[13] See *supra* note 11, at 712. *See also* Boggess v. Hogan, *supra* note 9. *Cf.* Condec Corp. v. The Lunkenheimer Co., 230 A.2d 769 (Del. Ch. 1967) discussed in text accompanying notes 105–108, *infra;* U.S. Smelting, Refining & Mining Co. v. Clevite Corp., Civ. Nos. C68-210, C68-345 (N.D. Ohio 1968), CCH FED. SEC. L. REP. ¶ 92,691 at pp. 99,046–47 where the offeror claimed that the resistance of the target's management to its offer constituted a breach of fiduciary responsibility. See also text accompanying note 61, *infra*.

SECTION 2. *PROCEDURES TO ALERT MANAGEMENT TO A POTENTIAL TAKEOVER ATTEMPT*

Where a company obtains knowledge of a proposed tender offer in advance of the actual bid, it gains valuable time in which to prepare an effective defense. Toward this end, there are a number of steps that a potential target may be able to take to reduce the risks of a surprise takeover attempt.[14]

A daily review of trading in the company's stock is an essential part of an early warning system and will enable the target to pinpoint any unusual trading activity. The "Fitch sheets," which provide a daily breakdown of each transaction in sequence for every security traded on the New York, American and National stock exchanges, serve as a valuable tool in analyzing trading activity. Regional exchange trading should also be reviewed regularly to determine if there are any unusual price or volume movements. Although information regarding individual trades on over-the-counter transactions is not available to the public, the newly automated NASDAQ quotation system will shortly make available volume figures on selected issues traded over-the-counter. In addition, close contact with the company's exchange specialist and/or OTC market makers [15] is advisable.

Stockholders' lists and transfer sheets should also be continuously reviewed to determine if there is any concentrated accumulation pattern in any individual or nominee names. An analysis of stock ownership by class of investor may also prove useful, particularly where there is some evidence of accumulation by institutional investors.[16] In this regard it should be noted that the

[14] *See* summary of a talk by Martin Zausner, presented before the Practising Law Institute, "Takeover Bids, Proxy Contests and Transactions in Control," Dec. 15, 1967, reprinted by Arthur Schmidt & Associates, Inc., N.Y.

[15] Those firms active in the third market, i.e., trading in NYSE-listed securities over-the-counter, should not be overlooked in reviewing trading activity. The SEC's "Statistical Bulletin" provides quarterly third market volume figures for individual securities. *See also* SEC 36th Annual Report (1970), at 81–82.

[16] "Vickers Guide to Investment Company Portfolios" (Vickers Associates, Inc., Huntington, L.I., N.Y., publishers), and the "International Securities Locator" (Scheinman Ciaramella International Ltd., N.Y., N.Y., publishers) may serve as valuable reference sources in identifying the most recently reported holdings of institutional investors.

degree of concentration of share ownership can be expected to bear an important relationship to the vulnerability of a particular company as a potential target.

A company which has developed a reputation for fair dealing and frankness with the professional investment community, financial institutions and the press, may often find these sources to be of assistance in locating and identifying a budding takeover attempt.[17] In addition, a company which develops a reputation of willingness to listen to and entertain legitimate acquisition offers may thereby reduce the odds of a surprise takeover attempt.

Information filed with the SEC pursuant to Section 13(d) of the 1934 Act may prove to be the most valuable reference source in uncovering a takeover attempt. A regular review of Schedule 13D reports, for example, may reveal a concert of action by a group of stockholders which would not be reflected by an analysis of individual holdings.[18]

SECTION 3. *DEFENSIVE MEASURES PRIOR TO THE TENDER OFFER*

If the potential target company hopes to offer any meaningful resistance to a takeover attempt, it is essential that it mobilize its defenses in advance of the actual offer. The inability to respond with a show of strength during the crucial first days of an offer may result in the loss of certain tactical advantages. It may also create the impression of ineptness or unpreparedness, with resulting loss of investor confidence in management.

Accordingly, consideration must be given to what can be done to insure that the target is prepared to respond effectively as soon as the offer is announced. Perhaps the best method of preparation is the fire-drill approach, whereby management assumes

[17] *See* Cheney, *Public Relations Considerations in Making and Fighting Tender Offers*, 42 OHIO ST. BAR ASSOC. REP. 771 (1969).

[18] Any person who acquires more than 5 percent of any equity security subject to the provisions of Section 13(d) of the 1934 Act must file a Schedule 13D report with the SEC, the issuer of such equity security and each exchange where the security is traded within ten days after such acquisition. *See* Rule 13d-1 (17 C.F.R. § 240.13d–1).

With regard to the information required by Schedule 13D (17 C.F.R. § 240.13d–101), see text accompanying notes 86–97, Chapter 4.

that a tender offer, the terms of which are unknown, will take place sometime within the next several weeks. Such an approach will necessarily require management to review its decision-making procedure as well as insure that the company has the ability to translate decision-making into effective action. In this regard it is recommended that the corporation obtain the advice and guidance of experienced experts at the earliest possible stage. The preparedness measures described below are truly a full-time occupation. It is highly recommended that these measures be delegated to qualified experts.

General policy discussions, establishing the realistic parameters as to the type of offer, if any, that would be acceptable to the board of directors, would be a useful starting point in planning a defense. If the offer does not meet the board's guidelines, consideration must be given to the tactics—legal, financial, and psychological—that the company will employ to defend against the bid. If acquisitions, private placements, or stock splits are a possibility, there should be sufficient authorized but unissued shares available. If the potential target chooses to consider the repurchase of its own shares as a defensive tactic, it must make certain that sufficient funds are on hand or that adequate financing is available. Drafts of sample letters to shareholders as well as advertisements and press releases should be prepared and available well in advance of the actual bid.

Mechanically, management must first insure that the board can be quickly convened. If there is a requirement in the charter or by-laws providing for a lengthy notice period in calling a board meeting, consideration should be given to reducing the notice period in order to prevent one or more directors from delaying action by refusing to give a waiver.[19] In addition, telephone

[19] *See* Chatlos, *What to Do Before the Tender Offer Comes*, PUB. REL. Q. (Spring 1969) at 5 (Reprint).

"In some states it has been held that if a quorum of the directors of a corporation meet specially, and act by a majority of the whole board, their action is valid, notwithstanding notice of the meeting was not given to the absent members of the board; but this view is contrary to the very decided weight of authority." 2 FLETCHER, CYC. OF CORPS. § 408 (rev. vol. 1969).

"The giving of notice may be excused because of an emergency which demands immediate attention, at least so far as absent or inaccessible directors are concerned." 2 FLETCHER, CYC. OF CORPS. § 408 (rev. vol. 1969). Query, whether a direc-

numbers of all board members, officers, and key operating and administrative personnel should be kept current and accessible. Emergency duplicating and printing facilities should be available on a stand-by basis. An extra set of pre-addressed shareholders envelopes should be maintained to eliminate any additional delays.

To insure that the offeror is not afforded any unintended advantage, the company should strictly limit access to its shareholders' lists. Items such as mailing plates or pre-addressed envelopes, which can form the basis for a shareholders' list, should also be carefully guarded. A review of the security procedures of the company's dividend disbursing and transfer agents is advisable to insure that appropriate steps are being taken to eliminate unauthorized access to shareholders' lists.[20]

The reaction of the well-drilled and well-prepared defense, once the offer is announced, has been described as follows:

> You freeze the opposition by a good, strong, firm, outright fighting attitude. If you have got your weaponry and strategy outlined in your little black book, you can optimize that posture. You have decided what you are going to do and you know what needs to be done. You have your statement out to Dow Jones. You have the letter in preparation to your stockholders.
>
> In your little black book every executive officer has his own timetable starting from Point Zero. The internal directors are called. The executive committee is called. Other directors are contacted. Bear in mind, all of this is premised on the fact that we act quickly and immediately and we are prepared with 14-D's. They are already in Washington, ready to be taken over to the SEC on a moment's notice, as quickly as we can do it.
>
> The shareholder list is immediately scanned to be sure it is up to date. But really, if you have this kind of a plan, you will know it is being continually brought up to date to meet any situation.
>
> Then the shareholder phone calling starts. This means that we know who is going to call whom, and we have their phone numbers.

---

tors' meeting to decide on what action is to be taken with respect to defending against a tender offer constitutes an emergency for purposes of satisfying this exception to the notice rule?

With regard to meetings of an executive committee, presumably notice must be given in the same manner as prescribed in the case of the full board of directors. *See* 2 FLETCHER, CYC. OF CORPS. § 407 (rev. vol. 1969).

[20] *See* Zausner, *supra* note 14.

In addition to that, we have the instructions that are to be given to those who are to make the phone calls. And we know who the alternates of those are who have been assigned to make the phone calls. These people don't know yet they have been assigned to make phone calls, but their supervisors do.

Simultaneously with all this, the lawyers start off on a Justice Department review to see if there is anything there that can help.

The letter to stockholders which has already been written, is very hurriedly revised and is at the printer's. We know exactly how long it will take to print the letter. We know where the stockholder envelopes are. We know how long it will take to print, insert, stuff and mail, and we know whether our post office has the capacity to send out that many letters overnight. If they don't, we will arrange to have it sent from two post offices.

Another team has the responsibility of looking at the financial community's response to see whether the volume of trading or anything else has an implication on the plan as we now have it drawn. The financial adviser has been brought into it and is already checking to see what sources of strength he can command in the financial community, whether brokerage houses or other banks or whatever.

Then there are press releases and answers to the Stock Exchange and press inquiries. As far as the press releases are concerned, they are prepared ahead of time and should be on their way.[21]

SECTION 4. *MANAGEMENT'S USE OF CORPORATE FUNDS FOR EXPENSES INCURRED IN DEFENDING AGAINST A TENDER OFFER*[22]

A. TYPES OF EXPENSES NORMALLY INCURRED IN CONNECTION WITH A TENDER OFFER DEFENSE

The expenses which management will incur in defending against a tender offer will in large measure depend upon the nature of the defensive tactics it chooses to employ. These tactics are described in detail in Section 5 of this chapter. There are, however, a number of basic commitments that management must normally be prepared to make if it hopes to offer any meaningful

[21] Chatlos, *supra* note 19. The above described procedures have often been referred to as the "black book procedures," referring to a hypothetical black book of defensive plans and procedures.

[22] The use of corporate funds to acquire capital assets (including the repurchase of the target's own shares) in defending against a tender offer is discussed in Section 5 of this chapter.

resistance to the takeover attempt. Initially, management should retain a team of specialists who will have the expertise to initiate planning and strategy as well as the knowledge and experience to anticipate potential problems which may arise. In many instances the team will include legal counsel, an accountant, a securities analyst, a public relations expert, and a soliciting group comprising a professional "proxy" solicitor and at least one brokerage firm acting as a soliciting dealer. In attempting to persuade shareholders to reject the offer, management must also be prepared to incur the costs of (1) preparing, printing, and mailing communications to shareholders; (2) advertising in newspapers of national daily circulation which generally publish financial news; and (3) travel, telephone, and entertainment in connection with the solicitation of shareholders.

B. General Principles Affecting Management's Right to Use Corporate Funds to Defend Against a Tender Offer

The right of management to use corporate funds for expenses in defending against a tender offer is not regulated by state or federal statute nor has there been any direct judicial expression on the issue to date. The applicable legal principles, however, have been enunciated in a number of cases where the incumbents avail themselves of the corporate treasury in a proxy contest.[23]

Most of the cases which have considered the issue in a proxy fight context have turned on the question of whether the expenditures were made to further some legitimate corporate policy as distinguished from expenditures made primarily to enable management to perpetuate itself in office.[24] The rule, however, is

[23] The right of the target company's management to use corporate funds to repurchase its own shares or to purchase stock or assets of other companies in exchange for cash and/or securities of the target in defending against a takeover attempt has also been reviewed by the courts. These cases have applied essentially the same legal principles set forth in the proxy expense cases. See subsections (a) and (f) of Section 5, *infra*.

[24] *See* Peel v. London & Northwestern Ry. Co. [1907], 1 Ch. Div. 5 (C.A. 1906); Lawyers' Advertising Co. v. Consolidated Ry. Lighting and Refrig. Co., 187 N.Y. 395, 80 N.E. 199 (1907); Steinberg v. Adams, 90 F. Supp. 604

easier to state than to apply and has been justly criticized as placing a premium on the inventiveness of management in disguising what is obviously a struggle for control in the guise of preserving corporate policy.[25] More important, this approach has served to obscure the importance of insuring that independent shareholders are kept fully informed. The recognition that all contested proxy contests and tender offers involve differences in policy would provide a much more workable and meaningful base from which to develop the guidelines for permissible corporate expenditures.[26]

While it is entirely possible that in some situations extravagance and waste will be encouraged by permitting the target's management to use corporate funds to defend against a tender offer that it considers to be against the target's best interests, there appears to be no better practical solution. The opportunity exists to challenge such abuses through judicial review of the "reasonableness" of both the nature and amount of such expenditures. Although the Courts may be reluctant to substitute their own views of reasonableness for those of management, they can be expected to condemn and hold management accountable in cases of flagrant abuse; and this should act as a limited deterrent. This more realistic approach would be better than doing lip service to the fictional distinction between management's use of corporate funds to further corporate policy and the use of such funds to perpetuate management.

(S.D.N.Y. 1950); Rosenfeld v. Fairchild Engine & Airplane Corp., 309 N.Y. 168, 128 N.E.2d 291 (1955). For an analysis and discussion of these and other cases as well as other problems in connection with management's use of corporate funds in proxy contests, *see* ARANOW AND EINHORN, PROXY CONTESTS FOR CORPORATE CONTROL (2d ed. 1968), at 547–68.

[25] *See* Steinberg v. Adams, *supra* note 24, at 608; Fleischer and Mundheim, *Corporate Acquisition by Tender Offer,* 115 U. PA. L. REV. 317, 364–65 (1967); Note, *Buying Out Insurgent Shareholders With Corporate Funds,* 70 YALE L.J. 308 (1960). *See also* dissent in Rosenfeld v. Fairchild Engine & Airplane Corp., *supra* note 24, at 176, 128 N.E.2d at 295.

[26] *Cf.* Levin v. Metro-Goldwyn-Mayer, Inc., 264 F. Supp. 797 (S.D.N.Y. 1967), where the court denied a motion for an injunction by stockholders of MGM to prevent the corporation from using its employees to solicit proxies and from expending corporate funds for the services of specially retained attorneys, a public relations firm, and "the four top proxy-soliciting concerns."

c. Tax Deductibility of Corporate Expenses

The deductibility of expenses incurred by the target in defending against a tender offer may depend on the purpose of the expense for which a deduction is claimed. However, deductibility can also be affected by the type of defensive tactic which is employed. In *Locke Manufacturing Companies v. U.S.*[27] the court held that certain legal, soliciting, and public relations fees incurred by the corporation in connection with a proxy contest were primarily concerned with a question of corporate policy and were therefore properly paid by the corporation. As to the question of deductibility, the court held, in a decision in which the Treasury has acquiesced,[28] that such fees were ordinary and necessary expenses deductible by the corporation as business expenses under Section 162 of the Internal Revenue Code ("Code") of 1964.[29]

Different considerations will apply, however, if the expenses are incurred in connection with the employment of specific substantive defensive tactics leading to the purchase or sale of property, such as the target's repurchase of its own shares, acquisitions for stock, or private placements of securities. It is well recognized, for example, that legal, brokerage, accounting, and similar costs incurred in the acquisition or disposition of capital assets are to be treated as capital expenditures.[30] If an expense is

[27] 237 F. Supp. 80 (D. Conn. 1964). For a discussion of the tax deductibility of corporate expenses in proxy contests, *see* Aranow and Einhorn, Proxy Contests for Corporate Control, pp. 566–68, (2d ed. 1968).

[28] *See* Rev. Rul. 67–1 (1967-1 Cum. Bull. 28). The ruling provides in essence that proxy expenses in contests over corporate policy may be deducted but that where the expenses are primarily for the benefit of individuals rather than in connection with corporate policy the expenses will be disallowed. Thus, deductions claimed by the corporation for expenditures which are in the nature of preferential dividends or excessive compensation will be disallowed. *Cf.* U.S. v. Smith, 418 F. 2d 589 (5th Cir. 1969).

[29] Section 162 provides that "There shall be allowed as a deduction all the ordinary and necessary expenses paid or incurred during the taxable year in carrying on any trade or business. . . ."

[30] "The law could hardly be otherwise, for such ancillary expenses incurred in acquiring or disposing of an asset are as much part of the cost of that asset as is the price paid for it." Woodward v. Commissioner, 397 U.S. 572, 576 (1970). *See* Rev. Rul. 69–561 (1969–2 Cum. Bull. 25), brokerage fees incurred and paid by a corporation upon the purchase of its outstanding stock for the purpose of holding

capital, it cannot be deducted as an ordinary and necessary business expense under Section 162 of the Code, or, in the case of individuals, as an ordinary and necessary expense under Section 212.[31] Instead, such expenditures are normally added to the basis of the capital asset, thereby reducing the gain or increasing the loss when the asset is sold.[32]

Difficulties arise in applying these principles in the context of a tender offer since an expenditure may be incurred for the purpose of preserving corporate policy in connection with the acquisition or disposition of a capital asset. Two recent Supreme Court cases would appear to pose strong obstacles to the current deductibility of expenses incurred in connection with the target's acquisition or sale of its own shares in defending against a tender offer.[33]

In *Woodward v. Commissioner*[34] and a companion case, *U.S. v. Hilton Hotels Corp.*,[35] involving the tax treatment of expenses

---

it as treasury stock or retiring it are not ordinary and necessary business expenses; Rev. Rul. 69–330 (1969-1 CUM. BULL. 51), accounting and legal expenses incurred in registering stock with the SEC are capital expenditures and not deductible as business expenses under Sec. 162 of the Code; Treas. Reg. § 1.263 (a)-2(e), commissions paid in purchasing securities are capital expenditures. Presumably, payment of solicitation fees to both securities dealers and professional soliciting firms in connection with a tender offer or other purchases of its own shares by the target will be treated or considered in the nature of "commissions" for deductibility purposes.

See also 4A MERTENS, LAW OF FEDERAL INCOME TAXATION, § 25A.15 (1966 rev.); Fireman's Insurance Co., 30 B.T.A. 1004 (1934); Atzingen-Whitehouse Dairy Inc. v. Commissioner, 36 T.C. 173 (1961), ¶ 36.17 P-H TC 1961; Helvering v. Winmill, 305 U.S. 79 (1938); Spreckels v. Commissioner, 315 U.S. 626 (1942); Spangler v. Commissioner, 323 F. 2d 913, 921 (9th Cir. 1963).

[31] Section 212 provides that "In the case of an individual, there shall be allowed as a deduction all the ordinary and necessary expenses paid or incurred during the taxable year (1) for the production or collection of income; (2) for the management, conservation, or maintenance of property held for the production of income. . . ." Section 212 is *in pari materia* with Section 162 so far as it relates to the term "ordinary and necessary."

[32] *See* Sections 263 and 1012 of the Code. Capital expenses may also be deducted through depreciation charges and through amortization of organization expenses. *See also* Section 1032 providing that no gain or loss is recognized on a corporation's sale of its own stock. Where a corporation sells its own stock, appropriate charges are normally made to the capital surplus account.

[33] Expenses incurred in connection with third-party merger negotiations entered into to defeat the tender offer would fall within the class of expenses which must be capitalized if the merger is in fact consummated. If the transaction is subsequently abandoned. the costs will be deductible.

[34] *Supra* note 30. [35] 397 U.S. 580 (1970).

incurred in certain appraisal litigation, the court held that expenses arising out of the acquisition of a capital asset are capital expenses, notwithstanding the taxpayers' purpose in incurring them. In the *Woodward* case, the taxpayers incurred legal, accounting, and appraisers' fees in connection with appraisal litigation arising out of the purchase of a dissenting shareholder's stock. Deductions were claimed for these expenses under Section 212 of the Code as "ordinary and necessary expenses paid—for the management, conservation or maintenance of property held for the production of income." The theory of the taxpayers' case was that the "primary purpose" test, "developed in the context of cases involving the costs of defending property, should be applied to costs incurred in acquiring or disposing of property as well." [36] Since the litigation involved the appraisal of the dissenters' stock, the taxpayers argued that the primary purpose of incurring such expenses was to establish a valuation for the stock rather than the acquisition of a capital asset. The court rejected the taxpayers' application of the "primary purpose" test to the regulation that makes the costs of acquisition of a capital asset a capital expenditure,[37] and held instead that since the origin of the claim litigated was part of the acquisition process, the expenses must be capitalized.[38]

In the *Hilton* case, the corporation retained a consulting firm to prepare a study to determine a fair rate of exchange in connection with a merger appraisal proceeding. Hilton then deducted the fees paid to the consulting firm as well as the cost of legal and other professional services arising out of the appraisal proceeding as ordinary and necessary expenses under Section 162.[39] The court rejected the claim and held, as in the *Wood-*

[36] Woodward v. Commissioner, *supra* note 30, at 577. Expenses incurred in defending or perfecting title to property are deemed to be capital in nature only where the taxpayers' "primary purpose" in incurring them is to defend or perfect title. Since the appraisal proceeding did not directly involve the question of title to the minority stock, the taxpayers and the court apparently reasoned that the "primary purpose" test did not require capitalization of these expenses.

See Treas. Reg. § 1.263(a) 2(c); Rassenfoss v. Commissioner of Internal Revenue, 158 F.2d 764, 767-78 (7th Cir. 1946); Industrial Aggregate Co. v. U.S., 284 F.2d 639, 645 (8th Cir. 1960). *See also* 4A MERTENS, *supra* note 30, § 25.24, § 25A.16.

[37] Treas. Reg. § 1.263(a)-2(a).

[38] Woodward v. Commissioner, *supra* note 30, at 579.

[39] Payments to the consulting firm for the "pre-merger determination of fair value" were conceded by Hilton to be nondeductible and the district court so held. See *supra* note 35, at 582.

ward case, that expenses arising out of the acquisition process are nondeductible regardless of the purpose in incurring them.

The *Woodward* and *Hilton* cases involve the question of whether an item of expense not directly a part of the acquisition cost but incidental to the entire acquisition process must be capitalized. A different issue may be presented, however, where the acquisition of the subject property is itself merely incidental to another plan designed to serve a purpose unrelated to the acquisition of property *per se*. In *Five Star Manufacturing Co. v. Commissioner*,[40] a deduction was allowed the company for the costs of its own shares which it repurchased to prevent liquidation by outside creditors. Similarly, in *Hogg v. Allen* [41] the court found that the sole purpose of a partnership's purchase of 600 shares of a supplier's stock was to insure a continued source of supply enabling the partnership to continue its business operations. Accordingly it was held that the acquisition of the shares was an ordinary and necessary expense incurred in carrying on a trade and business and as such was deductible. *In U.S. v. Smith*,[42] the company claimed that it assumed liabilities in the acquisition of certain assets to preserve its business, and took an ordinary deduction for the amount of the liabilities. In remanding the case to determine whether the liabilities were in fact assumed by the corporation, the court held that if there was an assumption, a determination of the reasons motivating the assumption must be made—and that "If this factual inquiry reveals a primary purpose other than acquisition of property, the court may properly allow a deduction to the corporation if all of the requirements of . . . Sec. 162, are met. . . ." [43]

The theory of this line of cases could seemingly be extended to permit a company to deduct not only incidental expenses but the full costs of acquiring assets or stock as well, at least where the acquisition is found necessary to preserve the continued existence of the corporate entity. It must be noted, however, that while a successful takeover attempt may involve a change in the form or structure of the target, it will generally not involve a threat to the target's continuing business operations. Thus, reli-

[40] 355 F.2d 724 (5th Cir. 1966).

[41] 105 F. Supp. 12 (M.D. Ga. 1952), *aff'd in part, sub nom.*, Edwards v. Hogg, 214 F.2d 640 (5th Cir. 1954).

[42] *Supra* note 28.

[43] *Id.* at 597.

ance on this line of cases to support the current deductibility of acquisitions or expenses incurred in connection with such acquisitions may be questionable in the absence of evidence that the offeror intends to liquidate the target if it obtains control.

SECTION 5. *SUBSTANTIVE DEFENSIVE TACTICS*

A wide variety of defensive tactics may be employed by the target company in defending against a tender offer.[44] The manner in which these tactics may be successfully employed as well as the limitations upon their use are the subject matter of this section. The following list identifies the defensive tactics which are discussed herein:

A. Repurchases of its own shares by the target;
B. Open-market purchases of the target's shares by friendly third parties;
C. Concentrated selling of the offeror's shares by friendly third parties;
D. Dividend increases;
E. Stock splits;
F. Issuance of additional shares;
G. Creation of incompatibility between the target and the offeror;
H. Defensive mergers;
I. Discriminatory voting provisions;
J. Triggering of state takeover statutes;
K. Legal action;
L. Publicity; and
M. Restrictive loan agreements.

[44] For articles on substantive defensive tactics generally, *see* Schmults and Kelly, *Cash Take-Over Bids—Defense Tactics,* 23 BUS. LAW 115 (Nov. 1967); Bradshaw, *Defensive Tactics Employed by Incumbent Managements in Contesting Tender Offers,* 21 STAN. L. REV. 1104 (1969); Kennedy, *Defensive Take-Over Procedures Since the Williams Act,* 19 CATHOLIC U. L. REV. 158 (1969); Comments, *Corporate Defenses to Takeover Bids,* 44 TUL. L. REV. 517 (1970). *See also* Mullaney, *Guarding against Takeovers—Defensive Charter Provisions,* 25 BUS. LAW 1441 (July 1970); Cary, *Corporate Devices Used to Insulate Management from Attack,* 25 BUS. LAW 839 (January 1970); Hayes and Taussig, *Tactics of Cash Takeover Bids,* 45 HARV. BUS. REV. 135, 142–47 (March–April 1967).

A. Repurchase Of Shares [45]

Acquisitions of its own shares, whether by open-market purchase or by tender offer, enable the target to reduce the number of shares available to the opposition [46] and may drive the price of the shares up to a level where the tender offer is no longer attractive.[47]

The prevailing rule in the United States is that corporations are authorized to repurchase their own shares provided that such purchases do not impair the capital or otherwise adversely affect the viability of the corporation.[48] Once the shares are reacquired, the corporation may have the option of retiring and restoring them to the status of authorized but unissued shares or carrying them as treasury stock and treating the shares as still being issued and subject to resale.[49] The corporation, however, cannot be a stockholder in itself, and shares of its own stock can neither

[45] As to corporate purchases of their own securities, *see* 33 BNA Sec. Reg. & L. Rep. B-1 (Jan. 14, 1970); Kennedy, *Transactions by a Corporation in Its Own Shares,* 19 Bus. Law 319 (Jan. 1964); Zilber, *Corporate Tender Offers for Their Own Stock: Some Legal and Financial Considerations,* 33 Cinc. L. Rev. 315 (1964); Note, *Corporate Stock Repurchases Under the Federal Securities Laws,* 66 Colum. L. Rev. 1292 (1966); Cohen, A *Note on Takeover Bids and Corporate Purchases of Stock,* 22 Bus. Law 149 (Nov. 1966); Israels, *Corporate Purchase of Its Own Shares—Are There New Overtones?,* 50 Cornell L.Q. 620 (1965); Fleischer and Mundheim, *Corporate Acquisition by Tender Offer,* 115 U. Pa. L. Rev. 317, 364–65; H. R. Rep. No. 1711, 90th Cong., 2d Sess 5 (1968).

[46] However, purchases of its own securities by the target also have the effect of decreasing the number of shares the offeror needs to acquire control. *See also* Section 5 subsection (B), *infra,* of this chapter.

[47] American Steel & Pump Corp. made an offer to purchase shares of Standard Products Co. at $13.50 per share. Standard scheduled a special stockholders' meeting to approve repurchases of its own stock at a higher price. When American raised its tender price to $15 per share, Standard shareholders authorized the company to repurchase its shares at $17.25. American then withdrew its offer. *Tender Offers Become a Much Favored Way To Acquire Companies,* Wall Street Journal, Feb. 11, 1966, at 1.

[48] 6A Fletcher, Cyc. of Corps. § 2848 (rev. vol. 1969); *Cf.* NY Insurance Law § 78 (3), as amended L. 1965, eff. June 28, 1965.

[49] 11 Fletcher, Cyc. of Corps. § 5088 (rev. vol. 1969). One commentator has suggested the tender of treasury shares as a possible defensive tactic in order to insure the target standing to sue under Rule 10b-5. *See* Lockwood, *Corporate Acquisitions and Actions Under Sections 10(b) and 14 of the Securities Exchange Act of 1934,* 23 Bus. Law 365, 375–76 (Jan. 1968).

be voted[50] nor counted in determining the number of shares outstanding for voting purposes.[51]

(1) Federal Regulation of Corporate Repurchases Pursuant to Section 13(e) of the 1934 Act and Rules Thereunder

Section 13(e)(1)[52] of the 1934 Act gives the SEC broad rule-making authority with regard to purchases by an issuer of its own equity securities. Although Section 13(e) became law as part of the tender offer legislation in 1968, its sweeping language grants the SEC power to regulate all repurchases of equity securities registered pursuant to Section 12 or issued by a registered closed-end investment company[53] regardless of whether such repurchases are made during the course of or in connection with any tender offer. However, the only rules adopted to date pursuant to Section 13(e) relate solely to repurchases during the course of a tender offer.[54]

Rule 13e–1 prohibits an issuer from reacquiring any of its equity securities [of a class specified in Section 13(e)(1)] during the course of a tender offer made by any other person[55] unless the issuer has filed an information statement with the SEC and has within the past six months transmitted the substance of the specified information to its shareholders. The statement filed with the

[50] 5 Fletcher, Cyc. of Corps. § 2020 (rev. vol. 1969). With regard to a corporation voting its own stock which it holds in trust or in which it otherwise has no beneficial interest, *see* Aranow and Einhorn, Proxy Contests for Corporate Control (2d ed., 1968), at 398–400.

[51] 5 Fletcher, Cyc. of Corps. § 2041 (rev. vol. 1969).

[52] 15 U.S.C. § 78m(e)(1).

[53] The 1970 amendments, which expanded the class of persons subject to the disclosure requirements of Sections 13(d) and 14(d) to include equity securities of insurance companies, did not contain any similar amendment of Section 13(e).

[54] Rule 13e-1 (17 C.F.R. § 240.13e-1), eff. July 30, 1968; Rule 10b-13 (17 C.F.R. § 240.10b-13) eff. Nov. 10, 1969.

A proposed Rule 13e-2 provides for comprehensive regulation of the prices, amounts, and circumstances under which an issuer may repurchase its shares at any time. *See* SEC Securities Exchange Act Release No. 8930 (July 13, 1970), CCH Fed. Sec. L. Rep. ¶ 77,837. The proposed rule is patterned after the detailed settlement arrangements in the *Georgia-Pacific* and *Genesco* cases (see note 76, *infra*), which restricted repurchases by these issuers to limit the impact of their purchases on the market.

[55] The Rule does not apply to a tender offer by an issuer for its own securities provided the offer is not made during the course of a competing tender offer.

Commission and transmitted to shareholders must include information regarding the amount of securities to be purchased, the purpose of the purchases, and the source and amount of funds to be used in making the purchases.[56]

Rule 10b-13,[57] adopted pursuant to Sections 10(b), 13(e), and 14(e) of the 1934 Act, prohibits a person making a tender offer for an equity security from purchasing such security (or any security immediately convertible into or exchangeable for such security) otherwise than pursuant to the tender offer itself. While adoption of this Rule was apparently inspired by the Commission's desire to safeguard the interests of tendering shareholders where the offeror is not the issuer of the securities which are the subject of the offer, the Rule applies equally to tender offers by an issuer for its own securities.[58] The Rule is discussed in detail in Chapter 4.[59]

(2) Judicial and Administrative Review of Corporate Repurchases

Purchases of its own shares by a corporation solely for the purpose of preventing outsiders from securing control have been held lawful under state law in a series of Delaware cases where the board of directors in good faith considered the purchases necessary to maintain proper business practice or corporate policy.[60] On the other hand, corporate repurchases have been viewed essentially as attempts by management to perpetuate itself in control and treated as a breach of management's fiduciary duty to the corporation where the board of directors acts in bad

[56] For further discussion of Rule 13e–1, see text accompanying notes 106–110, Chapter 4. *Cf.* N.C. Gen. Stat. § 55–52(e)(1)(1)(1969) prohibiting a corporation from repurchasing its own shares unless the offer is made to purchase pro rata from all of its shareholders or all of a class of shareholders.

[57] 17 C.F.R. § 240.10b-13.

[58] *See* SEC Securities Exchange Act Release No. 8712 (Oct. 8, 1969), CCH Fed. Sec. L. Rep. ¶ 77,745; SEC Securities Exchange Act Release No. 8595 (May 5, 1969), CCH Fed. Sec. L. Rep. ¶ 77,706.

[59] See text accompanying notes 163–176, Chapter 4.

[60] *See* Cheff v. Mathes, 41 Del. Ch. 494, 199 A.2d 548 (1964); Kors v. Carey, 39 Del. Ch. 47, 158 A.2d 136 (1960); Martin v. American Potash and Chemical Corp., 33 Del. Ch. 234, 92 A.2d 295 (1952). For notes commenting on Cheff v. Mathes, *see* 50 Cornell L. Rev. 302 (1965), 78 Harv. L. Rev. 1253 (1965), 65 Duke L.J. 412 (1965). For note criticizing Kors v. Carey, *see* 70 Yale L.J. 308 (1960), *Buying Out Insurgent Stockholders With Corporate Funds.*

faith or could not offer some meaningful evidence to support its claim that the repurchases were in the best interests of the corporation.[61]

Where the target can relate such purchases to some legitimate corporate purpose, the transactions more likely will withstand judicial scrutiny. Thus, if the target can show that purchases of its shares during a tender offer were but an extension of a long-standing program to reacquire shares for incentive stock bonuses, a corporate pension plan, charitable gifts or acquisitions, there would seem to be less question as to the legality of the purchases.[62]

Even where there is no past history of a regular repurchase program, the target may be justified in purchasing its shares during the course of a tender offer if management in good faith and with no ulterior motives simply considers the shares to be underpriced.[63] However, in such situations, all the surrounding facts and circumstances will be scrutinized to determine management's good faith.[64]

[61] *See* Bennett v. Propp, 41 Del. Ch. 14, 187 A.2d 405 (1962). *See also* dictum in Lawrence v. Decca Records, Inc., 20 Misc. 2d 424, 195 N.Y.S.2d 431 (Sup. Ct. 1959); Gottesman v. General Motors Corp., 279 F. Supp. 361, 384–85 (S.D.N.Y. 1967); Gilchrist v. Highfield, 140 Wis. 476, 123 N.W. 102 (1909) (dissent). *Cf.* Trainor v. Berner, 66 Civ. 2177 (S.D.N.Y. 1971), CCH FED. SEC. L. REP. ¶ 93,381 (application for court approval of a disputed settlement arrangement granted in a stockholders' derivative suit alleging, *inter alia,* waste of corporate assets in that certain directors of the target falsely informed other directors that an impending takeover attempt would be adverse to the target's interest, thereby resulting in the target purchasing, pursuant to a tender offer, over one million of its own shares at a price $10 above the prevailing market.

[62] *See* National Union Electric Corp. v. National Presto Industries, Inc., No. 69-C-148 (W.D. Wis. 1969), CCH FED. SEC. L. REP. ¶ 92,460. *Cf.* Davis v. Pennzoil Co., 438 Pa. 194, 264 A.2d 597 (1970).

[63] "Presumably, too, an insider is under no obligation to give the ordinary investor the benefit of his superior financial analysis." 3 LOSS, SECURITIES REGULATION 1463 (2d ed. 1961).

[64] Actions based upon repurchases by the target where the shares are selling below book value or net asset value may be difficult to sustain. Evidence of historic price/earnings ratios; prior purchases, if any, by the target and the correlation of p/e ratios with prior purchases, comparative p/e ratios of comparable companies as well as the growth record of the target—all may be important in proving or disproving management's purpose in repurchasing shares. *Cf.* Kennedy, *Transactions by a Corporation in Its Own Shares,* 19 BUS. LAW 319, 324 (Jan. 1964), where it is suggested that repurchases based solely upon the corporation's belief that the shares are underpriced may require disclosure of the basis upon which the decision was made. Absent material information concerning favorable developments not known by the public, this would not appear to be the prevailing view.

The company nevertheless stands in the shoes of an insider when repurchasing its own shares [65] and is obliged publicly to disclose facts about its business which in reasonable and objective contemplation might affect the price of its stock and which it should reasonably believe are unknown to the public.[66] Failure to disclose such material facts may constitute common law fraud as well as violations of Section 14(e) and Section 10(b) of the 1934 Act and Rule 10b-5 thereunder.[67]

Manipulative trading activities, as well as the failure to disclose the purpose and extent of the target's market activities in its own securities, may also constitute violations of the anti-fraud provisions of the federal securities laws. In *Crane Co. v. Westinghouse Air Brake Co.*,[68] the court found violations of both Sections 9(a)(2) [69] and 10(b) and Rule 10b-5 thereunder where purchases of the target's stock by a corporation acting in concert with the target and with whom it was on the verge of consummating a

[65] *See* Kohler v. Kohler Co., 208 F. Supp. 808 (E.D. Wis. 1962), *aff'g* 319 F.2d 634 (7th Cir. 1963); Northern Trust Co. v. Essaness Theatres Corp., 348 Ill. App. 134, 108 N.E.2d 493 (1952). *See also* 3 Loss, SECURITIES REGULATION 1453 (2d ed. 1961).

[66] "The proper test is whether plaintiff would have been influenced to act differently than he did act if the defendant had disclosed to him the undisclosed fact." List v. Fashion Park Inc., 340 F.2d 457, 463 (2d Cir. 1965), *cert. denied, sub. nom.* List v. Lerner, 382 U.S. 811 (1965). *See also* Speed v. Transamerica Corp., 99 F. Supp. 808 (D. Del. 1951).

The NYSE Listing Agreement (Part I, Section 8) requires listed companies to report all purchases of their own securities to the Exchange within ten days after the close of a fiscal quarter.

[67] *See* Strong v. Repide, 213 U.S. 419 (1909); *In re* Ward La France Trucking Corp., 13 S.E.C. 373 (1943). *But see* O'Neill v. Maytag, 339 F.2d 764 (2d Cir. 1964) (Purchases by corporation at excessive prices). Absent deception, no cause of action under 10b-5, rejecting dictum in McClure v. Borne Chemical Co., 292 F.2d 824 (3d Cir. 1961), *cert. denied*, 368 U.S. 939 (1961) to the effect that claim is stated where controlling directors acquired a large block of its own stock at an excessive price to secure control. *See also Hoover v. Allen*, 241 F. Supp. 213 (S.D.N.Y. 1965) (Purchases by the company at fraudulently depressed prices where the sellers were victims and not the company. Accordingly, a derivative action did not state a cause of action under 10b-5); List v. Fashion Park, Inc., *supra* note 66.

[68] 419 F.2d 787 (2d Cir. 1969), *cert. denied*, 400 U.S. 822 (1970).

[69] Section 9(a) (2) of the 1934 Act makes it unlawful "To effect, alone or with one or more other persons, a series of transactions in any security registered on a national securities exchange creating actual or apparent active trading in such security, or raising or depressing the price of such security for the purpose of inducing the purchase or sale of such security by others."

With regard to fraudulent market activity in over-the-counter securities, *see* Section 15(c) (2) of the 1934 Act.

merger constituted a manipulative trading scheme designed to defeat the takeover bid.

Air Brake, in an effort to thwart an offer by Crane to exchange $50 face amount of Crane stock and debentures for each share of Air Brake, agreed to merge with American Standard Inc. On the day Crane's tender offer was to expire, Standard purchased 170,000 shares of Air Brake on the New York Stock Exchange at an average cost of $49.50 per share and immediately sold 120,000 of those shares in two private transactions at an average price of $44.50 per share, taking a loss of more than $500,000 on its trading for the day.[70] The court rejected Standard's contention that its purchases of Air Brake were for the purpose of acquiring control; instead the court found that Standard failed to disclose its private sales at the time it was dominating trading on the NYSE in an effort to deter Air Brake shareholders from tendering to Crane. Since antitrust considerations would require Crane to dispose of the Air Brake shares which it held if the merger with Standard were consummated, the court held that Standard's market activity had the effect of inducing Crane to become a forced seller within the meaning of Section 9(a)(2). The court went on to hold that Standard's failure to disclose its manipulation operated as a fraud and deceit upon Crane under Rule 10b-5 quite apart from the violation of Section 9(a)(2).[71]

Purchases by the target company of its own securities may also

[70] The contemporaneous sales of the 120,000 shares at substantial losses were allegedly effected to avoid problems of pooling-of-interest accounting treatment and liability under Section 16(b) of the 1934 Act. Crane Co. v. Westinghouse Air Brake Co., *supra* note 68, at 792.

[71] Although the court found violations by Standard, it did not make specific findings regarding the participation of Air Brake or the broker-dealer which effected the NYSE purchases for Standard. Presumably, Air Brake's conduct was equally violative of Rule 10b-5 in light of the court's determination that Standard was acting in concert with Air Brake. *Id.* at 796. Regarding the broker-dealer, Crane alleged that the broker manipulated the market on Standard's behalf to deter tenders of Air Brake stock pursuant to the Crane exchange offer. *Id.* at 790.

While the court found that Crane had standing to sue under both Sections 9(a)(2) and 10(b), it apparently struggled to reach that conclusion. The court noted, however, that the passage of Section 14(e) of the 1934 Act should resolve all doubt regarding the standing of the tender offeror to maintain an action for damages or injunctive relief resulting from a target company's fraudulent efforts to defeat an offer. For a discussion of the standing issue in connection with the tender offer cases, see text accompanying notes 132–147, Chapter 4; text accompanying notes 38–43, Chapter 10.

raise problems under Rule 10b–6[72] of the 1934 Act. This Rule makes it unlawful (except where certain specified exemptions may apply) for participants in a distribution of securities, including the issuer of the securities, to bid for or purchase any security which is the subject of such distribution, or any security of the same class and series, or any right to purchase any such security, until completion of their participation in the distribution.

The term "distribution" has been rather broadly interpreted in the Rule 10b–6 context.[73] Accordingly, the Rule would appear to prohibit the target from purchasing its own securities where it agrees to a defensive merger which contemplates that the target company, as the surviving corporation, will exchange its securities for those of the merger partner.[74] The staff of the Commission has apparently also taken the position that a violation of Rule 10b–6 occurs where an issuer purchases its own securities when it has other outstanding securities convertible into the securities being purchased.[75] A proposed amendment to Rule 10b–6 provides that if the Rule prohibits an issuer from purchasing its own securities solely because it has outstanding other securities exchangeable for or convertible into such securities, then the prohibition of the Rule will not apply provided such pur-

[72] 17 C.F.R. § 240.10b-6, eff. Nov. 20, 1964. For the underlying rationale of the Rule, see discussion in text accompanying notes 168–175, Chapter 4.

[73] "As we have stated on prior occasions, the term "distribution" as used in Rule 10b-6 is to be interpreted in the light of the rule's purposes covering offerings of such a nature or magnitude as to require restrictions upon open market purchases by participants in order to prevent manipulative practices. . . ." *In the Matters of* Billings Associates, Inc., SEC Securities Exchange Act Release No. 8217 (Dec. 28, 1967), at 7, citing J. H. Goddard & Co., Inc., SEC Securities Exchange Act Release No. 7618 (June 4, 1965) at 4; Bruns, Nordeman & Company, 40 S.E.C. 652, 660 (1961). *See also* Lowenfels, *Rule 10b-13, Rule 10b-6 and Purchases of Target Company Securities during an Exchange Offer*, 69 COLUM. L. REV. 1392 (1969); Chris-Craft Industries, Inc. v. Bangor Punta Corp., 426 F.2d 569 (2d Cir. 1970) (*en banc*), *aff'g in part, sub nom.* Chris-Craft Industries, Inc. v. Piper Aircraft Corp., 303 F. Supp. 191 (S.D.N.Y. 1969); Chris-Craft Industries, Inc. v. Piper Aircraft Corp., 69 Civ. 2227 (S.D.N.Y. 1971), CCH FED. SEC. L. REP. § 93,301 at pp. 91,668–70.

[74] *Cf.* SEC v. Georgia Pacific Corp., 66 Civ. 1215 (S.D.N.Y. 1966), CCH FED. SEC. L. REP. § 91,692, discussed in note 76, *infra;* Chris-Craft Industries, Inc. v. Bangor Punta Corp., *id. See also* Kennedy, *Defensive Take-Over Procedures Since the Williams Act*, 19 CATHOLIC U. L. REV. 158, 173 (1969).

With regard to the application of Rule 10b-6 to purchases of the target's securities by a tender offeror, see text accompanying notes 168–176, Chapter 4.

[75] *See* Kennedy, *id.*

chases are made in accordance with the provisions of proposed Rule 13e–2.[76]

B. Open-Market Purchases of the Target's Shares by Friendly Third Parties

An attractive alternative to the target's purchasing its own shares is to encourage friendly third parties to make open-market purchases. In addition to eliminating the need of the target to use its own funds, purchases by third parties when compared to those made by the corporation have the effect of increasing the number of shares the offeror needs to acquire control. Thus, for example, where the target has one million shares outstanding and the offeror seeks majority control, repurchases of 20 percent of its stock by the target will reduce the total shares outstanding and give the offeror control upon obtaining 400,001 shares. Purchases of the same 200,000 shares by third parties will require the offeror to obtain 500,001 shares.

The practice of third parties in purchasing shares of the target to defeat a takeover attempt is not without its pitfalls and problems.[77] As described in the preceding subsection of this chapter, the failure to disclose a manipulative trading scheme in connection with large-scale open-market purchases and contemporaneous private sales of the target's shares by a proposed defensive merger partner was held to constitute violations of Section 10(b) of the 1934 Act and Rule 10b–5 thereunder.[78] The court also

[76] *See* SEC Securities Exchange Act Release No. 8930, July 13, 1970, CCH Fed. Sec. L. Rep. ¶ 77,837.

In SEC v. Georgia-Pacific Corp., 66 Civ. No. 1215 (S.D.N.Y. 1966), CCH Fed. Sec. L. Rep. ¶ 91,692, the defendant corporation and two of its officers were enjoined by consent from violating, *inter alia,* Section 10(b) and Rules 10b-5 and 10b-6 thereunder, based upon allegations that the corporation's purchase of substantial amounts of its stock for its employee stock bonus plan was designed to raise the price of the stock for the purpose of reducing the number of shares *Georgia-Pacific* would be required to issue in certain acquisitions. Undertakings limiting open-market purchases by the defendants were also imposed. For excerpts of the complaint in this case, *see* CCH Fed. Sec. L. Rep. ¶ 91,680.

Undertakings similar to those entered against the defendants in the *Georgia-Pacific* case were also "voluntarily" imposed by the SEC on *Genesco, Inc.* to avoid any possible violations of Sections 9(a)(2) and 10(b) of the 1934 Act and Rules 10b-5 and 10b-6 thereunder and Section 17(a) of the Securities Act of 1933. *See* Prospectus, Genesco, Inc., May 10, 1966, reprinted in relevant part in CCH Fed. Sec. L. Rep. § 77,354.

[77] With regard to third-party purchases for the benefit of the offeror, see text accompanying notes 45–55, Chapter 2.

[78] See text accompanying notes 68–71, *supra.*

found violations of Section 9(a)(2) of the 1934 Act in the *Crane* case in that the purpose and effect of the open-market purchases were to deter shareholders from tendering by driving up the price of the target's shares to a level where the offer would no longer appear attractive and to create the appearance of extraordinary demand for the target's stock.[79] While this case cannot be cited for the proposition that concentrated open-market purchases by third parties for the benefit of either the offeror or the target are *per se* illegal,[80] it does suggest that extreme caution should be exercised to insure that all material facts are properly disclosed prior to undertaking such purchases.[81]

Where the target arranges to repurchase the shares acquired by the third party, additional regulatory considerations come into play. Thus, purchases of the target's shares by a broker-dealer or other regulated lender pursuant to an agreement whereby the target will repurchase the shares at a later date[82] may be considered an unlawful extension of credit in violation of the margin rules of the Federal Reserve Board.[83] An arrangement of this kind may also be considered a repurchase by the target as of the date the buy-back agreement is signed for purposes of requiring the target to file a statement pursuant to Rule 13e–1 under the 1934 Act.[84]

Purchases of the target's securities by a friendly third party may also constitute violations of Rule 10b–6 under the 1934 Act where such third party proposes to issue its own securities in connection with a defensive merger.[85] Purchases by regulated investment companies for the purpose of aiding the target will raise additional issues under the Investment Company Act of

[79] *See* Crane Co. v. Westinghouse Air Brake Co., *supra* note 68.

[80] *See supra* note 68. at 793.

[81] Query, however, whether full disclosure of all material facts prior to consummation of the transactions in question in the *Crane* case would have cured the Section 9(a) (2) violation?

[82] Altruistic considerations play little, if any, role in motivating the third party to undertake an arrangement of this kind. In most instances, the agreement will provide that the third party can require the target to repurchase the shares at a price well in excess of its cost.

[83] *See, e.g.*, SEC v. Madison Square Garden Corp., 69 Civ. 4364 (S.D.N.Y. 1970), CCH FED. SEC. L. REP. § 92,649. For a summary of the complaint in this matter, *see* 19 BNA SEC. REG. & L. REP. A-2, A-3 (Oct. 8, 1969).

[84] See text accompanying notes 52–56, *supra*.

[85] See text accompanying notes 72–76, *supra*.

1940 and may require the investment company to obtain Commission approval prior to effecting such transactions.[86]

C. Concentrated Selling of the Offeror's Shares by Friendly Third Parties

Where a takeover attempt is effected by means of an exchange offer, a decline in the market price of the offeror's common stock will result in appropriate reductions in the value of the exchange package.[87] If the extent of the decline is substantial and the offeror is unable or unwilling to increase the consideration paid to tendering shareholders, the offer must inevitably fail. Recognizing this, the target may attempt to persuade large stockholders to liquidate their holdings of the offeror's shares in the open market.[88] This may be done, for example, by astute publicity regarding the financial and management affairs of the offeror.[89]

While economic considerations normally dictate investment decision-making, there are often more subtle factors which influence some investors when a change of control is at stake. Thus, there have been instances of large-scale dumping of entire investment positions where the offeror is regarded by the professional investment community as an impertinent upstart and the target is a well-established and respected industrial corporation or financial institution.

[86] In essence, the problems confronting an investment company in this regard are substantially the same as those where it attempts to befriend the offeror. For a discussion of these issues, see text accompanying notes 45–55, Chapter 2.

[87] The correlation in market price movement between the offeror's common stock and the exchange package will of course depend upon the nature of the securities which constitute the package.

[88] Similarly, the target's management may attempt to defeat the offer by using its business and social relationships with institutional lenders to persuade them not to lend the offeror the necessary funds to finance the takeover attempt. *See* Institutional Investor Study Report of the Securities and Exchange Commission, H.R. Doc. No. 92–64, Pt. 5, 92d Cong., 1st Sess. at 2801 (1971); Hayes and Taussig, *Tactics of Cash Takeover Bids*, 45 Harv. Bus. Rev. 135, 144 (March/April 1967).

[89] A *caveat*, however, is in order. The information that is circulated concerning the offeror must be true and accurate. Reckless statements containing unsupported conjectures will subject the target to a possible charge of manipulative, fraudulent or deceptive practices within the meaning of Sections 10(b) and 14(e) of the 1934 Act.

D. DIVIDEND INCREASES

One of the more common defensive responses to a tender offer is for the target to raise its dividend or declare an additional dividend for the purpose of discouraging shareholders from tendering their stock. By increasing the return to investors, the target also hopes to drive up the price of the stock to a level where the offer may no longer be attractive.[90]

The effectiveness of this technique, however, is subject to question and may prove to be a rather weak attempt to buy off shareholders.[91] The expectation that shareholders will be dissuaded from tendering because of a dividend increase which, in most cases, will be substantially less than the premium over market of the tender offer, fails to take into account the fact that the shareholder who would be tempted to tender for capital gains probably is a different investor from the one concerned about dividends. This is particularly so today with the growing influence of aggressive institutional investors that seek capital appreciation rather than dividends. In addition, the hoped-for rise in the market price of the stock in response to the announcement of an increased dividend may prove disappointing where the earnings of the target do not show a corresponding increase.[92] How-

[90] The timing of an extra or increased dividend should be given careful consideration. Where the target declares an extra dividend, an attempt should be made to establish the record date as of a date after the offer is to expire or after the date to which it can reasonably be extended. On the other hand, a record date which is six or nine months after the declaration date may not constitute a sufficient incentive to discourage shareholders from tendering. (*See also* DEL. CORP. LAW ANN. § 213; N.Y. BUS. CORP. LAW § 604.)

Different considerations may affect the timing of a regular dividend. Postponement of a regular, albeit increased, dividend which is customarily declared and paid to shareholders of record at the same time each year may only serve to antagonize shareholders.

[91] *Cf.* Hayes and Taussig, *supra* note 44, at 143, indicating that more than one-third of the companies in their study undertook this defense.

[92] An increase in the dividend should not be undertaken with an intention to reduce the rate after the offer is defeated. Such action would be the ultimate in effrontery to shareholders and could well constitute a breach of fiduciary responsibility as well as violations of Sections 14(e) and 10(b) of the 1934 Act.

See also Rule 10b-17, 17 C.F.R. § 240.10b-17(eff. July 12, 1971), requiring issuers of publicly traded securities to furnish specified advance information to the NASD or a national securities exchange regarding dividends or other distribu-

ever, where there is a declaration of a special cash dividend or dividend increase which is substantial in relation to the market price of the stock, the market price can be expected to reflect a corresponding increase which should prevail until the ex-dividend date.[93]

E. STOCK SPLITS

While stock splits or stock dividends create no real economic benefit for the shareholder, the technique is used primarily to capitalize on the frailties of investor psychology. Many investors are said to view such declarations as extra dividends.[94] Others consider the increase in the number of shares held without any corresponding investment to be of greater significance than the corresponding decrease in the market value of each share. The target may also benefit from the confusion created in the minds of shareholders as to the price they will ultimately receive for their shares should they decide to tender.[95]

The stock split mav also give the target an opportunity temporarily to take its certificates out of circulation during which time investors would be unable to deposit their shares pursuant to the tender offer.[96] In attempting to defeat a bid by American Elec-

---

tions; planned splits or reverse splits; and rights or other subscription offerings. Failure to give notice to the NASD at least ten days prior to the record date (with certain exceptions) or in accordance with substantially comparable procedures of a national securities exchange constitutes a manipulative or deceptive device within the meaning of Sec. 10(b) of the 1934 Act. For a description of Rule 10b-17 and the abuses it is designed to prevent, *see* SEC Securities Exchange Act Release No. 9192 (June 7, 1971), CCH FED. SEC. L. REP. ¶ 78,099.

[93] E.g., at the close of trading on June 24, 1970, Sinclair Venezuelan Oil Co. ("SVZ"), for reasons unrelated to a tender offer contest, declared a special dividend of $7.50 per share payable to shareholders of record July 6, 1970. SVZ stock, which is traded on the ASE, closed at 21½ on that day. During the next two trading sessions (June 25 and 28) SVZ traded as high as 33¾. The stock traded ex-dividend on June 29 and closed at 22½. *See* Wall Street Journal, June 25, 28–30, 1972.

[94] *See* Hayes and Taussig, *supra* note 44, at 143. With regard to the standards to be applied in determining whether a particular pro rata stock distribution is misleading, *see* SEC Securities Exchange Act Release No. 9618 (June 1, 1972), 155 BNA SEC. REG. & L. REP. A-6, D-1 June 7, 1972).

[95] In an effort to insure that the target does not give the offeror any unintentional advantages, the split should result in the issuance of a multiple of shares for each share then outstanding. A 5 for 4 split, for example, might make the offer appear more attractive to the unsophisticated investor by creating the misleading impression that a greater premium is being offered.

[96] While tenders of shares may sometimes be made without the concurrent de-

tric Power Co., the Michigan Gas & Electric Co. announced a 7 for 1 split and requested shareholders to surrender their shares for certificates representing seven shares for each share previously held. Customarily, shareholders would have received certificates representing the six additional shares while retaining their original shares.[97]

Another noteworthy consideration is the fact that lower-priced stocks often command a proportionately higher premium than shares selling at higher levels. In order to maintain the prospects of success, the offeror, after the split, may be compelled to raise his bid. Again, there is no economic rationale for this phenomenon, which apparently results simply because a $60 bid for stock selling at $50 appears to some people to be more attractive than a $12 offer for a $10 stock—despite identical 20 percent premiums for both offers.[98]

F. Issuance of Additional Shares

There are two principal techniques involving the issuance of additional shares which are employed in defending against tender offers—private placements of the target's shares for cash and acquisitions of securities or assets of third parties for the target's shares. Private placements, requiring neither shareholder approval nor SEC registration, offer a convenient and efficient method of increasing the number of shares which the offeror must acquire to achieve its objective. The target also benefits by placing stock in the hands of investors who have a significant stake in assuring that incumbent management retains control.[99]

---

posit of share certificates (see text accompanying note 10, Chapter 3), the problem of obtaining guaranties as well as the uncertainties surrounding the delivery date of certificates may make it impractical for shareholders to commit themselves to a tender.

[97] Berton, *Fighting Take-overs*, Wall Street Journal, July 11, 1967, at 1, 17.

[98] For a discussion of the factors in determining the premium, see Section 5, Chapter 2.

With regard to the information which issuers are required to furnish to the NASD or a national securities exchange in connection with stock splits, *see* Rule 10b-17 under the 1934 Act, discussed in note 92, *supra*.

[99] Potential investors, on the other hand, may be reluctant to commit themselves to a private placement where uncertainties regarding control exist. If the insurgents manage to win, the investors can hardly expect enthusiastic cooperation when they attempt to register their shares.

Where the target is unable to place its shares, it may consider the exercise of

The incumbents, however, must secure a price which adequately reflects the value of the target company. Private sales at deep discounts from market, particularly during the course of a tender offer, may raise serious questions regarding the purpose and intent of management in negotiating the sales and may form the basis for allegations of waste of corporate assets as well as violations of Rule 10b–5.[100]

Acquisitions of stock or assets of other companies for shares of the target involve many of the same considerations that affect the private sale of securities for cash.[101] Stockholder approval, however, is a prerequisite to the listing of the target's shares on the New York Stock Exchange, where a director, officer or substantial security holder has a direct or indirect interest in the stock or assets to be acquired or where the acquisition involves the issuance of common stock (for securities convertible into common stock) which could result in increasing the outstanding common shares by approximately 20 percent or more or having a combined fair value approximating 20 percent or more of the market value of the outstanding common shares.[102] In addition, where any shares issued by the target (for cash or for acquisitions) are of a class previously listed on the Exchange, the target will be re-

---

stock options by officers and employees as a means of increasing the total outstanding shares. For other possible defensive techniques involving the issuance of additional shares, *see* Schmults and Kelly, *supra* note 44, at 120.

[100] Several recent cases suggest an awakening concern regarding the responsibilities of officers and directors of the issuer in connection with the delicate art of pricing shares issued in private transactions. *See, e.g.*, Lewis v. Spiral Metal Co., Inc., CCH FED. SEC. L. REP. ¶¶ 92,827, 92,919 (S.D.N.Y. Jan. 11, 1971); Penn Mart Realty Co. v. Becker, 300 F. Supp. 731 (S.D.N.Y. 1969); Schoenbaum v. Firstbrook, 405 F.2d 215 (2d Cir. 1968) (*en banc*), *cert. denied*, 395 U.S. 906 (1970).

[101] Acquisitions of other companies for the target's shares have been considered to have "the additional advantage of possibly impressing shareholders that incumbent management is dynamic and promises further growth through diversification of the company's business." See Schmults and Kelly, *supra* note 44, at 120.

Announcement of an agreement on a proposed sale of additional shares may have as great a negative impact on the offer as the actual issuance of the shares. *See* Chris-Craft Industries, Inc. v. Piper Aircraft Corp., 303 F. Supp. 191, 193 (S.D.N.Y. 1969).

[102] NYSE COMPANY MANUAL, at A-283, 284. The minimum vote necessary to constitute stockholder approval for listing purposes is defined as "approval by a majority of votes cast on a proposal in a proxy bearing on the particular matter, provided that the total vote cast on the proposal represents over 50% in interest of all securities entitled to vote on the proposal." NYSE Company Manual, at A-285.

quired to apply for Exchange approval of the listing of such additional shares prior to the issuance thereof.[103]

Perhaps the most perplexing problem confronting incumbent management in connection with its consideration of the issuance of additional shares is the question of whether the issuance of such shares will be viewed under state law as a breach of management's fiduciary responsibility to the corporation. This is in many respects the same problem with which the Delaware courts have struggled for years in connection with corporate repurchases of their own shares.[104] Two relatively recent cases highlight the major problems in this area as well as the diversity in approach by the courts. These two cases merit extended discussion.

(1) Condec Corp. v. The Lunkenheimer Co.[105]

It is perhaps poetic justice that the Delaware courts were given an opportunity to express their views on this problem in a tender offer context in the case of *Condec Corp. v. The Lunkenheimer Co.* The background and facts of this case are as follows:

After several unsuccessful attempts to arrange a merger with the Lunkenheimer Co., Condec Corp., pursuant to a cash tender offer, acquired some 21,000 shares of Lunkenheimer. During the course of the offer, the latter arranged to sell its assets to Textron, Inc. Shortly thereafter, Condec made a combination cash and exchange offer to purchase at least an additional 190,000 shares of Lunkenheimer, which, together with the shares already owned, would give it majority control. Pursuant to the second tender offer, Condec purportedly acquired a sufficient number of Lunkenheimer shares to block the proposed sale to Textron, and by the

[103] *See* Sec. I, para. 17, NYSE Listing Agreement.

Piper Aircraft Corp. issued over 460,000 authorized but previously unissued shares for controlling blocks of stock in two other corporations without obtaining shareholder or NYSE approval. Piper had approximately 1.6 million shares listed and outstanding prior to consummation of these transactions. In addition to refusing to list these newly issued shares, the Exchange suspended trading in Piper shares and authorized delisting proceedings before the SEC. Piper's management thereafter agreed to rescind the transactions and trading was resumed. *See* Chris-Craft Industries Inc. v. Bangor Punta Corp., *supra* note 73 at 571.

[104] See text accompanying notes 60–61, *supra*.

[105] 230 A.2d 769 (Del. Ch. 1967).

time fixed for the Lunkenheimer stockholders' meeting the Textron proposal had been withdrawn.

The failure of the proposed sale to Textron constituted only a temporary setback to Lunkenheimer, which had still another eager suitor. After hurried negotiations, Lunkenheimer arranged to sell its assets to U.S. Industries, Inc. pursuant to an arrangement whereby Industries would make an exchange offer to Lunkenheimer shareholders. The stock purchase agreement was preceded by an agreement whereby a wholly owned subsidiary of Industries subscribed for 75,000 shares of authorized but unissued shares of Lunkenheimer in exchange for 75,000 shares of the same class of Industries preferred stock which constituted the stated consideration for the purchase of Lunkenheimer by Industries. The sale of the 75,000 Lunkenheimer shares was conditioned on the successful consummation of the sale of assets to Industries.

Condec thereupon brought suit for cancellation of the Lunkenheimer shares purchased by Industries, alleging that: (a) the sale of such shares served no legitimate corporate purpose and was designed to serve the personal interests of the officers and directors of Lunkenheimer; (b) the primary purpose of the proposed sale was to frustrate control of Lunkenheimer by reducing the percentage holdings of Condec below 50 percent of the outstanding common shares; and (c) the sale was not made in good faith or in the exercise of prudent business judgment. Evidence elicited during the course of the proceeding indicated that the then present officers and directors of Lunkenheimer would probably not be retained if the Condec offer was successful. On the other hand, it appeared that they would be retained if the agreement with Industries was consummated. Additional testimony, however, indicated that the decision of Lunkenheimer's management to reject the Condec offer was based upon much more than self-preservation. In summarizing the major objections to the Condec offer, the president of Lunkenheimer noted, *inter alia,* the following factors influencing its decision: (a) Condec's allegedly excessive debt, disproportionate government business, low profit ratio, and slow payment of bills; (b) Industries' proposal was fair and equitable and benefited all shareholders; (c)

Condec's offer ignored 49 percent of Lunkenheimer's shareholders; and (d) acceptance of Condec's offer would create a taxable transaction for tendering shareholders while Industries offer apparently would not.

In ordering cancellation of the 75,000 shares issued to Industries, the court found that in view of the haste with which the Lunkenheimer-Industries agreement was reached, the primary purpose of the issuance of such shares was to thwart Condec's offer by reducing its holdings below a majority. In describing such action as manipulation, the court considered the case as one "of a stockholder with a contractual right to assert voting control being deprived of such control by what is virtually a corporate legerdemain."[106]

While the legality of issuing additional shares for the purpose of thwarting a tender offer prior to the time the offeror obtains voting control was not really at issue in this case, the extensive dictum in the court's opinion may provide some meaningful guidelines for the future. The opinion, for example, stresses the court's conclusion that Lunkenheimer's management did not have a justifiable basis for believing that control by Condec represented a reasonable threat to the best interests of the target.[107] While it may be difficult to find more persuasive reasons for opposing a tender offer than those advanced by the defendants, the opinion nevertheless suggests that where the court may reasonably conclude that the offeror's takeover may not be in the best interests of the corporation, the issuance of additional shares for the primary purpose of thwarting the offer may not be unlawful.[108]

[106] *Id.* at 777.

[107] The court brushed off many of the defendant's reasons for opposing the Condec offer on the ground that the investigation into the affairs of Condec by the incumbent management lacked thoroughness and was not objective. *Id.* at 776.

[108] The semantics of the *Condec* case deserve special note. In applying the primary purpose test, the courts have traditionally based their decision on whether the primary purpose of incumbent management's action is to perpetuate themselves in office or to preserve some legitimate corporate objective. The *Condec* opinion states that the primary purpose of management's issuance of shares was to defeat the tender offer. The test applied in the *Condec* case, however, is essentially no different from the traditional approach because the court was still compelled to determine whether the primary purpose of thwarting the offer was to preserve corporate policy or to perpetuate management in office.

(2) NORTHWEST INDUSTRIES, INC. v. THE B. F. GOODRICH CO.[109]

On January 20, 1969, Northwest Industries announced its intention to make an exchange tender offer for common stock of Goodrich. At the time of the announcement, Goodrich was a 50 percent partner with Gulf Oil Corp. in a joint venture, Goodrich-Gulf Chemicals, Inc. During 1965, Goodrich and Gulf engaged in extensive negotiations regarding Chemicals with a view toward having one company buy out the other. The companies were unable to agree upon a sales price and accordingly the negotiations were terminated. As a result of Northwest's tender offer announcement, talks between Goodrich and Gulf on Chemicals were reopened in late January and February. After a single day of negotiations, Goodrich agreed to purchase Gulf's interest in Chemicals for 700,000 shares of Goodrich common stock. Goodrich management hastily prepared a two-page memorandum and a one-page statistical analysis of the transaction as support for its recommendation to the board of directors that it approve the purchase. The entire consideration and approval of the $35 million transaction by the board took place during the first hour of a directors' luncheon meeting on February 6, 1969, one day after the negotiations with Gulf.

Suing derivatively as a minority stockholder of Goodrich, Northwest sought a preliminary injunction prohibiting the listing and delivery of the stock to Gulf. Northwest claimed, *inter alia,* that the $35 million consideration, resulting in the issuance of 700,000 Goodrich common shares, was grossly inflated to guarantee that a substantial block of stock would be held by interests friendly to Goodrich's present management. Such action was alleged to be a waste of corporate assets by Goodrich's management constituting fraud under New York law.[110] In denying plaintiff's motion, the court found that the transaction was consummated at a fair price by officers and directors exercising honest business judgment and that while Northwest's offer

[109] 301 F. Supp. 706 (N.D.Ill. 1969).

[110] The court applied New York law to the transaction in question since Goodrich was a New York corporation.

"prompted" the purchase by Goodrich, Northwest had not established that the desire of Goodrich officials to maintain control was the sole or primary motivation for their decision.

The significance of this decision as a practical and recommended guideline regarding the extent of permissible activity by a target company in defending against a tender offer is perhaps best set forth in the following paragraphs of the court's opinion:

> More specifically, while Northwest's January 20 announcement prompted the purchase, such a catalyst does not invalidate the transaction if the exchange was in the best interests of Goodrich. As stated in Cummings v. United Artists Theatre Circuit, Inc., 237 Md. 1, 204 A.2d 795, 805–806 (1964):
>
> "Thus the cases relied on by the appellants [Northwest] do not support their contention that where a board of directors has as one of its motives manipulation for control the transaction is invalid, regardless of fairness, and regardless of whether a legitimate corporate purpose is also being served.
>
> * * * *
>
> "Therefore we hold that where a good corporate purpose is being furthered and is the principal motivation for an action by a board of directors, the fact that the consummation of such transaction may have some effect on the control of the corporation is immaterial and the agreement will stand or fall depending on whether it is fair to the corporation."
>
> Northwest's tender offer announcement galvanized Goodrich and Gulf to complete the purchase at this time. Although the officers of both Goodrich and Gulf claim there was no mutual agreement to defeat plaintiff's takeover bid, there was a remarkable empathy between the companies. On the other hand, Northwest appears unable to establish that Goodrich officials' desire to remain in office was the sole or the primary motivation for their decisions.
>
> Plaintiff has not shown any likelihood that it can prove that the transaction amounts to fraud. Considering all factors of value, the persuasive evidence indicates that $35 million is a fair price for Gulf's one half of Chemicals. Goodrich's officers and directors appear to have been exercising their honest business judgment, so that their decision is conclusive.
>
> Furthermore, whenever a tender offer is extended and the management of the threatened company resists, the officers and directors may be accused of trying to preserve their jobs at the expense of the corporation. The alleged conflict of interest was created by Northwest, not by Goodrich. Yet, management has the responsibility to oppose offers which, in its best judgment, are detrimental to the company or

its stockholders. In arriving at such a judgment, management should be scrupulously fair in considering the merits of any proposal submitted to its stockholders. The officers' and directors' informed opinion should result from that strict impartiality which is required by their fiduciary duties. After taking these steps, the company may then take any step not forbidden by law to counter the attempted capture.

Although the haste displayed by Goodrich officials casts some doubt on the management's actions, I find no violation of the preceding principles of sufficient magnitude to warrant judicial interference. The instant economic struggle should be resolved in the market place and by the stockholders at their meeting, not in the courts.[111]

G. Creation of Incompatibility Between the Target and the Offeror

Where the offeror skillfully plans and develops its takeover attempt, the target may have little success in attempting to block the offer by means of legal action. Notwithstanding the offeror's scrupulous attempts to perfect its bid, the target may still be able to *create* a situation whereby a takeover by the offeror will violate some regulatory statute. This approach was one of many attempted by B. F. Goodrich Co. in its battle with Northwest Industries, Inc. While Goodrich in this instance was unsuccessful in applying the technique, the facts of the case serve as a valuable example of the variety of alternatives that may be open to the target in creating impediments to a takeover attempt.

On January 20, 1969, Northwest announced an exchange tender offer for shares of Goodrich. Northwest was a widely diversified corporation whose interests at the time of the offer included a 99 percent interest in the voting stock of a common carrier which was subject to regulation under the Interstate Commerce Act. During the course of the offer, Goodrich purchased all of the outstanding shares of Motor Freight Corporation, a motor carrier also subject to the Interstate Commerce Act. Three days after its purchase, Goodrich advised the Interstate Commerce Commission of its action and complained that control of Goodrich by Northwest without ICC approval would violate Section 5(2) of the Interstate Commerce Act because it would result in control of Motor Freight by a company which was not a

[111] Northwest Industries, Inc. v. The B. F. Goodrich Co., *supra* note 109, at 712–13.

carrier but had control of one or more carriers.[112] Northwest responded to Goodrich's allegations, claiming that its acquisition of Goodrich would not violate the Interstate Commerce Act because it would agree to immediately divest itself of the Motor Freight stock if it acquired control. The ICC found that Northwest's plan of divestiture precluded a violation of the statute and accordingly denied Goodrich's petition. Thereafter, Goodrich filed a complaint in the Federal District Court in Delaware for a declaratory judgment and an injunction, alleging, *inter alia,* that Northwest's agreement to divest itself of Motor Freight did not prevent the acquisition, without prior approval of the ICC, from constituting a violation of the act. The District Court, however, dismissed the complaint and denied the motion for a preliminary injunction.[113] A subsequent appeal by Goodrich of the dismissal of the complaint resulted in an affirmance of the decision of the district court.[114]

A frequently cited article on the tactics employed in connection with cash tender offers described a successful application of this technique as follows:

> One company, on learning of an impending bid from another firm, promptly acquired a business that competed with the bidder in lines

[112] Section 5(2) of the Interstate Commerce Act provides in relevant part that "It shall be lawful, with the approval and authorization of the Commission . . . for a person which is not a carrier and which has control of one or more carriers to acquire control of another carrier. . . ."

[113] B. F. Goodrich Company v. Northwest Industries, Inc., 303 F. Supp. 53 (D. Del. 1969). The decision was based primarily on the ground that the court lacked jurisdiction since there is no private right of action for enforcement of Section 5(2) of the act. Anticipating an appeal on this issue, the court offered the following additional grounds for its decision with regard to the preliminary injunction: (1) the concept of "primary jurisdiction" compelled the court to give substantial weight to the administrative decision of the ICC; (2) in view of the vigorous defense of Goodrich to the takeover attempt and the absence of any evidence on the record regarding the number of shares acquired by Northwest pursuant to the tender offer, the court could not assume that control over Goodrich and Motor Freight was likely to pass to Northwest unless a preliminary injunction was issued; and (3) even assuming Northwest was about to violate the act, the issuance of a preliminary injunction would not be appropriate in light of the ICC's supervision of the matter and the limited likelihood that a preliminary injunction would be issued after a final hearing.

[114] B. F. Goodrich Company v. Northwest Industries, Inc. 424 F. 2d 1349 (3d Cir. 1970). The court of appeals found an additional basis for holding that the district court had no jurisdiction because the complaint was a collateral attack on an order of the ICC and, accordingly, should have been brought before a three-judge court convened pursuant to 28 U.S.C. § 2325.

accounting for 80% of its total sales. The move, of course, was designed to raise the specter of monopoly in connection with the expected bid. When the bid was announced, the subject company filed an anti-trust suit, confident that the bidder would be forced to withdraw. This proved correct, since to divest itself of the conflict of interest would have meant severing practically the whole company.[115]

Other possibilities may develop along these same lines where the prospective offeror was previously enjoined from acquiring an interest in a corporation engaged in a particular business or industry. In such circumstances, the target's management may give consideration to acquiring a company in that field.[116]

H. Defensive Mergers [117]

The defensive merger, whereby the target company agrees to merge into a company other than the offeror in order to defeat the takeover attempt, has been described as "a form of orderly retreat" rather than as a defensive tactic.[118] This description is particularly appropriate where the target company has not been

[115] Hayes and Taussig, *Tactics of Cash Takeover Bids*, 45 Harv. Bus. Rev. 135, 146 (March-April 1967).

[116] An attempted takeover of Columbia Pictures Corp. by a group of investors headed by a French bank offers yet another illustration of the potential of this defensive technique. A tender offer by the Banque de Paris et des Pays-Bas for Columbia stock resulted in tenders of over 30 percent of the target's outstanding shares. Columbia, which controlled several television stations, filed suit to prevent the takeover, alleging, *inter alia*, that the bank's purchases violated the Federal Communications Act. This Act prohibits: (1) foreign interests from taking substantial investment positions in the stock of companies which hold broadcasting licenses; and (2) transfers of control of radio and television stations, without prior Federal Communications Commission approval. Other defendants, including two American investment companies, were alleged to have acted in concert with the bank and to have committed violations of the Federal Communications Act, the Investment Company Act of 1940, and the Securities Exchange Act of 1934.

The case was eventually settled pursuant to an agreement whereby the incumbents maintained control, with the bank remaining a minority shareholder. The Federal Communications Commission subsequently approved the bank's ownership of approximately 37 percent of Columbia's outstanding shares, subject to certain specified conditions which included a stipulation by the bank that it would not attempt to assert direct or indirect control of Columbia. *See* complaint in Columbia Pictures Corp. v. Clairmont, Civ. No. 3581 (S.D.N.Y. 1966); *Columbia Sues Stock Buyers*, N.Y. Times, Oct. 28, 1966, at 57; *FCC Backs Sale of Movie Stock*, N.Y. Times, Dec. 30, 1966, at 31.

[117] While reference is made to mergers in this subsection, the discussion which follows applies equally as well to defensive consolidations and sales of assets.

[118] *See* Schmults and Kelly, *Cash Take-Over Bids—Defense Tactics*, 23 Bus. Law 115, 132 (Nov. 1967).

actively pursuing merger possibilities prior to the tender offer and the decision to effect such a merger is dictated more by desperation than by economics. Whatever one may choose to call it, the defensive merger has become an increasingly common response in defending against takeover attempts as the threat of losing all control over the target company will normally make it easier for incumbent management to reconcile itself to becoming a smaller cog in a larger wheel.[119]

The success of a defensive merger will in the first instance depend upon the ability of the target company to reach agreement on a proposed merger and publicly announce the terms of such agreement before substantial numbers of shares have been irrevocably tendered to the offeror.[120] Assuming agreement can be quickly reached, the terms of the proposed merger must be sufficiently attractive to discourage stockholders from tendering their shares. In some instances, the merger exchange package will consist of a newly issued class of income-producing debt or senior equity security which will be convertible into common shares on a basis which will provide each stockholder of the target company with that number of common shares which, in the aggregate, will have a market value at least equal to the consideration offered by the tender bid. Other merger packages, made up of combinations of common stock, warrants, and income-producing convertible or nonconvertible debt or equity securities, have apparently been structured to offer an attractive alternative to the tender bid but are extremely difficult to appraise in terms of a re-

[119] A compilation of some of the more noteworthy defensive mergers includes the following (the offeror appearing in parenthesis and the target in italics): *Westinghouse Air Brake Co.*-American Standard, Inc. (Crane Co.); *Dodge Manuf. Co.*-Reliance Electric Co. (Emerson Electric Co.); *Kern County Land Co.*-Tenneco, Inc. (Occidental Petroleum Co.); *Commercial Credit Corp.*-Control Data, Inc. (Loew's Theatres, Inc.).

[120] In addition to thwarting the offeror's attempted takeover, the successful consummation of a defensive merger may provide some unintended benefits. If the consummation of a merger agreement within six months of any purchases by the offeror is deemed a "sale" within the meaning of Section 16(b) of the 1934 Act, the target company or its successor may be able to recover short-swing profits from the offeror. *See* Reliance Electric Co. v. Emerson Electric Co., 404 U.S. 418 (1972). *Cf.* Abrams v. Occidental Petroleum Corp., 450 F.2d 157 (2d Cir. 1971), *rev'g* 323 F. Supp. 570 (S.D.N.Y. 1970). *See also* Newmark v. RKO General, Inc., 425 F.2d 348 (2d Cir. 1970), *cert. denied*, 400 U.S. 854 (1970). For a discussion of these cases, see Chapter 8.

alistic market evaluation. Simplicity of the defensive merger package, wherever possible, is therefore advisable, particularly where the tender offer is for cash, as a combination of different classes of securities, each with its own conditions and restrictions, may only serve to confuse stockholders and encourage them to tender their shares.

Tax considerations may also play a role in structuring the defensive merger. A tender of shares pursuant to a cash offer or an exchange offer where the offeror does not acquire at least 80 percent of the total combined voting power of all classes of the target's stock entitled to vote and at least 80 percent of the total number of shares of all other classes of stock of the target, will result in a recognizable taxable gain to the tendering shareholder.[121] On the other hand, an exchange of securities pursuant to a merger may be a non-taxable exchange of securities.[122] Thus the parties to the merger may agree to issue securities worth less than the tender bid in the expectation that the tax considerations will dissuade stockholders from tendering their shares.

It should be noted, however, that the rather widely held notion that the desire to postpone recognition of taxable gain will cause investors to continue to hold securities can prove illusory. Stockholders, for a variety of reasons, may no longer find it advisable to continue to hold the shares for investment purposes. Accordingly, the target company which is convinced that stockholders will reject the tender offer simply because no taxable gain will be recognized on the merger transaction, may well have made a serious and disappointing miscalculation. Instead, the target company should consider structuring its merger on a basis which offers its stockholders securities which will have a value in excess of the tender bid.

The announcement of a proposed defensive merger may also inspire the offeror to make its own merger proposal[123] or in-

[121] *See* Int. Rev. Code § 368(a)(1)(B)I.R.C.; Treas. Reg. 1.368-2(c).

[122] *See* Int. Rev. Code § 368(a)(1)(A)I.R.C.; Int. Rev. Code § 354(a)(2)I.R.C.

[123] If the target company is incorporated in a state which requires the board of directors to approve an agreement of merger or consolidation, the offeror will be required to obtain control of the board before it can effectuate its plans. *See, e.g.*, DEL. GEN. CORP. LAW § 251(b), § 252(c). A provision of this nature may require the offeror to undertake a full-scale proxy contest to accomplish the ultimate result.

crease its bid for the target's shares. Where a counter-merger proposal is made, the tender offer may take on the appearance of a proxy contest with the offeror undertaking a solicitation of proxies or, alternatively, requesting inclusion of its merger proposal in management's proxy statement.[124] In addition, the offeror may be required to permit shareholders who previously tendered their shares to return the consideration received for such shares in exchange for the securities package to be issued pursuant to the counter-merger proposal.[125]

I. Discriminatory Voting Provisions

A wide variety of voting restrictions have been employed by target companies to discourage potential takeover attempts. These restrictions, all designed to discriminate against both dissident shareholders and potential tender offerors, are effected by means of amendments to the articles of incorporation or by-laws of the target and are classic examples of overreaction to the tender offer phenomenon. In most instances these restrictions have served to compromise basic principles of corporate democracy by permitting incumbent management, under the guise of promoting corporate policy, to transform the will of the majority into what may best be described as the tyranny of the minority.[126] In addition, the use of discriminatory voting provisions has

[124] *But see* Rule 14a-8(a) [17 C.F.R. § 240.14a-8(a)], promulgated pursuant to the Securities Exchange Act of 1934, specifying the circumstances under which management must include security holders proposals in its proxy statement and providing in part that "This rule does not apply . . . to counter proposals to matters to be submitted by the management." *See also* Schmults and Kelly, *supra* note 118, at 133.

Query, whether the failure to describe an existing tender offer or a counter-merger proposal will cause management's proxy statement to be false and misleading within the meaning of Rule 14a-9 under the 1934 Act? *Cf.* Elgin National Industries, Inc. v. Chemetron Corp., 299 F. Supp. 367 (D. Del. 1969). *See also* Crane Co. v. Westinghouse Air Brake Co., *supra* note 68.

See also Rule 14a-12(a) [17 C.F.R. § 240.14a-12(a)] under the 1934 Act permitting the target company to solicit support for its defensive merger proposal prior to furnishing security holders with a written proxy statement if, *inter alia,* "the solicitation is made in opposition to a prior solicitation or an invitation for tenders or other publicized activity, which if successful, could reasonably have the effect of defeating the action proposed to be taken at the meeting. . . ."

[125] *See* Section 14(d)(7) of the 1934 Act. *See also Offer to Purchase Common Stock of Symington Wayne Corporation,* Wall Street Journal, July 10, 1967, at 23

[126] For an excellent article on discriminatory voting provisions, *see* Mullaney, *Guarding Against Takeovers—Defensive Charter Provisions,* 25 Bus. Law 1441

had the effect of alienating any number of institutional investors which view such provisions as fundamentally inconsistent with their fiduciary responsibility to seek optimum portfolio performance.

(1) FORMS OF DISCRIMINATORY VOTING PROVISIONS

The following compilation identifies some of the more discriminatory arrangements which have either been adopted or recommended by incumbent management to discourage takeover attempts:

(a) Approval by a minimum of 80 percent of the outstanding voting shares of the target company to effect a merger or similar transaction with a corporation which owns more than 10 percent of any class of the target's equity securities.[127]

(July 1970). *See also* Wetzel, *Defensive Tactics—Who Are the Goodies and Who Are the Baddies?* 25 BUS. LAW 545 (Jan. 1970).

[127] *See* letter of Philip L. West, Vice President, New York Stock Exchange to Presidents of Listed Companies, Dec. 26, 1968, reprinted in NYSE COMPANY MANUAL, at xxi–xxii; *Continental Airlines, Cyclops to Elevate Take-Over Hurdles,* Wall Street Journal, April 14, 1969, at 29; *United Nuclear Meeting Backs Proposal to Make Take-Over Bids Harder,* Wall Street Journal, July 22, 1969, at 29; *Firm Amends Charter in Hopes of Eluding the Corporate Raider,* Wall Street Journal, April 24, 1968, at 11. For other examples and variations of this type of provision, *see* Mullaney, *supra* note 126.

In order to make a proposed amendment of this type effective, management may also recommend an amendment requiring an 80 percent affirmative vote to amend or repeal the proposed amendment. *See, e.g.,* Masonite Corporation, *Notice of Annual Meeting of Shareholders November 25, 1969.* The Delaware General Corporation Law makes a provision of this type mandatory where the certificate of incorporation requires the vote of a greater percentage of shares than required by law. *See* DEL. GEN. CORP. LAW § 242(c)(4). See also note 129, *infra.*

A proposed amendment by the board of directors of the Masonite Corporation required an 80 percent affirmative vote for a merger or similar transaction with any other corporation without limitation on the percentage of its outstanding stock held by such other corporation. *See* Masonite Corporation, *Notice of Annual Meeting of Stockholders November 25, 1969.*

Provision has been made in a proposed amendment for waiver of the 80 percent voting requirement, if the transaction is approved by the board of directors where a majority of the directors voting for approval were elected prior to the time the proposed merger partner became the holder of more than 10 percent of the target's stock. *See* Masonite Corporation, *Notice of Annual Meeting of Stockholders November 25, 1969.*

A proposed amendment at the annual meeting of General Host Corp. on October 29, 1969, required an affirmative 80 percent vote to authorize a merger or similar transaction with an entity owning 5 percent or more of the Corporation's stock.

The express purpose of an amendment requiring increased stockholder approval for a merger transaction has been clearly stated in the proxy solicitation materials of one corporation as follows:

> The purpose of the proposed amendment is to discourage, in advance, a tender offer, or takeover bid, for the Company's shares by any offeror which has in mind the imposition upon the Company of a merger or asset transfer transaction following its acquisition of a substantial stock interest. Recently, several publicly held corporations have experienced the type of transaction which the proposed amendment is designed to discourage. Often, the offeror must in some manner utilize the assets of the target Company to finance the original tender offer. The effect is a radical change in the enterprise in which the stockholders have invested, made possible in part by the assets of the Company itself. Often, the corporation making the tender offer has little familiarity with the business of the target company. As a result, the stockholders of the target corporation are faced with a choice of having their investment shifted into a business and under a management not originally of their choice or liquidating their securities with, in many cases, substantial adverse Federal tax consequences. The Company has no information that any attempted takeover of the Company by way of tender offer or otherwise is contemplated by any other corporation.[128]

In a provision of this type, voting requirements on a merger or similar transaction with an entity owning less than the stipulated percentage of the target's stock would continue to be governed by the corporation law of the state in which the target was incorporated.[129] Accordingly, in most instances, an affirmative vote of only a majority or two-thirds of the voting shares would be required.

(b) Approval by a minimum of 80 percent of the shares of a

[128] Masonite Corporation, *Notice of Annual Meeting of Stockholders November 25, 1969*, at p. 5.

[129] The corporation laws of a number of states expressly permit the charter or articles of incorporation to provide for a vote of a greater percentage of shares than required by law. *See, e.g.*, DEL. GEN. CORP. LAW § 102(b)(4); N.Y. BUS. CORP. LAW § 616(a). Absent an express provision of this type, the issue becomes one of whether the stipulated percentage set forth in the statute is simply a minimum requirement as opposed to a provision which prohibits a vote greater than the stipulated percentage. *See* Mullaney, *supra* note 126, at 1446–50.

small class of preferred stock, privately placed in friendly hands, to effect a merger transaction.[130]

(c) Approval by two-thirds of the minority interest as well as two-thirds of all shares entitled to vote to effect a merger transaction.[131]

(d) Reduction of the necessary two-thirds approval required for a merger to a majority vote unless the other party to the transaction owns more than 5 percent of any class of voting stock of the target company. Where the party to the merger owns more than 5 percent of the voting stock, the target would require approval by holders of two-thirds of the common stock as a class in addition to two-thirds approval of the voting power of all classes of securities entitled to vote.[132]

(e) Election of directors who may not be removed for any reason during their three-year terms of office.[133]

(f) Elimination of cumulative voting or increasing the minimum cumulative vote necessary to obtain representation on the board.[134]

(g) Substitution of a classified or "staggered" board of directors for an annually elected board, thereby extending the time required to elect a majority of the board as well as diluting cumulative voting power.[135] In addition to creating a classified board, incumbent management may also choose to decrease the number of board members, thereby further diluting cumulative voting power.[136]

[130] *See* letter of Phillip L. West, *supra* note 127.

[131] *Id.* A provision of this type, however, may prove to be more beneficial to the offeror than to the target by preventing the target itself from consummating a defensive merger.

[132] *Id.* [133] *Id.*

[134] Westinghouse Air Brake Co., in an effort to prevent Crane Co. from obtaining representation on the board, changed its by-laws to increase the minimum cumulative vote necessary to obtain representation from 9.1 percent to 25 percent. *See* Crane Co. v. Westinghouse Air Brake Co. *supra* note 68, at 790.

In defending against a takeover attempt by Northwest Industries, Inc., management of B. F. Goodrich Co. sought and received shareholder approval of a proposal to initiate cumulative voting. The proposal was apparently recommended to insure that incumbent management would retain at least some board seats in the event that Northwest acquired control. *See Continental Airline, Cyclops to Elevate Take-Over Hurdles*, Wall Street Journal, *supra* note 127.

[135] *See* Masonite Corporation, *Notice of Annual Meeting of Stockholders November 25, 1969.*

[136] An increase in the size of the board may also be used to dilute cumulative voting. At the 1955 annual meeting of Western Air Lines, Inc., a minority group

(2) Regulation Affecting Discriminatory Voting Provisions

The concern of the New York Stock Exchange with regard to provisions of the type described above was reflected in a letter to presidents of listed companies in December 1968:

> Generally speaking, an arrangement which could be applied uniformly to all transactions of similar nature and without regard to the parties involved, normally, would not be viewed as objectionable. On the other hand, any proposal which results in either discrimination against an existing substantial stockholder or discouragement of anyone seeking to make a substantial investment would appear to raise substantial questions as to whether or not it constitutes an infringement upon the voting philosophy of the Exchange.
>
> At present, as a matter of policy, the Exchange will refuse to list common stock when restrictions are involved such as voting trusts, irrevocable proxies, disproportionate voting power, classification of boards of directors into more than three classes of approximately equal size and tenure, or unusual voting provisions which tend to nullify or restrict the voting of a class of stock or the right to veto the actions of another class.[137]

However, in February 1969 the Exchange reversed its previous position and advised listed companies that it would not adopt a formal policy prohibiting the listing of shares which are the subject of restrictive voting arrangements.[138]

---

cumulated its votes and elected one of thirteen directors. Immediately after the meeting, the board met and voted to increase its membership to fourteen. The board then filled the vacancy with the nominee who had been ousted by election of the minority candidate. N.Y. Times, April 23, 1955, at 27, col. 4.

Some states require prior approval by the board of directors before a vote upon a merger or similar transaction may be submitted to shareholders. *See, e.g.*, Del. Gen. Corp. Law § 251(b), § 252(c). Proposed amendments which provide for classified directors or which eliminate or restrict cumulative voting thus have the effect of creating additional insulation for incumbent management. With regard to classified directors generally, *see* Aranow and Einhorn, Proxy Contests for Corporate Control 348–59 (2d ed. 1968).

[137] *See* Letter of Phillip L. West to Presidents of Listed Companies, *supra* note 127.

[138] *See* Letter of Phillip L. West, Vice-President, New York Stock Exchange, to Presidents of Listed Companies, Feb. 21, 1969, reprinted in NYSE Company Manual, at xxiii–xxiv.

Exchange regulation of corporate voting requirements was opposed by a number of listed companies among others. *See Big Board to Study Curb on Firms' Efforts to Protect Themselves Against Take-overs*, Wall Street Journal, Feb. 20, 1969, at 6.

The Exchange's official position in this matter is presently set forth in the NYSE Company Manual as follows:

UNUSUAL VOTING PROVISIONS

The Exchange *may* (emphasis added) refuse to list any class of stock which has unusual voting provisions which tend to nullify or restrict its voting, or which is subject to unusual voting provisions of another class of stock having such effect, as, for example, a situation in which one class of stock has the right to veto the actions of another class.[139]

The SEC has attempted to deal with these restrictions by requiring the target company to make appropriate disclosures in proxy solicitation materials. Thus, where a provision of the type described in (a) above was recommended by management which controlled approximately 16 percent of the company's voting stock, the Commission required disclosure to the effect that management would acquire disproportionate voting power which would effectively give it a veto power over corporate merger proposals and assist its officials in retaining their present positions with the company.[140]

State law has also had an impact on some of the restrictions noted above. For example, where cumulative voting is made mandatory either by state constitution or by statute, management may be powerless to eliminate it by charter or by-law amendment.[141] Similarly, a provision for the classification of directors, although permitted by statute, has been construed to impair a state constitutional provision guaranteeing stockholders the right to cumulate their votes in the election of directors.[142] Charter or

[139] NYSE COMPANY MANUAL, at A-282, A-283. With regard to Exchange policy in connection with other provisions affecting voting rights and stockholder approval, *see also* NYSE COMPANY MANUAL, at A-280 to A-285.

[140] *See* Masonite Corporation, *Notice of Annual Meeting of Stockholders November 25, 1969*, at p. 5. *Cf.* Elgin National Industries, Inc. v. Chemetron Corp., *supra* note 124.

[141] To avoid mandatory cumulative voting, some corporations have reincorporated in other states which do not have such a requirement. *See* Western Air Lines, Inc. v. Sobieski, 191 Cal. App. 2d 399, 12 Cal. Rpt. 719 (1961). *See also* Maddock v. Vorclone Corp., 17 Del. Ch. 39, 147 A. 255 (1929); Sturdy, *Mandatory Cumulative Voting, An Anachronism*, 16 BUS. LAW 550 (April 1961). As to cumulative voting generally, *see* ARANOW AND EINHORN, *supra* note 136, at 331–47.

[142] *See* Wolfson v. Avery, 6 Ill.2d 78, 126 N.E.2d 701 (1955). *See also* State *ex rel.* Syphers v. McCune, 143 W.Va. 315, 101 S.E.2d 834 (1958). *Cf.* Bohannan v. Corporation Commission, 82 Ariz. 299, 313 P.2d 379 (1957); Humphrys v. Winous Co., 165 Ohio St. 45, 133 N.E.2d 780 (1956), rev'g 57 Ohio App. 44, 125

by-law amendments providing that directors may not be removed for any reason during their terms of office may also be struck down as conflicting with the inherent power of shareholders to remove directors for cause.[143] Proposals to reduce the size of the board of directors are also subject to statutory limitations designed to protect minority interests.[144]

J. State Takeover Statutes

Perhaps one of the most effective and prophylactic methods of combating a tender offer is for the target company, prior to inception of the offer, to take those steps necessary to trigger the application of a state takeover statute to the tender offer. At present, Ohio,[145] Virginia,[146] and, to a more limited extent, Nevada[147] have takeover statutes which compromise, if not eliminate, any tactical advantages which an offeror may have in its quest to obtain control of a target company.[148] These statutes appear to be primarily designed to prevent contested transfers of control of local industry rather than to protect the investing public and, accordingly, are weighted heavily in favor of the target company.

The Ohio statute applies to tender offers for equity securities of any company incorporated in Ohio or having its principal

---

N.E.2d 204 (1955). For an analysis of these cases and classification of directors generally, *see* Aranow and Einhorn, *supra* note 136 at 348–59. *See also* McDonough v. Copeland Refrigeration Corp., 277 F. Supp. 6 (E.D. Mich., 1967).

A by-law provision providing for removal of directors with or without cause by a majority vote of stockholders has been held invalid when the certificate of incorporation provides for a classified board, "because [the by-law provision] would permit the removal of directors without cause in a manner which would frustrate the plan and purpose behind the provision for staggered terms and because it is incompatible with the pertinent language of the statute and the certificate." Essential Enterprises Corp. v. Automatic Steel Products, Inc., 159 A. 2d 288, 291 (Del. Ch. 1960). *But see* Everett v. Transnation Development Corp., 267 A. 2d 627 (Del. Ch. 1970); Dillon v. Berg, 326 F. Supp. 1214 (D. Del. 1971), *aff'd per curiam*, 453 F.2d 876 (3d Cir., 1971).

143 *See* Campbell v. Loew's, Inc., 36 Del. Ch. 563, 134 A.2d 852 (1957).

144 *See, e.g.*, Mich. Stat. Ann. § 21.13(3); Cal. Corp. Code Ann. § 501,3640 (Deering). *See also* McDonough v. Copeland Refrigeration Corp., *supra* note 142.

145 Ohio Rev. Code Ann., § 1707.041, eff. Nov. 9, 1969.

146 Va. Code Ann., § 13.1–528 to § 13.1–541, as amended, eff. March 5, 1968.

147 Nev. Rev. Stat. § 78.376 to § 78.3778, eff. March 4, 1969.

148 The state of Wisconsin recently enacted a takeover bill similar to the Ohio and Virginia statutes. *See* Wisc. Stat. §§ 552.01 et seq., eff. July 1, 1972.

place of business and substantial assets within the state. The Virginia Take-Over-Bid Disclosure Act applies to offers for equity securities of companies incorporated and doing business in Virginia, while the Nevada takeover statute applies to cash offers for equity securities of companies incorporated in Nevada.

In addition to these statutes, which apply generally to all local industry, a number of states have passed similarly restrictive statutes regulating tender offers for domestic insurance companies.[149] A more detailed discussion of the broad local interest and insurance statutes, together with a review of other forms of state regulation of tender offers, appears in Chapter 5, *supra*.

K. Legal Action

There are very few contested tender offers where the target will not consider legal action as a method of resisting the offeror's advances. In large measure resort to the courts has resulted from the maze of federal regulation affecting tender offers—the application and interpretation of which are subjects on which reasonable men may differ. Where appropriate, legal action may be the surest method of bringing the offer to a grinding halt and while such action may serve only to delay the offer, the effect of such delay may often be enough to assure the ultimate defeat of the offer.[150]

In recent years, attempts at defeating tender offers through the judicial process have been based upon a wide variety of allegations, including the following:

(a) Failure of the offeror to disclose material facts regarding its plans to: (1) merge the target with other persons; (2) ob-

[149] *See, e.g.*, MD. ANN. CODE art. 48A § 494, eff. July 1, 1969; CONN. GEN. STAT. ANN. §§ 38–39b, c, d, and e, eff. June 30, 1969; 40 PA. STAT. ANN. § 459.6 (Purdon), eff. Nov. 25, 1968; N.H. REV. STAT. ANN. § 401-A, eff. June 30, 1969.

[150] In addition to initiating its own legal proceedings, the target may attempt to persuade federal and state regulatory authorities to take appropriate action. For a description of the efforts of Armour & Co., in this regard, *see* Armour & Co. v. General Host Corp., 296 F. Supp. 470, 473–75 (S.D.N.Y. 1969); *Armour Steps Up Legal Moves in States in Bid to Block Offer by General Host,* Wall Street Journal, Feb. 7, 1969, at 14; *Greyhound Lifts Armour Offer $2 to $72, Extends It; Wisconsin Bars General Host,* Wall Street Journal, Feb. 11, 1969, at 3.

For the use of a private tax ruling as a defensive tactic, *see* Shop Talk, *Interesting Use of Private Ruling in Tender Offers,* 28 J. TAX 319 (May 1968).

tain control of the target by electing a majority of its representatives to the target's board of directors; (3) use the target's cash assets as a source of funds to repay loans obtained by the offeror to finance the offer; [151]

(b) Failure of the offeror to submit copies of Schedule 13D to the target; [152]

(c) Failure of a "group" to make timely filings of Schedule 13D reports; [153]

(d) False and misleading press releases regarding the offeror's earnings; [154]

(e) Violations of the anti-trust laws; [155]

(f) Violations of Regulations G & T (promulgated under Section 7 of the 1934 Act) in connection with loans obtained by the offeror to finance the offer; [156]

(g) Violation of the Interstate Commerce Act; [157]

(h) Violation of the Public Utility Holding Co. Act; [158]

(i) Violation of the Federal Communications Act; [159]

[151] *See* Electronic Specialty Co. v. International Controls Corp., 409 F.2d 937 (2d Cir. 1969); The Susquehanna Corp. v. Pan American Sulphur Co., 423 F.2d 1075 (5th Cir. 1970), *rev'g* Pan American Sulphur Co. v. The Susquehanna Corp., No. SA-69-CA-67 (W.D. Tex. 1969), CCH FED. SEC. REP. ¶ 92,473. *Cf. Matter of* The Susquehanna Corp., SEC Admin. Proc. File No. 3-1868 (Aug. 5, 1969), CCH FED. SEC. L. REP. ¶ 77,741; *In the Matter of* Reports of The Susquehanna Corp., SEC Securities Exchange Act Release No. 8933 (July 17, 1970), CCH FED. SEC. L. REP. ¶ 77,842.

[152] *See* The Susquehanna Corp. v. Pan American Sulphur Co., *id.*

[153] *See* Bath Industries, Inc. v. Blot, 427 F.2d 97 (7th Cir. 1970). *Cf.* Ozark Air Lines, Inc. v. Cox, 326 F. Supp. 1113 (E.D. Mo. 1971); GAF Corp. v. Milstein, 453 F.2d 709 (2d Cir. 1971), *cert. denied* 406 U.S. 910 (1972); Sisak v. Wings & Wheels Express, Inc., 70 Civ. 2817 (S.D.N.Y. 1970), CCH FED. SEC. L. REP. ¶ 92,991.

[154] *See* Butler Aviation International, Inc. v. Comprehensive Designers, Inc., 425 F.2d 842 (2d Cir. 1970).

[155] *See* Allis-Chalmers Mfg. Co. v. White Consolidated Industries, Inc., 414 F.2d 506 (3d Cir. 1969), *cert. denied,* 396 U.S. 1009 (1970); Metro-Goldwyn-Mayer Inc. v. Transamerica Corp., 303 F. Supp. 1354 (S.D.N.Y. 1969); The Lunkenheimer Co. v. Condec Corp., 268 F. Supp. 667 (S.D.N.Y. 1967); Muskegon Piston Ring Co. v. Gulf & Western Industries, Inc. 328, F. 2d 830 (6th Cir. 1964). *See also* C. Leonardt Improvement Co. v. Southdown Inc., 313 F. Supp. 1146 (C.D. Calif. 1970).

[156] *See* Metro-Goldwyn-Mayer Inc. v. Transamerica Corp., *id.*

[157] *See* B. F. Goodrich Company v. Northwest Industries, Inc., *supra* note 114.

[158] *See* United Gas Corp. v. Pennzoil Co., 248 F. Supp. 449 (S.D.N.Y. 1965) *aff'd per curiam,* 354 F.2d 1002 (2d Cir. 1965).

[159] *See* complaint in Columbia Pictures Corp. v. Clairmont, Civ. No. 3581 (S.D.N.Y. 1966). See also note 116, *supra.*

(j) Violation of the Investment Company Act;[160]

(k) Violation of state securities laws.[161]

In most instances, the relief sought by the target will be in the form of a judgment requiring the offeror to divest itself of the stock acquired pursuant to the offer or, alternatively, an injunction prohibiting the offeror from voting the stock so acquired. In addition, the target will normally request an order restraining the offeror from purchasing additional shares.

Assuming a violation can be sufficiently proved on an application for a preliminary injunction, the court may shape the relief granted to the nature of the violation.[162] Thus, where the offeror has made false and misleading statements in the tender offer, press releases or in filings with the Commission, the court may prohibit renewal of the offer until full disclosure is made or it may compel full disclosure and require the offeror to give shareholders an opportunity to withdraw shares previously tendered.[163] Similarly, if there is sufficient evidence to indicate that the offeror has manipulated the price of the target's stock prior to the offer, the court may require recission and temporarily enjoin further solicitation, or alternatively, it may require the offeror to raise the offering price for all shares tendered.[164]

L. PUBLICITY

One of the least complicated and often most effective ways of defending against a tender offer is for the target to undertake an aggressive publicity campaign aimed at dissuading stockholders

[160] *See* Armour & Co. v. General Host Corp., *supra* note 150.

[161] See note 150, *supra;* Layritz v. Condec Corp., Civ. No. 6439 (S.D. Ohio 1967). With regard to state regulation of tender offers, see text accompanying notes 145–149, *supra.*, Chapter 5.

[162] ". . . the court has a variety of tools available to do equity at the stage of the temporary injunction. In using them, it is important both to protect stockholders against deceptive exchange offers and not to frustrate the desires of those who wish to exchange when all the facts are known." Butler Aviation International, Inc. v. Comprehensive Designers, Inc., *supra* note 154, at 844.

[163] *See* Butler Aviation International Inc. v. Comprehensive Designers, Inc., *id.* *See* Electronic Specialty Co. v. International Controls Corp., *supra* note 151, at 947.

[164] *See* Electronic Specialty Co. v. International Controls Corp., *id.* For a more detailed discussion of the remedies available for violations of the securities laws by tender offerors, see Chapter 10.

and professional arbitrageurs from tendering shares. In most instances the target, as a means of communicating with shareholders, will place large advertisements in newspapers of national daily circulation which publish financial news.[165] News releases, press conferences, and direct communication with stockholders by way of letter and telephone (perhaps with the assistance of a recognized "proxy" soliciting firm) normally complement an advertising campaign to insure effective dissemination of the target's position with regard to the offer.[166]

(1) Forms of Publicity to Thwart a Tender Offer

The substance of the target's statements will normally be designed to highlight the past progress and future potential of the target under present management as well as the adverse consequences that may befall shareholders if they choose to tender their shares. The specific nature of the target's response may be influenced in large part by whether the tender offer is one for cash or an exchange of securities. Where the target responds to an exchange offer, it may comment extensively on the probable adverse effects which the offeror's control of the target will have on its continued success and the resulting depreciation in investment values for shareholders. If the tender offer is for cash, however, there may be little point in a lengthy discussion of the ef-

[165] This method of communication is normally preferable to a direct mail solicitation, as large numbers of shares are likely to be traded during the offering period and the purchasers of such shares may not yet appear on the books of the corporation. In addition, a direct mail solicitation can prove ineffective with regard to those stockholders whose shares are held in street name. Moreover, a certain amount of delay must be expected in a direct mailing, in part because of the traffic problems of the transfer agent. In addition, some delay may be anticipated with the proxy clerks at brokerage firms with regard to shares held in street name.

[166] It has been suggested that prior to embarking on a plan of this nature, consideration should be given to the question of whether widespread publicity by the target may alert a substantial number of stockholders who might not otherwise have heard of the tender offer. As a practical matter, it can safely be assumed that large individual and institutional stockholders will be well aware of the offer and that smaller stockholders who may not have seen ads announcing the offer will be contacted by broker-dealers eager to earn a solicitation fee. The failure of the target to publicly announce its position on the offer may in fact do more harm than good by creating the impression that incumbent management does not oppose the offer. With regard to the availability of the target's stockholder list to the offeror, see text accompanying notes 1–26, Chapter 2.

fects on the target because the tendering shareholder will cease to be an investor in the target.

With the distinction between cash and exchange offers in mind, a typical response of the target may include reference to one or more of the following factors in attempting to discourage shareholders from tendering their shares:

(a) The inadequacy of the consideration being offered in relation to both the current market and future growth potential of the target;

(b) The conditional nature of the offer resulting from: (1) antitrust or other legal action seeking to enjoin the takeover attempt; and/or (2) the terms and conditions of the offer relating to the number of shares to be purchased, pro rata purchases and "out" clauses;

(c) The obvious incentive of broker-dealers to encourage shareholders to tender because of their receiving solicitation fees for shares tendered and accepted and brokerage commissions on reinvestment of proceeds;

(d) The tax consequences of tendering shares;

(e) The sources of financing of the offer, particularly where: (1) the cash flow of the offeror appears inadequate to cover interest and dividends on an exchange package; or (2) there is evidence indicating that the target's own assets will be the ultimate source of funds to finance the offer;

(f) The inexperience of the offeror in the type of business activities engaged in by the offeror;

(g) Poor past performance results of the offeror in operating its own business enterprises.

The sweeping attack which B. F. Goodrich Company made on the exchange offer of Northwest Industries, Inc., furnishes an excellent example of the use of defensive publicity in an actual tender offer contest. The July 24, 1969, editions of both the New York Times and the Wall Street Journal carried full-page ads entitled "B. F. Goodrich Stockholders: Ten Dangers in Tendering Even One Share to Northwest Industries." [167] The ten dangers

[167] N.Y. Times, July 24, 1969, at 55; Wall Street Journal, July 24, 1969, at 31. *See also,* defensive publicity statement of Colorado Interstate Corp., N.Y. Times, July 20, 1972, at 45.

related to what Goodrich considered to be the "principal internal troubles" of Northwest, which were identified as poor earnings and operating results and declining sales of Northwest and a number of its subsidiaries, the apparent inability of Northwest to pay interest and dividends on the securities which formed the exchange package, the "crash" in Northwest stock reflecting public recognition of its internal troubles, and an allegation that the Northwest announcement of the tender offer violated the federal securities laws. The Goodrich ad went on to disclose the following additional matters which it believed would have the effect of discouraging shareholders from tendering their shares: (1) the anti-trust action instituted by the Justice Department against Northwest in connection with its attempt to acquire control of Goodrich; (2) the investment banking firm managing the offer for Northwest had withdrawn its support; (3) the Northwest offer was fully taxable and did not include any money with which to pay the tax; (4) broker-dealer advisory opinions recommending against the offer; (5) the inadequacy of the consideration offered as reflected in the fact that the Northwest package was quoted at a price less than the price of Goodrich common stock; (6) Northwest might refuse to make the exchange unless shareholders paid over the June 1969 Goodrich dividend to Northwest; and (7) projected improvement in profit margins and earnings at Goodrich resulting from a capital expansion program.

Goodrich's publicity attack, containing a series of similar ads which began shortly after announcement of the Northwest offer in January 1969, did not stop with the ad noted above. Some two weeks later it took another large ad to advise shareholders of the following additional matters: (a) continued poor earnings of Northwest for the six-month period ending June 30, 1969; (b) the withdrawal of two other recently retained investment banking houses; and (c) the admission by Northwest that, aside from tenders by a corporation headed by a Northwest director, less than 3.5 percent of the Goodrich shares had been tendered as of July 29.[168]

[168] *B. F. Goodrich Stockholders: Additional Reasons Why Northwest's Offer Will Fail,* N.Y. Times, Aug. 7, 1969, at 53.

Some other interesting examples of defensive publicity are found in the following ads: (a) Sinclair Oil Corp. letter to stockholders entitled *Would you will-*

(2) Federal Regulation of Recommendations by the Target to Security Holders

(a) Filing and Disclosure Requirements

If the target proposes to respond to a tender offer subject to the provisions of Section 14(d) of the 1934 Act,[169] it must comply with the requirements of Rule 14d-4 under that Act before any recommendations may lawfully be made to security holders.[170] Rule 14d-4(a) provides that the target must file a statemement with the SEC containing the information specified by Schedule 14D [171] no later than the time copies of its recommendation to accept or reject the offer are first published or sent to security holders. Rule 14d-4(b) also requires the target to promptly file amendments to its statement if any material change occurs in the facts set forth therein. Rule 14d-4(c) relates to the substance of the recommendation itself and requires such statement to include

---

ingly exchange your stock in Sinclair and turn its management over to a company that is not in the oil business and could end up with 4 billion of debt? Wall Street Journal, Dec. 13, 1968, at 27; (b) National Presto Industries, Inc. response to the exchange offer of National Union Electric Corp. entitled *World's First Comic Prospectus. Read about "Funny Money," How Emerson Turned the Profit Corner and Other Factual but Hilarious Stuff*, Wall Street Journal, July 1, 1969, at 27. *See also* National Presto ad, Wall Street Journal, Oct. 31, 1969 at 23; (c) Hugoton Production Co. letter to stockholders claiming, *inter alia*, that Mesa Petroleum Corp. (the offeror) capitalizes the costs of drilling nonproductive wells and that an American Petroleum Institute study showed that only two of thirty-seven companies covered by the survey followed this practice. Wall Street Journal, Nov. 14, 1968, at 26. *See also* Mesa Petroleum Corp. letter to stockholders of Hugoton Production Co. advising that an API survey revealed that only three of thirty-seven companies followed the accounting practice of Reserve Oil & Gas (a proposed defensive merger partner) regarding retained production payments. Wall Street Journal, Nov. 11, 1968, at 25.

For citations of other examples, *see* Schmults and Kelly, *supra* note 118, at 123, n. 12; Bromberg, *Exchange Offers*, 2 Rev. of Sec. Reg. 805, 811–12 (Dec. 3, 1969). *See also* Shop Talk, *Interesting Use of Private Ruling in Tender Offer*, 28 J. Tax 319 (May 1968).

[169] With regard to the obligations, if any, of the target to respond to a tender offer, see text accompanying notes 1–13, *supra*.

[170] 17 C.F.R. § 240.14d–4, eff. July 30, 1968. Section 14(d)(4) provides as follows: "Any solicitation or recommendation to the holders of such a security to accept or reject a tender offer or request or invitation for tenders shall be made in accordance with such rules and regulations as the Commission may prescribe as necessary or appropriate in the public interest or for the protection of investors."

[171] 17 C.F.R. § 240.14d–101, eff. July 30, 1968.

the name of the person making the recommendation together with the information required by Items 1(b) and 2(b) of Schedule 14D or a summary thereof.

Compliance with Rule 14d-4 is not required, however, where the target's statement does no more than provide the following information:

(1) identify a tender offer or request or invitation for tenders made by another person, (2) state that the management of the issuer is studying the matter and will, on or before a specified date (which shall be not later than 10 days prior to the date specified in the offer, request or invitation, as the last date on which tenders will be accepted, or such shorter period as the Commission may authorize) advise security holders as to the management's recommendation to accept or reject the offer, request or invitation, and (3) request security holders to defer making a determination as to whether or not they should accept or reject the offer, request or invitation until they have received the management's recommendation with respect thereto.[172]

(b) Application of the Anti-fraud Provisions to False and Misleading Statements of the Target

Where the target responds to a tender offer, it is obliged to furnish shareholders with completely honest and accurate information. Accordingly, any statements containing fraudulent misrepresentations or omissions of material facts which dissuade security holders from tendering their shares would subject the target to potential liability under the anti-fraud provisions of the 1934 Act.

Prior to enactment of the Williams Bill, fraudulent statements by the target were actionable pursuant to Section 10(b) and Rule 10b-5 thereunder. The Williams Bill, however, has added a new anti-fraud provision, Section 14(e), which was apparently intended to "affirm" the applicability of the disclosure standards of Rule 10b-5 to tender offers.[173] This provision provides in relevant part as follows:

[172] *See* Rule 14d–2(f), 17 C.F.R. § 240.14d–2(f), eff. Aug. 30, 1968. For further discussion of federal regulation of recommendations in connection with tender offers, see text accompanying notes 111–122, Chapter 4.

[173] "This provision (Section 14(e)) would affirm the fact that persons engaged in making or opposing tender offers or otherwise seeking to influence the decision of investors or the outcome of the tender offer are under an obligation to make

It shall be unlawful for any person to make any untrue statement of a material fact or omit to state any material fact necessary in order to make the statements made, in the light of the circumstances under which they were made, not misleading or to engage in any fraudulent, deceptive, or manipulative acts or practices, in connection with any tender offer . . . or any solicitation of security holders in opposition to . . . any such offer.

Violations of Section 10(b) and Rule 10b-5 thereunder and Section 14(e) would thus subject the target to possible injunctive action by the Securities and Exchange Commission, tender offerors, or shareholders who were dissuaded from tendering their shares by the target's false and misleading statements. In addition, nontendering shareholders (and possibly tender offerors) could seek relief in the form of monetary damages for violations of these provisions.[174]

M. Restrictive Loan Agreements

Target companies which have relied upon the use of restrictive loan agreements as a means of thwarting a tender offer have enjoyed varying degrees of success over the years. Such an agreement will normally provide that any loans made to the target company will be immediately repayable at the option of the lender if the target company experiences a change in control. Where the continued success of the target company is dependent upon the preservation of continuous, reliable, and well-established lines of credit, a provision of this type may cause a prospective offeror to think twice about the efficacy of attempting a takeover.

In one noteworthy instance, the offeror's decision to withdraw an exchange offer was attributed to its being advised by the target company that the latter had amended its credit agreements with several banks by incorporating a provision of the type de-

---

full disclosure of material information to those with whom they deal." S. Rep. No. 550, 90th Cong., 1st Sess. 11 (1967); H.R. Rep. No. 1711, 90th Cong., 2d Sess. 11 (1968). *See also* Neuman v. Electronic Specialty Co., No. 68C1817, Dec. 31, 1969 (N.D. Ill.), CCH Fed. Sec. L. Rep. ¶ 92,591; Feit v. Leasco Data Processing Equipment Corp., 332 F. Supp. 544 (E.D.N.Y. 1971).

174 As to the important issues regarding standing to sue and the types of relief available for violations of Sections 10(b) and 14(e), see text accompanying notes 132–147, Chapter 4; text accompanying notes 38–43, Chapter 10.

scribed above.[175] Prior to the amendment, the target's credit agreements contained only standard protective clauses, including a provision giving the banks with a specified percentage of the loan commitment the option of requiring repayment if the target merged or consolidated with another company. The lenders, which included two banks that held a substantial amount of the target's outstanding shares, expressed concern that this provision would not apply in the tender offer situation and accordingly suggested that the target agree to a modification of the loan agreement to provide that if 30 percent of the outstanding stock of the target were owned or controlled by any single shareholder, the loans would be repayable at the option of 25 percent of the target's outstanding loans.[176]

Where a restrictive loan provision is negotiated and incorporated in a loan agreement at the request of the target's management, such an arrangement may be viewed essentially as an attempt by management to perpetuate themselves in control. Under such circumstances, the officers and directors may be subject to extensive liability for damages if the loan is in fact called. While no case has been found dealing with this issue, a provision of the type described herein which is incorporated at the request of incumbent management may well be viewed as fundamentally inconsistent with the best interests of the corporation even where management, in good faith, believes that the interests of the target will best be served by the perpetuation of existing management.

It should also be noted that the use of restrictive loan provisions as a defensive tactic may prove to be largely ineffective where the offeror has the ability to refinance the target's debt on

[175] *See* Institutional Investor Study Report of the Securities and Exchange Commission (hereinafter referred to as Institutional Investor Study), H.R. Doc. No. 92–64, Pt. 5, 92d Cong., 1st Sess. 2811 (1971).

[176] Query, whether the willingness of some banks to enter into arrangements of this nature has been motivated by their desire to protect themselves against transactions which might adversely affect the target's ability to service the debt or their interest in preserving the target as a customer? The SEC has questioned whether institutional lenders are not confronted with a basic conflict between its interest as a creditor and its fiduciary duty to other customers for which the institution is holding shares where the primary purpose of the restrictive loan provision is to preserve the present management in an effort to insure that the target will continue as a customer. *See* Institutional Investor Study, at 2841.

favorable terms. Similarly, institutional lenders, while having the option to call the loan, may be reluctant to do so, particularly where such action will have a detrimental effect on the target company.[177]

[177] *See* INSTITUTIONAL INVESTOR STUDY, at 2811.

CHAPTER 10. ENFORCEMENT AND REMEDIES FOR VIOLATIONS OF THE FEDERAL SECURITIES LAWS IN CONNECTION WITH TENDER OFFERS

SECTION 1. *SEC ENFORCEMENT AND REMEDIES*

Where there is an apparent violation of the federal securities laws, the Commission will first consider whether the nature and character of the violation make it necessary or appropriate to proceed with enforcement action. In making such a determination, the Commission can be expected to consider its obligations to insure compliance with the federal securities laws, the interests of investors in the case at bar, and the deterrent effect resulting from both the initiation of enforcement action and the imposition of sanctions on offenders.

Once a decision has been made to proceed, the Commission will have a variety of administrative and judicial enforcement techniques from which to choose in dealing with violations in connection with tender offers.[1] Before discussing these techniques, however, it is important to briefly note that the Commis-

[1] The initiation of enforcement action by the Commission or, in some instances, the mere prospect of such action, often leads to requests by respondents for a settlement of the charges. Where a settlement would be consistent with the public interest, it has generally been the policy of the Commission and the staff to give every consideration to an appropriate settlement arrangement, thereby perhaps sparing the respondent the more unfavorable consequences of litigation as well as the time and expense resulting therefrom. Accordingly, counsel representing a party subject to Commission enforcement action should be cognizant of the opportunities and implications of the Commission's settlement policies and procedures. *See generally* Mathews, *SEC Civil Injunctive Actions-II*, 5 REV. OF SEC. REG. 949, 955–56 (March 22, 1972). *See also*, the so-called Wells Committee Report, reprinted in 158 BNA (Extra Edition, June 28, 1972).

sion's enforcement machinery is used primarily to secure statutory compliance rather than to effect relief for investors. Thus, for example, an administrative or judicial order directing an offeror to amend its Schedule 13D statement because of false and misleading statements contained therein may have limited practical significance to shareholders who tendered pursuant to a misleading offer. Investors must, therefore, be prepared to seek their own relief for violations of the federal securities laws.

A. Administrative Enforcement

If the Commission chooses to proceed administratively for alleged violations in connection with tender offers, it can be expected, where appropriate, to weigh the following alternative courses of action:

(1) Administrative Proceedings Pursuant to Section 15(c)(4) of the 1934 Act

Section 15(c)(4) [2] provides as follows:

> If the Commission finds, after notice and opportunity for hearing, that any person subject to the provisions of section 12, 13, or subsection (d) of section 15 of this title or any rule or regulation thereunder has failed to comply with any such provision, rule, or regulation in any material respect, the Commission may publish its findings and issue an order requiring such person to comply with such provision or such rule or regulation thereunder upon such terms and conditions and within such time as the Commission may specify in such order.

This statutory provision enables the Commission to compel an offeror that has filed a false, misleading, or inadequate Schedule 13D statement to make appropriate revisions by way of an amendment to such statement.[3] Similarly, a tender offeror that has failed to file a Schedule 13D statement may be directed to do so pursuant to a Section 15(c)(4) proceeding.[4]

[2] 15 U.S.C. § 78o(c)(4).

[3] *See, e.g., In the Matter of* Reports of the Susquehanna Corp., SEC Securities Exchange Act Release No. 8933 (July 17, 1970), CCH Fed. Sec. L. Rep. ¶ 77,-842. *Cf.* Susquehanna Corp. v. Pan American Sulphur Co., 423 F.2d 1075 (5th Cir. 1970).

[4] The extent to which the Commission is empowered to fashion broad equitable relief under Section 15(c)(4) is unclear. Thus, for example, where a false or misleading Schedule 13D statement has been filed, it is questionable whether the

(2) TRADING SUSPENSIONS

The speed with which the Commission can effect a suspension of trading makes this technique one of the more potent weapons in its enforcement arsenal and, where appropriate, may well be the most effective method of protecting the interests of investors. The power of the Commission summarily to suspend trading in the securities of the offeror and the target company derives from Sections 15(c)(5) and 19(a)(4) of the 1934 Act.[5] These statutory provisions authorize the Commission, where the public interest and the protection of investors so require, summarily to suspend over-the-counter trading [Section 15(c)(5)] and trading on a national securities exchange [Section 19(a)(4)] in any security (other than an exempt security) for a period not exceeding ten days. The Commission has adopted the practice of issuing additional ten-day suspensions at the end of the original ten-day period if further suspensions are deemed necessary.[6]

Securities dealers who effect transactions in securities suspended from trading are subject to revocation of their broker-dealer registration. While Sections 15(c)(5) and 19(a)(4) may not prohibit a tender offeror from accepting shares tendered by persons other than broker-dealers during the course of a trading suspension, it is generally advisable that the offeror refrain from doing so, particularly where the suspension is prompted by some statement or activity of the offeror. The acceptance of tendered shares under such circumstances may well subject the offeror to liability under the anti-fraud provisions of the federal securities laws.

(3) STOP ORDER PROCEEDINGS PURSUANT TO SECTION 8(d) OF THE 1933 ACT

Section 8(d) of the 1933 Act[7] authorizes the Commission to issue a "stop order" suspending the effectiveness of a registration

---

Commission, pursuant to Section 15(c)(4), can compel the offeror to make a rescission offer to tendering shareholders.

[5] 15 U.S.C. § 78o(c)(5); 15 U.S.C. § 78s(a)(4).

[6] *See In the Matter of* Red Bank Oil Co., 21 S.E.C. 695 (1946), CCH FED. SEC. L. REP. ¶ 75,610.

[7] 15 U.S.C. § 77h(d).

statement if it appears "at any time" that such statement "includes any untrue statement of a material fact or omits to state any material fact required to be stated therein or necessary to make the statements therein not misleading." This provision thereby enables the Commission to suspend the effectiveness of a registration statement used in connection with an exchange offer either before or after the Commission declares such registration statement effective. When the registration statement has been amended pursuant to the provisions of the stop order, such stop order will be lifted.

Unlike the Commission's summary trading suspension power, Section 8(d) provides that a stop order may issue only after an opportunity for a hearing (at a time fixed by the Commission) within fifteen days after notice of such hearing has been given by personal service or telegraphic notification. However, the initiation of stop order proceedings prior to the effective date of the registration statement has the effect of suspending the effective operation of such statement pending the hearing and determination of the stop order proceeding.[8] Similarly, where a stop order proceeding is initiated subsequent to the effective date of the registration statement but during the course of the distribution, the exchange offeror can be expected to discontinue the offering unless, of course, it is willing to incur the risks of an anti-fraud liability inherent in proceeding with the distribution.

(4) Broker-Dealer Revocation Proceedings

The federal securities laws reserve perhaps the harshest administrative sanctions for broker-dealers and persons associated with broker-dealers who participate in unlawful activities in connection with securities transactions. Section 15(b)(5) of the 1934 Act authorizes the Commission, after notice and an opportunity for a hearing, to censure, suspend for a period not exceeding twelve months, or revoke a broker-dealer's registration if it finds that such action is in the public interest and that the broker-dealer willfully violated any provision of the federal securities laws. Similarly, Section 15(b)(7) of the 1934 Act empowers the Com-

[8] *See* Jones v. SEC, 298 U.S. 1, 15 (1936).

mission, after notice and an opportunity for a hearing, to censure, bar, or suspend, for a period not exceeding twelve months, any person from being associated with a broker-dealer if it finds that such action is in the public interest and that such person has engaged in activities prohibited by the federal securities laws.

B. Judicial Enforcement

(1) Injunctive and Other Equitable Relief [9]

The power of the Commission to obtain injunctive and other equitable relief for violations of the 1934 Act derives from Section 21(e) [10] of that act which provides in part as follows:

> Whenever it shall appear to the Commission that any person is engaged or about to engage in any acts or practices which constitute or will constitute a violation of the provisions of this title, or of any rule or regulation thereunder, it may in its discretion bring an action in the proper district court of the United States, the district court of the United States for the District of Columbia, or the United States courts of any Territory or other place subject to the jurisdiction of the United States, to enjoin such acts or practices, and upon a proper showing a permanent or temporary injunction or restraining order shall be granted without bond.[11]

While a literal reading of Section 21(e) would indicate that the power of the courts is limited to enjoining violations of the 1934 Act and the rules thereunder, the courts, once jurisdiction is properly invoked, may exercise their inherent equity powers to grant a measure of relief greater than that of merely enjoining violations. The discretionary power of the courts to grant broad equitable relief is based upon the very sound rationale that those who violate the securities laws should not be permitted to derive any benefit from their wrongdoing.

Both the Securities Act of 1933 and the Investment Company Act of 1940 contain provisions similar to 21(e) of the 1934 Act.

[9] For a comprehensive analysis of injunctive actions by the SEC, see Mathews, *SEC Civil Injunctive Actions*, 5 Rev. of Sec. Reg. 969 (Feb. 18, 1972) (Part I); 5 Rev. of Sec. Reg. 949 (March 22, 1972) (Part II).

[10] 15 U.S.C. § 78u(e).

[11] The jurisdiction of the federal district courts to hear such actions is conferred by Section 27 of the 1934 Act (15 U.S.C. § 78aa).

Section 20(b) of the 1933 Act is almost identical with Section 21(e) of the 1934 Act and Section 42(e) of the 1940 Act. In addition to authorizing injunctive action, it expressly grants the courts the power to appoint a receiver for a failure to comply with the Act's registration requirements, thereby providing essential elements in the Commission's comprehensive tender offer enforcement scheme. The Commission, for example, has had occasion to seek injunctive relief under Section 20(b) of the 1933 Act in connection with certain preregistration publicity in a proposed exchange offer.[12] Similarly, the Commission has sought injunctive relief under Section 42(e) of the 1940 Act in connection with "warehousing" activities by a prospective tender offeror.[13] The Commission has also sought injunctive and other equitable relief for violations of Section 17(a) of the 1933 Act and Section 10(b) of the 1934 Act in connection with an alleged misleading registration statement and prospectus relating to an exchange offer.[14]

In the tender offer context, however, the Commission has not had frequent occasion to initiate judicial enforcement of the securities laws. Apart from the fact that the statutes and regulations affecting tender offers only date from July 1968,[15] the infrequency of the Commission's appearances has apparently been caused by the aggressiveness of private litigants in pursuing appropriate relief rather than from any paucity of violations. Generally speaking, the Commission will not initiate judicial action where an alleged violation has been properly brought before the court by a private party.[16] However, where the legal issues in a

[12] *See* SEC v. Bangor Punta Corp., No. 1388–69 (D.D.C. 1969), CCH Fed. Sec. L. Rep. ¶ 92,428, discussed in note 17, *infra*.

[13] *See* SEC v. Talley Industries, Inc., 399 F.2d 396 (2d Cir. 1968), *cert. denied,* 393 U.S. 1015 (1969). For later proceedings, *see* SEC v. General Time Corp., 407 F.2d 65 (2d Cir. 1968), *cert. denied,* 393 U.S. 1026 (1969). *See also* General Time Corp. v. Talley Industries, Inc., 403 F.2d 159 (2d Cir. 1968), *cert. denied,* 393 U.S. 1026 (1969).

[14] In SEC v. Bangor Punta Corp., 331 F. Supp. 1154 (S.D.N.Y. 1971), the Commission alleged and the court found that Bangor Punta's registration statement and prospectus relating to an exchange offer for securities of Piper Aircraft Corp. was misleading. The court granted the Commission's request compelling Bangor Punta to make a rescission offer to securityholders who tendered their shares but denied injunctive relief on the ground that the Commission had not sustained the burden of proving that Bangor Punta and its officers, directors and employees have "a propensity or natural inclination" to violate the securities laws.

[15] Pub. L. No. 90–439 (July 29, 1968).

[16] *Cf.* SEC v. Talley Industries, Inc.; SEC v. General Time Corp.; General Time Corp. v. Talley Industries, Inc., *supra* note 13.

private suit are of a precedential nature or are otherwise of sufficient importance to make an expression of its views desirable, the Commission may seek or be requested by the court to participate as *amicus curiae*.[17]

Of the limited number of judicial actions initiated by the Commission in a tender offer context, perhaps the most interesting from the standpoint of the nature of the relief granted are the cases of *SEC* v. *Talley Industries, Inc.*[18] and *SEC* v. *Madison Square Garden Corp.*[19] While the *Talley* case involves relief fashioned to effectuate the purposes of the 1940 Act rather than the 1934 Act tender rules, the case is particularly important with regard to the form of relief which may be granted for violations in connection with the widespread practice of "warehousing"; i.e., purchases of the target's shares by institutional investors for the benefit of a prospective offeror.[20] The *Madison Square Garden* case is discussed in detail in Section 3(B) of Chapter 2. The various forms of equitable relief available to the Commission for violations of the 1934 Act tender rules are for the most part the same as those available to investors in private remedy actions and are discussed in Section 2 of this chapter.

(2) Criminal Enforcement

The imposition of criminal sanctions for willful violations of the federal securities laws is expressly provided for in each of the

[17] In one noteworthy instance the Commission instituted an action in which it obtained a consent injunction and thereafter proceeded to participate as *amicus curiae* in a private suit involving the same issue considered in its own action. In SEC v. Bangor Punta Corp., No. 1388–69 (D.D.C. 1969), CCH Fed. Sec. L. Rep. ¶ 92,428, the Commission obtained a consent injunction against Bangor Punta Corp. and Piper Aircraft Corp. based on allegations that the corporations engaged in unlawful preregistration publicity (gun-jumping) in violation of § 5(c) of the 1933 Act and Rule 135 thereunder in connection with a proposed exchange offer. Shortly thereafter, Chris-Craft Industries, Inc., which was competing with Bangor Punta for control of Piper, initiated its own injunctive action alleging, *inter alia*, a violation of the SEC's gun-jumping rule. The District Court held that the preregistration publicity did not constitute gun-jumping but the Circuit Court of Appeals reversed. The Commission appeared as amicus in the circuit court and urged that the district court's decision be reversed. *See* Chris-Craft Industries, Inc. v. Piper Aircraft Corp., 303 F. Supp. 191 (S.D.N.Y. 1969), *aff'd in part, sub nom.*, Chris-Craft Industries, Inc. v. Bangor Punta Corp. No. 33983 (2d Cir. 1969), CCH Fed. Sec. L. Rep. ¶ 92,510, *aff'd on rehearing*, 426 F.2d 569 (2d Cir. 1970) (*en banc*). *See also* SEC v. Bangor Punta Corp., 331 F. Supp. 1154 (S.D.N.Y. 1971).

[18] See *supra* note 13.

[19] 69 Civ. 4364 (S.D.N.Y. 1970), CCH Fed. Sec. L. Rep. ¶ 92,649.

[20] See Chapter 2, Section 3(B).

statutes administered by the Commission.[21] The Commission, however, is not empowered to initiate criminal proceedings on its own. Where the Commission deems such action appropriate, it will furnish a "criminal reference report" to the U.S. Attorney General setting forth its recommendations and detailing the acts and practices which are alleged to constitute criminal conduct.[22] The Attorney General's office, in its discretion, will then determine whether to initiate a criminal proceeding.[23] If criminal sanctions are deemed appropriate, the case will then be referred for prosecution to the U.S. Attorney in the appropriate federal district. In most instances, one or more members of the staff of the Commission will be assigned to assist the U.S. Attorney's office in the preparation and presentation of the case.

As noted previously, it is a criminal offense to "willfully" violate any of the federal securities laws. The term "willfully," however, does not lend itself to a hard and fast definition and in many instances may only be ascertained from the facts and circumstances of the particular case. Nevertheless, there is authority for the proposition that willfulness in a criminal prosecution for violation of the securities laws can be established merely upon proof that the defendant had factual knowledge of the act committed or statement made as opposed to knowledge of the law itself. Stated in other words, specific intent to violate the law would not be a requisite element of the offense. Instead, all that apparently need be shown is that the defendant intentionally (i.e., not accidentally, negligently, etc.) committed the act prohibited by statute, with the law implying the willful intention to do all that which is the natural consequence of such an act. Thus, it has been held that a willful violation is established by proof of the commission of an unlawful act, notwithstanding a defendant's lack of knowledge of the illegality of such conduct.[24] The practi-

[21] See, e.g., § 24 Securities Act of 1933 (15 U.S.C. § 77x); § 32 Securities Exchange Act of 1934 (15 U.S.C. § 78 ff); § 49 Investment Company Act of 1940 (15 U.S.C. § 80a–48).

[22] *See, e.g.*, § 20(b) Securities Act of 1933 (15 U.S.C. § 77t(b)); § 21(e) Securities Exchange Act of 1934 (15 U.S.C. § 78u(e)); § 42(e) of the Investment Company Act of 1940 (15 U.S.C. § 80a–41(e)).

[23] *Id.*

[24] *See* U.S. v. Custer Channel Wing Corp., 376 F.2d 675; 680–82 (4th Cir. 1967), *cert. denied*, 389 U.S. 850 (1967), *reh. denied*, 389 U.S. 998 (1967); U.S. v.

cal effect of these decisions therefore appears to make the term "willfully" superfluous in that a criminal prosecution may conceivably be sustained merely upon proof of a violation.

While there have been no reported criminal prosecutions involving tender offers to date, it is important to outline some of the types of unlawful conduct which could conceivably arise in a tender offer context and which have given rise to criminal prosecution in the past. Criminal prosecutions, for example, have been initiated for the following types of alleged violations: [25]

(a) Concealment of material information and filing of materially false information required pursuant to a form or report adopted by the Commission; [26] (b) filing of fraudulent financial statements; [27] (c) failure to comply with applicable margin regulations; [28] (d) distribution of securities without an effective registration statement; [29] (e) making of false statements to SEC staff members during the course of an official investigation; [30] and (f) market manipulation.[31]

Obviously, the particular facts and circumstances of future cases will ultimately determine the extent to which the Commis-

---

Sussman, 37 F. Supp. 294, 296 (E.D. Pa. 1941); Stone v. U.S., 113 F.2d 70, 75 (6th Cir. 1940); Norris & Hirshberg v. SEC, 177 F.2d 228, 233 (D.C. Cir. 1949), *cert. denied*, 333 U.S. 867 (1948) ("Conscious, knowing, and purposeful course of action" sufficient to establish a willful violation); Hughes v. SEC, 174 F.2d 969, 977 (D.C. Cir. 1949); Townsend v. U.S., 95 F.2d 352, 357–59 (D.C. Cir. 1938), *cert. denied*, 303 U.S. 664 (1938); Roe v. U.S., 287 F.2d 435 (5th Cir. 1961).

See also 3 Loss, SECURITIES REGULATION 1986–87 (2d. ed. 1961); 5 Loss, SECURITIES REGULATION 3367–73 (Supp. 1969).

[25] For summaries of the major criminal cases referred by the SEC to the Justice Department, *see* SEC "Annual Reports."

[26] U.S. v. Colasurdo 453 F.2d 585 (2d Cir. 1971) (indictment alleging criminal conduct in connection with attempt to obtain control of a target corporation), *cert. filed* Feb. 18, 1972 (Dkt. 71–1066); U.S. v. Wolfson, 405 F.2d 779 (2d Cir. 1968), *cert. denied*, 394 U.S. 946 (1969). For prior opinion, *see* 289 F. Supp. 903 (S.D.N.Y. 1968); U.S. v. Pope, 189 F. Supp. 12 (S.D.N.Y. 1960); U.S. v. Liggett & Myers Tobacco Co. (E.D. Pa.), March 4, 1946 (SEC Litig. Rels. 273, 328); U.S. v. Guterma, 189 F. Supp. 265 (S.D.N.Y. 1960), *aff'd in part*, 281 F.2d 742 (2d Cir. 1960), *cert. denied*, 364 U.S. 871 (1960).

[27] U.S. v. Callahan (D. Mass.), June 11, 1946 (SEC Litig. Rel. 358).

[28] U.S. v. Weisscredit Banca Commerciale E D'Investimenti, 325 F. Supp. 1384 (S.D.N.Y. 1971).

[29] U.S. v. Wolfson, *supra* note 26; U.S. v. Crosby, 294 F.2d 928 (2d Cir. 1961), *cert. denied, sub nom.*, Mittleman v. U.S., 368 U.S. 984 (1962).

[30] U.S. v. Colasurdo, *supra* note 26.

[31] U.S. v. Williams, 424 F.2d 344 (5th Cir. 1970), *cert. denied*, 405 U.S. 954 (1972).

sion will recommend criminal prosecution for violations in connection with tender offers. In summary, however, it may generally be stated that where a violation of the securities laws does in fact occur, the probability of criminal prosecution for such violation will be increased where there is an obvious or repeated failure to comply with the law for the purpose of inducing investors to purchase or sell securities or where the nature of the violation is the principal cause of investors suffering substantial losses.

Section 2. *PRIVATE ENFORCEMENT AND REMEDIES*

a. Existence of Private Rights of Action, Standing to Sue and Establishing a Cause of Action under the 1934 Act Tender Rules

While the 1934 Act expressly provides that the Commission may institute judicial enforcement proceedings whenever it appears that any person is engaged or about to engage in any violation of the act or the rules thereunder,[32] the statute contains no similar recognition of private rights of action.[33] The courts, however, in an effort to insure the protection of investors, have viewed private enforcement as a necessary and desirable supplement to Commission action and accordingly have recognized an *implied* right of private action for violations of a number of the provisions of the 1934 Act.[34] The landmark case of *J. I. Case Co.*

[32] *See* § 21(e) of the 1934 Act.

[33] The 1934 Act, however, expressly provides for private enforcement under certain limited circumstances. Section 18(a) of the 1934 Act, for example, expressly authorizes a private right of action for damages to any person who relied on a material misleading statement filed with the Commission under the Act and purchased or sold a security at a price which was affected by such statement—unless the person sued can prove he acted in good faith and had no knowledge that the statement was false or misleading. Similarly, Section 16(b) provides for a private right of action to recover short-swing profits, but the remedy is only available to the issuer or a securityholder who sues on behalf of the issuer. *See also* Section 9(e) of the 1934 Act. *Cf.* Sections 11 and 12 of the Securities Act of 1933 (15 U.S.C. §§ 77k and 77l). For an interesting recent case with regard to the question of whether there is an implied right of private action under Section 17(a) of the 1933 Act (15 U.S.C. § 77q(a)), *see* Dorfman v. First Boston Corp., 336 F. Supp. 1089 (E.D. Pa. 1972).

[34] *See, e.g.*, Geismar v. Bond & Goodwin, Inc., 40 F. Supp. 876 (S.D.N.Y. 1941) [§ 15(c)(1)]; List v. Fashion Park Inc., 222 F. Supp. 798 (S.D.N.Y. 1963) *aff'd* 340

v. Borak,[35] in which the U.S. Supreme Court recognized an implied right of private action under the SEC's proxy rules, placed the private right on a solid legal foundation and has left little doubt as to the existence of such right to enforce violations of the tender rules.[36] Many of the courts which have had occasion to consider private actions under the tender rules have, in fact, "assumed" the existence of a private right of action with little or no discussion of the issue.[37]

F.2d 457 (2d Cir. 1965), *cert. denied sub nom.*, List v. Lerner, 382 U.S. 811 (1965) [§ 10(b) & Rule 10b–5, 15(c)(1)]; *Mills v. Sarjem Corp.*, 133 F. Supp. 753 (D.N.J. 1955) [§§ 10(b), 15(c)(1) and rules thereunder]; *Kardon v. National Gypsum Co.*, 73 F. Supp. 798 (E.D. Pa. 1947), *add'l findings*, 83 F. Supp. 613 (E.D. Pa. 1947) [§ 10(b) and Rule 10b–5]; Opper v. Hancock Securities Corp., 250 F. Supp. 668 (S.D.N.Y. 1966), *aff'd per curiam*, 367 F.2d 157 (2d Cir. 1966) [§§ 10(b), 15(c)(1) & rules thereunder]; J. I. Case Co. v. Borak, 377 U.S. 426 (1963) [§ 14(a)]; Hawkins v. Merrill, Lynch, Pierce, Fenner & Beane, 85 F. Supp. 104 (W.D. Ark. 1949) [§ 10(b), Rule 10b–5, § 11(d), Rule 17a–5]; Standard Fruit & Steamship Co. v. Midwest Stock Exchange, 178 F. Supp. 669 (N.D. Ill. 1959) [§ 12(a)]; Appel v. Levine, 85 F. Supp. 240 (S.D.N.Y. 1948) [§ 7]; Serzysko v. Chase Manhattan Bank, CCH FED. SEC. L. REP. § 91,676 (S.D.N.Y. 1966) [§ 7]; Olson Bros., Inc. v. Albert, CCH FED. SEC. L. REP. ¶ 93,896 (S.D.N.Y. 1962) [§ 20(c)]. *See also* cases cited at 6 Loss, SECURITIES REGULATION 3871–73 (Supp. 1969); 5 Loss, *id.*, 3299–301.

[35] 377 U.S. 426 (1964). *See also* Dillon v. Berg, 326 F. Supp. 1214, 1218 (D. Del. 1971), *aff'd per curiam*, 453 F. 2d 876 (3d Cir. 1971).

[36] *Id.* at 430–32.

[37] *See* Electronic Specialty Co. v. International Controls Corp., 409 F.2d 937 (2d Cir. 1969), *rev.'g in part*, 295 F. Supp. 1063 (S.D.N.Y. 1968). For prior opinion in this case, *see* 296 F. Supp. 462 (S.D.N.Y. 1968); Susquehanna Corp. v. Pan American Sulphur Co., 423 F.2d 1075 (5th Cir. 1970), *rev'g*, No. SA–69–CA–67 (W.D. Tex. 1969). CCH FED. SEC. L. REP. ¶ 92,473. *Cf. In the Matter of* Reports of the Susquehanna Corp., SEC Securities Exchange Act Release No. 8933 (July 17, 1970), CCH FED. SEC. L. REP. ¶ 77,842; Butler Aviation International, Inc. v. Comprehensive Designers, Inc., 425 F.2d 842 (2d Cir. 1970), *aff'g*, 307 F. Supp. 910 (S.D.N.Y. 1969); Neuman v. Electronic Specialty Co., No. 68C 1817 (N.D. Ill. E.D. 1969), CCH FED. SEC. L. REP. ¶ 92,591; Fabrikant v. Jacobellis, No. 69–C–880 (E.D.N.Y. 1970), CCH FED. SEC. L. REP. ¶ 92,686; MGM v. Transamerica Corp., 303 F. Supp. 1354 (S.D.N.Y. 1969); *See also* Crane Co. v. Westinghouse Air Brake Co., 419 F.2d 787 (2d Cir. 1969), *cert. denied*, 400 U.S. 822 (1970); Iroquois Industries, Inc. v. Syracuse China Corp., 417 F.2d 963 (2d Cir. 1969), *cert. denied*, 399 U.S. 909 (1970).

But see Washburn v. Madison Square Garden Corp., 340 F. Supp. 504 (S.D.N.Y. 1972), a class action for damages and injunctive relief brought by a stockholder of MSG alleging, *inter alia*, violations of Section 13(d)(1), Rule 13d–1, Section 14(d)(4), Rule 14d–4 and Section 14(e) of the 1934 Act, in that MSG engaged in unlawful activities in an effort to defeat a tender offer by a corporation which was competing with MSG for control of a target company. In dismissing the complaint for failure to state a claim on which relief could be granted, the court suggests that the Section 13(d) and Section 14(d) filing requirements *do not* create private rights of action

The apparently well-settled principle that there is an implied right of private action to enforce violations of the tender rules must be distinguished from the question of just who has standing to enforce such rules. The approach of the courts to the standing issue under the tender rules reflects an attempt to fully implement the Congressional intent—that being to protect the interests of investors by assuring that their ability to make informed investment judgments has not been compromised by unlawful activity on the part of the tender offer combatants. Thus, quite unlike the restrictive readings given Section 10(b) and Rule 10b–5 in a number of jurisdictions [38] the courts have uniformly been far more generous in conferring standing under the tender rules.

It has been held, for example, that nontendering shareholders of the target have standing under Section 14(e) to bring an action for damages or injunctive relief based upon allegations that the target fraudulently discouraged them from tendering their shares.[39] Similarly, a nontendering shareholder has been found to have standing under Section 14(e) to maintain a derivative action on behalf of the target for damages against an offeror,[40] and a target has been held to have standing under Sections 13(d) and 14(e) to enjoin alleged fraudulent conduct by an offeror.[41] The dicta in other opinions likewise suggest that offerors, nontendering shareholders, and target companies have standing to enjoin fraudulent conduct under all provisions of the tender rules.[42]

---

where the plaintiff cannot show injury resulting from the alleged violations. In dismissing the Section 14(e) allegation, the court found that the plaintiff was not the subject of any tender offer or solicitation and did not have standing under Section 14 (e) to represent the target's shareholders.

Cf. Dyer v. Eastern Trust and Banking Co., 336 F. Supp. 890 (D. Me. 1971), expressly recognizing an implied right of private action for damages under Section 14(e). For accord in a related case, *see* Emmi v. First-Manufacturers National Bank of Lewiston and Auburn, 336 F. Supp. 629 (D. Me. 1971).

[38] See text and accompanying notes 132–47, Chapter 4.

[39] *See* Neuman v. Electronic Specialty Co., *supra* note 37. For a more detailed discussion of standing to sue under Section 14(e), see text accompanying notes 132–147, Chapter 4. *Cf.* Textron, Inc. v. American Woolen Co., 122 F. Supp. 305 (D. Mass. 1954).

[40] *See* Fabrikant v. Jacobellis, *supra* note 37.

[41] *See* Butler Aviation International, Inc. v. Comprehensive Designers, Inc., *supra* note 37. *See also* GAF Corp. v. Milstein, 453 F.2d 709 (2d Cir. 1971), *cert. denied,* 406 U.S. 910 (1972).

[42] *See* cases cited in note 37, *supra. See also* Grow Chemical Corp. v. Uran, 316 F. Supp. 891 (S.D.N.Y. 1970). In addition, with respect to the standing of the offeror, *see* H.K. Porter Co., Inc. v. Nicholson File Co. (D.R.I. Nov. 30, 1972) as discussed in 182 BNA Sec. Rec. & L. Rep. at A-4–A-6. The court *held* that Sec-

A recently reported case has also held that a shareholder of the tender offeror has standing to maintain an action for damages against the offeror under Section 14(e).[43]

Assuming the existence of a private right of action and standing of a private party to maintain such action, consideration must be given to whether the plaintiff's allegations establish a cause of action upon which relief can be granted. Assuming proof of a violation can be established, the issue will become one of whether proof of a violation, by itself, establishes a cause of action on which relief can be granted or whether the private litigant must show causal connection between the violation and the alleged injury before the question of remedies is considered.[44]

Where an action is initiated in time for the court to institute preventive measures, proof of a violation, standing alone, should ordinarily be deemed sufficient to establish a cause of action.[45] In the tender offer context, such an approach would clearly advance the Congressional purpose of insuring full and fair disclosure to investors. However, where an action is initiated subsequent to the consummation of a transaction which was effected by means of some unlawful practice, the courts, in an apparent effort to avoid academic exercises in the judicial process, have generally required proof of both a violation and a causal connection between the violation and the alleged injury.[46] The U.S. Supreme Court, in *Mills v. Electric Auto-Lite Co.*,[47] has added a subtle

---

tion 14(e) clearly gives a tender offeror standing to seek damages for misrepresentation made by the target corporation.

[43] *See* Dyer v. Eastern Trust and Banking Co., *supra* note 37. With regard to the interrelationship of the standing issue and the extent of extraterritorial application of the 1934 Act, *see* Schoenbaum v. Firstbrook, 405 F. 2d 215 (2d Cir. 1968) (*en banc*), *cert. denied*, 395 U.S. 906 (1969) and Travis v. Anthes Imperial Limited, No. 69 C 367 (E.D.Mo. 1971), CCH FED. SEC. L. REP. ¶93,303.

[44] The "causal connection" test is simply the common law fraud test of reliance, i.e., whether the injured party relied upon the unlawful act thereby denying such party the opportunity to make an informed investment decision. *See* Mills v. Electric Auto-Lite Co., 396 U.S. 375, 380 (1970), *rev.'g* 403 F.2d 429 (7th Cir. 1970).

[45] *See* Mills v. Electric Auto-Lite Co., *id.*

[46] *See, e.g.*, Mills v. Sarjem Corp., 133 F. Supp. 753, 768–69 (D.N.J. 1955); Lapchak v. Sisto, CCH FED. SEC. L. REP. ¶ 90,721 (S.D.N.Y. 1955); Hoover v. Allen, 241 F. Supp. 213 (S.D.N.Y. 1965); Robbins v. Banner Industries, Inc., 285 F. Supp. 758 (S.D.N.Y. 1966); Laurenzano v. Einbender, 264 F. Supp. 356 (E.D.N.Y. 1966); List v. Fashion Park, Inc., 340 F.2d 457 (2d Cir. 1965), *cert. denied sub nom.*, List v. Lerner, 382 U.S. 811 (1965); O'Neill v. Maytag, 339 F.2d 764 (2d Cir. 1964).

[47] 396 U.S. 375 (1970).

and important refinement to this latter principle. The court had occasion to consider the causation question in connection with an injunctive action brought subsequent to the consummation of a merger which was effected pursuant to a materially misleading proxy statement which violated Section 14(a) of the 1934 Act and Rule 14a–9 thereunder. While the court found that proof of a causal relationship was necessary to establish a cause of action, it held that such proof could be established simply on a showing "that the proxy solicitation itself, rather than the particular defect in the solicitation materials, was an essential link in the accomplishment of the [merger] transaction."[48] The court went on to state that "This objective test will avoid the impracticalities of determining how many votes were affected, and by resolving doubts in favor of those the statute is designated to protect, will effectuate the congressional policy of ensuring that the shareholders are able to make an informed choice when they are consulted on corporate transactions."[49]

In applying the *Mills* holding to a typical tender offer fraud situation it would appear that a private plaintiff may well be able to show a causal relationship and thereby establish a cause of action, simply upon proof of a violation. For example, if a tender offer is successfully consummated pursuant to a materially misleading invitation for tenders which violates Section 14(e) of the 1934 Act, there can be little doubt that the invitation was "an essential link in the accomplishment" of the tender offer. Similarly, a cause of action may be established upon proof that the offeror failed to file a Schedule 13D statement at the commencement of the offer, since the requisite filing requirement is essential to the lawful consummation of the offer.[50]

Thus, as stated above, the practical impact of the *Mills* case,

[48] *Id.* at 385. *Cf.* Emmi v. First-Manufacturers National Bank of Lewiston and Auburn, *supra* note 37; Bangor Punta Corp. v. Chris-Craft Industries, Inc., 337 F. Supp. 1147 (S.D.N.Y. 1971); Chris-Craft Industries, Inc. v. Piper Aircraft Corp., 337 F. Supp. 1128 (S.D.N.Y. 1971).

[49] *Id.* at 385.

[50] Proof that the target company made materially misleading statements in violation of Section 14(e) would also appear to enable the private plaintiff to establish a cause of action, since the statement might well be considered "the essential link" in the target's efforts (whether successful or unsuccessful) to defeat the offer.

when viewed in light of the remedial purposes of the tender rules, would appear to suggest that if a private plaintiff can prove a violation, he will also be able to meet the causal connection test as enunciated in *Mills*. However, three lower court cases involving tender offers which were decided after the *Mills* case have resulted in the denial of damages to plaintiffs who failed to show a specific causal connection between the claimed violation and the injury.[51]

B. Types of Relief

Where there has been a violation of the Federal securities laws, it is clear that the courts have the power to enforce compliance with the law and to make use of any available remedy in securing some meaningful measure of relief to undo the wrong done.[52] This well-settled principle has been stated as follows:

> the power *to enforce* implies the power to make effective the right of recovery afforded by the Act. And the power to make the right of recovery effective implies the power to utilize any of the procedures or actions normally available to the litigant according to the exigencies of the particular case.[53]

(1) Injunctive and Other Equitable Relief

The problem of fashioning appropriate relief for violations in connection with tender offers represents a particularly imposing challenge to the judiciary.[54] In many instances the difficulties stem from requests for preliminary injunctive relief, generally by

[51] *See* Chris-Craft Industries, Inc. v. Piper Aircraft Corp., *supra* note 48; Emmi v. First-Manufacturers National Bank of Lewiston and Auburn, *supra* note 37; Bangor Punta Corp. v. Chris-Craft Industries, Inc., *supra* note 48.

As noted, the *Mills* case involved an injunctive action. Query, whether proof of reliance on the specific act or misrepresentation is a more appropriate or desirable test in an action for damages?

[52] *See* J. I. Case Co. v. Borak, 377 U.S. 426 (1964).

[53] Deckert v. Independence Shares Corp., 311 U.S. 282, 288 (1940).

The specific relief which will be granted in a particular tender offer case will depend in large measure on the court's evaluation of the deterrent efficacy of imposing sanctions, the nature and extent of the violation in relation to the injury resulting therefrom, the status of the tender offer at the time the suit is initiated, and the materiality of the unlawful conduct (e.g. whether shareholders who tendered would or would not have done so if the violation had not occurred).

[54] *See* Young, *Judicial Enforcement of the Williams Amendments: The Need to Separate the Questions of Violation and Relief*, 27 Bus. Law 391 (Jan. 1972).

the target company, during the course of the tender offer.[55] In the acrimonious imbroglio of the contested tender offer, it is normally at this time when relief is most desperately sought and when the courts must be most vigilant to guard against suits initiated for the purpose of delaying and thereby defeating legitimate tender offers.[56] Against this background, the court should be prepared to act quickly for if a violation is sufficiently proved on an application for a preliminary injunction, the opportunity for promptly doing equity and fashioning a meaningful remedy may then be considerably better than it would be later on.[57]

Accordingly, the court may be requested to rule (very often without the benefit of a full evidentiary hearing) on a claim that the offeror has either manipulated the market price in order to effect the tender offer at an artificially low price or has made a materially misleading offer.[58] Thus, it has been suggested by one court that if the offer is found to be misleading, the court could require the offeror to make a corrective statement, give shareholders the opportunity to withdraw shares previously tendered, and enjoin further solicitations until the withdrawal period expires.[59] Similarly, where there is a showing that the offeror ma-

[55] Generally speaking a preliminary injunction, which is considered to be in the nature of an extraordinary remedy, will not be granted unless there is some showing of irreparable harm together with some evidence of a probability of success at trial. *See* Electronic Specialty Co. v. International Controls Corp., 409 F.2d 937, 947 (2d Cir. 1969); Butler Aviation International Inc. v. Comprehensive Designers, Inc., 307 F. Supp. 910, 915 (S.D.N.Y. 1969), *aff'd*, 425 F.2d 843 (2d Cir. 1970); Walston & Co., Inc., v. Haven Industries, Inc., 69 Civ. 793 (S.D.N.Y. 1969), CCH FED. SEC. L. REP. ¶ 92,364.

[56] *See* Electronic Specialty Co. v. International Controls Corp., *supra* note 55. *Cf.* North American Car Corp. v. The Flying Tiger Corp., No. 70C 2008 (N.D. Ill. 1970), CCH FED. SEC. L. REP. ¶ 92,757, discussed more fully in note 61, *infra. See also* Young, *supra* note 54, at 413.

[57] Electronic Speciality Co. v. International Controls Corp., *supra* note 55, at 947.

[58] Similarly, the offeror may seek a preliminary injunction against the target, based on allegations that the target artificially effected an increase in the market price or made material misrepresentations in an effort to thwart the offer. In many instances, however, the damage to the offeror resulting from such activity by the target may be irreparable, with injunctive relief having a limited practical effect. Thus, the offeror may well have difficulty in securing any meaningful relief unless it is able to prove actual damages. See text accompanying notes 67–76, *infra*.

[59] *See* Electronic Specialty Co. v. International Controls Corp., *supra* note 55, at 947.

nipulated the market prior to the offer, it has been suggested that the court could compel the offeror to return all shares tendered and enjoin any further solicitations for a period of time or alternatively permit the offeror to raise the price paid for tendered shares.[60]

This approach represents a meaningful attempt to fashion relief in a manner consistent with the best interests of investors. Where at all possible, investors should not be deprived of an opportunity to dispose of their shares at an attractive price. Thus, where time permits the offeror to cure the violation, it would appear appropriate for the court to fashion a remedy which will permit the offer to continue.[61]

On the other hand, it can be argued with some persuasion that relief in the form of harsh sanctions against the offeror, such as divestiture or deprivation of voting rights of the target's shares, may be the only effective method of deterring potential offenders and securing voluntary rather than enforced compliance with the law; for if the relief granted will not prevent the offender from achieving its ultimate objectives, there will be little incentive to comply in the first instance.[62] It is patently obvious, however, that while relief in the form of divestiture or deprivation of voting rights may be just what the doctor ordered for the management of the target company, such relief would be of little, if any, benefit to investors who tendered their shares.[63]

The issue confronting the courts on an application for injunc-

[60] *Id.*

[61] *See* Butler Aviation International, Inc. v. Comprehensive Designers, Inc., 425 F.2d 842, 844–45 (2d Cir. 1970). *See also* North American Car Corp. v. The Flying Tiger Corp., *supra* note 56 discussed in 64 BNA SEC. REC. & L. REP. A–13 (Aug. 19, 1970), where the court denied the target's request for an interlocutory injunction restraining the offeror from proceeding with its offer, but instead issued a preliminary injunction prohibiting the offeror from pledging, hypothecating, selling, transferring or voting any tendered shares until final disposition of the case. In addition, the court ordered the offeror to segregate all tendered shares to facilitate the return of such shares to tendering stockholders in the event the court should so order.

[62] *See* Bath Industries, Inc. v. Blot, 427 F.2d 97, 113 (7th Cir. 1970); Committee for the New Management of Butler Aviation v. Widmark, 335 F. Supp. 146 (E.D.N.Y. 1971); complaint in Chemetron Corp. v. Sun Chemical Corp., No. 72 Civ. 1824 (S.D.N.Y. May 3, 1972).

[63] *See* Electronic Specialty Co. v. International Controls Corp., 295 F. Supp. 1063, 1082 (S.D.N.Y. 1968), *rev'd in part,* 409 F.2d 937 (2d Cir. 1969).

tive and other equitable relief thus becomes one of balancing the interests of the offeror, the investors, and the incumbent management of the target company as well as promoting statutory compliance. The balancing of these often conflicting interests is not easily accomplished. However, the recognition that the Williams Act is designed to protect the investing public within a statutory framework which favors neither the offeror nor the target company suggests that the court's primary concern should be that of fashioning relief to promote the protection and interests of security holders. Along these lines, the flexibility inherent in permitting the offer to continue—under conditions which provide, where appropriate, for sterilization of the violation, full disclosure, and a temporary denial of voting rights until such time as all shareholders have had an adequate opportunity to withdraw their shares—appears to represent a more balanced approach to the problem of relief for violations by the offeror.[64] In this regard, it should be added that the uncertainties which will confront the offeror from a court-enforced withdrawal offer should be more than sufficient to encourage voluntary statutory compliance.

While the withdrawal offer may be the key to the fashioning of truly meaningful relief, it must be recognized that there are circumstances where such an offer would be impractical. For example, where the market price of shares tendered pursuant to a cash offer is below the tender price at the time the suit is considered by the court, a withdrawal offer would simply be an idle gesture.[65] In such circumstances the court must then consider whether the nature of both the violation and the injury sustained justify divestiture, deprivation of voting rights, damages, or simply an injunction against future violations.[66]

[64] Similarly, where an action is initiated against the offeror subsequent to the consummation of the offer, the court may find it appropriate to adopt the same basic approach. However, the extent to which this approach will be practical will depend largely on the timing of the suit and whether the facts and surrounding circumstances have materially changed since the offering period. *Cf.* Mills v. Electric Auto-Lite Co., No. 63C 1138 (N.D. Ill. 1972), CCH FED. SEC. L. REP. ¶ 93,354.

[65] *Cf.* Butler Aviation International, Inc. v. Comprehensive Designers, Inc., *supra* note 37.

[66] *Cf.* Cattlemen's Investment Company v. Fears, Civ. 72–152 (W.D. Okla., May 3, 1972), CCH FED. SEC. L. REP. ¶ 93,487.

(2) DAMAGES

Consideration of the damage remedy will be appropriate where there is a calculable measure of damages and where the causal relationship between the alleged violation and the plaintiff's loss can readily be determined.[67] While the difficulties in proving actual damages are often substantial, particularly where the plaintiff is a nontendering shareholder, the damage remedy nevertheless represents a viable form of relief. In *Neuman v. Electronic Specialty Co.*,[68] the plaintiffs, who were nontendering shareholders of the target company, instituted an action for damages alleging that the target company fraudulently discouraged them from tendering their shares. In discussing the availability of both injunctive relief and the damage remedy, the court stated:

> In other words, though injunctive relief may be justified, a damage remedy is inappropriate when there can be no exact proof and measure of damages, and when the causal connection between the alleged wrong and plaintiff's loss is not determinable. As defendant notes, such is generally the case where a security holder is suing in relation to past transactions. In particular, this is illustrated in the tender-offer situation. If the private damage remedy were allowed without restriction, the shareholder who decided not to tender when the offer was outstanding, could, after the expiration of the offer, file a claim for damages which were a result of his own decision not to accept the offer rather than any misdeeds of the defendants.
>
> It cannot be denied that generally it would be impossible for a court to determine whether a nontendering shareholder was in actual fact damaged as a direct result of any misrepresentation relating to a tender offer. It is also true that, without knowing whether and when the stockholder suing in hindsight relied on the alleged misrepresentations, it would normally be impossible to measure any damages suffered by the non-tender-shareholder. It follows, however, that these difficulties may be obviated when, as a condition of any recovery under the private damage remedy, the shareholder must prove that his reliance on any alleged misrepresentations was the cause of his re-

[67] Where it would be impractical to unscramble a successfully consummated tender offer, an award of money damages may in fact be the only practical method of providing appropriate relief. *Cf.* Mills. v. Electric Auto-Lite Co., *supra* note 64; Gottlieb v. Sandia American Corp., 304 F. Supp. 980 (E.D. Pa. 1969).

[68] *Supra* note 37.

fusal to tender. In light of such proof, it should be no great task to determine when and if the shareholder would have accepted the offer, and thereby attain a calculable measure of damages. The damage remedy thus limited because [sic] viable both in regards to the determination of causation and damages.[69]

While the *Neuman* opinion suggests that a showing of an *exact* proof and measure of damages will be required in order for the plaintiff to prevail, other courts, exercising their equitable discretion, have fashioned appropriate awards of money damages where the measure of damages was somewhat speculative in nature [70] or where traditional methods of computing damages would be impractical or would not adequately redress the injury sustained.[71] In *Feit v. Leasco Data Processing Equipment Corp.*,[72] the plaintiff, a former shareholder of the target company who exchanged his shares pursuant to a *Leasco* exchange offer, initiated a class action suit for damages resulting from alleged misrepresentations in the *Leasco* registration statement. The court found that the registration statement filed in conjunction with the exchange offer omitted to state material facts and accordingly held that the plaintiff was entitled to money damages pursuant to Section 11 of the 1933 Act. While recognizing the difficulties in calculating actual damages in an exchange offer context, the court stated:

> We recognize that once a plaintiff has shown that the defendant has violated his substantive rights and that he is entitled to damages, he ought not to be held to the high level of proof required for other elements of this case. The somewhat speculative nature of damages ought not to prevent a plaintiff from recovering; where there is a substantial question, the facts must be construed, within reasonable limits, against the tort feasor.[73]

[69] *Id.* at pp. 98,703–704.

[70] *See* Feit v. Leasco Data Processing Equipment Corp., 332 F. Supp. 544 (E.D.N.Y. 1971).

[71] *See* Gottlieb v. Sandia American Corp., *supra* note 67.

[72] *Supra* note 70.

[73] *Id.* at p. 585. For an excellently detailed discussion of the actual calculation of damages in this exchange offer, *see id.* at 584–88. *See also* Gottlieb v. Sandia American Corp., *supra* note 67 at 989–92 and cases and authorities cited therein; Mitchell v. Texas Gulf Sulphur Co., 446 F.2d 90,104–106 (10th Cir. 1971); Reynolds v. Texas Gulf Sulphur Co., 309 F. Supp. 548, 562–65 (D. Utah 1970).

Where the plaintiff is a tendering shareholder, the damage remedy may, in some circumstances, be the only form of effective relief. In the *Leasco* case, for example, a rescission offer as an alternative to money damages would have been highly impractical because many members of the class had already divested themselves of the securities received in the exchange offer and those who still held the *Leasco* package, if granted rescission, would have "the dubious benefit of being a minority shareholder in a corporation totally controlled by *Leasco*." [74]

Similarly, where a cash tender offeror fraudulently depresses the market price of the target's shares in order to purchase tendered shares at an artificially low price, money damages may be the only feasible method of making investors whole where the market price of shares tendered is below the tender price at the time the plaintiff's suit is considered by the court. However, the dictum in one appellate opinion suggests that even in such circumstances damages would not be appropriate, on the theory that the offeror should not be required to purchase tendered shares at a price it was never willing to pay.[75]

Where the plaintiff is either the target company or the offeror, actual damages may be difficult to prove. If the offeror manipulates the market price in order to obtain tendered shares at an artificially low price, the target may have difficulty in proving a causal connection between any losses it may have sustained and the alleged violation. Similarly, whether the target company fraudulently increases the market price of its shares, thereby causing the offeror to withdraw its bid, the latter would in most instances stand little chance of proving actual losses other than perhaps its cost and expenses in undertaking the offer. On the other hand, where the offeror nevertheless goes ahead with its offer and is successful, it may seek to obtain damages for the difference between the price it paid for tendered shares and the lower price it would have been able to pay had the target company not fraudulently increased the market price.

Superimposed on the whole damage issue, even where an

[74] *See* supra note 70, at 584.

[75] *See* Electronic Specialty Co. v. International Controls Corp., *supra* note 55, at 948.

exact proof and measure of actual damages can be shown, is the overriding public policy issue of whether a full measure of damages should be awarded where such damage liability will effectively destroy the continued viability of a publicly owned corporate defendant.[76]

[76] *See* Mitchell v. Texas Gulf Sulphur Co., 446 F.2d 90, 105 (10th Cir. 1971); SEC v. Texas Gulf Sulphur Co., 401 F.2d 833, 867–68 (2d Cir. 1968) (concurring opinion), *cert. denied, sub nom.*, Kline v. SEC, 394 U.S. 976 (1969); *Cf.* Electronic Specialty Co. v. International Controls Corp. 409 F.2d 937, 947–48 (2d Cir. 1969). *See also* Ruder, Texas Gulf Sulphur—The Second Round, 63 Nw U.L. Rev. 423, 428–29 (1969).

With regard to the question of punitive damages or, as it is sometimes referred to, "smart money" (i.e., damages granted to a plaintiff over and above actual losses as a means of punishing a fraudulent act and to deter others from committing similar fraudulent acts), the Second Circuit Court of Appeals has held that the 1934 Act specifically precludes an award of damages under that Act. *See* Green v. Wolf Corp., 406 F.2d 291 (2d Cir. 1968); Globus v. Law Research Services, Inc., 418.F.2d 1276 (2d Cir. 1969), *cert. denied,* 397 U.S. 913 (1970). *Contra,* de Haas v. Empire Petroleum Co., 302 F. Supp. 647 (D. Col. 1969); Hecht v. Harris, Upham & Co., 283 F. Supp. 417 (N.D. Cal. 1968).

APPENDIXES

PART 1. APPENDIXES A–K: *Statutes and SEC Rules and Regulations Pertaining to Tender Offers*

- A. Sections 13(d) and (e)—Securities Exchange Act of 1934.
- B. Sections 14(d), (e), and (f)—Securities Exchange Act of 1934.
- C. Regulation 13D—1934 Act.
- D. Regulation 14D—1934 Act.
- E. Schedule 13D—1934 Act.
- F. Schedule 14D—1934 Act.
- G. Rule 10b–4—1934 Act.
- H. Rule 10b–13—1934 Act.
- I. Rule 10b–13 Interpretative Release No. 9395.
- J. Rule 434B—Securities Act of 1933.
- K. Proposed Rule 13e–2—1934 Act.

PART 2. APPENDIX L: *Compilation of Representative Examples of Invitations for Cash Tender Offers, Notices of Exchange Offers, and Defensive Publicity*

PART 1. STATUTES AND SEC RULES AND REGULATIONS PERTAINING TO TENDER OFFERS (AS OF JULY 1, 1972)

APPENDIX A. SECTIONS 13(d) AND (e)— SECURITIES EXCHANGE ACT OF 1934

SEC. 13(d)(1) Any person who, after acquiring directly or indirectly the beneficial ownership of any equity security of a class which is registered pursuant to section 12 of this title, or any equity security of an insurance company which would have been required to be so registered except for the exemption contained in section 12(g)(2)(G) of this title, or any equity, security issued by a closed-end investment company registered under the Investment Company Act of 1940, is directly or indirectly the beneficial owner of more than 5 per centum of such class shall, within ten days after such acquisition, send to the issuer of the security at its principal executive office, by registered or certified mail, send to each exchange where the security is traded, and file with the Commission, a statement containing such of the following information, and such additional information, as the Commission may by rules and regulations prescribe as necessary or appropriate in the public interest or for the protection of investors—

(A) the background and identity of all persons by whom or on whose behalf the purchases have been or are to be effected;

(B) the source and amount of the funds or other consideration used or to be used in making the purchases, and if any part of the purchase price or proposed purchase price is represented or is to be represented by funds or other consideration borrowed or otherwise obtained for the purpose of acquiring, holding, or trading such security, a description of the transaction and the names of the parties thereto, except that where a source of funds is a loan made in the ordinary course of business by a bank, as defined in section 3(a)(6) of this title, if the person filing such statement so requests, the name of the bank shall not be made available to the public;

(C) if the purpose of the purchases or prospective purchases is to acquire control of the business of the issuer of the securities, any plans or proposals which such persons may have to liquidate such issuer, to sell its assets to or merge it with any other persons, or to make any other major change in its business or corporate structure;

(D) the number of shares of such security which are beneficially owned, and the number of shares concerning which there is a right to acquire, directly or indirectly, by (i) such person, and (ii) by each associate of such person, giving the name and address of each such associate; and

(E) information as to any contracts, arrangements, or understandings with any person with respect to any securities of the issuer, including but not limited to transfer of any of the securities, joint ventures, loan or option arrangements, puts or calls, guaranties of loans, guaranties against loss or guaranties of profits, division of losses or profits, or the giving or withholding of proxies, naming the persons with whom such contracts, arrangements, or understandings have been entered into, and giving the details thereof.

Sec. 13(d)(2) If any material change occurs in the facts set forth in the statements to the issuer and the exchange, and in the statement filed with the Commission, an amendment shall be transmitted to the issuer and the exchange and shall be filed with the Commission, in accordance with such rules and regulations as the Commission may prescribe as necessary or appropriate in the public interest or for the protection of investors.

Sec. 13(d)(3) When two or more persons act as a partnership, limited partnership, syndicate, or other group for the purpose of acquiring, holding, or disposing of securities of an issuer, such syndicate or group shall be deemed a "person" for the purposes of this subsection.

Sec. 13(d)(4) In determining, for purposes of this subsection, any percentage of a class of any security, such class shall be deemed to consist of the amount of the outstanding securities of such class, exclusive of any securities of such class held by or for the account of the issuer or a subsidiary of the issuer.

Sec. 13(d)(5) The Commission, by rule or regulation or by order, may permit any person to file in lieu of the statement required by paragraph (1) of this subsection or the rules and regulations thereunder, a notice stating the name of such person, the number of shares of any equity securities subject to paragraph (1) which are owned by him, the date of their acquisition and such other information as the Commission may specify, if it appears to the Commission that such securities were acquired by such person in the ordinary course of his business and were not acquired for the purpose of and do not have the effect of changing or influencing the control of the issuer nor in connection with or as a participant in any transaction having such purpose or effect.

Sec. 13(d)(6) The provisions of this subsection shall not apply to—

(A) any acquisition or offer to acquire securities made or proposed to be made by means of a registration statement under the Securities Act of 1933;

(B) any acquisition of the beneficial ownership of a security which, together with all other acquisitions by the same person of securities of the same class during the preceding twelve months, does not exceed 2 per centum of that class;

(C) any acquisition of an equity security by the issuer of such security;

(D) any acquisition or proposed acquisition of a security which the Commission, by rules or regulations or by order, shall exempt from the provisions of this subsection as not entered into for the purpose of, and not having the effect of, changing or influencing the control of the issuer or otherwise as not comprehended within the purposes of this subsection.

Sec. 13(e)(1) It shall be unlawful for an issuer which has a class of equity securities registered pursuant to section 12 of this title, or which is a closed-end investment company registered under the Investment Company Act of 1940, to purchase any equity security issued by it if such purchase is in contravention of such rules and regulations as the Commission, in the public interest or for the protection of investors, may adopt (A) to define acts and practices which are fraudulent, deceptive, or manipulative, and (B) to prescribe means reasonably designed to prevent such acts and practices. Such rules and regulations may require such issuer to provide holders of equity securities of such class with such information relating to the reasons for such purchase, the source of funds, the number of shares to be purchased, the price to be paid for such securities, the method of purchase, and such additional information, as the Commission deems necessary or appropriate in the public interest or for the protection of investors, or which the Commission deems to be material to a determination whether such security should be sold.

(2) For the purpose of this subsection, a purchase by or for the issuer, or any person controlling, controlled by, or under common control with the issuer, or a purchase subject to control of the issuer or any such person, shall be deemed to be a purchase by the issuer. The Commission shall have power to make rules and regulations implementing this paragraph in the public interest and for the protection of investors, including exemptive rules and regulations covering situations in which the Commission deems it unnecessary or inappropriate that a purchase of the type described in this paragraph shall be deemed to be a purchase by the issuer for purposes of some or all of the provisions of paragraph (1) of this subsection.

Appendix B. SECTIONS 14(d), (e), AND (f)—SECURITIES EXCHANGE ACT OF 1934

Sec. 14(d)(1) It shall be unlawful for any person, directly or indirectly, by use of the mails or by any means or instrumentality of interstate commerce or of any facility of a national securities exchange or otherwise, to make a tender offer for, or a request or invitation for tenders of, any class of any equity security which is registered pursuant to section 12 of this title, or any equity security of an insurance company which would have been required to be so registered except for the exemption contained in section 12 (g)(2)(G) of this title, or any equity security issued by a closed-end investment company registered under the Investment Company Act of 1940, if, after consummation thereof, such person would, directly or indirectly, be the beneficial owner of more than 5 per centum of such class, unless at the time copies of the offer or request or invitation are first published or sent or given to security holders such person has filed with the Commission a statement containing such of the information specified in section 13(d) of this title, and such additional information as the Commission may by rules and regulations prescribe as necessary or appropriate in the public interest or for the protection of investors. All requests or invitations for tenders or advertisements making a tender offer or requesting or inviting tenders of such a security shall be filed as a part of such statement and shall contain such of the information contained in such statement as the Commission may by rules and regulations prescribe. Copies of any additional material soliciting or requesting such tender offers subsequent to the initial solicitation or request shall contain such information as the Commission may by rules and regulations prescribe as necessary or appropriate in the public interest or for the protection of investors, and shall be filed with the Commission not later than the time copies of such material are first published or sent or given to security holders. Copies of all statements, in the form in which such material is furnished to security holders and the Commission, shall be sent to the issuer not later than the date such material is first published or sent or given to any security holders.

Sec. 14(d)(2) When two or more persons act as a partnership, limited partnership, syndicate, or other group for the purpose of acquiring, holding, or disposing of securities of an issuer, such syndicate or group shall be deemed a "person" for purposes of this subsection.

Sec. 14(d)(3) In determining, for purposes of this subsection, any percentage of a class of any security, such class shall be deemed to consist of the amount of the outstanding securities of such class, exclusive of any securities of such class held by or for the account of the issuer or a subsidiary of the issuer.

Sec. 14(d)(4) Any solicitation or recommendation to the holders of such a security to accept or reject a tender offer or request or invitation for tenders shall be made in accordance with such rules and regulations as the Commission may prescribe as necessary or appropriate in the public interest or for the protection of investors.

Sec. 14(d)(5) Securities deposited pursuant to a tender offer or request or invitation for tenders may be withdrawn by or on behalf of the depositor at any time until the expiration of seven days after the time definitive copies of the offer or request or invitation are first published or sent or given to security holders, and at any time after sixty days from the date of the original tender offer or request or invitation, except as the Commission may otherwise prescribe by rules, regulations, or order as necessary or appropriate in the public interest or for the protection of investors.

Sec. 14(d)(6) Where any person makes a tender offer, or request or invitation for tenders, for less than all the outstanding equity securities of a class, and where a greater number of securities is deposited pursuant thereto within ten days after copies of the offer or request or invitation are first published or sent or given to security holders than such person is bound or willing to take up and pay for, the securities taken up shall be taken up as nearly as may be pro rata, disregarding fractions, according to the number of securities deposited by each depositor. The provisions of this subsection shall also apply to securities deposited within ten days after notice of an increase in the consideration offered to security holders, as described in paragraph (7), is first published or sent or given to security holders.

Sec. 14(d)(7) Where any person varies the terms of a tender offer or request or invitation for tenders before the expiration thereof by increasing the consideration offered to holders of such securities, such person shall pay the increased consideration to each security holder whose securities are taken up and paid for pursuant to the tender offer or request or invitation for tenders whether or not such securities have been taken up by such person before the variation of the tender offer or request or invitation.

Sec. 14(d)(8) The provisions of this subsection shall not apply to any offer for, or request or invitation for tenders of, any security—

(A) if the acquisition of such security, together with all other acquisitions by the same person of securities of the same class during the preceding twelve months, would not exceed 2 per centum of that class;

(B) by the issuer of such security; or

(C) which the Commission, by rules or regulations or by order, shall exempt from the provisions of this subsection as not entered into for the purpose of, and not having the effect of, changing or influencing the control of the issuer or otherwise as not comprehended within the purposes of this subsection.

Sec. 14(e) It shall be unlawful for any person to make any untrue statement of a material fact or omit to state any material fact necessary in order to make the statements made, in the light of the circumstances under which they are made, not misleading, or to engage in any fraudulent, deceptive, or manipulative acts or practices, in connection with any tender offer or request or invitation for tenders, or any solicitation of security holders in opposition to or in favor of any such offer, request, or invitation. The Commission shall, for the purposes of this subsection, by rules and regulations define, and prescribe means reasonably designed to prevent, such acts and practices as are fraudulent, deceptive, or manipulative.

Sec. 14(f) If, pursuant to any arrangement or understanding with the person or persons acquiring securities in a transaction subject to subsection (d) of this section or subsection (d) of section 13 of this title, any persons are to be elected or designated as directors of the issuer, otherwise than at a meeting of security holders, and the persons so elected or designated will constitute a majority of the directors of the issuer, then, prior to the time any such person takes office as a director, and in accordance with rules and regulations prescribed by the Commission, the issuer shall file with the Commission, and transmit to all holders of record of securities of the issuer who would be entitled to vote at a meeting for election of directors, information substantially equivalent to the information which would be required by subsection (a) or (c) of this section to be transmitted if such person or persons were nominees for election as directors at a meeting of such security holders.

APPENDIX C. REGULATION 13D

RULE 13d–1. FILING OF SCHEDULE 13D.

Any person who, after acquiring directly or indirectly the beneficial ownership of any equity security of a class which is registered pursuant to Section 12 of the Act, or any equity security of an insurance company which would have been required to be so registered except for the exemption contained in Section 12(g)(2)(G) of the Act, or any equity security issued by a closed-end investment company registered under the Investment Company Act of 1940, is directly or indirectly the beneficial owner of more than 5 per centum of such class shall, within 10 days after such acquisition, send to the issuer of the security at its principal executive office, by registered or certified mail, send to each exchange where the security is traded, and file with the Commission, a statement containing the information required by Schedule 13D. Eight copies of the statement shall be filed with the Commission. Where an acquisition, not heretofore subject to this Rule, was made subsequent to December 22, 1970 but prior to January 18, 1971 the specified statement shall be sent to the issuer and any exchange and filed with the Commission not later than January 28, 1971. At the time of filing the statement, the person making the filing shall pay to the Commission a fee of $100, no part of which shall be refunded.

RULE 13d–2. FILING OF AMENDMENTS.

If any material change occurs in the facts set forth in the statement required by Rule 13d-1, the person who filed such statement shall promptly file with the Commission and send to the issuer and the exchange an amendment disclosing such change.

Eight copies of each such amendment shall be filed with the Commission.

RULE 13d–3. DETERMINATION OF OWNERSHIP OF SPECIFIED PERCENTAGES OF A CLASS OF EQUITY SECURITIES.

In determining, for the purposes of Section 13(d) or Section 14(d), whether a person is directly or indirectly the beneficial owner of securities of any class, such person shall be deemed to be the beneficial owner of securities of such class which such person has the right to acquire through the exercise of presently exercisable options, warrants or rights or through the conversion of presently convertible securities, or otherwise. The securities subject to such options, warrants, rights or conversion privileges held by a person shall be deemed to be outstanding for the purpose of computing the percentage of outstanding securities of the class owned by such person but shall not be deemed to be outstanding for the purpose of computing the percentage of the class owned by any other person.

RULE 13d–4. EXEMPTION OF ACQUISITIONS PURSUANT TO PRE-EMPTIVE RIGHTS.

Acquisitions of securities of an issuer by a security holder who prior to such acquisition was the beneficial owner of more than 5 percent of the outstanding securities of the same class as those acquired shall be exempt from Section 13(d) of the Act if the following conditions are met:

(a) The acquisition is made pursuant to pre-emptive subscription rights in an offering made to all holders of securities of the class to which the pre-emptive subscription rights pertain;

(b) The purchaser does not, through the exercise of such pre-emptive subscription rights, acquire more than his or its pro rata share of the securities offered; and

(c) The acquisition is duly reported pursuant to Section 16(a) of the Act and the rules and regulations thereunder.

RULE 13e–1. PURCHASE OF SECURITIES BY ISSUER THEREOF.

When a person other than the issuer makes a tender offer for, or request or invitation for tenders of, any class of equity securities of an issuer subject to Section 13(e) of the Act, and such person has filed a statement with the Commission pursuant to Rule 14d–1 and the issuer has received notice thereof, such issuer shall not thereafter, during the period such tender offer, request or invitation continues, purchase any equity securities of which it is the issuer unless it has complied with both of the following conditions:

(a) The issuer has filed with the Commission eight copies of a statement containing the information specified below with respect to the proposed purchases:

(1) The title and amount of securities to be purchased, the names of the persons or classes of persons from whom, and the market in which, the securities are to be purchased, including the name of any exchange on which the purchase is to be made;

(2) The purpose for which the purchase is to be made and whether the securities are to be retired, held in the treasury of the issuer or otherwise disposed of, indicating such disposition; and

(3) The source and amount of funds or other consideration used or to be used in making the purchases, and if any part of the purchase price or proposed purchase price is represented by funds or other consideration borrowed or otherwise obtained for the purpose of acquiring, holding, or trading the securities, a description of the transaction and the names of the parties thereto.

(b) The issuer has at any time within the past six months sent or given to its equity security holders the substance of the information contained in the statement required by subparagraph (a). *Provided, however,* that any issuer making such purchases which commenced prior to July 30, 1968 shall, if such purchases continue after such date, comply with the provisions of this rule on or before August 12, 1968.

Appendix D. REGULATION 14D

Rule 14d–1. Filing of Schedule 13D and Furnishing of Information to Security Holders.

(a) No person, directly or indirectly, by use of the mails or by any means or instrumentality of interstate commerce or of any facility of a national securities exchange or otherwise, shall make a tender offer for, or a request or invitation for tenders of, any class of any equity security which is registered pursuant to Section 12 of the Act, or any equity security of an insurance company which would have been required to be so registered except for the exemption contained in Section 12(g)(2)(G) of the Act, or any equity security issued by a closed-end investment company registered under the Investment Company Act of 1940, if, after consummation thereof, such person would, directly or indirectly, be the beneficial owner of more than 5 per centum of such class, unless, at the time copies of the offer or request or invitation are first published or sent or given to security holders, such person has filed with the Commission a statement containing the information and exhibits required by Schedule 13D: *Provided, however,* that any person making a tender offer, or a request or invitation for tenders, not heretofore subject to this rule, which commenced prior to January 18, 1971 shall, if such offer, request or invitation continues after that date, file the statement required by this rule on or before January 28, 1971.

(b) If any material change occurs in the facts set forth in the statement required by paragraph (a) of this rule, the person who filed such statement shall promptly file with the Commission an amendment disclosing such change.

(c) All tender offers for, or requests or invitations for tenders of, securities published or sent or given to the holders of such securities shall include the following information:

(1) The name of the person making the tender offer, request or invitation;

(2) The exact dates prior to which, and after which, security holders who deposit their securities will have the right to withdraw their securities pursuant to Section 14(d)(5) of the Act, or otherwise:

(3) If the tender offer or request or invitation for tenders is for less than all of the outstanding securities of the class and the person making the offer, request or invitation is not obligated to purchase all of the securities tendered, the date of expiration of the period during which the securities will be taken up pro rata pursuant to Section 14(d)(6), or otherwise; and

(4) The information required by Items 2(a), (c) and (e), 3, 4, 5, and 6 of Schedule 13D, or a fair and adequate summary thereof.

(d) Any additional material soliciting or requesting such tender offers subsequent to the initial solicitation or request shall contain the name of the persons making such solicitation or request and the information required by Items 2(a), (c) and (e), 3, 4, 5 and 6 of Schedule 13D, or a fair and adequate summary thereof: *Provided, however*, that such material may omit any of such information previously furnished to the persons solicited or requested for tender offers. Copies of such additional material soliciting or requesting such tender offers shall be filed with the Commission not later than the time copies of such material are first published or sent or given to security holders.

(e) Eight copies of the statement required by paragraph (a), every amendment to such statement, and all other material required by this rule, shall be filed with the Commission.

(f) If any securities to be offered in connection with the tender offer for, or request or invitation for tenders of, securities with respect to which a statement is required to be filed pursuant to paragraph (a) of this rule have been or are to be registered under the Securities Act of 1933, a copy of the prospectus containing the information required to be included therein by Rule 434B under that Act shall be filed as an exhibit to the statement required by paragraph (a). Any information contained in such prospectus may be incorporated by reference in such statement.

RULE 14d–2. CERTAIN COMMUNICATIONS TO WHICH RULES DO NOT APPLY.

The rules contained in this regulation do not apply to the following communications:

(a) offers to purchase securities made in connection with a distribution of securities permitted by Rule 10b–6, 10b–7 or 10b–8.

(b) the call or redemption of any security in accordance with the terms and conditions of the governing instruments.

(c) offers to purchase securities evidenced by a script certificate, order form or similar document which represents a fractional interest in a share of stock or similar security.

(d) offers to purchase securities pursuant to a statutory procedure for the purchase of dissenting shareholders' securities.

(e) the furnishing of information and advice regarding a tender offer to customers or clients by attorneys, banks, brokers, fiduciaries or investment advisers, who are not otherwise participating in the tender offer or solicitation, on the unsolicited request of a person or pursuant to a general contract for advice to the person to whom the information or advice is given.

(f) A communication from an issuer to its security holders which does no more than (1) identify a tender offer or request or invitation for tenders made by another person, (2) state that the management of the issuer is studying the matter and will, on or before a specified date (which shall be not later than 10 days prior to the date specified in the offer, request or invitation, as the last date on which tenders will be accepted, or such shorter period as the Commission may authorize) advise security holders as to the management's recommendation to accept or reject the offer, request or invitation, and (3) request security holders to defer making a determination as to whether or not they should accept or reject the offer, request or invitation until they have received the management's recommendation with respect thereto.

(g) offers to purchase securities in transactions exempt from registration under the Securities Act of 1933 pursuant to Section 3(a)(10) thereof.

RULE 14d–4. FILING OF SCHEDULE 14D.

(a) No solicitation or recommendation to the holders of a security to accept or reject a tender offer or request or invitation for tenders subject to Section 14(d) of the Act shall be made unless, at the time copies of the solicitation or recommendation are first published or sent or given to holders of the security, the person making such solicitation or recommendation has filed with the Commission a statement containing the information specified by Schedule 14D: *Provided, however,* that this rule shall not apply to (1) a person required by Rule 14d–1(a) to file a statement, or (2) a person, other than the issuer or the management of the issuer, who makes no written solicitations or recommendations other than solicitations or recommendations copies of which have been filed with the Commission pursuant to this rule of Rule 14d–1: *And, provided further,* that any person making a solicitation or recommendation to the holders of a security to accept or reject a tender offer or request or invitation for tenders which solicitation or recommendation commenced prior to July 30, 1968 shall, if such solicitation or recommendation continues after such date, file the statement required by this rule on or before August 12, 1968.

(b) If any material change occurs in the facts set forth in the statement required by paragraph (a) of this rule, the person who filed such statement shall promptly file with the Commission an amendment disclosing such change.

(c) Any written solicitation or recommendation to the holders of a security to accept or reject a tender offer or request or invitation for tenders subject to Section 14(d) of the Act shall include the name of the person making such solicitation or recommendation and the information required by Items 1(b), 2(b) of Schedule 14D or a fair and adequate summary thereof: *Provided, however,* that such written solicitation or recommendation may omit any of such information previously furnished to the persons to whom the solicitation or recommendation is made.

(d) At the time of filing of the statement the person making the filing shall pay to the Commission a fee of $100, no part of which shall be refunded.

RULE 14f–1. CHANGE IN MAJORITY OF DIRECTORS.

If, pursuant to any arrangement or understanding with the person or persons acquiring securities in a transaction subject to Section 13(d) or 14(d) of the Act, any persons are to be elected or designated as directors of the issuer, otherwise than at a meeting of security holders, and the persons so elected or designated will constitute a majority of the directors of the issuer, then, not less than 10 days prior to the date any such person takes office as a director, or such shorter period prior to that date as the Commission may authorize upon a showing of good cause therefor, the issuer shall file with the Commission and transmit to all holders of record of securities of the issuer who would be entitled to vote at a meeting for election of directors, information substantially equivalent to the information which would be required by Items 5(a), (d), (e) and (f), 6 and 7 of Schedule 14A of Regulation 14A to be transmitted if such person or persons were nominees for election as directors at a meeting of such security holders.

APPENDIX E. SCHEDULE 13D—INFORMATION TO BE INCLUDED IN STATEMENTS FILED PURSUANT TO RULE 13d-1 OR 14d-1

NOTES. A. The item numbers and captions of the items shall be included but the text of the items are to be omitted. The answers to the items shall be so prepared as to indicate clearly the coverage of the items without referring to the text of the items. Answer every item. If an item is inapplicable or the answer is in the negative, so state.

B. If the statement is filed by a partnership, limited partnership, syndicate, or other group, the information called for by Items 2 to 6, inclusive, shall be given with respect to (1) each partner or any partnership or limited partnership, (2) each member of such syndicate or group and (3) each person controlling such partner or member. If a person referred to in (1), (2) or (3) is a corporation or the statement is filed by a corporation, the information called for by the above-mentioned items shall be given with respect to each officer and director of such corporation and each person controlling such corporation.

ITEM 1. SECURITY AND ISSUER.

State the title of the class of equity securities to which this statement relates and the name and address of the issuer of such securities.

ITEM 2. IDENTITY AND BACKGROUND.

State the following with respect to the person filing this statement:

(a) Name and business address;

(b) Residence address;

(c) Present principal occupation or employment and the name, principal business and address of any corporation or other organization in which such employment is carried on;

(d) Material occupations, positions, offices or employments during the last 10 years, giving the starting and ending dates of each and the name, principal business and address of any business corporation or other organization in which each such occupation, position, office or employment was carried on; and

(e) Whether or not, during the last 10 years, such person has been convicted in a criminal proceeding (excluding traffic violations or similar misdemeanors) and, if so, give the dates, nature of conviction, name and location of court, and penalty imposed, or other disposition of the case. A negative answer to this subitem need not be furnished to security holders.

ITEM 3. SOURCE AND AMOUNT OF FUNDS OR OTHER CONSIDERATION.

State the source and amount of funds or other consideration used or to be used in making the purchases, and if any part of the purchase price or proposed purchase price is represented or is to be represented by funds or other consideration borrowed or otherwise obtained for the purpose of acquiring, holding, or trading the securities, a description of the transaction and the names of the parties thereto.

ITEM 4. PURPOSE OF TRANSACTION.

State the purpose or purposes of the purchase or proposed purchase of securities of the issuer. If the purpose or one of the purposes of the purchase or proposed purchase is to acquire control of the business of the issuer, describe any plans or proposals which the purchasers may have to liquidate the issuer, to sell its assets or to merge it with any other persons, or to make any other major change in its business or corporate structure, including, if the issuer is a registered closed-end investment company, any plans or proposals to make any changes in its investment policy for which a vote would be required by Section 13 of the Investment Company Act of 1940.

ITEM 5. INTEREST IN SECURITIES OF THE ISSUER.

State the number of shares of the security which are beneficially owned, and the number of shares concerning which there is a right to acquire, directly or indirectly, by (i) such persons, and (ii) each associate of such person, giving the name and address of each such associate. Furnish information as to all transactions in the class of securities to which this statement relates which were effected during the past 60 days by the person filing this statement and by its subsidiaries and their officers, directors and affiliated persons.

ITEM 6. CONTRACTS, ARRANGEMENTS, OR UNDERSTANDINGS WITH RESPECT TO SECURITIES OF THE ISSUER.

Furnish information as to any contracts, arrangements, or understandings with any person with respect to any securities of the issuer, including but not limited to transfer of any of the securities, joint ventures, loan or option arrangements, puts or calls, guaranties of loans, guaranties against loss or guaranties of profits, division of losses or profits, or the giving or withholding of proxies, naming the persons with whom such contracts, arrangements, or understandings have been entered into, and giving the details thereof.

ITEM 7. PERSONS RETAINED, EMPLOYED OR TO BE COMPENSATED.

Where the Schedule 13D relates to a tender offer, or request or invitation for tenders, identify all persons and classes of persons employed, retained or to be compensated by the person filing this Schedule 13D, or by any person on his behalf, to make solicitations or recommendations to security holders and describe briefly the terms of such employment, retainer or arrangement for compensation.

ITEM 8. MATERIAL TO BE FILED AS EXHIBITS

Copies of all requests or invitations for tenders or advertisements making a tender offer or requesting or inviting tenders, additional material soliciting or requesting such tender offers, solicitations or recommendations to the holders of the security to accept or reject a tender offer or request or invitation for tenders shall be filed as an exhibit.

SIGNATURE

I certify that to the best of my knowledge and belief the information set forth in this statement is true, complete and correct.

__________________ ____________________________
(*Date*) (*Signature*)

If the statement is signed on behalf of a person by an authorized representative, evidence of the representative's authority to sign on behalf of such person shall be filed with the statement.

Appendix F. SCHEDULE 14D

Item 1. Security and Issuer.

(a) State the title of the class of equity securities to which this statement relates and the name and address of the issuer of such securities.

(b) Identify the tender offer or request or invitation for tenders to which this statement relates and state the reasons for the solicitation or recommendation to security holders to accept or reject such tender offer, request, or invitation for tenders.

Item 2. Identity and Background.

(a) State the name and business address of the person filing this statement.

(b) Describe any arrangement or understanding in regard to the solicitation with (i) the issuer or the management of the issuer or (ii) the maker of the tender offer or request or invitation for tender of securities of the class to which this statement relates.

Item 3. Persons Retained, Employed or to be Compensated.

Identify any person or class of persons employed, retained or to be compensated, by the person filing this Schedule 14D, or by any person on his behalf, to make solicitations or recommendations to security holders and describe briefly the terms of such employment, retainer or arrangement for compensation.

Item 4. Material to be Filed as Exhibits.

Copies of all solicitations or recommendations to accept or to reject a tender offer or request or invitation for tenders of the securities specified in Item 1 shall be filed as an exhibit.

SIGNATURE

I certify that to the best of my knowledge and belief the information set forth in this statement is true, complete and correct.

__________________ __________________________
(*Date*) (*Signature*)

If the statement is signed on behalf of a person by an authorized representative, evidence of the representative's authority to sign on behalf of such person shall be filed with the statement.

ITEM 5. ADDITIONAL INFORMATION TO BE FURNISHED.

(a) Furnish information as to all transactions in the class of securities to which this statement relates which were effected during the past 60 days by the issuer and its subsidiaries and their officers, directors and affiliated persons.

Appendix G. RULE 10b-4—SHORT TENDERING OF SECURITIES

Rule 10b–4. (a) It shall constitute a "manipulative or deceptive device or contrivance" as used in Section 10(b) of the Act for any person, in response to an offer for, or to a request or invitation for tenders of, any security,

(1) to tender any security for his own account unless (A) he owns the security or, (B) he owns a security convertible into or exchangeable for, or owns an option, warrant or right to purchase the tendered security, intends to acquire the tendered security, by conversion, exchange, or exercise of such option, warrant or right to the extent necessary to deliver the tendered security, and, upon the acceptance of his tender, he does convert, exchange, or exercise such option, warrant or right to the extent necessary to deliver the tendered security, *Provided, however,* that if he tenders a security on the basis of his ownership of an option to purchase such security, he shall have reason to believe that the maker or writer of the option has title to and possession of such security and will promptly deliver it upon exercise of the option; or,

(2) to tender or guarantee the tender of any security on behalf of another person, unless (A) such security is in the possession of the person making the tender or giving the guarantee, or (B) the person making the tender or giving the guarantee, upon information furnished by the person on whose behalf the tender or guarantee is made, has reason to believe that such person owns the security tendered and, as soon as possible, without undue inconvenience or expense, will deliver the security for the purpose of the tender to the person making the tender or giving the guarantee, or (C) the person on whose behalf the tender or guarantee is

made owns a security convertible into, or exchangeable for, or owns an option, warrant or right to purchase the tendered security and the person making the tender has reason to believe that such other person intends to acquire the tendered security, by the conversion, exchange, or exercise of such option, warrant or right to the extent necessary to deliver the tendered security. *Provided, however,* that if the tender or guarantee of the tender of a security is made on the basis of the ownership of an option to purchase such security, the person making the tender or guarantee shall have reason to believe that the maker or writer of the option has title to and possession of such security and will promptly deliver it upon exercise of the option.

(b) For the purposes of this section, a person shall be deemed to own a security if (1) he or his agent has title to it; or (2) he has purchased, or has entered into an unconditional contract, binding on both parties thereto, to purchase it but has not yet received it; or (3) he owns a security convertible into or exchangeable for it and has tendered such security for conversion or exchange; or (4) he has an option to purchase or acquire it and has exercised such option; or (5) he has rights or warrants to subscribe to it and has exercised such rights or warrants. *Provided, however,* that a person shall be deemed to own securities only to the extent that he has a net long position in such securities.

Appendix H. RULE 10b-13—PROHIBITING OTHER PURCHASES DURING TENDER OFFER OR EXCHANGE OFFER

Rule 10b–13. (a) No person who makes a cash tender offer or exchange offer for any equity security shall, directly or indirectly, purchase, or make any arrangement to purchase, any such security (or any other security which is immediately convertible into or exchangeable for such security), otherwise than pursuant to such tender offer or exchange offer, from the time such tender offer or exchange offer is publicly announced or otherwise made known by such person to holders of the security to be acquired until the expiration of the period, including any extensions thereof, during which securities tendered pursuant to such tender offer or exchange offer may by the terms of such offer be accepted or rejected; *provided, however,* that, if such person is the owner of another security which is immediately convertible into or exchangeable for the security which is the subject of the offer, his subsequent exercise of his right of conversion or exchange with respect to such other security shall not be prohibited by this rule.

(b) The term "exchange offer" as used in this rule shall include a tender offer for, or request or invitation for tenders of, any security in exchange for any consideration other than for all cash.

(c) The provisions of this rule shall not apply to a purchase of a security of the same class as that which is the subject of a cash tender offer or exchange offer (or of any other security which is immediately convertible into or exchangeable for such security) if such purchase is made by the issuer, by participating employees of the issuer or the employees of its subsidiaries, or by the trustee or other person acquiring such security for the account of such employees, pursuant to (1) a stock option plan involving only "qualified stock options", or qualifying as an "employee stock purchase plan" as those terms are defined in Sections 422 and 423 of the Internal Revenue Code of 1954, as amended, or "restricted stock options" as defined in Section 424(b) of the Internal Revenue Code of 1954, as amended: *provided, however,* that for the purposes of this paragraph an option which meets all of the conditions of that section other than the date of issuance shall be deemed to be "restricted stock options"; or (2) a savings, investment, pension or other stock purchase plan providing for both (A) periodic payments (or payroll deductions) for acquisition of securities by or on behalf of participating employees and (B) periodic purchases of the securities by participating employees, or the person acquiring them for the account of such employees.

(d) This rule shall not prohibit any transaction or transactions if the Commission, upon written request or upon its own motion, exempts such transaction or transactions, either unconditionally or on specified terms or conditions, as not constituting a manipulative or deceptive device or contrivance or a fraudulent, or deceptive or manipulative act or practice comprehended within the purpose of this rule.

Appendix I. INTERPRETATION OF RULE 10b-13—PAYMENT OF SOLICITATION FEES IN TENDER OFFERS

SECURITIES AND EXCHANGE COMMISSION
Washington, D.C. 20549

Securities Exchange Act of 1934
Release No. 9395, Nov. 24, 1971.

The Commission has received a number of inquiries from broker-dealers regarding the circumstances in which a broker-dealer may receive a "soliciting dealer's fee" from a person making a tender offer. Specifically, questions have arisen as to whether an arbitrageur who purchases securities which are the subject of a tender offer in the open market and subsequently tenders such shares may sign a soliciting dealer's agreement and receive a soliciting dealer's fee for the tender of such shares.

Arbitrageurs in a tender offer typically make money on the differential between the market price at the time the tender offer is announced and the tender price, which normally includes a premium above market. Their purchases enable the public investor to elect to avoid the risk that the tender will not be consummated or that it will be prorated. The receipt of a soliciting dealer's fee by an arbitrageur enables him to enhance his profit by tendering his shares at the tender price plus the soliciting dealer's fee.[1]

The language of Rule 10b–13 under the Securities Exchange

[1] The anticipation of receipt of the soliciting dealer's fee may induce the arbitrageur to purchase the stock to be tendered at prices up to, and possibly even in excess of, the tender price.

Act of 1934 prohibits a person making a tender offer from, directly or indirectly, purchasing or making any arrangement to purchase the securities which are the subject of the tender offer otherwise than pursuant to the tender offer. The intent of this language is to protect public investors who, if the tender offer were prorated, might lose the opportunity to tender all their shares whereas those whose shares were purchased outside the tender offer would not be prorated. In view of that intent, the Commission views purchases and subsequent tenders by arbitrageurs, accompanied by receipt of a soliciting dealer's fee, as permissible activities, provided that the payment of such soliciting dealer's fees is adequately disclosed in the context of the tender offer.

Appendix J. RULE 434b—SECURITIES ACT OF 1933

Rule 434B. Additional Information Required to be Included in Prospectuses Relating to Tender Offers.

Notwithstanding the provisions of any form for the registration of securities under the Act, any prospectus relating to securities to be offered in connection with a tender offer for, or a request or invitation for tenders of, securities which is subject to Section 14(d) of the Securities Exchange Act of 1934 shall, if used after January 28, 1971, include all of the information, not otherwise required to be included therein, required by Rule 14d–1(c) under such Act to be included in all such tender offers, requests or invitations, published, sent or given to the holders of such securities.

Appendix K. PROPOSED RULE 13e-2 —REACQUISITION OF SECURITIES BY ISSUER THEREOF— SECURITIES EXCHANGE ACT OF 1934

Rule 13e–2. (a) It shall be unlawful as acts and practices which are fraudulent, deceptive, or manipulative and as a manipulative or deceptive device or contrivance for an issuer whose securities are registered pursuant to Section 12 of the Act or for any close-end investment company registered under the Investment Company Act directly or indirectly to purchase by use of any means or instrumentality of interstate commerce, or of the mails, or of any facility of any national securities exchange any equity security it has issued unless:

(1) if bids or purchases are made on any national securities exchange:

(A) such bids and purchases are made on its behalf under the supervision and control of only one broker on any one day;

(B) no bid or purchase is made until after the opening transaction or within one-half hour before the close of trading on such exchange;

(C) no bid or purchase is made at a price higher than the highest current independent bid price, or the last sale price, on such exchange, whichever is higher;

(D) the amount of securities purchased on any one day on such exchange does not exceed 15% of the average daily volume of trading in such security on such exchange in the four calendar weeks preceding the current week, and the broker employed to effect the purchase is instructed to endeavor to keep the amount of securities purchased during the day equal to or below 15% of that day's volume of trading on such exchange; *provided, however,* that these volume limitations shall not prohibit (i) the purchase of one unit of trading in any security on any exchange on any day, or (ii) the purchase of a block of securities involving not less than 10 units of trading at an aggregate price of not less than $250,000, if the price per unit is not higher than the highest current independent bid or the last sale price on such exchange, whichever is lower.

(2) If bids or purchases are made otherwise than on a national securities exchange from or through a broker or dealer:

(A) such bids and purchases are made on its behalf by only one broker on any one day; or if purchases are not made through a broker, purchases may be made directly by the issuer from one dealer; and other purchases may be made directly from other dealers on any day in compliance with subparagraphs (B) and (C) below of this paragraph (a)(2) of this rule if the issuer establishes that such purchases were not solicited, directly or indirectly, by the issuer or on its behalf;

(B) no bid or purchase is made at a total cost to the issuer higher than the following: (i) if the principal market for such security is a national securities exchange: the higher of the highest current independent bid or the last sale price on such exchange, plus an amount equal to the minimum stock exchange commission on such exchange, except that, with respect to the purchase of a block of securities involving not less than 10 units of trading and not less than $250,000, the total cost to the issuer of each trading unit involved does not exceed the lower of the highest current independent bid or the last sale price on such exchange, plus an amount equal to the minimum stock exchange commission, or (ii) if the principal market for such security is otherwise than on a national securities exchange: the mean between the highest current independent bid price and the lowest current independent asked price for such security, plus an amount equal to a minimum stock exchange commission.

(C) (i) if the principal market for such security is a national securities exchange, the amount of securities purchased on any one day on one or more national securities exchanges, plus the amount of such securities purchased otherwise than on national securities exchange from or through brokers or dealers, does not exceed 15% of the average daily volume in such security on all such exchanges in the four calendar weeks preceding the current week; *provided, however,* that this volume limitation shall not apply to a block of securities involving not less than 10 units of trading and an aggregate price of not less than $250,000 if the price per unit is not higher than the highest current independent bid or the last sale price on the exchange which is the principal market for such security, whichever is lower plus an amount equal to the minimum stock exchange commission, or

(ii) if the principal market for such security is otherwise than on a national securities exchange, the amount of securities purchased in any one week does not exceed 1/25 of 1% of the number of units of the security of the same class outstanding, *provided, however,* that this volume limitation shall not prohibit the purchase of one unit of trading on any day, and shall not apply to a block of securities involving not less than 10 units of trading and an aggregate price of not less than $250,000, if the total cost per unit does not exceed the highest current independent bid plus an amount equal to a minimum stock exchange commission.

(3) if any of such securities are purchased in transactions otherwise than on a national securities exchange and not involving a broker or dealer:

(A) if the principal market for such security is a national securities exchange, no purchase is made at a price higher than the last sale price or the highest current independent bid on such exchange, whichever is higher;

or

(B) if the principal market for such security is otherwise than on a national securities exchange, no purchase is made at a price higher than the mean between the highest current independent bid and the lowest current independent offer for such security in such market.

(b) The provisions of this rule shall not apply:

(1) to the purchase of "exempted securities" as defined in Section 3(a)(12) of the Act.

(2) to the purchase of redeemable securities issued by an open-end management company or unit investment trust, as defined in the Investment Company Act of 1940.

(3) to the purchase of securities issued by a public utility holding company registered under the Public Utility Holding Company Act of 1935 or by any subsidiary company.

(4) to bids for or purchases of securities by the issuer in compliance with Rule 10b–7 or Rule 10b–8 in connection with a distribution of securities being made by the issuer.

(5) to the repayment, call or redemption of any security in accordance with the terms and conditions provided for in applicable indentures, corporate charters or other governing instruments.

(6) to the purchase of any security issued by a person organized and operated exclusively for religious, educational, benevolent, fraternal, charitable or reformatory purposes and not for profit, no part of the net earnings of which inures to the benefit of any person, private stockholder or individual.

(7) to the purchase of any security, evidenced by a scrip certificate, order form or similar document which represents a fractional interest in a share of stock or similar security, if the fractional interest (i) resulted from a stock dividend, stock split, reverse stock split, conversion, merger or similar transaction, and (ii) is purchased pursuant to arrangements for the purchase and sale of fractional interests among the persons entitled to such fractional interests for the purpose of combining such interests into whole shares or for the purpose of compensating security holders for any such fractional interest not so combined.

(8) to the purchase by an issuer of securities of dissenting shareholders who have asserted rights of appraisal with respect to their shares in the course of a proceeding instituted in accordance with statutory provisions.

(9) to the purchase of a specified class of security pursuant to a bona fide tender offer made to all holders of such security or to all holders of less than a specified number of units of such security.

(10) to the purchase of a security otherwise than on a national securities exchange not made from or through a broker or dealer, if the transaction is not solicited directly or indirectly by the issuer.

(11) to any purchase or purchases which the Commission, upon written request or upon its own motion, exempts either un-

conditionally or upon specified terms or conditions, as not constituting a manipulative or deceptive device or contrivance comprehended within the purpose of this rule.

(c) For the purpose of this rule, a purchase by or on behalf of any bonus, profit-sharing, pension, retirement, thrift, savings, incentive, stock purchase, or similar plan of the issuer or its employees shall be deemed to be a purchase by the issuer, unless the plan is operated and purchases are made by a trustee who is independent of the issuer. A trustee shall not be deemed independent of the issuer if the trustee or the issuer, or an affiliate of either, directly or indirectly controls, is controlled by, or is under common control with the other (provided that a common directorship shall not alone affect the trustee's independence), or if the issuer directly or indirectly has any control or influence over the time when or the price at which securities may be purchased, the amount of securities to be purchased, or the selection of the broker or dealer through or from whom they are to be purchased.

PART 2. APPENDIX L. COMPILATION OF REPRESENTATIVE EXAMPLES OF INVITATIONS FOR CASH TENDER OFFERS, NOTICES OF EXCHANGE OFFERS, AND DEFENSIVE PUBLICITY

1. International Controls Corp. offer to purchase for cash shares of common stock and certain convertible subordinated debentures of Electronic Specialty Co., Wall Street Journal, August 19, 1968 at 15.
2. International Controls Corp. extension of offer to purchase for cash shares of common stock and certain subordinated debentures of Electronic Specialty Co., New York Times, September 4, 1968 at 67.
3. Rapid-American Corp. offer to purchase for cash shares of common stock of J. J. Newberry Co., New York Times, January 26, 1972 at 51.
4. Coastal States Crude Gathering Co. offer to purchase for cash shares of common stock of Colorado Interstate Corp., New York Times, July 10, 1972 at 46.
5. General Host Corp. offer to purchase for cash shares of common and preferred stock of Cudahy Co., New York Times, June 29, 1971 at 57.
6. Studebaker-Worthington, Inc. offer to purchase for cash shares of its own common stock, New York Times, April 26, 1972 at 64.

7. Tracy Investment Co. offer to purchase for cash shares of common stock of Metro-Goldwyn-Mayer, Inc., Wall Street Journal, July 23, 1969 at 33.
8. Cleveland-Cliffs Iron Co. extended offer to purchase for cash shares of common stock of Detroit Steel Corp., New York Times, June 9, 1970 at 59.
9. Allegheny Beverage Corp. offer to purchase for cash shares of common stock of Arrowhead and Puritas Waters, Inc., New York Times, October 15, 1968 at 69.
10. Allegheny Airlines, Inc. notice of exchange offer to holders of certain subordinated debentures of Mohawk Airlines, Inc., New York Times, January 11, 1972 at 54.
11. Standard Oil Corp. notice of exchange offer to holders of common stock of Midwest Oil Corp., New York Times, March 6, 1972 at 51.
12. Slick Corp. notice of further extension of exchange offer to holders of common stock of Filtrol Corp., New York Times, March 11, 1969 at 69.
13. B. F. Goodrich defensive publicity notices re: exchange offer of Northwest Industries, Inc., Wall Street Journal, July 24, 1969 at 31; New York Times, August 7, 1969 at 53.
14. Arrowhead and Puritas Waters, Inc. defensive publicity notice re: cash tender offer of Allegheny Beverage Corp., Wall Street Journal, October 23, 1968 at 25.
15. Butler Aviation, Inc. defensive publicity notice re: exchange offer of Comprehensive Designers, Inc., Wall Street Journal, December 1, 1969 at 35.

INDEX

NOTE: For main subjects, the Rule, Schedule, and Section referred to in the text will be found under the heading "Tender Offer Rules and Regulations"

GPSR Authorized Representative: Easy Access System Europe, Mustamäe tee 50, 10621 Tallinn, Estonia, gpsr.requests@easproject.com

www.ingramcontent.com/pod-product-compliance
Lightning Source LLC
LaVergne TN
LVHW101457200926
848483LV00001B/148

* 9 7 8 0 2 3 1 0 3 6 7 1 9 *